REREADING THE CITY/
REREADING DICKENS

Gustave Doré, "The New Zealander"

REREADING THE CITY/ REREADING DICKENS

REPRESENTATION, THE NOVEL, AND URBAN REALISM

SECOND EDITION, REVISED AND UPDATED

EFRAIM SICHER

AMS PRESS, INC.

NEW YORK

AMS Studies in the Nineteenth Century

ISSN 0196-657X

Series ISBN-13: 978-0-404-61480-5

No. 50

Rereading the City/ Rereading Dickens

Representation, the Novel, and Urban Realism

ISBN-13: 978-0-404-64480-2

Contents

Illustrations   vii

Abbreviations   ix

Acknowledgments   xi

Preface to the Second Edition   xiii

Introduction: Mapping the Territory   1

1. The "Attraction of Repulsion": Walking the Streets   25

2. The Railway and the Body of the City: *Dombey and Son*   51

3. House and Home: *Bleak House*   87

4. The Factory: Fact and Fancy in *Hard Times*   123

5. Labyrinths and Prisons: *Little Dorrit*   163

6. The Waste Land: Salvage and Salvation in *Our Mutual Friend*   195

Index   231

Library of Congress Cataloging-in-Publication Data
Sicher, Efraim.
    Rereading the city/rereading Dickens : representation, the novel, and urban realism /
Efraim Sicher. — Second Edition, Revised and Updated.
    pages cm.— (AMS Studies in the Nineteenth Century, ISSN 0196-657X ; no. 50)
    Includes bibliographical references and index.
    ISBN 978-0-404-64480-2 (pbk. : alk. paper) 1. Dickens, Charles, 1812–1870—
Knowledge—London (England) 2. London (England)—In literature. 3. City and town life
in literature. 4. Cities and towns in literature. 5. Realism in literature. I. Title.
    PR4592.L58S53   2015
    823'.8—dc23

                                                              2012050482

All AMS books are printed on acid-free paper that meets the guidelines for performance
and durability of the Committee on Production Guidelines for Book Longevity of the
Council on Library Resources.

AMS Press, Inc.
Brooklyn Navy Yard, 63 Flushing Ave. – Unit #221
Brooklyn, New York 11205-1073, U.S.A.
www.amspressinc.com

MANUFACTURED IN THE UNITED STATES OF AMERICA

Illustrations

Frontispiece: Gustave Doré, "The New Zealander," in Gustave Doré and Blanchard Jerrold, *London: A Pilgrimage*. London: Grant & Co., 1872, facing p. 188.

1. George Cruikshank, "London Going Out of Town, or The March of Bricks and Mortar" [1829], *Scraps and Sketches*. London: published by the author, 1832, unpaginated. By permission of The British Library, LR.410.PP24.   11

2. George Cruikshank, title page, *Sketches by Boz*. London: Chapman and Hall, 1839. By permission of The British Library. 180.b.8.   30

3. Jules Arnout, "View from a Balloon of Westminster, River Thames, and Lambeth." Imprimeries Lemercier, ca. 1846. Lithograph on paper. Guildhall Library, Corporation of London. © 2002.   31

4. Paul Gavarni, illustration for Angus B. Reach, "The Regent Street Lounger," in *Gavarni in London: Sketches of Life and Characters*, ed. Albert Smith. London: O. Bogue, 1849, plate facing p. 70. By permission of The British Library, 1456.k.7.   34

5. Wrapper for the serial installments of *Dombey and Son*, number 14 (June 1847). Bodleian Library, Oxford University (Johnson collection d.1702/9).   57

6. Gustave Doré, "Over London—By Rail," Gustave Doré and Blanchard Jerrold, *London: A Pilgrimage*. London: Grant, 1872, plate facing p. 120.   64

7. John Cooke Bourne, "Early Stages of the Excavations toward Euston" [1836–37], *Drawings of the London & Birmingham Railway*. London: Ackermann, 1839. By courtesy of the Guildhall Library, Corporation of London. © 2002.   70

8. George Cruikshank, "The Railway Dragon," in *Cruikshank's Table Book*, ed. Gilbert Abbott A. Beckett. London: Punch, 1845, plate facing p. 261. By permission of The British Library, PP.5985.ba.   73

9. H. K. Browne ("Phiz"), frontispiece, *Dombey and Son* (1848). Reprinted in *Dombey and Son*, ed. Alan Horsman (Oxford: Clarendon Press, 1974).   77

10. "Condition of the Poor," *Pictorial Times*, 10 October 1846, p. 1. By permission of The British Library, newspaper collection.   102

11. "The Great Barbarian Dragon That Will Cut the 'Brother of the Moon,' &c &c &c," *Punch*, 3 September 1853, pp. 99–100.   115

12. Gustave Doré, "Ludgate Hill—A Block in the Street," in Gustave Doré and Blanchard Jerrold, *London: A Pilgrimage*. London: Grant, 1872, plate facing p. 116.   117

13. George Cruikshank, "London Crammed and Manchester Deserted," in Henry Mayhew and George Cruikshank, *1851 or, The Adventures of Mr. and Mrs. Sandboys and Family Who Came Up to London to See the Great Exhibition*. London: George Newbold, 1851, p. 59, plate 2. By permission of The British Library, 12620.d.15.   117

14. Lockwood and Mawson, Salts Mill, Saltaire, 1851–53. Photograph by Martin Ruffe, ©Martin Ruffe www.martinruffe.com 2002. Used by kind permission of Martin Ruffe.   129

15. Augustus Pugin and Thomas Rowlandson, "Astley's Amphitheatre," *The Microcosm of London, or, London in Miniature*. London: Ackermann, 1808–1810, vol. 1, plate facing p. 23. By permission of The British Library, 190e.1.   147

16. Augustus Pugin, "Contrasted Residences for the Poor," *Contrasts, or A Parallel Between the Noble Edifices of the Middle Ages, and the Corresponding Buildings of the Present Day; Shewing the Present Decay of Taste*. 2nd ed., London: Dolman, 1841, unpaginated plate [p. 123]. By permission of The British Library, 560.d.33.   179

17. "Modern Resurrection—East London, 19th Century," in "London Burials," *Pictorial Times*, 19 September 1846, p. 185. By permission of The British Library, newspaper collection.   208

18. "Nova Scotia Gardens and What Grew There," in George Godwin, *Town Swamps and Social Bridges*. London: Routledge, Warner, & Routledge, 1859, p. 22. By permission of The British Library, 8276.d.39.   211

19. "Metropolitan Traffic Relief" (1850). Anonymous lithograph on paper, Wakefield Collection, Guildhall Library, Corporation of London. © 2002.   213

20. "The 'Silent Highway'-Man," *Punch*, 10 July 1858.   215

Abbreviations

References to Dickens's novels are to the following editions (book numbers are given in large Roman numerals, chapters in small capitals):

BR *Barnaby Rudge.* Ed. Gordon Spence. Penguin English Library, 1973.

BH *Bleak House.* Ed. Norman Page. Penguin English Library, 1971.

CB *The Christmas Books.* Oxford Illustrated Dickens edition, 1954 (1968 reprinting).

D&S *Dombey and Son.* Ed. Alan Horsman. Oxford: Clarendon Press, 1974.

DC *David Copperfield.* Ed. Trevor Blount. Penguin English Library, 1966.

DJ *The Dent Uniform Edition of Dickens' Journalism.* Ed. Michael Slater and John Drew. 4 vols. London: Dent, and Columbus OH: Ohio State University Press, 1994–2000.

GE *Great Expectations.* Ed. Angus Calder Penguin English Library, 1965.

HT *Hard Times.* Ed. David Craig. Penguin English Library, 1969.

LD *Little Dorrit.* Ed. John Holloway. Penguin English Library, 1967.

Letters = The Letters of Charles Dickens. Ed. Madeline House, Graham Storey, and Kathleen Tillotson. 12 vols. Oxford: Oxford University Press, 1965–2002.

MB *Charles Dickens' Book of Memoranda: A Photographic and Typographic Facsimile of the Notebook Begun in January 1855.* Transcribed and annotated by Fred Kaplan. New York: New York Public Library, 1981. Unpaginated.

MC *Martin Chuzzlewit.* Ed. P. N. Furbank. Penguin English Library, 1968.

MHC *The Mystery of Edwin Drood and Master Humphrey's Clock.* London: Dent, 1915.

NN *Nicholas Nickleby.* London: Dent, 1907.

OCS *The Old Curiosity Shop.* Ed. Angus Easson. Penguin English Library, 1972.

OMF *Our Mutual Friend.* Ed. Stephen Gill. Penguin English Library, 1971.

OT *Oliver Twist.* Ed. Peter Fairclough. Penguin English Library, 1966.

PP *The Pickwick Papers.* Ed. Robert L. Patten. Penguin English Library, 1972.

SB *Sketches by Boz.* Ed. Dennis Walder. Penguin Classics, 1995.

Speeches = The Speeches of Charles Dickens: A Complete Edition. Ed. K. J. Fielding. Atlantic Highlands NJ: Humanities Press International, 1988.

TTC *A Tale of Two Cities.* Ed. George Woodcock. Penguin English Library, 1970.

UT *The Uncommercial Traveller.* Oxford: Oxford University Press, 1958.

UW *The Uncollected Writings of Charles Dickens: Household Words, 1850–1859.* Ed. Harry Stone. 2 vols. Bloomington: Indiana University Press, 1968, and London: Allen Lane, 1969.

For Thomas Carlyle I have used *The Works of Thomas Carlyle in Thirty Volumes.* Ed. H.D. Traill. London: Chapman and Hall, 1898–1907.

Although articles in Victorian magazines such as *Household Words* were usually unsigned, I have supplied authors' names where these are known or have been traced.

Acknowledgments

Seeds of this book were sown at international conferences in 1982 on "Loci of Writing"; in 1987 on "Landscape—Artifact—Fact: Reading the Environment"; and in July 1992 on "Homes and Homelessness." An embryo of chapter 4 first struggled into existence as "Acts of Enclosure: The Moral Landscape of Dickens's *Hard Times*," in *Dickens Studies Annual: Essays on Victorian Fiction*, ed. M. Timko, F. Kaplan, E. Guiliano, volume 22 (New York: AMS Press, 1993); a "fearful abortion" of chapter 3, under the title "Bleak Homes and Symbolic Houses: Athomeness and Homelessness in Dickens," found its way into a book edited by Murray Baumgarten and H. M. Daleski, *Homes and Homelessness in the Victorian Imagination* (New York: AMS Press, 1998). A version of chapter 6 was published as "A Waste of Money? Recycling and the Economy of *Our Mutual Friend*," *New Comparison* [continued as *Comparative Literary Criticism*] 32–33 (2003). Parts of chapter 1 have previously seen the light of day as "The 'Attraction of Repulsion': Dickens and Other *Flâneurs*" in *A Mighty Mass of Brick and Smoke: Victorian and Edwardian Representations of London*, ed. Lawrence Phillips (Amsterdam and New York: Rodopi, 2007); used by permission of Rodopi Publishers.

I am grateful to Alexander Gelley for sharing with me a manuscript version of his essay on urban epistemologies, in which he argues that the city has long ceased to be merely a theme and has become more than a locus of writing, a text which cannot be reduced to any one sign. The public lectures and published writing of W. J. T. Mitchell and Wendy Steiner provoked me into rethinking representation of landscape and its reverberations for knowledge and power, while my conviction in the visibility of the written text was reinforced by working with the semiotician and art historian Claude Gandelman, whose untimely death robbed me of a dear friend and colleague. My personal and intellectual debt to Harold Fisch will never be repaid in this world, and his passing after the completion of the final revision meant the loss of a friend and mentor. In Western Australia, Michael O'Toole encouraged my impatience with theoretical categories of spatial ordering in fiction, while David Newman was an outstanding example of interdisciplinary study of human geography in his Toronto office during a sabbatical leave from the hot and arid desert as wind chill dropped to minus 36°C—like Simon Pugh, David Feldman, and Gareth Stedman Jones, his work shows that the perception of our world is formed by discourses which map out political, cultural, and class boundaries. Additionally, I am indebted to Clare Loughlin, for checking references in *Household Words*, and Eitan Bar-Yosef, for photocopying at the "Bod." Barbara Hardy, J. Hillis Miller, the late Mark Spilka, and Hanna Wirth-Nesher suffered preliminary and premature prefigurations of some of the chapters and were generous with their sharp criticism. Special thanks to Murray Baumgarten, Tony Nuttall, and Bill Daleski, who endured the entire manuscript prior to its final revision and suggested "Improvements." Some of my ideas were tested on unsuspecting colleagues and students, who were most helpful in forcing me to clarify some of them or to abandon others. Finally, Dr. David Parker, the former curator, and the staff of the Charles Dickens Museum in London were helpful, as ever, and the British Library was an invaluable storehouse of Fact. Jeremy Bentham kept watch over me each time I passed through the portals of University College London, and gave me to understand that he hoped my writing would be useful. I hope it is.

Preface to the Second Edition

This is a book about Dickens's discursive practices in major novels which confront the modernity of the city, above all London, the primary site of modernity in the nineteenth century. To reread Dickens's reading of the city is to reread the city as an interstice of diverse and divergent competing discourses about public health, education, industrialization, urbanization, and political, as well as artistic, representation. While informed by a Bakhtinian understanding of the dialogic relationship between texts and the dialogic nature of the novel genre, the discussion benefits from the insistence of Catherine Gallagher, Mary Poovey, and other new historicists on the inseparability of ideology and literature in Victorian polemics. However, these competing discourses function in a polyphonic culture, and the heteroglossia built into the text can be heard in the contrasting and contradictory voices of the ideological debate. The approach is multidisciplinary and pluralist in its engagement with the textual web to which Dickens responded in ways that were surprisingly radical but not always consistent.

What is missing from previous studies is the context of contemporary debates which would allow us to glimpse the cultural micro-history of the city. Recently art historians, geographers, and sociologists have begun asking how the image of the city is constructed in the popular imagination and how its ideology is disseminated. Interdisciplinary approaches to the crisis of modernity in urban studies have focused on representation as both an ideological and cartographical issue. Some literary scholars such as Carol Bernstein and Julian Wolfreys have also examined the Victorian representation of the city in theoretical terms, as distinct from the former trend of thematic studies of the city in individual authors. Kate Flint and others have studied the Victorian preoccupation with a controlling gaze, but also drawn attention to Dickens's resistance to the mania for classification and to his insistence on the powers of the imagination to meet its inadequacy. But all too often Dickens's anticipation of modernist views of the city (by now a given of studies of the later Dickens) has tempted scholars into an anachronistic reading of Dickens's city through the eyes of T. S. Eliot. This modest contribution to the unceasing flood of Dickens studies tries to redress a neglect of a major issue in our reading of Dickens and of the nineteenth-century novel—representation. Representation is the key to any understanding of the rival modes of realism and of the engagement of urban realism with politics and society.

Rereading the City/Rereading Dickens aims to push back the frontiers of the study of the city in literature, which generally begins with modernism and often with American anti-urbanism, and to identify London as the site of modernity well before Baudelaire celebrated Paris as the modern metropolis. Modern London is often dated from the beginnings of municipal government, starting with the 1855 Metropolitan Works Act, but the anxieties of modernity arise much earlier in the century with the phenomenal growth of the city, the arrival of the railway, and the development of a popular culture.

Dickens was one of the first English novelists to explore the modern city as a central theme of his fiction. His brand of urban realism gives form and shape to a vision of an entire world, but raises fundamental issues in a crisis of representation—artistic as well as political after 1832—that underlies Victorian debates about the city and the nation. Who is reading the city and how it is being read are questions that reveal as much about epistemology of the city as about perceptions of modernity as it transformed the city beyond recognition and made conventional forms of representation seem inadequate. How is the city being read? And how does Dickens's reading of the city relate to the epistemology and politics of representation at a turning point in English cultural history?

Rereading the city *through* rereading Dickens, then, is to return to something of the sense of what the city meant to Dickens's contemporary readers. In shifting the focus, we may discover concerns that are familiar to us, because the problems of modernity are at the core of the social and political problems of Western urban society. Postmodern London is much changed (not always for the worse), but to understand Dickens's reading of the city, in particular his awareness of its illegibility, we must attempt to recover Victorian London as it was imagined — imagined not only as a common experience, but experienced through the mediation of perceptions produced by rival discourses. Perception, after all, is a social and cultural construct, not always answerable to Mr. Gradgrind and facts.

Apart from an excursion to Coketown, I focus on the city with which Dickens is most associated as an urban novelist and which has long been so central to the English cultural imagination—London. Dickens was one of the first city novelists and arguably the greatest. He grew up in Chatham but spent his formative years in the great metropolis. The legendary incident in Warren's Blacking Factory, which for many years was the mainstay of Dickens's biography, has given credence to a mythic loss of an innocent childhood in Nature. Yet Dickens never lived in the country until his retirement to Gad's Hill. The romanticized or neo-romantic idyll of escape from the city, glimpsed at the Maylies' in *Oliver Twist* and in Little Nell's flight and death, or later located in the pastoral cottage that displaces Bleak House, gradually narrows down to Plornish's Bleeding Heart Yard and Mr. Riah's rooftop. The question (explored in my reading of *Our Mutual Friend*) of whether salvation can be found in or beyond the city and whether recycling can redeem more than economic value remains relevant in the year of Dickens's bicentenary in our cities of effluence and in the postmodern waste land.

Sadly, Tony Nuttall was lost to us in January 2007, followed in December 2010 by Bill Daleski. This revised edition is dedicated to the memory of two true scholars.

Introduction: Mapping the Territory

Reading the City

Toute description littéraire est une vue.
—Roland Barthes, *S/Z* (1970)

The real hues are delicate, and need a clearer vision.
—Dickens (OT 307)

[Dickens] describes London like a special correspondent for posterity.
—Walter Bagehot (1858)

This book rereads Dickens by relating his fiction to key issues in social discourse and re-placing the novels in the epistemology of mid-Victorian Britain. While Dickens's novels have been aligned with ideology, little attention has been paid to their precarious negotiation of competing social discourses in the crisis of representation. That crisis brought into question the relation between fiction and reality at a time when Victorian writers and artists tried to reconcile the real and the ideal and when fictional representations entered a competition in the public discourse, not just of claims over the reality of Jacob's Island, or Nancy and Fagin, but over the function and propriety of art in representing them.[1] Dickens's novels had to compete within the diversity of modes of realism, in particular in relation to what has sometimes been labeled "critical realism," or, since the urban perspective includes in the comprehensiveness of its vision a critique of the new industrial and urban society, what can be loosely termed "urban realism" or the "urban aesthetic." This assumes there is an "urban novel," an assumption which has implications for Dickens's reading of the city as well as for his brand of realism.[2]

Beyond the critical cliché that Dickens's novels are "realist" and "urban," the two terms are inextricably intertwined and problematic. This is because, although they are fiction, Dickens's novels nevertheless relate to ideological and literary debates in mid-Victorian England and must be seen in their intellectual as well as artistic context. Within the transitions and transactions in which they were written, Dickens's novels necessarily participate in the debate between the mechanical and the organic (*Frankenstein* being the outstanding example), or between agnosticism and religious beliefs (as exemplified by Newman's biography or George Eliot's response to Higher Biblical Criticism and her penchant for Feuerbach and Comte). It would nevertheless be fruitless to seek consistency in Dickens's ideological positions, and anyone intent on "theorizing" Dickens would do well to heed John Lucas's warning to remember his was "an undisciplined genius," though Raymond Williams has usefully distinguished polemic and political propaganda from social

1

analysis and vision, without expecting from Dickens the intellectual range and richness of George Eliot.[3]

Dickens's imaginary cityscape cannot, for example, be fully understood outside the contemporary debates over the "Condition of England."[4] His public statements, correspondence, journalism, and fiction enter the competing discourses of that controversy under different guises and personas. Each of these modes of writing manipulates rhetorical strategies and plays to readers' ideological expectations while consciously shaping public opinion and engaging with rival representations. Overriding conventional generic distinctions, these modes borrow from each other: Dickens cites his observation and reading, while social investigators cite Dickens, and both flaunt the claim to show "life as it is" in the exposure of the city's mysteries. The dangerous streets of the city with its dens of crime and sinks of vice were prominent in the popular imagination, and Oliver Twist, Jane Eyre, Heathcliff and other orphans peopled the moral allegories of the bildungsroman. Yet, while there was a perception of a real situation that posed a serious threat to public health and middle-class security, discussions of literature and the city have all too often been locked in a descriptive referentiality that depends on a mimetic relationship to the real world (how real places or events are "mirrored" in fiction), so that "realism" is misunderstood as measurable against some historical reality. Alternately, a cultural materialist approach would reread history from a politicized position. Either way, we lose the cut and thrust of the contemporary debates over the city and its representation in medical reports, political speeches, poetry and the novel.

To scour Dickens's novels for "information" about Victorian life is to presume that the "facticity" of the text guaranteed the author was faithful to history, as if "history" were itself not a trope of the realist novel. In his classic study, *The Dickens World*, Humphry House deplored the way Dickens had been read as a historian or taken as a synonym of Victorianism. Yet House is himself ready to identify the novelist with Jeremy Bentham without pausing to consider the complex relations of fact and fiction. On the other hand, I do not agree with Alexander Welsh's complaint in *The City of Dickens* that Dickens lacked "historical imagination" and that the journalist and the satirist could not share the same views.[5] One of the difficulties besetting those who label Dickens as a "realist" is their great expectations of factual precision. They are disappointed by impressionistic generalizations and superficial descriptions of historical processes. We are not told (nor do we need to be told) what is produced in Doyce's factory, exactly how Merdle's bank swindle works, why Fagin and Monks do not leave footprints, and so forth. Such details are left to the imagination, or subsumed in a larger, more symbolic scheme of things. The exchange between Dickens and George Lewes over the scientific basis of "spontaneous combustion" in *Bleak House* is a case in point. And it is precisely Dickens's emblematic use of a moral landscape that thwarts attempts to divorce the figurative and the literal.

Dickens is too often read for an evocation of what Victorian London was like, yet despite the naming of streets and the wealth of incidental detail, Dickens can be notoriously vague in locating places. Sometimes he refuses to name in order to universalize and to render locations more topical, as in the libelously unnamable workhouse in the opening of *Oliver Twist*, originally located (in the serial publication) in "Mudfog." That description playfully defies conventional naming of place and hero to comically do neither: Oliver is named quite arbitrarily by the beadle, Mr. Bumble, and the mystery of Oliver's true identity is left for the denouement of the plot. The workhouse and Fagin's den are memorably visible, thanks to Cruikshank's illustrations and Dickens's talent for dramatization, but the *scenes* described with such comic irony come across vividly not because of any topographical details of the *places* where they are set. We know no more of Fagin's den than that it is a "house near Field Lane"; indeed, the reader may feel as lost as poor Oliver following the devious route taken by the Artful Dodger. J. Hillis Miller calls this, in his discussion of *Pickwick Papers*, Dickens's "topographical circumstantiality."[6] To presume a readership with a similarly exact map of London's alleys and byways who shared Mr. Weller's "extensive and peculiar" knowledge of London is to restrict the meaning of the text to a relatively small interpretive community who had access to such detailed toponymical and topological knowledge and to the even smaller number among them who also read novels; significantly, less than half of the reading population lived in London. The fact that most of Dickens's readers did not have this detailed information and could not, like Little Dorrit's brother, be expected to be "streetwise" does not, in my view, lessen the knowledge gained by the "realism" of such circumstantiality, but then neither does it make it any more useful as a street map of London.

Balzac is no more helpful in his classically "realist" description of Madame Vauquet's boarding house which places it in the rue Neuve-Sainte-Geneviève, obscure and unknown, grim and gloomy. Yet it is unmistakably and uniquely Paris, Balzac tells us, just as we think of Fagin's underworld as indescribably and unforgettably London. Dickens spares us even these sparse picturesque details in *Sketches by Boz* or *Oliver Twist*; all is small, dark, or dirty. The first glimpse Oliver Twist gets of London, when he runs away from the supposed benevolence of the Poor Law, anticipates the mortal danger that awaits him at the hands of Fagin.

> A dirtier or more wretched place he had never seen. The street was very narrow and muddy, and the air was impregnated with filthy odours.... Covered ways and yards, which here and there diverged from the main street, disclosed little knots of houses, where drunken men and women were positively wallowing in filth; and from several of the door-ways, great ill-looking fellows were cautiously emerging, bound, to all appearance, on no very well-disposed or harmless errands. (OT VIII; 103)

Oliver's native parish was not exactly clean and he was almost starved to death in the children's farm and the workhouse, but in Fagin's hands the danger is moral, not merely physical. The city which, according to the old men in the workhouse, was just the place for a homeless boy and offered ways of living undreamt of in the country, turns out to be dark and dangerous, a disillusion for the latter-day Dick Whittington. Dickens has chosen the poorest districts to characterize London— Saffron Hill, Spitalfields, and the area around Smithfield first encountered by Noah Claypole on his entry into the capital. This, we are told, is the worst part of London, untouched by improvement, while Jacob's Island is rock-bottom destitution.[7] That is the setting for Sikes's gruesome end, a site of such poverty and degradation that it must astonish the stranger.

The effect is to create a binary opposition in the mapping of the city, a mythical world that is divided into what Graham Greene once called a Manichean universe of good and evil: on the one hand, a hell ruled by the infernal Fagin, who is several times given all the attributes of the stage Jew, the Judas and anti-Christ of medieval legend, a Shylock brought to judgment, and, on the other hand, Mr. Brownlow's virtual Eden of rest and tranquility, which seemed to Oliver "like Heaven itself" (143), the site of middle-class benevolence and moral agency. Fagin's habitat of thick mud and slime, as he glides stealthily through the dark, damp streets of Whitechapel, like some "loathsome reptile" (186), engenders a mythopoeic presence of evil. But the well-lit broad streets of middle-class respectability lie dangerously close to the narrow alleys of Saffron Hill and Smithfield, where Oliver is recaptured when he takes a wrong turn on his errand to the bookseller's in Clerkenwell: the maze of streets reveals the mysteries of London's underworld that fill the avid reader of the Gothic with terror at the proximity of crime and poverty in the city's terra incognita of filth and vice.[8] Such horrors, later exploited by Reynolds in *The Mysteries of London* and exposed by Henry Mayhew in *London Labour and the London Poor*, were instinctively associated by the reader with an atavistic criminality in the paupers and outcasts of the city, who lived uncomfortably close to civilization and who elicited the darker side of the human psyche. Hence the shudder at the uncanny vision of Fagin and Monks in the paradise of Oliver's refuge at the Maylies' among pastoral fields and flowers.

Only in Dickens's later novels do we get anything approaching the feel of a *place* in the grotesque interiors and comic eccentricities of *Great Expectations* and *Our Mutual Friend*, or the visualized city of *Bleak House* and *Little Dorrit*. But even the famous opening of *Bleak House*, "London," introduces a foggy view of mud which thematically hints at the incoherent muddle of things and people in the city's legal tangle and contagious streets. A similar thematic characterization of the city in chapter three of *Little Dorrit* describes London's maddening bell-clanging Sunday monotony as "Nothing to see but streets, streets, streets. Nothing to breathe but streets, streets, streets" (67–68); the blank deadness of a plague city seems to hint at the amoral and anonymous "Circumlocution Office" in its religion, morality, and government.

Nevertheless, the nineteenth-century novel's evocation of place, in particular its connection of character and plot with atmosphere and setting, has been thought of as the embodiment of "realism," though, besides Gothic conventions, there may be a confusion with Romantic use of the picturesque. Certainly, a concern with social and industrial processes placed within specific locales sounds to us distinctly "realist." By contrast, twentieth-century modernist consciousness tends to present a feeling of place, or placelessness, through an estranged point of view as displacement.[9] In moving beyond place as setting to give an index of an entire social situation, Dickens's pioneering representations of the city, like Balzac's description of Paris in *Le Père Goriot*, create an intentional location.[10] We should note that Balzac's detailed description was not only one of the longest to date but carefully linked characterization and setting with a synecdoche of society and the human condition. This is something which Dickens attempts to do on an epic scale beginning with *Dombey and Son*, where a microcosm is represented structurally as well as symbolically, so that the locus of writing exceeds the exigencies of mere setting. Dickens's mature novels achieve a unity of vision lacking in his earlier descriptions of the city, and, although it never attains the monumental "organism" of Balzac's Paris[11] or the grand scale of *La Comédie humaine*, Dickens's representation of the city reveals labyrinthine connections which cut across social divisions and geographical space.

Peter Ackroyd has turned the fiction into an imaginative reconstruction of the real in *Dickens's London: An Imaginative Vision* (1987), so that (as in his biography of Dickens) fantasy stalks larger than life when the creatures of Dickens's imagination ghost walk into sepia photographs of Victorian London. This says a lot about the power of Dickens's imagination to immortalize a fictional London, to constantly return us to the sites of his childhood and his literary life, inhabited by the spectral presence of the Dickens myth, which was already being created and marketed in the Immortal's lifetime. That Dickens helped shape the image of the city was recognized in his own day. Kevin Lynch has held Dickens responsible for creating our experience of London "as surely as its actual builders."[12] And, although this does not necessarily impair our enjoyment of Dickens's writing, guides to "Dickens's London"[13] point to the invention of a cultural past forming a collective identity in the heritage industry described by David Lowenthal.[14] From Doré and Jerrold's *London: A Pilgrimage* (1872) to Thomas Burke's *The English Townsman as He Was and as He Is* (1947), Victorian city streets and city types have been remembered through Dickens's novels and other literary quotation. "Literary Geography" speaks to our need to place fictions in real settings, and at the beginning of the twentieth century it was a respectable field for both intellectual or academic study and, for the fit and adventurous, exploration.[15] Philip Collins has, in fact, warned against the tendency to reconstruct Dickens's knowledge of London by excerpting from the novels and summed up Dickens's description of London as selective, concluding that he never went beyond the areas of his boyhood memory and early career.[16]

The tendency to historicize "Dickens's London" in a chronological context has essentially little to do with Dickens or his writing, just as one might speak of

"Shakespeare's London" as if that represented some body of knowledge available to the author,[17] though it is probably true that Dickens's novels greatly popularized "knowledge" of London. Such was its verisimilitude that Dickens's London, like Balzac's Paris, acquired a life of its own, sometimes one more believable than the real.[18] As early as 1837 Mary Russell Mitford was writing from her remote Berkshire village to persuade a friend in Ireland to read *Pickwick Papers*, which she found so true to life that one could curtsey to the people as you met them in the streets; she noted that Sir Benjamin Brodie took it to read in his carriage between patients and Lord Denman studied it on the bench while the jury deliberated. This small example demonstrates just how much the fictional representation of the streets was becoming part of the experience of the city, and it illustrates the complex production and dissemination of cultural perceptions.

In a way that would bring glee to a postmodernist writer, London has become "Dickensian," and "Dickens" has become part of the literary itinerary of the tourist who doesn't mind fiction mixed up with fact and who might enjoy the fantasy life of real places. For example, the "original" Old Curiosity Shop in Lincoln's Inn Fields vaunted on tourist postcards is the product of a quite untrue claim by an enterprising Victorian shopkeeper. The Marshalsea Prison is preserved in the form of a sacred relic of the debtors' Bastille and displayed at the Charles Dickens Museum, which has become an object of pilgrimage when the original site has long vanished. By the time *Little Dorrit* was written, the prison was gone and the world none the worse for it, as Dickens noted, but his whimsical search for the birthplace of his fictional child in the preface to the novel provides one of several examples of places on Dickens's memory map that no longer existed or had changed beyond recognition. There are also several cases of fanciful reconstruction of memory. Bayham Street, for example, is presented by John Forster as "about the poorest part of London" and associated in Dickens's reminiscence with the severance from Chatham and a happy rural childhood. Yet at the time the Dickens family lived in this fairly recent suburb on the edge of Regency London this was far from the introduction to "struggling poverty" to which Dickens attributes his early aptitude for acute observation. Indeed, though Camden Town may have been as seedy and déclassé as it appears in *David Copperfield*, it was certainly not the run-down slum in a photograph preserved in the Charles Dickens Museum of Dickens's back room garret in Bayham Street shortly before its demolition at the turn of the twentieth century. Warren's Blacking Warehouse, the site of painful remembrance of childhood shame, was erased by the rebuilding of Hungerford Market, which disappeared in turn when demolished in 1862. The imaginative recovery of memory may, in fact, account for the transformations of the city experience into the fictional landscape of the novels, not least the construction of home and a lost pastoral idyll.[19]

Zooming in on the Saracen's Head on Snow Hill, in *Nicholas Nickleby*, Dickens noted how toponyms generated false perceptions very different from the "reality" of London. In London's toponymic cartography, naming has become divorced from reality—in *Bleak House*, Mount Pleasant is anything but pleasant, and Lincoln's Inn Fields are far from any fields.[20] Some places are remembered today only from Dickens's writings, and probably bear little if any resemblance to anything that ever existed. Although Forster's house, Dickens's own in Doughty Street, and some of the Inns and Courts of the City of London are still recognizable, many of the locations immortalized in Dickens's work exist now only in a subterranean archeology of toponyms, a jumble of arbitrary signifiers on buses or the tube map, which mingle with the multilingual babble of postmodern London in Penelope Lively's 1991 novel *City of the Mind*. In the dead signs on a historical memory map in Graham Swift's *Last Orders* (1996), Smithfield is remembered for its proximity both to the long-gone Newgate Prison and Bart's Hospital: the "three M's: Meat, Medicine and Murders." This true "bleeding heart" of London is to be understood in a no less mythical sense than Dickens's symbolic portrayal of Smithfield in *Oliver Twist* and *Great Expectations* as the legal and bestial center of a labyrinthine underworld.[21] To describe the heart of the city as a notorious prison and as a cattle market infamous for breeding filth and disease is to criticize a central trope in Victorian discourse of the healthy city-body, though Dickens was hardly unique: for example, William Moncrieff's melodrama *The Heart of London, or The Sharper's Progress* (1830) also uses Newgate to characterize the crime and violence at the heart of the city.

The past is indeed a foreign country, but, even as Dickens was writing, memory could barely grasp hold of a fast changing topography. Kit, for example, is hard put to say exactly where the Old Curiosity Shop stood after it was pulled down in favor of progress and a broader street. We cannot help noticing the characteristic time lag in representation of London in novels such as *Little Dorrit*, where the bars of the Marshalsea and the gaping churches stand at ambivalent distance from the hustle and bustle of the streets, railways, and river of the 1860s. We must retrace our steps to an unknown London. The palpable sense of historical change is heard in the heteroglossia of social class, types, and voices. Dickens's London can scarcely be said to exist as a recognizably shared experience except (to adopt G. H. Martin's term for the traces of the vanished institutions and topography of the English town) as a palimpsest.[22] The trace of the vanished past, however, is often in Dickens no more than a mythical construct of the pastoral, like the rural memory of Theobald's Road in *Little Dorrit* or Grewgious's legal nook with its obscure founder's date and Tartar's nautically rigged window-garden amid the depressing "gritty" streets of Holborn in *The Mystery of Edwin Drood*. In chapter four of *Barnaby Rudge*, Dickens looks back a mere sixty-six years to the eighteenth century, before the horror of urban sprawl was imagined, and fondly reconstructs a "purer place" in the clean suburb of Clerkenwell, with nature and fresh, open fields close at hand.

It is well known that Dickens's novels present a belated view of social problems, sometimes with a lapse of decades during which reform removed the worst of the injustices, such as the debtors' prison in *Little Dorrit* or the penal code in *Great Expectations*. Dickens's fictional representation of society nevertheless offers the judgment of moral satire and a fine sense of history, though not in the usual meaning of historical writing (which Dickens, following Carlyle, regarded as "dry-as-dust"). Alexander Welsh seems only too aware of the difficulty of reconciling the metaphorical and literal in his allegorical reading of the "City" of Dickens when he expresses discomfort about the relationship between the city as a social problem and its mythical function, especially in satire. He warns us that to impose an allegorical reading of the Christian tradition of the two cities is to read into the novels Puritan attitudes with which the writer would not necessarily have agreed.[23] The tensions we will note between the literal and the figural, between metaphor and metonym, allow us to imagine larger structures while playfully revising conventions such as the inheritance plot or allegory, for example in rereadings of *Pilgrim's Progress*.

The line dissolves between the real city and the imaginary one, inhabited by a fantasized persona. Dickens acts out the lives of his protagonists, identifies with them in mind and body, splits his flamboyant identities among them, and fantasizes various social and moral personalities, as well as different sexual and gender roles. This may obscure any authorial position—indeed, since Barthes announced the "death of the author" we might be tempted to dismiss it altogether—yet the biographical and historical contexts are too insistent for us to do so in perfect safety. In particular, we cannot ignore formative events in the development of Dickens's personality, not least those that affected his perception of the city. From a biographical standpoint, F. S. Schwarzbach has shown in *Dickens and the City* that there was a sense in which Dickens was using therapeutic regression to reorder his childhood experiences to alleviate the traumatic effects of Mary Hogarth's death.[24] A number of critics, among them Edmund Wilson, Stephen Marcus, and Gwen Watkins, have explored recurrent themes in Dickens's writings which reveal traumatic experiences of his childhood, and have found transformations of Warren's Blacking Warehouse in a number of novels.[25] Yet the use of that episode as the basis of biographical criticism has been called into question.[26] Dickens's *performance* of the city may be a working through of several memories, but its celebration of the urban spectacle says more about the city than a psychoanalysis of the real-life writer allows. Schwarzbach does credit the inner world of the author's mind with the creative power to transform the city, but in claiming that Dickens is "representative,"[27] he fails to distinguish between Dickens's mythical re-creation of London and its biographical basis. More significantly, the inadequate distinction between representation of the world and the world as a source of representation glosses over the complex ways the novelist works through social and personal crises in the all too common dislocation of the move from country to city.

The picture we get of the city in Dickens is more complex than the usual opposition of town and country. While it owes much to Romantic conventions of the sublime and the grotesque, it looks to moral and social dimensions of the everyday. The tension between the literal and the figural points up the fluidity and instability of definitions of realism and enlarges the referentiality of the novel from the local and anecdotal to the epic and social. Instead of documentary detail, symbolic patterns imbue the literal with metaphysical significance and symbolic meaning. In order to appreciate the complexity and contradictions of Dickens's "urban realism" it will be necessary to do more than summarize Dickens's descriptions of urban scenes or catalog the urban themes and imagery of Dickens's novels. That would reduce the study to a celebration of "historical" place and it would miss the intertextuality of the city at key cultural moments. In order to place an urban realism within the politics of representation, it is necessary to break from the opposition of literary to nonliterary texts and to reread Dickens through the context of social discourse and cultural practice. In a dialog of the written and the spoken, the visible and the experienced, the intertext of painting, architecture, medical reports, parliamentary commissions, and legislation will serve as a cipher to rereading the city/rereading Dickens.

The Metropolis of Modernity

> Our age is preeminently the age of great cities.
> —Robert Vaughan, *The Age of Great Cities* (1843)

The city was felt to be the site of modernity even if it was not agreed what modernity was or looked like. "Modern" and "new" were terms, like "spirit of the age," which acquired an ambiguous and judgmental meaning in the mid-nineteenth century and suggest both novelty and the replacement of the old-fashioned.[28] As Robert Southey observed in *Letters from England* (9), "modern" meant to the Romantics the ugliness of machinery and the commercial system, in contradiction of Macaulay and other progressive liberals. The speed of technological change and the visible alteration of the landscape underscored the unprecedented sensation of modernity that eroded social hierarchies, while traditional belief systems seemed to be breaking down and familiar patterns of life were disappearing. The pressures of modernity challenged basic class assumptions in the very language of social discourse.

Urban realism in particular was a product of these changes. The city was acquiring major social and artistic importance as a locus of writing, cultural base, and sociopolitical microcosm, not just in England, but increasingly in France and other European countries. London was the first and largest modern metropolis, the commercial and ideological powerhouse of an empire, and it underwent immense reconstruction in the middle of the century with the coming of the railway and with the spread of suburbia. Between 1841 and 1891, London's population grew from 1.8 million (11.45% of the total population of England and Wales) to 4.2 million (14.52%). At the beginning of the century, there had been no city outside London with more than 100,000 inhabitants; by Queen Victoria's coronation there were five and by 1891 twenty-three. At the end of the century, over a third of the population of England and Wales lived in cities.

In the north of England, "Coketown" came to represent the new industrial town, with its restless masses and ugly, noisy machinery. Here was the source of Britain's new prosperity, but also an entirely new form of social existence, regulated by the factory system. It was unfamiliar to the provincial in the south or the Londoner, who often had vague, imprecise impressions of manufacturing towns. The North-South divide and the polarity of "masters" and "men" were further parameters in the shifting definitions of class and nationhood in middle-class attitudes to the city. Only in *Hard Times* does Dickens devote a novel to the notorious Lancashire mill-town; elsewhere he describes the industrial wasteland in *The Old Curiosity Shop*. However, the effects of the industrial system spread throughout Dickens's writings and are felt in the urban consciousness that pervades *Dombey and Son*.

The representation of the city required a new mode of realism not least because, as Raymond Williams and other Marxist critics have reminded us, the fleeting and fragmentary nature of street life contradicted the ideological assumptions underlying the sedate country house or rural village that had dominated cultural norms and the literary landscape.[29] In England the chronotope of the country house clashed with the values of the modern urban culture that was beginning to dominate society. As Hana Wirth-Nesher suggests in her study of the city in modernist fiction, the country house was no longer the secure home it was for Jane Austen because it was threatened with violation by the forces of modernity.[30] We will see that for Dickens the country house was an idealized home when it had ceased being a place of origin, a refuge from the menacing site of homelessness in the city and a last bulwark against the inhuman demands of capitalism. In *Bleak House*, on the other hand, the mysteries of the country estate cannot withstand the penetration of privacy by the figure of the detective, while Esther's narration both reveals the intimate secrets of the country house and creates a space of seclusion and safety in middle-class homemaking.

Within a relatively short time the traditional baroque and neoclassical shape of the city was obscured as a result of the concentration of labor in mass production, the influx of rural poor, and the rapid development of new forms of communication, such as the railway. The hurried jerry-building of ugly lower-class housing and the higgedly-piggedly expansion of the city into fields and tea gardens left George Cruikshank to bemoan, in a famous comic visualization of the cliché of the city monster, the ugly assault of bricks and mortar as the city ate up the disappearing countryside, disturbing sheep and haystacks alike (fig. 1). The vanishing of the countryside was a shared cultural perception of what urbanization and modernization meant—the irreparable loss of an Englishness rooted in a natural environment and its destruction by the monster-city.

We will see that this sense of loss lends a deceptively romantic nostalgia to Dickens's realism. London had sprawled as a hybrid cluster of parishes and suburbs, Regency terraces and slums, populated by a highly diverse population (as Addison had noticed a century earlier) of St. James' and St. Giles', the nouveaux riches and the underworld. Unlike Sennacherib's Babylon or contemporary

Versailles, there was little monumentality about London, though it was a capital of a world empire. Foreign observers from the eighteenth century on remark that all was rush and turmoil. A common complaint in eighteenth-century descriptions of London's monstrous growth invariably singles out unpassable streets and stinking sewers, riotous violence and debauchery, crime and commotion.[31] The problem was not simply the unprecedented immensity of the city, with its leveling effects, crowds, diverse social demography, or the loosening hold of religion (as evidenced in the 1851 census returns).[32] The dynamism of accelerated change caused many who moved to the city to experience a traumatic break in the sense of a communal belonging, a social hierarchy, and a shared past. Spatial order broke down. The unified view of the physical and social environment in the sense it had been represented, for example, in the harmony of Renaissance portrayals of the walled town with its castle, citadel, and surrounding fields was effectively effaced, and the relationship between country and city was no longer stable in the amorphous towns of nineteenth-century Europe. London was not simply the biggest city in the world and the fastest growing metropolis (having tripled its population in the eighteenth century alone); it was a city of change and of strangers. In the 1850s, forty percent of all Londoners had been born elsewhere.[33] London was swept up in the huge migrations of workers to the cities that resulted from the agrarian and industrial revolutions, as well as from the enormous growth of commerce and trade since the end of the seventeenth century. Newcomers faced the cultural shock of modernity, particularly its feel of accelerated transition and a strange unfamiliarity. The variety of urban experience, moreover, with its contrasts of good and evil, could not be contained in one view, so it is no wonder that a common trope in representation of the city was the inability to read the city.

Fig. 1: George Cruikshank, "London Going Out of Town" (1829)

Modernist tropes of alienation and fragmentation may be traced back to nineteenth-century poetic responses to the modernity of the city, not just because of changes in perception of time and space brought about by industrialization and the coming of the railway, but also, as Walter Benjamin has explained, because changes in the technology of reproduction, such as the daguerrotype and, later, photography, contributed to a fundamental transformation of perception.[34] The urban experience came to shape cultural discourse by the end of the century, and the city was identified as the site of modernity, associated with exciting change alongside disoriention and dislocation, new modes of living, and new technologies alongside tumble-down slums and inhuman misery. Modernization meant both construction and destruction. To say that the transformation of the perception of time and space, of social experience, and of the landscape affected modes of realism and shaped the novel is to repeat a cliché that ignores the fact that many English novels of the nineteenth century are set in country houses or the provinces, not in the city.[35] However, the representation of Jane Austen's or George Eliot's England, or for that matter Hardy's, would be incomprehensible without some understanding of the urban center of its culture—the political, intellectual, and commercial hub of the nation, as well as the marketplace for dissemination and reception of artistic and literary works.

The city became synonymous with modernity, and the novel was, in Mikhail Bakhtin's defining characteristic of the genre,[36] a surrogate through which the reader could enter and identify with the experience of modernity in linguistic constructs that are shaped by cultural practice, but also shape it, that act out social problems, but also act on them.[37] Modernity is a generic feature of the novel because, since the eighteenth century, time has been perceived as contemporaneity and the past has been reevaluated from an implicit belief in progress and empiricism. In such a perception, the fragmentation of modernity was opposed to a static idyll located in the country, repository of the values of the past,[38] though modernization, as Marshall Berman has proposed, was a complex and gradual process that was globalized beyond the city's boundaries.[39]

Rereading Dickens today, one is often struck by Dickens's modernity. On his death, Ruskin, in a letter from Venice of 19 April 1870, thought Dickens a "pure modernist" in a pejorative sense, "a leader of the steam-whistle party *par excellence.*"[40] John Forster was probably nearer the mark when he remarked of Dickens's domestic crisis in the 1850s that he never had a "city of the mind" to which to escape, but only the city of realities to which he was forced to return.[41] Those urban realities are symptomatic for us of the dis-ease of modernity, and it is often encountered by the outsider, the stranger, or the new arrival. Philip Fisher has commented, "As matter totalized within an outside mind the city is the subject, the antagonist even, of that classical nineteenth-century form, the novel of entrance, in which the individual immigrant biography condenses the slower, less recordable transition of the society as a whole."[42]

In his mammoth study of the city, Lewis Mumford has shown the growth of the modern metropolis to be largely unplanned, unlike the rational design of visionary cities or imagined utopias. Rather, the doctrinal emphasis in laissez-faire policies on profit and loss in the name of a larger good encouraged the unchecked and uncontrolled exploitation of natural resources and cheap labor in a particularly sporadic way that was environmentally destructive. The Industrial Revolution, which brought about the growth of urban population in unsanitary and overcrowded conditions, depended on mining that scarred the land and ruined it beyond repair or replacement. While we tend to think of the machine age as one of rational order, such destruction indicates the opposite trend was simultaneously at work, a form of "unbuilding" that the biologist William Morton Wheeler termed "Abbau," which Mumford borrows as his arch-metaphor for the industrial city, based as it was on mining and excavation that eroded the environment.[43] Despite the generalization in Mumford's apocalyptic view of global self-destruction, "Abbau" is a useful notion which he applies to the development and meaning of the modern city; it is a word which elsewhere resounds for Derrida with the Heideggerian origins of deconstruction.[44] "Abbau" is the process of demolition, erosion, destruction, and loss of meaning of and in the city, and thus well describes the upheaval of the city in a chaotic and constant rebuilding, as in London, a sprawling metropolis with various Georgian and Regency accretions, not a planned architectural whole. The rebuilding, or "improvements," dictated by the building of railways or road-widening were often destructive, sometimes displacing lower-class populations. Improvement could be especially disruptive and chaotic because street cleaning, garbage collection, lighting, and repairs were handled by different, often conflicting authorities in dozens of parishes which made up what was called London; there was no unified municipal government or overall planning authority until the end of the nineteenth century, when the London County Council replaced the Metropolitan Board of Works which since 1856 had been responsible for building London's sewers, streets, and parks. In Paris, where Haussmann's plans were somewhat more violent transformations of social and political space, to read the city was also to read its illegibility—"délire" in Flaubert's definition of a delirium.[45] The modern city was not a thing of beauty or a coherent whole, but was divorced from the meaningful cultural forms of living handed down through the ages. As an abstraction of a diversity of fluid meanings, the city was on the way to becoming T. S. Eliot's "unreal city"[46]—hence the hallucinatory quality of some of the Urban Gothic in *Bleak House* and *Our Mutual Friend*.

The city provided an unprecedented variety of character and incident, a dynamic poetic microcosm. The chance meetings on its streets mirrored a widening range of social contact and demographic representation, which opened up radical and transcendental possibilities, while providing material for the intricate connections of melodramatic and Gothic plots. The deformed urban monster drew the attention of social reformers and novelists alike (including

Dickens, Mrs. Gaskell, Eugène Sue, and Zola), who saw the city for the first time as a fascinating object of study that uncovered hidden aspects of the human character.[47] Yet Dickens's brand of realism employs a fanciful mode to suspend our disbelief in the mysteries and dangers of the city, a popular topic of countless books and sketches that attempted to explain the "world" of London to outsiders as part of a new ethnographic attention paid to street life. London's "wild tribes" formed a growing urban subculture, which by midcentury helped to redefine the limits of artistic representation, along with a more democratic awareness of social realities in the emphasis on everyday things in the Pre-Raphaelite movement or in George Eliot's pronouncements on genre painting in *Adam Bede*. Surprisingly, in his attack on the Pre-Raphaelites in "Old Lamps for New Ones" (*Household Words*, 15 June 1850), it is precisely the unidealized picture of the carpenter's shop in Millais's *Christ in the House of his Parents* that Dickens finds so loathsome, because the scene, which reminded him of St. Giles', failed to inspire him with any transcendence and, curiously, represented "the great retrogressive principle" that threatened to put the clock back in science and art (DJ 2: 246). Since Fielding, the inclusion of "low life" had been associated with verisimilitude in the novel, a claim taken up by Dickens in his 1841 preface to *Oliver Twist*, but whether the poor, criminals, and prostitutes were legitimate subjects for literature was hotly contested.

In fact, Dickens disabuses us of the assumption that the "ordinary" is representative of the everyday. More representative of London or any big city was the strangeness of its perception, as Dickens noted in his *Memoranda Book* in 1857:

> Representing London—or Paris, or any other great place—in the new light of being actually unknown to all the people in the story, and only taking the colour of their fears and fancies and opinions—so getting a new aspect, and being unlike itself. An *odd* unlikeness of itself. (MB, 14; emphasis in the original)

The key to representation (as distinct from description) of the modern city is here presented as a problem of characterization. The construction of subjectivity through estrangement from the city is an encounter with its newness and difference, but the ambience of a place is also an exteriorization of inner consciousness, so that the contrasts of evil and good, fetish-worship, or whimsical individualism seep into the narrative through the workings of a fanciful imagination. Because character is "placed" through the exteriorization of subjectivity, feeling and place are connected, allowing no simple definition of a realistic description, but making the reader visualize the city as a polyphony of voices and images. Yet this is also a fragmentary, often estranged vision, that reflects the crisis of subjectivity in a metonymic reading of place which enables us to experience spatially the personality and functions of the protagonists. Knowledge of the city comes only with formation of self, so that, for example, Esther (in *Bleak House*) or Little Dorrit read themselves into the city as they develop as conscious persona in the novel. Their moral reformation of self must reread the city in ways that circumscribe the conventional legal, political, and economic institutions of representation, which have failed to account for the self or a transcendental vision of society.

From an early review of *Sketches by Boz* to Walter Bagehot's journalistic trope for Dickens's coverage of the city twenty years later it was remarked that readers of Dickens's novels discovered an unknown urban world for the first time.[48] Yet Bagehot's point was that Dickens's was a fragmentary, unsymmetrical genius which delighted in "graphic scraps" of city streets. Bagehot was criticizing Dickens for reading London as a newspaper:

> Everything is there, and everything is disconnected. There is every kind of person in some houses; but there is no more connection between the houses than between the neighbours in the lists of 'births, marriages, and deaths.' As we change from the broad leader to the squalid police-report, we pass a corner and are in a changed world. This is advantageous to Mr. Dickens's genius. His memory is full of instances of old buildings and curious people, and he does not care to piece them together. On the contrary, each scene, to his mind, is a separate scene,—each street a separate street. He has, too, the peculiar alertness of observation that is observable in those who live by it. He describes London as a special correspondent for posterity.[49]

This is to read the fragmentariness of the urban experience as a visible perception, a text peopled by bizarre and unforgettable characters. Dickens's novels are, as one critic commented cryptically, "essays on the illegibility of London,"[50] and it is remarkable how much the urban narrator is preoccupied with reading and readers in order to decipher the illegibility of the city and its illiterate masses. What Volker Klotz has called the "narrated city," however, raises questions of what is being narrated and how, and the larger issues of referentiality and ideology can only be addressed when we do not take representation as a given.

AN ITINERARY

> To put it polemically, there is no such *thing* as a city.... *The city*, then, is above all a representation.
> — James Donald, "Metropolis as Text"

While I have followed a generally chronological order of Dickens's career and the major novels, this study will proceed by selecting key issues and themes which, though far from exhaustive, illustrate Dickens's representation of the city. Organized around clusters of interlocking discussions, each chapter explores the most blatant and significant spaces of the city through structuring images and metaphors in a particular novel. None of these spaces is discrete or unconnected and not all are uniquely or exclusively urban spaces; the streets, the railway, the home, the factory, the prison, and the dustheaps are, however, significant economic, social, and epistemological sites which came to represent for Dickens the network of connections in the commercial and materialistic culture of modernity. These spaces overflow into fields of metonym and project meanings which cannot be confined to the real places of the city, nor can they satisfy our desire that they contain the meaning of the city. The railway, for example, functionally an extension of the street in time and space, connects narratives and places in a way that symbolizes the social and economic machine of the city in conflict with the flow of natural values represented by the eternity of the sea. Though its full horror is only hinted at, the factory represents the clash between rival models of social change and individual growth. Such chronotopes reflect the changing relationship of the individual with the *agora*, the private and the public, as the country house becomes less representative,[51] and they form conflict zones where generic rules come into dialogic relationship with ideologically hostile epistemologies. But they are also metaphorical spaces in which the novel negotiates its own ontology (the house of fiction as Victorian home, the production of the novel as factory, the prison as real and figurative, and so forth). In such classic chronotopes of the nineteenth-century novel, polyphony mimics conventional discourses in a parodic satire of society (as in Bakhtin's examples of social hypocrisy in *Little Dorrit*), creating a judgmental distance not found in Fielding, Sterne, or Smollett, and subversively introducing other voices (*chuzhaia rech'*) in the comic stylization of public discourse.[52]

The first chapter introduces us to the street as contiguous with narrative and explores the analogy of walking and writing in the figure of the flâneur, though Walter Benjamin's labeling of Dickens as a flâneur requires some qualification and reservation which should put into sharper perspective the differences between London and Paris, as well as between Dickens and Baudelaire. The flâneur is generally associated with the solitude of the individual in the alienating urban crowd, but a comparison with Poe soon reveals Dickens's street walker to be a purposeful spectator, not an introspective dreamer and not the leisurely rambler or dandyish loiterer of Regent Street. The city's geography is mapped out through the reading of signs—linguistic as well as topographical—but the itinerary works against mimesis and represents the city's illegibility by making it visible, by constructing a narrative out of the confusion of its signs. Dickens's reading of the city challenges the validity or coherence of other representations of the city, such as the conventional panorama. The risky venture of a balloon ascent provides an alternate moral overview to that of the tourist lookout from St. Paul's and interrogates the epistemology of the bird's-eye view. Nevertheless, the theatricality of the city's spectacle provides a feast for the narrator's eyes. However, over the years the limitations of vision bring a somber appraisal of the city. London becomes obscured in mist or fog, but this does not mean that there is no meaning in the city, simply that there is no single viewpoint that can hold the perspective seen from Todgers's.

The traumatic transformation of memory brought about by the move to the city reveals the "trace" of Nature in the city in a backward movement from the city into a pastoral time and space. The loss of the countryside and the childhood innocence associated with it leaves its trace in the city of the dead in *The Old*

Curiosity Shop. In *Dombey and Son*, on the other hand, the "natural" is established as an antitype to the "mechanical" which threatens subjectivity and femininity. Representation of the commercial emporium of the world metropolis in *Dombey and Son* exposes a colonizing repression of the subject, who can be freed only by the nurturing of a maternal figure. Calculating business management is opposed to a romantic humane reading, to natural values rooted in the notion of "eternity." Time and space are visibly altered by the coming of the railway, but the question is whether progress is fundamentally destructive or can accommodate the uneconomic, natural values of benevolence and love. Providence, whose eternal Time of divine judgment is represented by the sea, suggests an alternative Nemesis here to that of the monstrous locomotive.

To what extent the novelist feels "at home" in the city and in the novel form is a question lurking beneath the bleak landscape of *Bleak House*. The synecdochal procedure of representation in that novel establishes radical connections between classes, as well as between city and country, while the metaphor of fog devalues privileged systems of representation—legal as well as linguistic, social as well as moral. Bleak House playfully parodies domestic ideology, but also serves as a metonym for the construction of the novel, in which the novelist wishes to feel at home. Anxieties of "at-home-ness" interrogate Victorian constructs of gender, domesticity, and nation. The Crystal Palace, an architectural construction of modernity and epitome of triumphant capitalism at mid-century, is shown to be an unnamed figure in *Bleak House*, and its ideological constructs of science and progress are opposed in the novel's counterexhibition of the noncirculation and blockage of language and law in fog, as well as regression to primeval conditions. The panoptic transparency of the Crystal Palace is implicitly resisted by the Gothic counter-architecture of Bleak House, and the novel's closure projects an idyllic home in the alternate space to the squalor of London slums and country houses of a dead aristocracy—in the pastoral.

The novel questions its own practice nowhere more than in *Hard Times*, where the tensions of Work and Art, or Fact and Fancy, provide an exemplary self-reading. The ideology behind the factory system shows Dickens engaged in debate with utilitarian attitudes which would deny imagination—and the novel—a place in the new industrial city. The juxtaposed models of "Fact" and "Fancy" are in binary opposition of *open* to *closed* systems, and the spatial oppositions operate dynamically to generate alternatively false and true expectations of social space. *Hard Times* is to be seen in the thick of the public discourse on Science and Culture in the Condition of England debate that was dominated by utilitarian thinking on social reform and personal liberty. The changes wrought by the Industrial Revolution altered the terms of political as well as artistic representation, and the novel had now to defend its usefulness as well as its productivity in the modern industrial society.

The labyrinth of the city turns out to be an ambiguous sign of the confusion of the city, as well as a maze, which only the novel can negotiate. The labyrinth of the streets is a narrative maze, with mysterious false starts and dead ends, which leads to its inversion in the prison in transformations of urban space that are geographical, metaphysical, and figurative. The real space of the prison cannot be separated from Dickens's childhood memories or his attitude toward reform. Since crime and prostitution were perceived as urban problems, the question of whether the criminal or the fallen woman can be redeemed once corrupted on the streets depends on whether the conditions of the modern city are seen to be determinist or whether human behavior and the character of the city can be altered. To what extent can the novel be said to be enforcing social norms and policing the streets? Or is the novel breaking out of its own prison-house to challenge power and gender relations?

The question of whether the city can be redeemed is one that can be asked in *Our Mutual Friend*, a novel which might well be regarded as a grand finale of Dickens's thematic and stylistic virtuosity. It is in this novel, I contend, that the literal and figural come into the most complex tensions. In *Our Mutual Friend*, the river is both a natural flow and a polluted carrier of death. The ambiguity of the river, the playful subversion of its scriptural associations as an agent of change and transformation, and the gloomy vision of the river at night do not make it easier to arrive at an assessment of regeneration in the city. The satire of Society, however, inverts the values and hierarchy of a city that makes money out of waste. Waste is a key word in the economy of the novel as well as the city, and the concern for efficiency is shared with Chadwick's sanitation reform, for the city is a body in which circulation must flow freely. But the principle of recycling in the system emphasizes, for all Dickens's support of public health reform, what Dickens attacked in utilitarianism. *Our Mutual Friend* allows for other possibilities in the city, such as John Harmon's refashioning of self and moral reformation in a religion of selfless love and benevolence. This final chapter attempts to answer, however tentatively, the question behind the enigma of the city with its dustheaps and corruption, its affluence and effluence: can some sort of salvation be salvaged from the urban wasteland?

Speaking of Dickens's "moral art," Barbara Hardy reminds us that the "Victorian art of fiction is essentially a moral art. It questions the nature and purpose of moral action, and, at its best, shows the difficulty and complexity of giving, loving, and growing out from self in an unjust, commercialized, and denaturing society."[53] What distinguishes Dickens's moral art according to Barbara Hardy, "is his combination of social despair and personal faith, his capacity to distrust both society and social reform while retaining and perhaps deepening a faith in the power of human love."[54] Barbara Hardy's analysis of *Little Dorrit, Hard Times, Great Expectations*, and *Tale of Two Cities* emphasizes just how much Dickens's realism is concerned with a broad view of society and hidden connections, rather than with nitty-gritty details that can be held up to the test of verisimilitude. It is surely not naive to say that in the very tensions between *récit* and *discours*, between failure of signification and the meaningful signification of that failure, between the pressures of autobiographical confession and its concealment in fiction, we may find the moral compulsion of narrative which seeks to represent truth through the lies of fiction.

It is by now a commonplace of literary theory to say that the rise in the eighteenth century of an urban monied middle class not based on land ownership largely shaped the novel form from Defoe onwards, especially because its construction of private individuality stabilized the multiple identities required by the city.[55] Of course, the novel is not reducible to a mere commodity in a capitalist economy, however much market forces dictated modes and forms, but it was both a vehicle and a product of social change, as much producer of cultural meaning as subject of social and economic production. Richard Lehan comments on Dickens's search for redeeming qualities in a hard-hearted urban capitalism that the sentimentalism which many critics feel weakens his novels was a failed attempt to read the possibility of a human community back into the city.[56] Yet the commercial center that emerged in the City of London after the Great Fire of 1666 was not the only city, and the cultural constructions built on the opposition of town and country did not offer the only possibilities and realities which coexisted within London and within the literary tradition, while the imperial project envisaged by Dryden in "Annus Mirabilis" belied the crowded, pestilent streets satirized by John Gay and Jonathan Swift. Conventional modes of representation based on preindustrial rural ways of thinking proved inadequate, and it took a remarkable imagination to make art out of the diversity of the city. There is no doubt, however, that Dickens's complex and sometimes contradictory artistic expression of the modern city experience tested modes of realism we have too often taken for granted.

NOTES

1   See John P. McGowan, *Representation and Revelation: Victorian Realism from Carlyle to Yeats* (Columbia: University of Missouri Press, 1986); Kate Flint, *The Victorians and the Visual Imagination* (Cambridge: Cambridge University Press, 2000).

2   Diane Levy believes Balzac, Dickens, and Zola wrote about character in the city, not of the city; it is not till the *nouveau roman*, she writes, that the novel takes on the experience of the city ("City Signs: Towards a Definition of Urban Literature," *Modern Fiction Studies* 24.1 [1978]: 65–74). A different term that has been used to describe Dickens's art is "urban grotesque," which connects him to Romanticism, as will be seen in chapters one and three below. One of the difficulties has been the lack of a consistent and historically precise methodological language in discussion of the modern city and the inevitable obtrusion of metaphorical displacement by postmodernist attitudes to the city (see William Sharpe and Leonard Wallock, "From 'Great Town' to 'Nonplace Urban Realm,'" in *Visions of the Modern City: Essays in History, Art, and Literature*, ed. William Sharpe and Leonard Wallock [Baltimore: Johns Hopkins University Press, 1987], 8–9).

3   John Lucas, *The Melancholy Man: A Study of Dickens's Novels* (London: Methuen, 1970), ix; Raymond Williams, "Dickens and Social Ideas," in *Dickens 1970: Centenary Essays*, ed. Michael Slater (London: Chapman & Hall, 1970), 77–98.

4   The "industrial" or "social" novels of the period between the Reform Acts have attracted much critical attention, most notably in Patrick Brantlinger's *The Spirit of Reform: British Literature and Politics, 1832–1867* (Cambridge, MA: Harvard University

Press, 1977); Catherine Gallagher's *The Industrial Reformation of English Fiction: Social Discourse and Narrative Form, 1832-1867* (Chicago: University of Chicago Press, 1985); and Rosemarie Bodenheimer's *The Politics of Story in Victorian Fiction* (Ithaca: Cornell University Press, 1988). Not all these studies treat the "social problem" novel as a separate genre or sub-species, and there is little agreement on the relation of the fictional text to social debates. Mary Poovey, for instance, follows Gallagher's lead in her *Making a Social Body: British Cultural Formation, 1830-1864* (Chicago: University of Chicago Press, 1995) and shows how social documents inform the text and texture of novels such as Dickens's *Our Mutual Friend*. More traditional studies, such as Igor Webb's *From Custom to Capital: The English Novel and the Industrial Revolution* (Ithaca: Cornell University Press, 1981), have fallen into a trap of remaining almost entirely within the world of the novel without resolving the "realness" of the characters and stories it describes. Webb does go beyond the industrial novels and relates Jane Austen, the Brontës and Charles Dickens to the general transformation of English society, but our idea of how that social transformation is expressed in their writing is barely advanced beyond general statements such as the assertion that Coketown placed an impediment on the formation of emotional individuality essential to the novel form. In this respect, Josephine M. Guy's *The Victorian Social Problem Novel* (London: Macmillan, 1996) is a useful corrective in its delineation of the complex relationship between literary value and historical knowledge: several of the texts with which Dickens's novels such as *Hard Times* are frequently lumped may be of differing aesthetic interest, and their interest to the economist or social historian may not necessarily coincide with their interest for the literary scholar. Guy's critique of "contextualist," Marxist, and new historicist approaches shows up anachronisms and contradictions in these positions, not least some false assumptions about Victorian views of society and the individual.

5   *The City of Dickens* (Oxford: Oxford University Press, 1971), 10–11.

6   *Topographies* (Stanford: Stanford University Press, 1991), 105. See also J. Hillis Miller, "The Topography of Jealousy in *Our Mutual Friend*," in, *Dickens Refigured: Bodies, Desires, and Other Histories*, ed. John Schad (Manchester: Manchester University Press, 1996), 218–35.

7   See pp. 96 below.

8   Robert Mighall, *A Geography of Victorian Gothic Fiction: Mapping History's Nightmare* (Oxford and New York: Oxford University Press, 1999), 39–40. See pp. 79–80 below.

9   Leonard Lutwack, *The Role of Place in Literature* (Syracuse: Syracuse University Press, 1984), 1–20. Lennard Davis postulates that whereas the Greek epic knew place only as backdrop to the action of the protagonists, a mythical "somewhere," the realist novel gives symbolic meaning to landscape because the representation of space carries within it ideological presuppositions, similar to those in landscape painting which gave symbolic meaning to space in painting in the eighteenth century (*Resisting Novels: Ideology and Fiction* [London: Methuen, 1987]).

10   Davis, *Resisting Novels*, 61.

11   Donald Fanger, *Dostoevsky and Romantic Realism: A Study of Dostoevsky in Relation to Balzac, Dickens, and Gogol* (Chicago: University of Chicago Press, 1967), 82.

12   Kevin Lynch, *The Image of the City* (Cambridge, MA: MIT Press, 1960), 147–50.

13   For example, Francis Miltoun's 1903 book and Cumberland Clark's 1923 lantern lecture of that title, or William Kent's 1935 *London for Dickens Lovers* and the London Transport guides to "Dickens's London." After Dickens's death, a plethora of articles and books explored the "country" peopled by his fictional characters or associated with his life, for example, T. Edgar Pemberton, *Dickens's London or London in the Works of Charles Dickens* (1876); Richard Allbut, *London Rambles "en zigzag" with Charles Dickens* (1886).

E. D. Whipple's imaginary "Dickens-land" (in *Scribner's Magazine*, 1887) gave William Hughes and Frederic Kitton plenty of space to roam in William Hughes (with Frederic Kitton), *A Week's Tramp in Dickens-Land* (London: Chapman & Hall, 1891), and Frederic Kitton, *The Dickens Country* (London: Adam and Charles Black, 1905); sixty years later William Addison was still following *In the Steps of Charles Dickens* (London: Rich & Cowan, 1955). More recently, Ed Glinert has taken us on a tour from the Charles Dickens Museum to Fagin's Den in his *Literary Guide to London* (London: Penguin, 2000), which, like other such tourist guides, looks for a factual basis for fiction.

14   *The Past is a Foreign Country* (Cambridge: Cambridge University Press, 1985).

15   See William Sharp, *Literary Geography* (New York: Scribner, 1904). A bibliography of such studies of "literary landmarks" may be found in Edith J. Roswell Hawley, *Literary Geography: A Bibliography* (Boston: Boston Book Company, 1917).

16   "Dickens and London," in *The Victorian City: Images and Realities*, ed. H. J. Dyos and Michael Wolff (London: Routledge, 1973), 2: 537–57.

17   For example, Aldon D. Bell, *London in the Age of Dickens*, 1967; Jacob Korg, *London in Dickens's Day*, 1960; the chapter "Charles Dickens's London" in R. J. Mitchell and M. D. R. Leys, *A History of Life in London*, 1958. In his lifetime Dickens was identified with "London character," and after his death Charles Dickens Junior cashed in on his father's notoriety to issue a gazetteer and alphabetical guide to the capital entitled *Dickens's Dictionary of London 1879: An Unconventional Handbook* (London: All the Year Round, 1879). A somewhat more historical account is Michael and Mollis Hardwick, *Dickens's England* (London: Dent, 1970), while Tony Lynch's 1986 book of the same title serves as an illustrated guide to the novels. For a partial correction see Anne Humpherys, "London," in *Charles Dickens in Context*, ed. Sally Ledger and Holly Furneaux (Cambridge: Cambridge University Press, 2011), 227–34. Dickens's bicentenary saw continued attempts to re-create from the novels a gazetteer or site of real knowledge—for example, Michael Paterson, *Inside Dickens's London* (Newton Abbot: David and Charles, 2011), and Andrew Sanders, *Charles Dickens's London* (London: Robert Hale, 2010). Exceptionally, Jeremy Tambling's *Going Astray: Dickens and London* (London: Pearson Longman, 2009) combines topography and biography with a textual reading informed by Walter Benjamin, Derrida, and Nietzsche.

18   See Lennard Davis's comments on Hugo's Paris sewers in *Les Misérables* and Saffron Hill in *Oliver Twist* as simulacra which took on a life of their own (*Resisting Novels*, 91–92).

19   John Forster, *The Life of Charles Dickens* (London: Dent, 1969), 1: 12.

20   Michael Ragussis, "The Ghostly Signs of *Bleak House*," *Nineteenth-Century Fiction* 34.4 (1980): 276–80.

21   See similar associations in a piece Dickens wrote with W. H. Wills, "The Heart of Mid-London," *Household Words*, 4 May 1850. On the bleeding heart of the city in *Little Dorrit*, see chapter 5 below.

22   See G. H. Martin, "The Town as Palimpsest," in *The Study of Urban History*, ed. H. J. Dyos (London: Edward Arnold, 1968), 155–64. Murray Baumgarten relates Carlyle's use of the palimpsest to Dickens's reading of the modern city in "Reading Dickens, Writing London," *Partial Answers* 9.2 (2011): 227.

23   *The City of Dickens*, vi–vii.

24   F. S. Schwarzbach, *Dickens and the City* (London: Athlone Press, 1979).

25   Edmund Wilson, *The Wound and the Bow: Seven Studies in Literature*. (London: Methuen, 1961); Steven Marcus, *Dickens: From Pickwick to Dombey* (London: Chatto & Windus, 1965); Gwen Watkins, *Dickens in Search of Himself* (New York: Barnes & Noble,

1987). Edmund Wilson's use in his essay "Dickens: The Two Scrooges" of the clinical term "trauma" to describe Dickens's experiences at the Blacking Warehouse is not precise. See also Albert Hutter, "Reconstructive Autobiography: Dickens's Experience at Warren's Blacking," *Dickens Studies Annual* 6 (1977): 1–14; Angus Easson, "The Mythic Sorrows of Charles Dickens," *Literature and History* 1 (1975): 49–61.

26   Notably by Alexander Welsh, *From Copyright to Copperfield: The Identity of Dickens* (Cambridge, MA: Harvard University Press, 1987).

27   Schwarzbach, *Dickens and the City*, 4–9.

28   Richard D. Altick, *The Presence of the Present: Topics of the Day in the Victorian Novel* (Columbus: Ohio State University Press, 1991), 11–13.

29   See Raymond Williams, *Culture & Society* (London: Chatto & Windus, 1966); Terry Eagleton, "Critical Commentary," in Charles Dickens, *Hard Times*, ed. Terry Eagleton (London: Methuen, 1987), 291–317.

30   Hana Wirth-Nesher, *City Codes: Reading the Modern Urban Novel* (Cambridge: Cambridge University Press, 1996), 18–20, 211 n. 20. I will discuss this insecurity in more depth in chapter 3 below.

31   See Max Byrd, *London Transformed: Images of the City in the Eighteenth Century* (New Haven: Yale University Press, 1978), ch. 1.

32   Asa Briggs, *Victorian Cities* (New York: Harper and Row, 1965), 62–63.

33   Robert Newsome, *The Victorian World Picture: Perceptions and Introspections in an Age of Change* (London: John Murray, 1997), 21–22. Compare the similar figures for the population of London and sixty-one other English towns in 1851 who had been born outside the metropolis (Lewis Mumford, *The City in History: Its Origins, Its Transformations, Its Prospects* [New York: Harcourt Brace, 1961], 467).

34   Walter Benjamin, *Illuminations*, trans. Harry Zohn (London: Collins, 1973), 188–9. See Raymond Williams, "The Metropolis and the Emergence of Modernism," in *Unreal City*, ed. Edward Timms and David Kelley (New York: St. Martin's Press, 1985), 13–24.

35   See John H. Ralegh, "The Novel and the City: England and America in the Nineteenth Century." *Victorian Studies* 11 (1968): 290–328.

36   *The Dialogic Imagination: Four Essays*, trans. Caryl Emerson and Michael Holquist (Austin: University of Texas Press, 1981), 32–33. There has been some recognition of polyphony in Cates Baldridge, *The Dialogics of Dissent in the English Novel* (Hanover, NH: University Press of New England, 1994); Peter Garrett, *The Victorian Multiplot Novel: Studies in Dialogical Form* (New Haven: Yale University Press, 1980); Ilinca Zarifopol-Johnston, *To Kill a Text: The Dialogic Fiction of Hugo, Dickens, and Zola.* Newark: University of Delaware Press, 1995). Lynne Pearce briefly surveys the beneficial influence of Bakhtin on some feminist readings of Dickens (*Reading Dialogics* [London: Edward Arnold, 1994], 62), and Michael Hollington has explored Bakhtin's approach to the grotesque in his *Dickens and the Grotesque* (London: Croom Helm/Totowa, NJ: Barnes & Noble, 1984), 1–34.

37   Gunter Gebauer, and Christoph Wulf, *Mimesis: Culture—Art—Society*, trans. Don Reneau (Berkeley: University of California Press, 1995).

38   Bakhtin, *The Dialogic Imagination*, 31, 229.

39   *All That Is Solid Melts into Air: The Experience of Modernity* (New York: Penguin Books, 1988).

40   Ruskin, *Letters to Charles Eliot Norton* (Boston and New York: Houghton, Mifflin, 1904), 2: 5.

41   Forster, *The Life of Charles Dickens*, 2: 200.

42   Philip Fisher, "City Matters: City Minds," in *The Worlds of Victorian Fiction*, ed. Jerome Buckley (Cambridge, MA: Harvard University Press, 1975), 373.

43   Mumford, *The City in History*, 450–51; see Rosalind Williams, *Notes on the Underground: An Essay on Technology, Society, and the Imagination* (Cambridge, MA: MIT Press, 1990), 4–5.

44   See *A Derrida Reader: Between the Blinds*, ed. Peggy Kamuf (New York: Columbia University Press, 1991), 270–71.

45   Cited Philippe Hamon, *Expositions: Literature and Architecture in Nineteenth-Century France*, trans. Katia Sainson-Frank and Lisa Maguire (Berkeley: University of California Press, 1992), 2.

46   Raymond Ledrut, "Speech and the Silence of the City," in *The City and the Sign: An Introduction to Urban Semiotics*, ed. M. Gottdiener M. and A. Lagopoulos (New York: Columbia University Press, 1986), 114–34. On the influence of Dickens's imagined city on T. S. Eliot, see Karl Smith, *Dickens and the Unreal City: Searching for Spiritual Significance in Nineteenth-Century London* (Houndmills: Palgrave Macmillan, 2008).

47   Françoise Choay, *The Modern City: Planning in the Nineteenth Century* (New York: George Braziller, 1969), 8–10.

48   Cited Collins, "Dickens and London," 539.

49   Walter Bagehot, *Literary Studies* (London: Dent, 1911), 2: 176.

50   Ralegh, "The Novel and the City," 324.

51   Bakhtin, *The Dialogic Imagination*, 245–50.

52   *The Dialogic Imagination*, 303–08.

53   Barbara Hardy, *The Moral Art of Dickens* (London: Athlone Press, 1970), 3.

54   Ibid.

55   See Ian Watt, *The Rise of the Novel: Studies in Defoe, Richardson, Fielding* (London: Chatto & Windus, 1957).

56   *The City in Literature: An Intellectual and Cultural History* (Berkeley: University of California Press, 1998), 4, 39–47.

1

The "Attraction of Repulsion": Walking the Streets

KNOWLEDGE AND SURVEILLANCE

I ... gazed
On this and other Spots, as doth a Man
Upon a Volume whose contents he knows
Are memorable, but from him locked up,
Being written in a tongue he cannot read,
So that he questions the half-mute leaves with pain,
And half-upbraids their silence.
—Wordsworth, *The Prelude* x, 57–62

es lässt sich nicht lesen
—Edgar Allan Poe, "The Man of the Crowd"

The nineteenth-century debate over London's primacy as the urban center of cultural production occupied the best talents in art, literature, and the theater. They set the "taste" for the literate public in an age of declining patronage, yet they held opposing views on whether, as some Romantics believed, urban civilization was corrupt and produced what Wordsworth deplored as an artificial culture. The nation's capital was vaunted as a world metropolis at the heart of an empire, but not all shared Robert Vaughan's confidence in *The Age of Great Cities* (1843) that the imperial project necessarily improved arts and literature on the model of Greece and Rome. The Enlightenment discourse of progress and prosperity was countered, in apocalyptic warnings by missionaries and conservative die-hards, by images of a new Babylon of corruption and vice.

These debates are reflected in a proliferation of books and pamphlets that (unlike engravings and guidebooks celebrating London's neoclassical architecture) investigated the terra incognita of the modern city, of which London was the paramount archetype: mammoth and boundless, the city had merged into the suburbs beyond the eighteenth-century boundary of the New Road. The city transgressed boundaries of class, creed, and race, and its enormity encompassed ways of life and people who had not before come into contact. London lured the curious in search of knowledge of the human character, whether utilitarians in search of statistics, or missionaries in search of lost souls. Anyone requiring "intelligence" of the present condition of the city had to walk its streets. The city's streets were a health hazard, often identified with the poor (who were criminalized), or the Irish (who were racialized and criminalized), yet the danger of the streets was tantalizingly inviting. The question was whether the knowledge they yielded could contain the problem of poverty and the problem of London.

Dickens's writing should be seen in a polemical context, which was dominated by the utilitarian insistence that only a scientific observation based on statistical representation could ensure the necessary surveillance and policing of the urgent urban problems of poverty, disease, and crime. London had a long reputation of crime and danger, evidenced in *vade mecum* books since the Restoration, like Ward's *London Spy* and its imitations or parodies (among the best known, Gay's *Trivia*, which opposed disorder to a sanitized image of the streets).[1] Dickens, however, presents a subversive gaze of the observer who walks the city streets and whose imagination evades police surveillance, thus resisting the discipline of rational inquiry that dominated most representations of the city.

Dickens's *Sketches by Boz* began to appear in newspapers and magazines from 1833, and several of them can be placed in the genre of the Hours, the round the clock tour of the capital. Here was a parliamentary reporter seeking to transform himself into a writer and to accommodate the changing political conditions in the wake of the Great Reform,[2] but Boz also engaged with the ideological assumptions of the genre and tried to give an entertaining sketch a more literary and critical turn. Some reviewers thought the first sketches too "clever" or politicized; in revising them for collection in the first series, Dickens toned down the style for a more genteel audience and generally reduced topicality.[3]

One of the most popular texts in this genre, Pierce Egan's *Life in London* (1821), celebrated the adventures of a couple of gentlemen about town who take a peek at the life of the poor. However, their slumming uncovers the supposed truth that beggars are shamming, and fashionable society can be easy about the invisible underside of the capital. The first edition of *Sketches by Boz*, which appeared in 1837, illustrated by George Cruikshank, who had also illustrated *Life in London* along with his brothers Isaac and Robert, shows, to the contrary, the realities of both progress and poverty. *Sketches by Boz* demonstrates the instabilities of London's social geography, though Cruikshank and Boz himself follow conventions of pictorial representation of London scenes, notably Hogarth and Egan's *Life in London*. Yet, as J. Hillis Miller has demonstrated, Boz draws attention to the inadequacy of conventional devices of novels and melodramas, thus exposing the ambiguous relationship between the fictional and the real.[4] The generic hybridity of the *Sketches* reflects the polyphony of the modern city, while the introduction of double-voicing and stylization creates a ventriloquy that enables Boz to maintain distance and comic irony in performing London's multiple voices.[5]

Dickens represents the Victorian city at a critical moment of modernity. Modernity is usually identified with Haussmann's Paris in the 1860s, not least thanks to Walter Benjamin's study of Baudelaire. Although Benjamin acknowledged the different conditions of modernity in London, Paris, and Berlin, his reading of Baudelaire's Paris has become the standard reference point for discussion of the modern city in literature. Gareth Stedman Jones and Lynda Nead[6] have shown London's similar modernization, albeit slower and not completed till the next century: "The history of modernity lies also in the experiences and journeys of individual men and women through the city streets, which round out the official story and uncover the contradictions of the streets in this period of improvement and the confusion of urban identities embedded in the process of modernization."[7] Representation is very much in question as the walker on the street tries to make the chaotic city legible by deciphering the vast, endless metropolis with its disparate crowds, diverse inscriptions, and changing social identities—which modernity made it impossible to subordinate to a fixed taxonomy, to the much advertised "intelligence" or "knowledge" of London.[8]

In his postmodernist reading of Dickens's city, Julian Wolfreys writes of the liminal urban experience of placelessness in *Sketches by Boz* that evokes a London which is ineffable and cannot be sketched.[9] What I am arguing is that, to the contrary, Boz does succeed in sketching the illegibility of the modern city without succumbing to "negativity." "Boz" functions as a rhetorical vehicle that posits an alternative theory of representation, one based on quite different ideological and aesthetic assumptions which are visibly modern in the *visuality* of what is represented. If, in Walter Benjamin's Marxist analysis of Paris and London, the stress is on the *unreadability* of modernity,[10] Dickens, I believe, makes us see that illegibility.

While *Sketches by Boz* cannot serve as a general statement of Dickens's position on art or on the city, it may nevertheless be useful to focus on the way the *Sketches* reflect tensions of modern urban life that arise in the 1820s and 1830s well before the establishment of a putative municipal government, the Metropolitan Board of Works, when radical shifts took place in perceptions of the city in literary, artistic, and popular representations of London. These shifts were accompanied by new technologies of representation, such as the magic lantern, the diorama, and photography, which radically altered the versatility of the optical image and the visibility of the observer:

> [The] palpable opacity and carnal density of vision loomed so suddenly into view that its full consequences and effects could not be immediately realized. But once vision became relocated in the subjectivity of the observer, two intertwined paths opened up. One led out toward all the multiple affirmations of the sovereignty and autonomy of vision derived from this newly empowered body, in modernism and elsewhere. The other path was toward the increasing standardization and regulation of the observer ... toward forms of power that depended on the abstraction and formalization of vision.[11]

Panoramas afforded the illusion of a controlled, objectively viewed real landscape, yet, like the one at the Colosseum, these were constructed in such a way as to hide the ugliness of urban poverty behind Regency façades.[12] Panoramas, dioramas, and magic lanterns made representation a marketable commodity, an entertainment for the wealthy that reassured them of the power and comfort they enjoyed. Such entertainment became so fashionable in Paris that Balzac jokes in *Le Père Goriot* (1834) about the mania for all kinds of "ramas." Yet the impossibility of a full view of the illimitable metropolis was something of a commonplace, and it was often accompanied by the concern about the resulting difficulty in controlling the proliferation of disease and poverty, which threatened the safety and security of the propertied classes.

The illegibility of the great metropolis baffled the attempts of many contemporaries to explain it and attracted a lucrative genre for which there was a profitable market. However, it is not hard to see the ideological bias in the reports by engineers and medical experts, while the falsity of panoramic views, whether from St. Paul's or the Monument, was evident to many observers. Dr. John Hogg, in his scientific and statistical survey, *London as It Is* (1837), described the artificial and unnatural way of life of a polluted Babylon, yet it is evident the scientific view is not totally clear when Hogg complains that the fog prevented London being seen at all from St. Paul's, the favorite observation post from which to view the great metropolis and a collecting station for data on pollution and the miasmic gases that were thought to carry epidemic disease. The irony is especially acute when we recall that the view from St. Paul's, as in Robert Mudie's *Babylon the Great* (1825), offered a panorama of life and industry. Indeed, London was, in Egan's words in *Life in London*, a "complete cyclopaedia," captured by a *camera obscura* that represented the nation's wealth and health, without the viewer being seen and far safer than Asmodeus's aerial view.[13]

The bird's-eye view of Asmodeus, familiar from Lesage's *Diable boiteux* (1707), was common in popular prints and literary sketches of Paris and London in the first half of the nineteenth century. Charles Sedley published *Asmodeus, or The Devil in London* in 1808, and a penny periodical of that title was launched in 1832; there are references to the lame devil ripping off roofs in Hawthorne, Carlyle, and Ruskin. Contemporary French examples include Janin's "Asmodée" (1831), or Bertall's *Le diable à Paris: Paris et les Parisiens* (1845–46), two volumes of contributions by Balzac, Eugène Sue, and other leading authors illustrated with humorous cartoons by Gavarni and others.[14] Less licentious use of this peep-show device is found in exposures of London's houses in James H. Friswell's *Houses with the Fronts Off* (1854), as well as Watts Phillips's *The Wild Tribes of London* (1855). In Bulwer-Lytton's *Asmodeus at Large* (1833), the devil relieves the narrator's boredom on a tour of London, but when invited to peer through walls with a magic salve, he does not report what he sees there.

Asmodeus and his cohorts peeled away walls and roofs, making the domestic interiors scandalously contiguous with the public gaze of the streets, luring the reader's curiosity to pry into intimate privacy. In *Dombey and Son*, Dickens peers into the unnatural spirit of the city:

> Oh for a good spirit who would take the house-tops off, with a more potent and benignant hand than the lame demon in the tale, and show a Christian people what dark shapes issue from amidst their homes, to swell the retinue

of the Destroying Angel as he moves forth among them! For only one night's view of the pale phantoms rising from the scenes of our too-long neglect; and from the thick and sullen air where Vice and Fever propagate together, raining the tremendous social retributions which are ever pouring down, and ever coming thicker! Bright and blest the morning that should rise on such a night: for men, delayed no more by stumbling-blocks of their own making, which are but specks of dust upon the path between them and eternity, would then apply themselves, like creatures of one common origin, owing one duty to the Father of one family, and tending to one common end, to make the world a better place! (D&S xlvii; 620)

However, this was neither the gaze of Milton's Satan from above and beyond the city, nor the demonic laughter of a destructive satire, but the view of a benign angel, which ripped open the vice and degradation lurking behind the panorama of conventional mimesis. In a review essay on prison reform, Dickens rejected the panoptic surveillance of a Benthamite warder in favor of a panorama of a good spirit, a beneficent Asmodeus, who would include every humble subject in the panorama and not exclude the human, so that the true needs of prisoners could be assessed (written with Henry Morley and W. H. Wills, "In and Out of Jail," *Household Words*, 14 May 1853; UW 2: 488). The aerial view assumes the superior moral position of authorial omniscience which penetrates the depths of wickedness in the unnatural city, in which there might lay some seeds of humanity and natural relations, if only that vision could be seen.

In the absence of effective policing, aerial views seemed to promise a more panoptical method of discipline and surveillance the overall view offered by statistical analysis. Ballooning remained, however, largely a promotional novelty and an attraction in pleasure gardens from the 1830s (briefly mentioned by Boz in "Vauxhall Gardens By Day"). Views from balloons were effective in controlling representation because they reduced the slums and untidy mess of an unplanned sprawling modern city to a legible map of social, demographic, and ideological order.[15] The aerial view was the superior moral overview of Dickens's intrepid contemporary, Henry Mayhew, flying high in Mr. Green's final ascent in his Royal Nassau Balloon in 1852, whose bird's eye perspective reduced the jumbled landscape to a "diorama" of toy-like, festooned patterns and brought into resolution what had evaded the eye.[16] However, the balloon view also afforded the thrill of physical risk, an entertainment for the new bourgeoisie offered by Astley's circus. It was a safer vantage point for the middle-class observer than the diseased and crime ridden streets trodden by Mayhew, the *Morning Chronicle's* own correspondent for the poor, whose exposés of the life of London's outcasts from 1849 onwards helped make them more visible as individualized types, no longer mere picturesque figures on the margins of a landscape or theatrical curiosities in amusing prints.[17]

George Cruikshank's frontispiece illustration of the 1839 edition of Dickens's *Sketches by Boz* (fig. 2) presents the author and the artist in their "pilot" balloon, trusting, as Dickens had written in the preface to the first edition of the first series in 1836, that "it may catch favourable current, and devoutly and earnestly hoping it may *go off well*" (SB, 7; emphasis in the original). This was a commercial risk but also a literary one too, since Boz was venturing into an alternate mode of representation of the city. The commercial risk in this launch of the partnership of a young writer and an experienced illustrator had paid off by the time Cruikshank's illustration appeared, and Dickens could build on his new popularity and warrant the success of the edition which marketed the fame of the author of *Pickwick Papers* and *Nicholas Nickleby*.

Fig. 2: George Cruikshank, title page, *Sketches by Boz* (1839)

There is no doubt that balloon flights and balloon views helped to change perceptions of the city, and "aerial" views of London's panorama (not actually taken from the air) were already popular before aerial photography was pioneered by Nadar from 1856 (fig. 3).[18] The panorama from above, Michel de Certeau has remarked, creates a fiction about the city; only the view down below can tell of the real experience of daily life.[19] In fact, *Sketches by Boz* present the city as a specular theater, an arena of speculation and spectacle. Speculation is both intellectual and financial, yet it rarely relies on scientific or empirical knowledge, as we can see in Boz's parody in "Our Next-Door Neighbour" of the flood of different theories propagated by phrenologists, who explained the relation of physiological appearance to moral character, a mainstay of both literary realism and criminology. Boz contributes his own theory of representation, a mock-discourse on the correlation of door-knockers to character:

> The various expressions of the human countenance afford a beautiful and interesting study; but there is something in the physiognomy of street door knockers, almost as characteristic, and nearly as infallible. Whenever we visit a man for the first time, we contemplate the features of his knocker with the greatest curiosity, for we well know, that between the man and his knockers, there will inevitably be a greater or less degree of resemblance and sympathy. (SB 58)

Fig. 3: Jules Arnout, "View from a Balloon of Westminster, River Thames, and Lambeth," lithograph (ca. 1846)

Boz imbibes the conventional relation of physiognomy and exterior appearance to social and moral typology as much as he mocks it as failing to offer a portrait of the whimsical, the eccentric, the individual. Yet Boz goes beyond comic scenes and penetrates the domestic interior of a personal as well as social tragedy; the story concludes with the chilling statement, "The boy was dead" (SB 66). Such compassion more than anything else marks off Boz from other contemporary observers of London, for whom the lower classes represented a danger to the stranger new to the "sinks" and "dens" of the capital. The stranger was warned, in the words of the anonymous author of *How to Live in London* (1828), that reality had given way to appearances, and especially so in the profusion of confidence tricksters. In a dismissal of the fictions of Egan and his imitators, John Duncombe claimed to be the first to describe at first hand a night spent in St. Giles', in *The Dens of London* (1835).[20] However, the usual empirical method of investigation in the stylized verbatim report, adopted, for example, by evangelical journalist James Grant, in *Sketches in London* (1838), evinces little sympathy for the lower classes. Similarly, Grant's description of Greenwich Fair has none of the vivacity and identification with popular entertainment shown by Boz, nor (with the exception of the humorous illustrations by "Phiz") his sense of pathos in the comic unmasking of social aspirations.

Consuming the City

> Where has spleen her food but in London! Humor, Interest, Curiosity, suck at her measureless breasts. Nursed amid her noise, her crowds, her beloved smoke, what have I been doing all my life, if I have not lent out my heart with usury to such scenes!
>
> —Charles Lamb (1802)

> My walking is of two kinds: one, straight on and to a definite goal at a round pace; one, objectless, loitering, and purely vagabond. In the latter state, no gipsy on earth is a greater vagabond than myself; it is so natural to me, and strong with me, that I think I must be the descendant, at no great distance, of some irreclaimable tramp.
>
> —"Shy Neighborhoods," (UT 95)

Boz might have said with Balzac in *Les Petits bourgeois*, "Flâner c'est la gastronomie de l'oeil." Michael Hollington has likened this ocular gastronomy to Boz's exclamation in "Shops and Their Tenants" about the "inexhaustible food for speculation" in the streets of London.[21] Charles Lamb also evoked the cornucopian metaphor in a letter to Wordsworth on 30 January 1801 in which he declined an invitation to tour the Lake District. Like Hazlitt, Lamb preferred the crowds of the city which gave him all the knowledge and morality he needed! His imagination and body feasted on the shop-window displays and the crowds of London streets, on the beggars, the prostitutes, and theater spectators: "all these things work themselves into my mind, and feed me, without a power of satiating me."[22] This insatiable desire was, of course, precisely what Wordsworth in *The Prelude* thought most unnatural and monstrous in the city's spectacle. Like Lamb, who boasted he was "born ... in a crowd,"[23] Dickens has followed Richard Steele's spectator out of the coffee-house into the streets, yet he never remains a mere spectator gazing at the theater of street life—in Dickens's adaptation of the Shakespearian trope of all the world a stage—but instead Boz engages in imaginative empathy with the players in domestic melodramas who act out their lives. Indeed, the use of melodramatic effects, the illusion of a magic lantern, and the movement of a diorama turn the imagined city into "the transformative optimism of theatrical experience."[24]

In an early review of *Sketches by Boz* attributed to G. H. Lewes, the novelty of Boz's generically hybrid approach was explained by the individuality that his satirical eye lent to characters in the scenes he depicted.[25] Yet there is here a paradox, noted by Walter Benjamin in *Das Passagen-Werk*, in the numerous "physiognomies" of the city: the flâneur scouted the crowd for a new, unique type, but was himself sucked into the crowd of typical characters. As in Baudelaire's "Les sept veillards," the city dweller cannot break the "magic circle" of typification, despite his cultivation of the most eccentric dualities, and his preoccupation with the new reveals multiple sameness. Walter Benjamin comments, "This points to an agonizing phantasmagoria at the heart of *flânerie*."[26] It is, indeed, phantasmagoria which unlocks the enigma in Dickens's own version of *flânerie*. The flâneur's observation of the city's ephemeral impressions and shifting scenes was particularly important for Benjamin's record of the cultural history of capitalism. The city transformed human relations because, as Georg Simmel explained in his lecture on "The Metropolis and Mental Life," the swiftly changing scenes of street life caused an intensification of nervous stimulation, so that the city dweller reacts with the head and not the heart.[27] In the nineteenth century, the flâneur negotiates the space of modernity in a paradigm of this psyche transfixed by "a fascinated alienation amidst urban spectacle."[28]

The city is a site of consumption, not production, where a commodified object of desire is fetishized by the gaze of the ultimate urban observer of nineteenth-century capitalism, the flâneur. The flâneur was a figure of the *Tableaux de Paris* in the 1830s to 1840s, a cultural construction Walter Benjamin later identified with the politics of the middle class during the Second Empire,[29] when he was an endangered species and an object of nostalgia, since he was about to fall prey to the commodity fetishism described by Marx, though he was himself a participant in the commerce of the city; his epistemological position as observer of urban life was precarious.[30]

The observer of life on the streets was in some respects a progeny of the strollers of the eighteenth century, the Idler, the Rambler, the Spectator, or the Lounger, whose speculations offered amusement and instruction; indeed, the contiguity of walking and writing was a trope common among Romantics such as Wordsworth and Hazlitt. However, only the paving of streets and the building of gas-lit boulevards or shopping arcades in the nineteenth century made *flânerie* possible, so that the flâneur is ideally situated as a *feuilleton*-sketcher of a modernity with which he is dialectically "out of step."[31] Looking back nostalgically from a railway age to Tom and Jerry in *Life in London*, Thackeray reminisced about the various styles of *flânerie* of these dandies in Regency London, "now a *stroll*, then a *look-in*, then a *ramble*, and presently a *strut*."[32] Angus B. Reach's Regent Street Lounger (in the 1849 collection, *Gavarni in London: Sketches of Life and Character*) is such a London "type" (fig. 4). Unlike the arcade lounger, in his hunger for intimate knowledge of good society, his gaze consumes not the goods in shop windows but the dress and pedigree of ladies in their carriages and of gentlemen in the elegant shopping street that was the showpiece of Regency London. What these types have in common is a position in a leisure class that is being eroded by modernity which radically shifts social stratification, most visibly on the streets.

Fig. 4: Gavarni, illustration for Reach, "The Regent Street Lounger" (1849)

Since Benjamin's discussion in *Illuminations* of Baudelaire's reading of a sketch by Edgar Allan Poe of a London street, "The Man of the Crowd" (1840), it has been axiomatic to speak of the flâneur as the urban observer driven by *ennui* to satisfy the urge for sensation of the new. In Baudelaire's definitive portrait of the perfect flâneur, the artist Constantine Guys, in his essay "Le peintre de la vie moderne," the flâneur is in the same condition as Poe's convalescent, in "The Man of the Crowd," who is compelled by irresistible passion to merge with the crowd and observe modernity; the artist can be compared with "a mirror as vast as this crowd; to a kaleidoscope endowed with consciousness."[33] The mirror, of course, has been an ambivalent trope of social mimesis, not least in Stendhal's mirror on the highway, for it reflects in a remarkably narcissistic manner the observer as well as dividing him from the object of observation. When the flâneur crosses the mirror's boundary between self and the crowd, he finds himself pulled by the crowd's ebb and flow: "To be away from home and yet to feel at home anywhere; to see the world, to be at the very centre of the world, and yet to be unseen of the world."[34] Baudelaire's incognito artist-flâneur thus enjoys the pleasure of being one with the crowd and does not recoil from such identification, as does Poe's narrator, who is *in* the crowd and who fears losing his identity and selfhood as one *of* the crowd. As Rignall has noted, Benjamin apparently misreads Baudelaire's understanding of who is the flâneur in Poe's story—the narrator, or the man of the crowd whom he pursues—and thus reveals the problematic nature of the epistemology of knowledge through observation; for Baudelaire this is an aesthetic issue, whereas for Benjamin it is a socio-economic phenomenon.[35]

This is an illuminating point for understanding the strolling narrator in *Sketches by Boz*, not least because of the correspondence—epistolary as well as literary—between Dickens and Poe, especially if both texts are considered as experiments in reading character, where reading is a kind of *flânerie*.[36] For Benjamin, Dickens is another flâneur who walked the streets of London and simply could not write when he was away from them.[37] The letter which Benjamin quotes from Lausanne, where Dickens was working on *Dombey and Son*, speaks of the impossibility of keeping up with his usual fast pace without the "magic lantern" of London's streets: "the difficulty of going at what I call a rapid pace, is prodigious: it is almost an impossibility. I suppose this is partly the effect of two year's ease, and partly of the absence of streets and numbers of figures. I can't express how much I want these. It seems as if they supplied something to my brain, which it cannot bear, when busy, to lose. For a week or a fortnight I can write prodigiously in a retired place (as at Broadstairs), and a day in London sets me up again and starts me. But the toil and labour of writing, day after day, without that magic lantern, is IMMENSE!!" (letter to John Forster, 30 August 1846, *Letters* 4: 612). Benjamin cites the comment on this in Edmond Jaloux's "Le dernier flâneur" (*Le Temps*, 22 May 1936), "in order to write his novels, Dickens needed the immense labyrinth of London streets where he could prowl about continuously," just as Thomas De Quincey was, according to Baudelaire, a wandering street philosopher pondering his way through the vortex of the city.[38] This sets up a mimetic relation of the streets with the imagination, enabling Benjamin to present the writer as a flâneur whose streetwalking is an allegory of reading.[39]

Dickens needs the crowds, not, like Baudelaire in "Paysage," the solitude of an attic. They feed his imagination and people the spectacle of the "magic lantern." The illusion of the magic lantern holds a mesmerized fascination with the inverted image and with the phantasmagorical effect of an artifice. It is, as Dickens tells us, the crowds which he misses, because they give his imagination the figures he needs for his writing, as he complains to John Forster in a letter from Lausanne in September 1846, when he could lose the "spectres" of his imagination walking the streets at night (*Letters* 4: 622).

This indicates not so much a mimetic, passive observation of the city's streets, but rather a peopling of the night-time crowds with phantasmagorical creatures, which brings us back to Benjamin's paradox of the flâneur's observation of unique types in the crowd who nevertheless conform to the collective identity of the city street. The flâneur in *Das Passagen-Werk* is a dreamer who, like the hashish user, perceives multiple faces in each passerby and yet reads into each one their profession and character. In Benjamin's reading of Poe's story, "The Man of the Crowd," the flâneur cannot help merging with the crowd. The boundaries of self and Other, like the mimetic glass which divides the coffee-lounger from the street, have been transgressed.[40]

Poe's story opens with the observer sitting in a coffee-house looking out on the street, not strolling. Under the peculiar effect of a recent illness and the unpleasant damp weather, he suffers from "the very converse of *ennui*" when the "film" departs from his mental vision and he enjoys the most delicious sensation of impressions. The window is a distorting reflection of passing figures who exist only during their passage through the observer's field of vision, as in Baudelaire's "Une Passante." These are external stimuli which cannot match Benjamin's criterion for "social realism."[41] However, the fascination of one figure pulls Poe's observer onto the street, taking him from the isolation of privacy into the public sphere. There his gaze is no longer feeding fetishized desire (like the strollers in Walter Benjamin's arcades), but the gazer becomes himself the object of the gaze and, in a recognition of the uncanny, comes back to his point of origin in his pursuit of the illegible "es lässt sich nicht lesen" ("it does not permit itself to be read") in the story's epigraph. The true horror is that he cannot separate himself from the secrets at the depths of the psyche or fail to recognize his own self in the mirroring gaze of the crowd, as in Goethe's observation that every human being carries a secret that would render that person hateful in the eyes of others if it were known, a remark that passes through Eugene Aram's thoughts as he strolls in a London crowd in 1758, indulging the curious gaze of passersby:

> What an incalculable field of dread and sombre contemplation is opened to every man who, with his heart disengaged from himself, and his eyes accustomed to the sharp observance of his tribe, walks through the streets of a great city! What a world of dark and troublous secrets in the breast of every one who hurries by you! Goethe has said somewhere, that each of us, the best as the worst, hides within him something—some feeling, some remembrance that, if known, would make you hate him.[42]

Poe's flâneur is "captivated" by the object of his pursuit, and, in a kind of compulsive repetition, he comes back repeatedly to his point of origin, to the Hotel D—, with a frisson of recognition, not unlike Dickens's whenever he visits coffee-rooms and recalls his repressed childhood memories of having to live on his own in the city and the shame of having to work for a living. Dickens's view of the street from a coffee-house is one he remembered because of the reverse image "MOOR-EEFFOC" in the boy's perverse backward reading of "dismal reverie."[43] Poe, however, is testing whether the imagination can be stretched beyond the limits of a literal mimesis and whether character can be read by the flâneur. The typology of physiognomic representation does not succeed in telling the old man's story, yet, in characterizing him as "the man of the crowd," Poe is establishing a collective identity beyond absolute knowledge, one which challenges the commonplace equation of the urban with the criminal, based on a non-rural space beyond Raymond Williams's community of knowledge. Poe is in effect rereading the city text.[44]

The metafictional ploy is hard to miss in the alliteration of "*d*agger and *d*iamond" which leads back to the D— Hotel and in the story's epistemological self-questioning, as well as the emphasis on the irrational forces of the *d*emon and *D*eath. The text subverts the finality of closure by teasingly allowing for the possible interpretation that the text is itself "illegible" or impervious to interpretation, except in as much as we have read its illegibility and are thankful for the small mercy that the darkest secrets of the human heart are not to be read. For this reason, the true parallel between Poe and Dickens is in the testing of realism: whether the observer on the streets (unlike the coffee lounger) can read the city streets without being swallowed by the crowd and robbed of his leisure to gaze freely on passersby.[45] In this lies the anticipation in realism itself of the end of its epistemological assumptions:

> In seeing the story as prefiguring the end of the *flâneur* in the development of the department store, [Benjamin] points to a change that has its literary equivalent in the transition from realism to naturalism; that is, to a mode of fiction that is at once the product and the critique of developed consumer society.[46]

When the homeless fugitive in chapter 18 of *Barnaby Rudge* plunges into the labyrinth of London's business district, the City, in order to lose himself and "baffle pursuit," he feels "a kind of suffering, on which the rivers of great cities close full many a time, and which the solitude in crowds alone awakens." Klotz speaks of this passage as probably the first example of the literary description of the lonely man among city crowds.[47] Only in modernism, however, does the urban observer become the lone figure *in* the crowd, no longer *of* the crowd,[48] and the horror of losing identity to the masses gives way to the alienated artist's perverse and stubborn insistence on individuality in a hostile collective mass.

In "The Man of the Crowd," the observer's fascinated gaze is observed by the object of fetishized desire; he is detective and detected. Similarly, in *Sketches by Boz*, Boz attracts the suspicions of the policemen on the opposite corner in "Meditations in Monmouth-Street" as he imagines the clothes dancing into life.

> We have gone on speculating in this way, until whole rows of coats have started from their pegs, and buttoned up, of their own accord, round the waists of imaginary wearers; lines of trousers have jumped down to meet them; waistcoats have almost burst with anxiety to put themselves on; and half an acre of shoes have suddenly found feet to fit them, and gone stumping down the street with a noise which has fairly awakened us from our pleasant reverie, and driven us slowly away, with a bewildered stare, an object of astonishment to the good people of Monmouth-street, and of no slight suspicion to the policemen at the opposite street corner. (SB 98)

Like Benjamin's flâneur, Boz is observer and under observation, detective and detected, a dialectic which Benjamin suspects underlies Poe's "The Man of the Crowd."[49] Boz's speculations give life to a motley group of characters who include a juvenile delinquent and a drunkard, the outcasts of London who are marginalized as dirty, dangerous, and not productively useful. By externalizing character in clothes and resurrecting stories from the cemetery of fashion, Boz establishes a mode of realism that risks blurring the lines between fact and fiction. He may indeed be committing a literary as well as literal felony, and his idle (though not profitless) speculations are rudely ended by the old woman minding the store who does not appreciate being stared at. Boz flees for safety to the "deepest obscurity" of Seven Dials, where he can observe unobserved in the linguistic, social, and topographical labyrinth of the city. The gaze of Dickens's and Poe's urban observers is surreptitious because they realize that conventional representation cannot read the city's illegibility, though what it is that cannot be read is the elusive secret hidden within the city's mystery.

ATTRACTION AND REPULSION

> The attraction of repulsion being as much a law of our moral nature, as gravitation is in the structure of the visible world, operates in no case (I believe) so powerfully, as in this case of the punishment of death.
> —Dickens, letter to the *Daily News* (28 February 1846)

Dickens's biographer John Forster sums up Dickens's life with the comment that he was "equally at home" on the narrow back-streets as the main thoroughfares of London,[50] because it was in the lanes and alleyways that he could know what was going on in the city and could read its stories. Similarly, in *Das Passagen-Werk*, Benjamin speaks of the "storied streets" of Paris read by the flâneur and quotes G. K. Chesterton, who also cites Dickens's letter of 30 August 1846 in his biography, as declaring that Dickens had the "key of the street." There may be some exaggeration in Chesterton's turn of phrase ("He walked in darkness under the lamps of Holborn, and was crucified at Charing Cross"), but he wants us to understand that as a child Dickens made the streets scenes for the "monstrous drama" in his miserable soul and not an exercise in the improvement of statistical knowledge.[51] These are the scenes which, for Benjamin, explain the psychology of the flâneur, because Dickens stamped his mind on these places, rather than allowing these places to stamp his mind.[52]

The grimmest parts of the city, Forster relates, fascinated Dickens: he had "a profound attraction of repulsion" for St. Giles'. Seven Dials, Dickens exclaimed, conjured up "wild visions of prodigies of wickedness, want, and beggary."[53] The "attraction of repulsion" is a Newtonian term which Forster applies to Dickens's romantic enchantment with the grotesque and his deep sympathy for the destitute and homeless. Forster ascribes it to the boyhood dreaminess in Chatham that Dickens brought to the city. The ugly could be an "attraction" in its magnetic appeal to the middle-class tourists of the day, whether they were the armchair readers of guides to the dens and sinks of vice, or those who preferred to venture out under protection of a policeman. The repulsion of what was morally and epidemically dangerous gave a similar pleasure of risk to that of ballooning.

The expression is found also in Dickens's 1846 protest against public hangings in the *Daily News*, in the sense of the fascination in the human psyche with such spectacles. In "The City of the Absent," the Uncommercial Traveller describes a lone stroller drawn by the "attraction of repulsion" on his tour of City churchyards to a particularly Gothic cemetery surrounded by grinning skulls that decorate the railings. These are given a particularly grotesque effect by the thunder and lightning at midnight. In *Oliver Twist*, a similar attraction is found in the patrons of *The Three Cripples*, "whose countenances, expressive of almost every vice in almost every grade, irresistibly attracted the attention, by their very repulsiveness" (chapter 26). Miss Flite experiences a "dreadful attraction" to the court of Chancery in *Bleak House*, and in *Great Expectations* Pip is "fascinated by the dismal atmosphere" of Jaggers's office, with its ghastly heads of dead convicts (chapter 20). In *David Copperfield*, the repulsive Uriah Heep exerts a mesmerizing attraction—Copperfield is "attracted to him in very repulsion" and identifies his murky, creepy presence with the night and the nightside of humanity which has invaded his own room (chapter 25). This is a fascination familiar from romantic constructions of the abnormal, associated elsewhere in Dickens with grotesque descriptions of the city, whose unknowable mystery reveals the evil in the human psyche. It speaks to a Freudian understanding of the uncanny, the compulsive return to the womb, at once familiar and strange, that recalls Poe's description of a similarly compulsive attraction in "The Man of the Crowd."

The phrase "attraction of repulsion" may have been current coin, and the Anglo-Irish journalist John Fisher Murray applies it in the early forties to the London crowd in *The World of London*, making the point that the crowd offers the delusion of sociability while alienating the lonely man who is pulled and absorbed: "the attraction of London life is an attraction of repulsion: the power of repulsion and being lost in an ocean of human beings is ever at hand, and the possession of that power generates an indifference to the use of it."[54] Herein lies the terrible ambivalence of the lonely man's fear of being *of* the crowd, where repulsion is both aesthetic and social.

Murray, like others before him, tried to explain the "physiognomy" of London, the synecdoche of the modern city and of the nation, but, in the second series (1845), what he wanted to know from the face of the capital of empire was where the money was coming from, wherein lay the power of knowledge, and how might it be made profitable. He saunters along the streets, a lounger enjoying the spectacle of hunger performed by beggars, genuine enough but still a performance. Presumably, his own writing staved off hunger and gave him the leisure to observe it in others.

Such hunger artistry marks the contrast between the lounging of flash gentlemen and the city walks of Boz. In "Thoughts about People," Boz notes how strange it is, "with how little notice, good, bad, or indifferent, a man may live and die in London" (SB 251). Such lonely men have lost any connection they had with the countryside and have no friends or companions in the city. They do not die forgotten, Boz quips, because there is nobody to remember them. However, the office drudge devoid of curiosity is one of a type, characteristic of a new class, alongside the wealthy bachelor and the apprentices, worthy of the attention of the roving reporter who is attempting to represent the variety and interest of everyday life on the streets of the city. Dickens has little sympathy for the flash London flâneur who derives no amusement or instruction from a walk between Covent Garden and St. Paul's Churchyard: "Large black stocks and light waistcoats, jet canes and discontented countenances, are the characteristics of the race; other people brush quickly by you, steadily plodding on to business, or cheerfully running after pleasure. These men linger listlessly past, looking as happy and animated as a policeman on duty. Nothing seems to make an impression on their minds: nothing short of being knocked down by a porter, or run over by a cab, will disturb their equanimity" ("Shops and their Tenants," SB 80). Their main amusement is flirting with a servant-girl in a cigar-shop, unlike Boz who, instead of staring like most visitors at the new smartly decorated interiors and plate-glass of London's gas-lit stores, explores gin-shops, maritime and pawnbrokers' shops, or dilapidated retail stores on the seamier Surrey side of the river and observes their progress from elegance to degradation and ruin. The gas-lit shop windows in "The Streets—Night" render stark contrast between the "whiskered dandyism" of Regent Street (SB 255) and the darkness and poverty of the nocturnal city.

We recall that Friedrich Engels, coming to London from provincial Germany, was shocked by the "enormous concentration" of population in London, the open class-warfare and the "brutal indifference" of an atomized modern society.[55] The indifference and indifferentiation of anonymous strangers who jostle past each other have the same dehumanizing effect, in Walter Benjamin's view, as factory production because of the reflex action brought on by mechanization and because of the regulation in the control of labor. Of course, the passersby include stockbrokers, entrepreneurs, and aristocrats, not only unskilled laborers, but the overall alienation is produced in an analogical way. Viewed by Baudelaire, in Benjamin's reading of *Les Fleurs du Mal*, the passersby are in turn forced to scrutinize each other, while themselves watched by the ultimate streetwalkers—the prostitutes and the police— who share an animal vigilance and sense of protection. The stroller and the prostitute are similar types of streetwalkers, and in both cases the relationship is uninvolved, a strictly commercial negotiation of desire in a crowd that spells both anonymity and danger of contagion. To cite one example, De Quincey in his *Confessions of an English Opium Eater* declared his affinity with a young prostitute, Ann, who succours him in his desperate loneliness among the crowd, a romantic figure whom he loses sight of and who remains a fleeting memory.

As in *Confessions of an English Opium-Eater*, the streets indelibly inscribe scenes on Dickens's imagination. Even the slums become a site of imagination, attractively picturesque yet accurately observed, free of the reformist rhetoric that took over in *Bleak House*, and free from the pathos of Charles Kingsley's *Alton Locke* or Elizabeth Gaskell's *Mary Barton*.[56] One cannot help thinking of the attraction of repulsion which Dickens found in Seven Dials, yet there is a better comparison than Baudelaire with Dickens in Hugo. As in Hugo, it is a sense of a new class that permeates Dickens's representation of London, a new vantage point with very different economic and social interests than that of the landed gentry and more established novelists. Moreover, Dickens's representation of London in *Little Dorrit* and *Our Mutual Friend* seems to have more in common with Hugo's attempt in *Les Misérables* to show all France in Paris than with Baudelaire's landscape of ennui (parodied in Eugene Wrayburn's view of London in *Our Mutual Friend*).

The "attraction of repulsion" may be understood as a mesmerized fascination with the grotesque, with the moral character of the ugly and the wicked,[57] but it also says something about the ambiguity of the writer's relationship with the crowd. Benjamin emphasizes the fact that the crowd was not an amorphous mass for Baudelaire, but permeates his poetry from within; in *Les Fleurs du mal* Benjamin reads "the trace of his defensive reaction to their attraction and allure."[58] Benjamin's flâneur idled his way through the crowds, pulled by laissez-faire, a counterpart to the universal law of attraction in vogue among supporters of Saint-Simon.[59] Nonetheless, Benjamin was aware that the principle of mass-production speeded up city life, leaving little space or time for *flânerie*. Yet it is the perceptive attitude, rather than Benjamin's all-inclusive definition of the figure of the flâneur, which persists in its "ur-form."[60] The flâneur should be understood as an ironic standpoint within an epistemological, as well as socioeconomic, crisis in representation of the city. As Chris Jenks remarks, the flâneur both enables and privileges a vision of modernity and is envied for the perceived power to walk freely through different social spaces, yet remains little more than a critical stance that cannot be pinned down.[61]

Dickens's pace through the city streets is, perhaps, too brisk, too hurried and purposeful, for the leisurely stroll of the gentlemanly flâneur; he is no idler.[62] Like Master Humphrey on his obsessive nocturnal walks, Dickens exhausted himself walking through "the cold wet shelterless midnight streets of London" (OT, preface to the 3rd ed., 35), along which Blake had wandered similarly observing "marks" of character, the marks of poverty and woe.[63] Boz probes the mysteries of the dark in space and mind and reminds us that the city vision is fantastic, a vision of "weird hauntings and dreadful intimacy" that owes something to the grotesque style of both Gothic novels and the Gothic revival in architecture.[64] Nevertheless, lounging down Oxford-street, Holborn, Cheapside, Coleman-street, and Finsbury Square in "The Parlour Orator" leads Boz not to observation of types in a crowd in the usual representation of urban "characters" and "knowledge" of the city, but to a red-faced character in a public house parlour. Boz takes his "likeness," noting that he is not going to follow the "established precedent" and is not in the mood for romantic modes of representation which would "invest the furniture with vitality" (SB 276), an indication, surely, of the tensions within realism between an enlightenment discourse and a phantasmagorical vision. Boz admits to "a most extraordinary partiality for lounging about the streets. Whenever we have an hour or two to spare, there is nothing we enjoy more than a little amateur vagrancy—walking up one street and down another, and staring into shop windows and gazing about as if, instead of being on intimate terms with every shop and house in Holborn, the Strand, Fleet-street and Cheapside, the whole were an unknown region to our wandering mind" (SB xxi). This excised passage in "The Prisoners' Van" allows Boz to pass through the crowd and enter into sympathy with the prisoners, instead of merely feeding his curiosity on the scene, as would be expected of the typical observer of a street brawl or accident. These are, as the subtitle of the collected volume tells us, sketches "Illustrative of Everyday Life, and Everyday People," and the author's object was "to present little pictures of life and manners as they really are" (1836, preface to the 1st ed. of the first series, SB 7). Dickens was exploring the uncharted territory of the lower classes in ways that defined and refined the social and political attitudes of a new readership from his own social background.

Later, Dickens would follow Poe and present the figure of a new urban observer, the detective. The detective is, to Benjamin's way of thinking, a "preformation" of the flâneur, who explored the labyrinth of the city, humanity's "ancient dream."[65] The detective hunts down malefactors in the urban jungle, in a manner not so different from Balzac's use of the Asmodeus device to unmask the savagery of civilization.[66] Mr. Bucket in *Bleak House* seems "to lurk and lounge" (chapter 22), but his pursuit through the labyrinth of contaminated streets is purposeful. His is the new "intelligence" of the city streets that are now efficiently policed and under surveillance. Yet only the novelist knows the true secrets of the city's dark mysteries which draw him with the "attraction of repulsion."[67]

LONDON, SEEN IN A FOG

> Fog everywhere. Fog up the river, where it flows among green airs and meadows; fog down the river, where it rolls defiled among the tiers of shipping, and the waterside pollutions of a great (and dirty) city. (BH 49)

Dickens was not alone in doubting whether the omniscience of the panoramic view contained an adequate epistemology for the modern city. Mudie notes in *Babylon the Great* that the variety and vastness seen from St. Paul's cannot be contained in one view. The "View from Todgers's," in *Martin Chuzzlewit*, on second sight seems less a touchstone for realism than an intuition that the city cannot be seen in absolute definition or clear resolution. As a city within a city, like most London boroughs, it is both of the city and separate from it, peculiar when compared with the peculiarities of London, so singular as to be typical of the city's indescribable uniqueness and to render London worthy of Todgers's:

> You couldn't walk about in Todgers's neighbourhood, as you could in any other neighbourhood. You groped your way for an hour through

> lanes and bye-ways, and court-yards, and passages; and you never once emerged upon anything that might be reasonably called a street. A kind of resigned distraction came over the stranger as he trod these devious mazes, and, giving himself up for lost, went in and out and round about and quietly turned back again when he came to a dead wall or was stopped by an iron railing, and felt that the means of escape might possibly present themselves in their own good time, but that to anticipate them was hopeless. (MC ix; 185)

The maze is so impenetrable that the streets themselves are not discernible, and, while the city-prison will attain its fullest expression in *Little Dorrit*, here too there is no escape from the hopelessness of finding one's way. Like the labyrinth of the city streets in *Oliver Twist* and *Hard Times*, the devious maze seems designed to prevent knowledge.

The view from the "observatory" of Todgers's rooftop is no less obscure and no less dizzying than the bird's-eye view of the medieval city in *Notre-Dame de Paris*, which Hugo used to penetrate the chaos of Babel in order to show the deterioration from a medieval city of stone to the modernity of plaster, an instance of the Urban Gothic to which we will return in chapter 3.[68] The initial impression of a conventional panorama of the Monument (itself a favorite spot for a bird's-eye view as well as suicides) reveals a frightening forest of disassociated objects and a wilderness, rather than a civilization, with enough smoke and noise "for all the world at once." A giddy loss of perspective follows, as the cityscape gets skewed out of proportion:

> the revolving chimney-pots on one great stack of buildings seemed to be turning gravely to each other every now and then, and whispering the result of their separate observation of what was going on below. Others, of a crooked shape, appeared to be maliciously holding themselves askew, that they might shut the prospect out and baffle Todgers's. The man who was mending a pen at an upper window over the way, became of paramount importance in the scene, and made a blank in it, ridiculously disproportionate in its extent, when he retired. (MC ix; 188)

So vertiginous is the view of the city that the observer is overwhelmed by the tumult amid an expanding mass of objects. Miss Pecksniff has to withdraw before falling headfirst. Any one view is ultimately untenable and subjective. No sense can be made of the detail within the whole and the figurative bursts the bounds of the real to acquire life of its own. Dorothy van Ghent finds that this is what distinguishes this commercial boardinghouse from Balzac's representation of Madame Vauquer's, which never goes beyond the limits of the rigidly human. The view from Todgers's rooftop is so unstable as to break down into insignificance, so that the nonhuman acquires an indiscriminate life of its own and the pathetic fallacy reveals a neurotic insecurity in the city.[69]

The Gothic atmosphere of mysterious cellars undermining the buildings points to a decay and collapse imminent in the city connected with a memory of Merry Olde England lost to steam and balloons. Though the narrator scoffs at such old men's talk, the represented view plainly resists a discourse of legibility and progress as the novel searches for the elusive Eden and rejects the planned American utopia as a fraud. We have to come back from the regular geometry of a planned city (which exists only on a paper map) to the real geography of London's labyrinth until we arrive at the final destination of the Temple Fountain, an enchanted garden of love in a celestial city far from the streets of the earthly city. The truer perspective is not to be found in the perspective from the top of the Monument, at a shilling a time, but in the novel form, which must bring coherence to the labyrinth of plot and human existence, an apparent muddle that, as I shall argue in an analysis of *Little Dorrit*, continues cultural and allegorical traditions. Tom's arrangement and cataloging of the library in the Temple would then be a counterbalance to the disconnected view from Todgers's, a trope for the book itself that makes sense out of disorder, yet nevertheless foregrounds its fictionality and questions the possibilities of mimesis.[70] In the view from the novel, the city spreads out in an endless labyrinth that exposes the falsity of the architectural monumentality with which London, Paris, and Vienna were promoted as capitals of the nineteenth century. Ironically, the congested streets observed from the Monument testify to the failure to fully implement Wren's plans after the Great Fire for a commercial world capital centered on the Royal Exchange, rather than the more spiritual St. Paul's; any planned monumentality is more likely to be found in art and the novel.[71]

London is shrouded in mist and mystery when Little Nell and her grandfather look back on it and they are glad to be "clear" of what Mr. Micawber called the "arcana of the modern Babylon." The nightside of the city is reflected, as in a Gothic mystery, in the fog that brings about Quilp's violent end, legally a suicide since he is victim of his own evil element. Fog was a real nuisance and health hazard which, as Dr. John Hogg observed in *London as It Is* (1837), obscured the panoramic vision of the city, rendering it invisible, but it also obscures the demarcation between classes and ranks so essential to correct social behavior. Thomas Miller's well-dressed gentleman in *Picturesque Sketches of London, Past and Present* (1852), for example, blunders along blindly in oblivion, bumping against the lower orders, and soiling himself with soot and lime. When fog obscures the bird's-eye view, our comprehension of the urban landscape is also obscured, yet we are pulled by the invisible and incomprehensible mystery of the unknown real city lurking behind its ideological construction.

The memorable opening of *Bleak House* makes fog more than the usual result of London's notorious pollution by coal-fires and gives the city its spectral appearance. It introduces the mystery that turns on deciphering illegible legal texts and rereading urban identities. However, Dickens seems to suggest both penetration of mysterious secrets and the limitations of aerial views when the crowds peeping over the parapets get a glimpse of London's all-enshrouding fog "as if they were up in a balloon and hanging in the misty clouds." Fog, that

"London particular" (BH III; 76), is the dense brown smoke which makes Esther Summerson think the city is on fire.

> The raw afternoon is rawest, and the dense fog is densest, and the muddy streets are muddiest, near that leaden-headed old obstruction, appropriate ornament for the threshold of a leaden-headed old corporation: Temple Bar. And hard by Temple Bar, in Lincoln's Inn Hall, at the very heart of the fog, sits the Lord High Chancellor in his High Court of Chancery. (BH I; 50)

Fog obscures the heart of this darkness like the legal ink of Chancery which muddles lives and truth. Jo's view of the cross atop St. Paul's Cathedral "glittering above a red and violet-tinted cloud of smoke" transforms it into an emblem, not of the Church or London's imperial and commercial power, but "the crowning confusion of the great confused city;—so golden, so high up, so far out of his reach" (BH XIX; 326).

In his later novels, Dickens visualized the illegibility of the city in the fog that blurs the text of its streets. In *Our Mutual Friend* the city has merged with the fog and contagious disease, thus dissolving any dividing line between visible and invisible, between the real and the figural, between the tangible and the imagined, between animate and inanimate:

> It was a foggy day in London, and the fog was heavy and dark. Animate London, with smarting eyes and irritated lungs, was blinking, wheezing and choking; inanimate London was a sooty spectre, divided in purpose between being visible and invisible, and to being wholly neither. Gaslights flared in the shops with a haggard and unblest air, as knowing themselves to be night-creatures that had no business abroad under the sun; while the sun itself, when it was for a few moments dimly indicated through circling eddies of fog, showed as if it had gone out and were collapsing flat and cold. Even in the surrounding country it was a foggy day, but there the fog was grey, whereas in London it was about the boundary line, dark yellow, and a little within it brown, and then browner, and then browner, until at the heart of the City—which call Saint Mary Axe—it was rusty-black. From any point of the high ridge of land northward, it might have been discerned that the loftiest buildings made an occasional struggle to get their heads above the foggy sea, and especially that the great dome of St. Paul's seemed to die hard; but this was not perceivable in the streets at their feet, where the whole metropolis was a heap of vapour charged with the muffled sound of wheels, and enfolding a gigantic catarrh. (OMF III, I; 479)

The opposition of city and country has faded into a difference of degree, though it is an all-important difference. The visible sign of the city is now its abstraction into what represents it—the fog that obscures the view from St. Paul's and threatens to submerge that landmark into the general "sea" of darkness, sickness, and death. Yet the city has not become totally invisible; it is just that its illegibility has to be represented in order for it to be imagined coherently.

The orphaned waif lost in the crowd in *Bleak House* is a far cry from Baudelaire's fashionable flâneur, and his insignificance in the indifferent stream of passersby speaks both for Jo's illiterate existence and for the inadequacy of conventional modes of representation to read the city streets. The unbearable conditions of city life are endowed with an imaginative and therefore emotive existence by narrative coherence. David Copperfield, it might be noted, cannot reconcile his unloved abandonment to the bottling warehouse in London with his reading of eighteenth-century novels and his perverse self-dependency except as "a romantic boy" storying the streets in his imagination (DC xi; 224). The rereading of the streets tells a romanticized story of traumatic severance from home and countryside which forces a reevaluation of the text of the city and uncovers the trace of Nature in the unnatural character of urban life.

The view of the city from the ground may resemble a sea of mud in *Bleak House*, just as Paris is a sea of mud in *Le Père Goriot*, and it may often look like a jumbled chaos, but its meaning is never unfathomable or unchartable. Simply, its signs have to be reread for us to make our way in the unfamiliar maze of city streets. Jo's view of London from Blackfriars Bridge is feverish and confused, yet it affords a truer perception of a chaos in which he can never have a home. Londoners do not need to be told that a crossing sweeper's view from Blackfriars' Bridge of the City of London (the financial center of capitalism) cannot be further from Wordsworth's view upriver of the City of Westminster and the Houses of Parliament (the powerhouse of empire). However, in contrast to Rastignac's overview of Paris from the necropolis of the cemetery which closes *Le Père Goriot*, Dickens does not throw down the gauntlet to society but transcends the view with other possibilities—the radical vision of mutual responsibility and benevolence which will be explored in the following chapters.

NOTES

1   See Alison O'Bryne, "The Art of Walking in London: Representing Urban Pedestrianism in the Early Nineteenth Century," *Romanticism* 14.2 (2008): 94–107. On the transgressive literature that grew out of the ideological and socio-economic tensions of the capital, see John Marriott, *The Other Empire: Metropolis, India and Progress in the Colonial Imagination* (Manchester: Manchester University Press, 2003).
2   Kathryn Chittick, *Dickens and the 1830s* (Cambridge: Cambridge University Press, 1990).
3   See Paul Schlicke, "Revisions to *Sketches by Boz*," *The Dickensian* 101.1 (2005): 29–38; Schlicke, "Risen Like a Rocket," *Dickens Quarterly* 22.1 (2005): 3–18; John Butt and Kathleen Tillotson, *Dickens at Work* (London: Methuen, 1957), 35–61.
4   "The Fiction of Realism: *Sketches by Boz*, *Oliver Twist* and Cruikshank's Illustrations," in *Dickens Centennial Essays*, ed. Ada Nesbet and Blake Nevius (Berkeley: University of California Press, 1971), 85–153. See also Sambudha Sen, "Hogarth, Egan, Dickens, and the Making of an Urban Aesthetic," *Representations* 103 (Summer 2008): 84–106.
5   Ian Wilkinson, "Textual Ventriloquy: Dickens's *Sketches by Boz* through Bakhtin," *Dickens Quarterly* 20.4 (2003): 225–39.

6   Gareth Stedman Jones, *Outcast London: A Study in the Relationship between Classes in Victorian Society* (Oxford: Clarendon Press, 1971); Lynda Nead, *Victorian Babylon: People, Streets and Images in Nineteenth-Century London* (New Haven: Yale University Press, 2000).

7   Nead, *Victorian Babylon*, 75.

8   Geoffrey Hemstedt, "Inventing Social Identity: *Sketches by Boz*," in *Victorian Identities: Social & Cultural Formations in Nineteenth-Century Literature*, ed. Ruth Robbins and Julian Wolfreys (London: Macmillan, and New York: St. Martin's Press, 1996), 216, 225.

9   Julian Wolfreys, *Writing London: The Trace of the Urban Text from Blake to Dickens* (London: Macmillan, and New York: St. Martin's Press, 1998), 164.

10   *Illuminations*, trans. Harry Zohn (London: Collins, 1973), 168.

11   Jonathan Crary, *Techniques of the Observer: On Vision and Modernity in the Nineteenth Century* (Cambridge, MA: MIT Press, 1990), 150. Also see Kate Flint, *The Victorians and the Visual Imagination* (Cambridge: Cambridge University Press, 2000), 21–22.

12   Christine M. Boyer, *The City of Collective Memory: Its Historical Imagery and Architectural Entertainment* (Cambridge, MA: MIT Press, 1994); Deborah Epstein Nord, *Walking the Victorian Streets: Women, Representation, and the City* (Ithaca: Cornell University Press, 1995); Stephan Oetterman, *The Panorama: History of a Mass Medium*, trans. Deborah L. Schneider (New York: Zone Books, 1997). For a dissenting view see Alan Robinson, *Imagining London, 1779–1900* (Houndsmill: Palgrave, 2004), 10–13.

13   On the use of optical tropes see John Plumkett, "Optical Entertainments and Victorian Literature," in *Literature and the Visual Imagination*, ed. David Seed (Cambridge: D. S. Brewer for the English Association, 2005), 1–28.

14   Priscilla Parkhurst Ferguson, *Paris as Revolution: Writing the Nineteenth-Century City* (Berkeley: University of California Press, 1994), 36–79. See also Sharon Marcus, *Apartment Stories: City and Home in Nineteenth-Century Paris and London* (Berkeley: University of California Press, 1999), 36–37; Jonathan Arac, *Commissioned Spirits: The Shaping of Social Motion in Dickens, Carlyle, Melville, and Hawthorne* (New Brunswick: Rutgers University Press, 1970), 85–86; and Philippe Hamon, *Expositions: Literature and Architecture in Nineteenth-Century France*, trans. Katia Sainson-Frank and Lisa Maguire (Berkeley: University of California Press, 1992).

15   Elaine Freedgood, *Victorian Writing about Risk: Imagining a Safe England in a Dangerous World* (Cambridge: Cambridge University Press, 2000), 74–98.

16   Mayhew, "In the Clouds," *Illustrated London News*, 18 September 1852; see Elaine Freedgood, *Victorian Writing about Risk*, 86–89. Kate Flint has expounded on the implications of Mayhew's balloon flight for the Victorian preoccupation with the panoptic gaze in *The Victorians and the Visual Imagination*, 9–11. However, as Flint points out in her study, Dickens and others resisted panoptic classifications in their writing and recorded how the visible could be misread.

17   See Sean Shesgreen, *Images of the Outcast: The Urban Poor in the Cries of London* (Manchester: Manchester University Press, 2002); Marriott, *The Other Empire*, 119.

18   See Walter Benjamin, "The Work of Art in the Age of its Technological Reproducibility (Second Version)," in *Walter Benjamin: Selected Writings, Volume 3, 1935–1939*, trans. Edmund Jephcott et al., ed. Howard Eiland and Michael J. Jennings (Cambridge, MA: Harvard University Press, 2002), 101–33.

19   "Practices of Space," in *On Signs*, ed. Marshall Blonsky (Baltimore: Johns Hopkins University Press, 1985), 123–24.

20   On how Duncombe, Bee, Smeeton and others reflected changes in the literary representation of London see Marriott, *The Other Empire*, 104–05.

21   Michael Hollington, "Dickens the Flâneur" *The Dickensian* 77 (1981): 76–77.

22   *The Complete Works and Letters of Charles Lamb* (New York: Random House, 1935), 687.

23   "The Londoner," *The Complete Works and Letters of Charles Lamb*, 375.

24   Baumgarten, "Dickens, London, & the Invention of Modern Urban Life," in *Dickens: The Craft of Fiction and the Challenges of Reading*, ed. Rossana Bonadei, Clotilde de Stasio, Carlo Pagetti, and Alessandro Vescovi (Milan: Unicopli, 2000), 196. J. Hillis Miller similarly points to Dickens's indebtedness to the theater and stresses the performance of scenes reminiscent of melodrama, pantomime, or farce ("The Fiction of Realism," 109).

25   *National Magazine* 1 (December 1837), 455–59; reprinted in *Charles Dickens: Critical Assessments*, ed. Michael Hollington (Mountfield, East Sussex: Helm), 1: 245–49.

26   *The Arcades Project*, trans. Howard Eiland and Kevin McLaughlin (Cambridge, MA: Harvard University Press, 1999), 22.

27   Georg Simmel, *Simmel on Culture: Selected Writings*, ed. David Frisby and Mike Featherstone (London: Sage, 1997), 175–76.

28   Lawrence Buell, *Writing for an Endangered World: Literature, Culture, and Environment in the U.S. and Beyond* (Cambridge, MA: Harvard University Press, 2002), 89.

29   *The Arcades Project*, 417–20.

30   John Rignall, *Realist Fiction and the Strolling Spectator* (London: Routledge, 1992), 3–12.

31   Graeme Gilloch, *Myth and Metropolis: Walter Benjamin and the City* (Cambridge: Polity Press, 1997), 155. See Susan Buck-Morss, *The Dialectics of Seeing: Walter Benjamin and the Arcades Project* (Cambridge, MA: MIT Press, 1991), 308.

32   "De Juventute," *Roundabout Papers from the Cornhill Magazine* (London: Smith, Elder, & Co., 1869), 85; see Hollington, "Dickens the *Flâneur*," 72–73.

33   Charles Baudelaire, *Selected Writings on Art and Artists*, trans. P. E. Charvet (Cambridge: Cambridge University Press, 1981), 400.

34   Baudelaire, *Selected Writings*, 399–400; see Benjamin, *The Arcades Project*, 443; Sara Hackenberg, "'Loitering Artfully': Reading *Flânerie* in *Our Mutual Friend*," in *Dickens: The Craft of Fiction and the Challenges of Reading*, ed. Rossana Bonadei, Clotilde de Stasio, Carlo Pagetti, and Alessandro Vescovi (Milan: Unicopli, 2000), 234. Hollington likens Baudelaire's characterization of Guys as an unseen observer of the crowd to both Balzac and Dickens ("Dickens the *Flâneur*," 74), and Lyn Pykett, too, cites Baudelaire's essay in her description of Dickens as a flâneur (*Charles Dickens* [Houndmills: Palgrave, 2002], 21, 28–29), but in a context in which Dickens would not have seen himself as a flâneur.

35   Rignall, *Realist Fiction and the Strolling Spectator*, 13–14.

36   Sara Hackenberg interprets *Our Mutual Friend* as a revision of Poe's story ("'Loitering Artfully,'" 230–39).

37   Benjamin, *Charles Baudelaire: Ein Lyriker im Zeitalter des Hochkapitalismus.* (Frankfurt-am-Main: Surhkampf, 1974), 68–69; Benjamin, *The Arcades Project*, 426.

38   *The Arcades Project*, 436.

39   *Charles Baudelaire*, 48.

40   *Illuminations*, 174.

41   *Illuminations*, 173.

42   Edward Bulwer-Lytton, *Eugene Aram* (London: Chapman & Hall, 1849), 180. See Benjamin, *Arcades Project*, 440.

43   John Forster, *The Life of Charles Dickens* (London: Dent, 1969), 1: 25.

44   Alexander Gelley, "City Texts: Representations, Semiology, and Urbanism," in *Politics, Theory, and Contemporary Culture*, ed. Mark Poster (New York: Columbia University Press, 1993), 255.

45   Benjamin, *Illuminations*, 174.
46   Rignall, *Realist Fiction and the Strolling Spectator*, 18.
47   Volker Klotz, *Die erzählte Stadt: Ein Sujet als Herausforderung des Romans von Lesage bis Döblin* (München: Carl Hanger, 1989), 154.
48   Burton Pike, *The Image of the City in Modern Literature* (Princeton: Princeton University Press, 1981), 100–17.
49   Benjamin, *The Arcades Project*, 20.
50   Forster, *The Life of Charles Dickens*, 2: 397.
51   G. K. Chesterton, *Dickens* [1906] (New York: Schocken, 1965), 45–46, 49.
52   Benjamin, *The Arcades Project*, 438.
53   Forster, *The Life of Charles Dickens*, 1: 14.
54   John Fisher Murray, *The World of London* (London: Blackwood, 1843), 1: 52–53; see Rick Allen, "John Fisher Murray, Dickens, and 'The Attraction of Repulsion,'" *Dickens Quarterly* 16.1 (Spring 1999): 139–59.
55   Engels, *The Condition of the Working Class in England*, trans. W. O. Henderson and W. H. Chaloner (Oxford: Blackwell, 1972), 30–31.
56   Hemstedt, "Inventing Social Identity," 219, 222.
57   Phillip Collins, "Dickens and London," in *The Victorian City: Images and Realities*, ed. H. J. Dyos and Michael Wolff (London: Routledge, 1973), 2: 537–40.
58   *Illuminations*, 169.
59   Benjamin, *The Arcades Project*, 420.
60   Buck-Morss, *The Dialectics of Seeing*, 344–47.
61   Chris Jenks, "Watching Your Step: The History and Practice of the *Flâneur*," in *Visual Culture*, ed. Chris Jenks (London: Routledge, 1995), 142–60.
62   Hollington, "Dickens the *Flâneur*," 74; Hemstedt, "Inventing Social Identity," 216. Eveline Kilian has traced the flâneur in *Sketches by Boz* to Fielding ("Charles Dickens' London and the Eighteenth-Century Tradition of Realism," *Zeitschrift für Anglisitk und Amerikanistik* 53 [2005]: 317–32), while. David Seed, on the other hand, places Dickens in the context of the nineteenth-century urban sketch ("Touring the Metropolis: The Shifting Subjects of Dickens's London Sketches," *Yearbook of English Studies* 34 [2004]: 155–70). Alan Robinson, in fact, distinguishes Boz from the disaffected bohemian Parisian flâneur because he identifies with the upwardly mobile middle class, yet he senses an affinity with the streetwalker that arises from an autobiographical experience of poverty and degradation (*Imagining London, 1779–1900*, 77–79). See also Michael Hollington, "Dickens, Sala and the London Arcade," *Dickens Quarterly* 28.4 (2011): 273-284.
63   Hollington, "Dickens the *Flâneur*," 75. I am not suggesting Dickens was reading Blake's "London," merely that he was following a conventional trope of sin and vice. In *Bleak House*, Mr. Bucket clatters over the midnight streets at a gallop, but nevertheless nothing escapes his keen eyes (BH LVI; 822).
64   Christine M. Boyer, *The City of Collective Memory: Its Historical Imagery and Architectural Entertainment* (Cambridge, MA: MIT Press, 1994), 279.
65   Benjamin, *The Arcades Project*, 429.
66   Ibid., 440–43.
67   On the transition from the casual gaze of Boz to the purposeful detection of the city's dark mysteries in *Bleak House* see Rignall, *Realist Fiction and the Strolling Spectator*, 62–79. See also Mark Willis, "Dickens the *Flâneur*—London and *The Uncommercial Traveller*," *Dickens Quarterly* 20.4 (2003): 240–56.

68   See Richard Maxwell, *The Mysteries of Paris and London* (Charlottesville: University Press of Virginia, 1992); Robert Mighall, *A Geography of Victorian Gothic Fiction: Mapping History's Nightmare* (Oxford: Oxford University Press, 1999), 53.

69   Dorothy Van Ghent, "The Dickens World: A View from Todgers's," in *Dickens: A Collection of Critical Essays*, ed. Martin Price (Englewood Cliffs, NJ: Prentice-Hall, 1987), 28–29. Insecurity can be seen in the anxiety connected with leaving the city in "Early Coaches" and in the opening of chapter 15 of *The Old Curiosity Shop*.

70   Gerhard Joseph treats the library as a *mise en abîme* and makes the point that the labyrinth is unfathomable. Cruikshank's illustration of Old Martin's unmasking of Pecksniff in chapter 52, showing books falling out of the library, including a copy of *Paradise Lost*, is surely an allusion to the loss of Pecksniff's Eden and the fall into the real world ("The Labyrinth and the Library: A View from the Temple in *Martin Chuzzlewit*," *Dickens Studies Annual* 15 [1986]: 1–22).

71   Donald J. Olsen, *The City as a Work of Art* (New Haven: Yale University Press, 1986), 9–34. In a counterargument to van Ghent's, Joseph has suggested that the trope of architectural monumentality is itself an object of representation ("The Labyrinth and the Library," 4–10).

2

The Railway and the Body of the City:
Dombey and Son

CIRCULATION AND THE BODY OF EMPIRE

> the circulation that is made in the heart of London ... moves
> more briskly in the blood of the citizens.
> —Tom Brown, *Amusements Serious and Comical,*
> *Calculated for the Meridian of London* (1700)

> But what is to be the fate of the great wen of all? The monster,
> called ... "the metropolis of the empire"?
> —William Cobbett, *Rural Rides* (1830)

"As the metropolis of the British Empire, it is the centre whither all the sensations of the Empire tend, and whence the motive currents issue that thrill to the extremities."[1] Writing in 1859, the Victorian critic David Masson uses a commonplace anthropomorphic analogy of the city as an organic system, its streets the veins of its body, to promote Dickens and Thackeray as founders of the urban novel that mined the inexhaustible resources of London. Since Harvey's discovery of the function of the heart in blood circulation, the danger to circulation of clogged streets and poor ventilation were frequent complaints of urban writers concerned with both physiological and moral health in the city.[2] The city-body trope was invigorated by Enlightenment notions of natural law and applied to the man-made artificial power structure of nineteenth-century capitalism, so that the circulation of the system was of overriding concern in discussions of the economic, ideological, and public health of the nation. Circulation was a common metaphor of economic health in particular, and Adam Smith in *The Wealth of Nations* warned that unnatural swelling of commerce might stop up the nation's blood vessels. In the nineteenth century the medical trope naturalized the city-body and (as will be seen again in chapter 6) became a commonplace metaphor in the discourse of Political Economy, particularly in the campaign for sanitary reform.[3]

The heart of the imperial body, London, was a grand emporium by the end of the forties, though Master Humphrey found the heart of London beating inside St. Paul's to be that of an unnatural body, like all cities. The arterial growth of the railways made London the largest consumer market in the country, while thanks to lower taxes, free trade, and colonial expansion, it was becoming a global port. Appearing at a crucial juncture in Dickens's career and in English politics, *Dombey and Son* (1846; one-volume ed., 1848) is Dickens's first novel to have London not just as location but as conceptual center, *the* metropolis of empire. The city is both the geographical and ideological center of a commercial and financial body. Yet in *Dombey and Son* it is the cold heart of an unfeeling monstrous body. The capital of empire has become an empire of capital that commodifies the bodies of its subjects, disciplining them to the iron will of economic principles and the railway timetable. The shift from private enterprise to large-scale investment by huge corporate bodies signaled a change in the character of the city, and nowhere was the anonymity and amoral calculation of modern business felt more than in the railway boom of the mid-forties.[4]

In Romantic constructions of the nation, the city is perceived as usurping an organic Nature associated with Englishness. The selfish drive for profit and gain had uprooted old-fashioned traditions. The commodity exchange of modern capitalism threatened the sacred portals of the home (a theme to which we will return in the following chapter), and the incursion of fetishized money and goods reinforced Romantic hostility toward urban culture as the railway reached into every part of the country. Touched by this Romantic sensibility, *Dombey and Son* attempts to incorporate in its characters a radical subjectivity that resists colonization by the business and railway empire. This is an act of resistance against the commodification of interpersonal relations by mass production, but also a rearguard action against mass production of literature that recalls Jane Austen's spirited defense in a prerailway age of the "injured body" of the novelist against cheap anthologies and the denigration of her literary production in *Northanger Abbey*. Robert Mudie, in his *Babylon the Great* (1825), also criticized the steam-powered printing presses as machines for the production of cheap literature. This resistance to the stifling competition of a materialist, consumer market can be seen in Dickens's attempt to ride both Pegasus and the steam engine in a somewhat different cultural matrix in *Dombey and Son* and, later, in *Hard Times*.

From a Freudian standpoint, *Dombey and Son* introduces the ontology of the Romantic self, "evolving its unity in and through time, a unity never fully achieved and always subject to revisions and regressions."[5] It takes a pivotal turn in both Dickens's life and works in "an engagement on new terms with another set of issues: the conjunction of the discourses of adult sexuality and middle-class economic desire, and the ambiguous role of art in rendering them."[6] The old-fashioned Romanticism represented by Paul and Florence and symbolized by the natural flow of a river is a kind of pleasure principle opposed to the calculated network of railway lines converging on the monstrous city. That amoral agent of death (though not Death itself), the locomotive, represents modernity as a phallic monster which simulates as well as represses desire. In her diatribe against the steam engine in chapter 40 of *Martin Chuzzlewit*, "especially them screeching railroad ones," Mrs. Gamp swears that only a man thinking of woman's "weak" nature could have invented such a monster since she somehow holds its hysterical noise responsible for the many women passengers who went into unexpected labor![7] In this parody of Victorian constructions of female sexuality, the steam engine is dangerously liable to run out of control in a euphemistic analogy with unnatural reproduction and liaisons of dubious morality (presumably resulting from the unbridled libido of railway navvies and such like).[8]

Such fears of rampant promiscuity were commonly associated with Victorian London, whose sheer size at midcentury (twice that of Paris) evoked both pride in the achievement and fear of the uncontrollable outcast population breeding immorality.[9] The Malthusian need to check population growth and medical attitudes toward reproduction, combined with class prejudice, tended to link street life with aberrant physiology and sexuality.[10] In the debate over regulation of industry and the railways, the central question was whether the city was a natural body subject to scientific investigation and reform, as William Cooke Taylor assumed in his *Natural History of Society* (1840), where he expressed a Unitarian belief in William Paley's natural system and in the material and cultural progress of urban life.[11] The biological metaphor assumes the city really works as a natural system. That London was proof of the natural laws at work was doubted by the Owenite James Hole when he endorsed Cobbett's counter-image of London as a swollen tumor on the pure body of the countryside and scathingly mocked a Malthusian approach to feeding London's teeming masses:

> That the people of London, or the major part of them, do somehow or other get fed, is true,—but that this is done in the best and wisest manner would be a pure assumption, were it not a downright falsehood. The real fact is, that in the large 'wen'—this sponge which sucks up so much of the wealth of the nation—there are tens of thousands who scarcely know from whence the next day's subsistence shall come,—multiplied thousands who lie on their beds inferior to those which the farmer gives to his cattle—and a thousand at least, who, night after night, have no shelter whatever![12]

The hopeless "bungle" of "un-'natural' law" perverted social justice and increased want and suffering, making the utilitarian model of the city-body look more like the "muddle" of unnatural Coketown with its polluted canal and interminable smoke-snakes. Machines were replacing the human body—"manufacture" no longer signified production by hand—and the insanitary conditions of overcrowded cities threatened the social body. The assumption that material prosperity would ameliorate conditions in the city is certainly not found in the indictment of the legal fog and the appalling slums in *Bleak House* or the attack on Circumlocution in *Little Dorrit*. The "unnatural humanity" (D&S xlvii; 620) of so-called natural laws is nowhere more evident than in Dombeyism.

The question was all the more topical since definitions of the social body and the relations between state intervention and free enterprise were shifting in the conflict between personal liberty and national interest.[13] Utilitarians favored free enterprise and competition, but the national interest in the rapid development of the railways also required control and coordination that were not always consistent with unfettered laissez-faire economics. For example, the regulation of traffic and the possibility of changing from one company's line to another were considerations behind parliamentary recommendations on such matters as a uniform gauge or cooperation between companies, but all too often the national interest was ignored by vested business interests.[14] The heartless System, deaf and blind to initiative, was much attacked in Dickens's *Household Words*, which was not slow to point out the moral and economic consequences of ignoring railway safety.[15]

The medieval worldview of a microcosmic hierarchy of man and nation, heaven and earth, or the cosmological allegory of the city of the spirit, could not be maintained when the "monster city" emptied the body of any meaning beyond its productive value in an alienating economic system of materialist profit and loss. The old vertical stratification could not survive when Newtonian physics had replaced cyclical time with linear progression and horizontal space.[16] Time and space were now measured in railway lines and production quotas. It is, as Mrs. Chick remarks, "a world of change" (D&S xxix; 396). This chapter will show how the natural body is being pitted against the monstrous city in competing, dialogic representations that express anxiety about the urban condition and a fear, common to nineteenth-century writers, of a denaturing, dehumanizing science that threatens the body. Mary Shelley's *Frankenstein* was the most famous example of the threat to the natural perceived in science and industrial production, but throughout the nineteenth century and well into the twentieth the threat of the alien and the monstrous was shown to lay within the human psyche, as in Pip's horror at what the monstrous Magwitch had made him into (GE xl; 354). That fear of the repressed coming to haunt Pip in Barnard's Inn parallels the monstrous creation of Estella by Miss Havisham, who, like E. T. A. Hoffmann's Olympia, is a seductive and unfeeling doll (she has also been fathered by Magwitch, though in a different sense to his creation of Pip as a gentleman). It would be misleading, however, to reduce *Dombey and Son* to a head-on collision of the natural with the monstrous, but the complexities and paradoxes involved in containing the destructiveness within the "progress" of modernity will be seen to inform the novel's rhetoric of representation and its modes of realism.

CORPORATE, CORPORATION, INCORPORATED

> Hence charter'd burghs are such public plagues;
> And burghers, men immaculate perhaps
> In all their private functions, once combined,
> Become a loathsome body, only fit
> For dissolution, hurtful to the main.
> Hence merchants, unimpeachable of sin
> Against the charities of domestic life,
> Incorporated, seem at once to lose
> Their nature; and, disclaiming all regard
> For mercy and the common rights of man,
> Build factories with blood, conducting trade
> At the sword's point, and dyeing the white robe
> Of innocent commercial Justice red.
>
> —Cowper, *The Task*

> ... every man *in corpore suo*, complete and comfortable ...
> —Robert Mudie, "The Corporation of London," *Babylon the Great*

Dombey and Son is a novel cited for its verisimilitude, yet only exceptionally have critics recognized that representation is thematized in the novel's epistemology in countless ways—not just in the commercial sense (Dombey's representation of his firm), or the representations that are offered in polite society. The novel is filled with people gazing, viewing, spying, surveying, peeping, and looking through windows, with and without eyeglasses. These various spectacles, however, actually show the limitations of their representation. Captain Cuttle's survey of Walter's prospects at Dombey & Son, for example, shows no more than Lady Skettles's panoramic view of Doctor Blimber's study through her eyeglasses.[17] In the novel's rhetoric of representation neither Edith nor Dombey can see what is revealed by the angel's view when the house tops are removed "rousing some who never have looked out upon the world of human life around them, to a knowledge of their relation to it, and for making them acquainted with a perversion of nature to their own contracted sympathies and estimates" (D&S XLVII; 620). They each become trapped in their blind representation of the world around them and are enslaved by their obsessive pride. Dickens characterized the new social order of Victorian England as managed on strictly business-like principles and controlled by the unbending, unnatural will of the businessman who is blind to the proliferation of suffering and misery in the city.

The more comic bird's-eye view of Miss Tox's dwelling shows an equally limited vision. Dickens has a lot of fun in the interpolated comic scenes with the overview of the parvenus who have squeezed their way into the society of the well-to-do and, like Dr. Blimber into his breeches, with as tight a fit. The tightness of the fit is as unnatural as the state of man in the "chartered boroughs" of William Cowper's *The Task*, likened to the flower crowded in the artificial vase, where corporations combine otherwise immaculate burghers into a "loathsome body." "Corporation" carried political and economic weight. The powerful political and economic body of the City of London is a chartered corporation which charters (hires) out bodies on a strictly commercial basis. In "London," that master-text which participates in the political debate over liberty in the 1790s, Blake responds to Cowper's and Thomson's conventional synecdoche of the city corrupted by commerce and trade: the "chartered streets" and "chartered Thames" set topographical knowledge (charting) against the control by privileged corporate business interests (chartering). Their enslaving hold and vested interests contravene the "charter of the land" in Thomson's "Rule Britannia," the hymn of British naval supremacy and world rule sung by the drowning sailors in chapter 4 of *Dombey and Son*, a celebration of constitutional monarchy that makes Podsnap proud he is British (OMF I XI; 179).

In *Babylon the Great*, Robert Mudie describes the Corporation of London as a type of empire whose ninety-one colonies are the chartered companies of

Freemen. This is an artificial culture enslaved to the gratification of appetites by an imperialist body that feeds on the female character of the crowd. The clarity of Wordsworth's view from Westminster Bridge was challenged by Arthur Clough in his poem "To the Great Metropolis" when he wrote, "if that Competition and display / Make a Great Capital, then thou art one"—perhaps the greatest one under the sun—but his "stranger's fancy" saw "Anything but a Nation's heart." The city-body metaphor exposes a heartless monstrous empire that was based on ruthless competition and display of the "chartered" body for profit and gain; it was hardly the true spirit of the nation.

The colonized, chartered body, stripped of subjectivity and agency, loses all but commercial value. It is thus also stripped of its mimetic power to make meaning and to shape social practice.[18] Several characters exhibit their bodies or abilities and sell themselves. Edith complains to her mother that she has been "hawked and vended here and there," submitting to the "licence of look and touch," until she loathes herself (D&S xxvii; 382). Edith's display of her talent at sketching is one mimetic ability that makes her desirable for purchase, while the display of her portrait is a claim by Dombey and later by Carker to subject her body to their gaze and representation.

Dombey's corporation (like that of the City) similarly both colonizes the body and controls its representation (in Bakhtin's understanding, invariably a discourse of both culture and society).[19] The monstrous empire was, at the time of the writing of *Dombey and Son*, resisting the attempts of the Chartists to change the rules of political representation and challenge the control of representation by the "chartered monopolies" which Thomas Paine had depicted as repressing the Englishman's civil liberties in his attack on Burke in *The Rights of Man*. Paine believed London was an exception, unlike Blake, who, at a time of political reaction and protectionism, recognized in "London" the implications for personal and civil liberty of the interested (chartered) monopoly of the Corporation of London.[20] Since the 1832 Reform Act, the middle class represented the City in both political and commercial senses, and the bust of Pitt in Dombey's drawing room looks down in mute contrast of national leadership, "the pilot," as Cousin Feenix puts it in a display of his own antiquated irrelevance, "who had weathered the storm" (D&S lxi; 821).

Pitt "represents" the world as Dombey represents Dombey & Son, but these representations are both limited and unstable. In the wrappers for the serial numbers of the novel (fig. 5), Dombey is depicted sitting precariously on top of a tottering house of cards, a Tower of Babel under construction, sure of his power and destiny; the right hand column comprises playing cards, but the left-hand column pictures them as business ledgers, account books, and check books that are falling with Dombey's own destruction. The cover resembles a commercial prospectus and announces "dealings" with the House of Dombey, "Wholesale, Retail and for Exportation," a significant and provocative title that was part of the overall design and plan of the novel.[21]

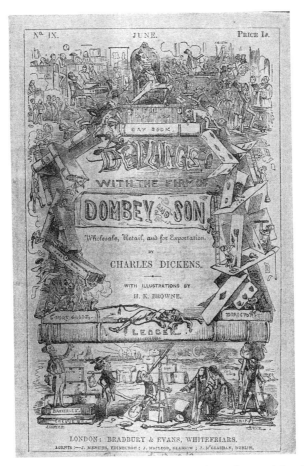

Fig. 5: Wrapper for the serial installments of *Dombey and Son* (1847)

"Wholesale" in Dickens's vocabulary refers to the commercialization of political representation, as in Sir Leicester's wholesale order of his own parliamentary candidacy and retailing of two pocket boroughs in *Bleak House*. And Mrs. Pardiggle's wholesale charity in the same novel seems as despicable as the retailing of society gossip. "Wholesale" is the statistical view of society in aggregate (a false one in Louisa's knowledge of the Hands in *Hard Times*) which was the characteristic of Political Economists such as Edwin Chadwick who favored laissez-faire and commercial interests. The later self-styled "Uncommercial Traveller" works hard against such wholesale solutions to social problems in a hardened commercial world, in which natural feelings are neither profitable nor practical. Yet the novel's retailing of its tale appears no less commercial in its own trade, since the public had to be persuaded to buy the next serial part. Hardsell promotion helped bring impressive profits and freed Dickens from financial worries. Boosting the commodification of the novel, serial parts included advertisement of commercial products, which were occasionally tied in to the text or to topical issues of the day.[22] The novel is no less commercial in its representation of the rival firm's epistemology (the playing cards of its account books and paperwork) as unstable and unreliable, a collapse which the novel must succeed in constructing. As a packaged commercial product, *Dombey and Son* carries the brand of a commercial enterprise, but one that contrasts with the old-fashioned and natural trade and merchandise of *The Old Curiosity Shop*. The novel's dealings with its subject create a dialogic encounter of ideology and form, and Dickens's practice of opposing the vitality and sincerity of his "good" characters to the reified spiritless villains obsessed by fetishized passions and objects (like Dombey, or Merdle the money-idol) must not be allowed to deteriorate into fetishized imagery.[23] The natural corpus of Dickens's work promotes itself as a rival competitor to Dombey's calculating trade, in fact to Hobbesean competition.

The commodities in which Dombey trades are, surprisingly, unnamed. This makes them all the more ephemeral and abstract, products of the Steam Age that have lost any connection with their origin and no longer have any identity as unique products, just as the railway has robbed the landscape of its aura of place (in Walter Benjamin's theory of "mechanical reproduction" of the art object in photography).[24] Indeed, the firm's shipping interests are represented as cards in the cunning paws of the feline manager, Carker. Carker does in the end precipitate the fall of the House and embodies a grotesque caricature of the economy of consumption who preys on Edith and whose desire is almost carnivorous (the table is set at Dijon). This beast of prey, like the monstrous body of the commercial and railway network in contemporary caricature, feeds on the subject-body and commodifies it. Such cannibalistic reification is typical of Dombey's business, which is described as being as mysterious as the creatures at the bottom of the ocean, a curious image that undoes any privileged representation of the calculating clear-headedness of business and reveals instead something monstrous:

> Such vapid and flat daylight as filtered through the ground-glass windows and skylights, leaving a black sediment upon the panes, showed the books and papers, and the figures bending over them, enveloped in a studious gloom, and as much abstracted in appearance, from the world without, as if they were assembled at the bottom of the sea; while a mouldy little strong room in the obscure perspective, where a shaded lamp was always burning, might have represented the cavern of some ocean-monster, looking on with a red eye at these mysteries of the deep. (D&S XIII; 170–71)

The unfeeling cruelty of the commodity culture is also evident in the fleeting images of "sparkling jewelry, silks and velvets of the richest colours, the most inviting delicacies, and most sumptuous articles of luxurious ornament" that meet Nicholas Nickleby's eye on his return to London. *Nicholas Nickleby* (1838) is a novel that describes a cynical business empire which displays Kate's body to the gaze of lecherous aristocrats for profit or a wager and offers bargain deals for the disposal of "natural" children in Squeers's Academy. There is nothing durable or stable in the "shifting scene" of "quickly-changing and ever-varying objects" on display, only a bewildering succession of images, as unconnected as the noisy, bustling crowd streaming past. The list of commodities in London's shop-fronts punctures the conspicuous display of consumption of the world emporium in which everything tends to death, itself a commodity:

> Emporiums of splendid dresses, the materials brought from every quarter of the world; tempting stores of everything to stimulate and pamper the sated appetite and give new relish to the oft-repeated feast; vessels of burnished gold and silver, wrought into every exquisite form of vase, and dish, and goblet; guns, swords, pistols, and patent engines of destruction; screws and irons for the crooked, clothes for the newly-born, drugs for the sick, coffins for the dead, churchyards for the buried—all these jumbled each with the other and flocking side by side, seemed to flit by in motley dance like the fantastic groups of the old Dutch painter, and with the same stern moral for the unheeding restless crowd. (NN xxxii; 413–14)

The moral of Holbein's *Danse Macabre* need not be spelled out when rags are placed next to riches. The riches speak for a greater poverty in the contrast they offer and the desire they deny:

> The rags of the squalid ballad-singer fluttered in the rich light that showed the goldsmiths' treasures; pale and pinched-up faces hovered about the windows where was tempting food; hungry eyes wandered over the profusion guarded by one thin sheet of brittle glass—an iron wall to them; half-naked shivering figures stopped to gaze at Chinese shawls and golden stuffs of India. There was a christening party at the largest coffin-maker's, and a funeral hatchment had stopped some great improvements in the bravest mansion. Life and death went hand in hand; wealth and poverty stood side by side; repletion and starvation laid them down together. (NN xxxii; 414)

Dryden's "famed emporium" is a bankrupt enterprise when it displays goods disconnected from their production, and the corporate/corporeal city has "renewed her charter's date" in the negative sense of Blake's lines bemoaning the fate of the hired bodies of soldier and whore. Nevertheless, the moral is far from the political chartism currently taking the streets, to the alarm of Carlyle in "Chartism," published the year following Dickens's novel.

Not just the sharp tongue of Susan "Spitfire" Nipper but the very walls of Dombey's grand house near Portland Place speak for the barrenness of his empire. The dismal, cold atmosphere seems to drive out the summer sun from the street; the "cellars frowned upon by barred windows, and leered at by crooked-eyed doors leading to dustbins" (D&S iii; 24) reveal the measure of authorial disapproval. The rooms are in icy-cold mourning not only because Mrs. Dombey has died in childbirth. Humanity itself is dead, and Paul grows up in the cold shadow of his father. His old-fashioned natural affection is almost stifled by modern calculating commerce. Paul decides his ambition is to put all his money in the bank, never make more, and live with Florence in the country. In a rare conversation with his father, Paul asks for a definition of money. The question puts Dombey in a difficulty because he can only think in terms of exchange value, which, as Georg Simmel puts it, reduces all quality and individuality to a question of how much, for in the economy of the metropolis, where goods are supplied from unknown producers for unknown consumers, all relations are strictly commercial.[25] This is human relationship reduced to the "cash payment" of Carlyle's analysis of the cold calculation of Political Economy, the new national creed, in *Past and Present* (1843), whose gospel of Mammonism teaches that hell is not having money (10: 146). Dombey answers in terms a child could be expected to understand, in tokens of currency, but base metals and coins do not satisfy Paul's presumptuous wish to know what money is. Dombey replies that money can do anything.

> "Anything, Papa?"
> "Yes. Anything—almost," said Mr. Dombey.
> "Anything means everything, don't it, Papa?" asked his son: not observing, or possibly not understanding, the qualification.
> "It includes it: yes," said Mr. Dombey.
> "Why didn't money save me my Mama?" returned the child. "It isn't cruel, is it?"
> "Cruel!" said Mr. Dombey, settling his neckcloth, and seeming to resent the idea. "No. A good thing can't be cruel."
> "If it's a good thing, and can do anything," said the little fellow, thoughtfully, as he looked back at the fire, "I wonder why it didn't save me my Mama."
> (D&S VIII; 94)

The child cannot logically reconcile Dombey's blind faith in the cruel economic determinism of Mammonism with a moral and just universe. When Walter begs money for his bankrupt uncle, Dombey demonstrates to his son, instead of compassion or reward for Florence's rescue, the arbitrary power of the money god.[26]

Even the family conference that decides on sending Paul down to Mrs. Pipchin's is run like a board meeting deciding on company policy. Paul is, after all, "& Son," and his destiny must be planned. Florence, in Dombey's patriarchal economy, is a base coin not worth investing. When Paul dies, Florence is cut off even more than previously from being a child of Dombey and is abandoned to the desolate house, haunted by the frozen curse of its master and conscious, in the anthropomorphic description in chapter XXIII, of slipping into neglect and decay. Holding tenaciously to her love for the father who has coldly rejected her, Florence looks to the rosy children in the house opposite for a different representation of fatherhood, one clearly dependent on an almost religious faith in the natural values of family and femininity. Her selfless affection is indeed a religious act of devotion and faith, like Paul's, and similarly inspired by haloed apostles.

Florence is not merely abandoned to loneliness but thrown onto the city streets. This is where she loses her subjecthood and, symbolically, her femininity.

She is first lost in the city during the commotion caused by a mad bull (a phallic monster) after Polly's surreptitious visit to her family (natural values in breach of contract). Her ordeal of being stripped and shorn by Good Mrs. Brown proves a symbolic stripping of identity before she is providentially rescued by Walter. He keeps her shoes as a keepsake, like the Prince in the Cinderella story (though she has been transformed from riches to rags, not rags to riches, by her experience). Florence represents the antitype of the self-interested drive for commercial profit and stubborn pride of Dombey, which becomes his undoing, just as it is pride that makes Edith and Alice self-destructive. Florence carries within her the spirit of her dead brother's compassionate and spontaneous benevolence, echoing the ethical capitalism of the Cheeryble brothers and the spirit of Carlyle's condemnation of the cruelty of "fair competition" in *Past and Present* (10: 146). Compassion and benevolence are what save Dombey at the end of the day, reconciling him to love for his children and awakening remorse for the past. A similarly uneconomic impulse on the part of Carker's delinquent brother John to make up for his past, with assistance from that deus ex machina, Mr. Morfin, shows that moral obligation pays off and that there is a duty beyond one's own strip of responsibility.

RAILWAY TIME

> I rejoice to see it, and think that feudality is gone for ever.
> —Thomas Arnold, on seeing a train on the Rugby line

> From west to east, and from north to south, the mechanical principle, the philosophy of the nineteenth century, will spread and extend itself. The world has received a new impulse. The genius of the age, like a mighty river of the new world, flows onward, full, rapid, irresistible.
> —Henry Booth, treasurer of the Liverpool and Manchester Railway, 1830.

The representation of Dombeyism brings into play radical shifts in the relations of time and space which must be understood in the context of the railway's impact not just on the morphology of the city, but on social, political, and gender relations within the nation's body. The railway remaps the nation as a circulatory system. Its colonization of land and its commodification of the bodies of passengers (who travel on a contractual basis) play out tensions between natural, mechanical, old-fashioned traditions and modernity, town and country. This was the technological breakthrough that more than any other changed perception of the world and knowledge of it. Anne Brontë's *Agnes Gray* had not traveled above twenty miles from home all her life. Now the sky was the limit, or so it seemed to the visionaries who spoke in missionary and colonialist terms of a great highway which would spread the light of civilization and science and which, true to the city-body trope, would stimulate the circulation of the fresh blood of commerce.

The discourse of the railways is instructive for the polarized construction of nation, class, and gendered bodies. For John Francis, writing his *History of the English Railway* from the economic high-water mark of 1851 and the vantage point of the Bank of England, which was assuming its new centralized position in the circulation of currency, the development of the railways was a matter of common sense, enterprise, and endeavor. Its opponents were Romantics resisting change (Francis names Wordsworth and Southey) or reactionaries seeking regulation (such as the ignorant Members of Parliament who cross-examined the railway engineer George Stephenson with obstructive and abusive questions). Samuel Smiles, in his 1857 biography of George Stephenson, placed the blame for the rampant speculation in railway shares of 1844–45 along ideological and regional lines on London capitalists who acted out of self-interest in the face of utility and steam, first pooh-poohing the northern engineers and entrepreneurs and then acting unscrupulously to get rich quickly. Nevertheless, in a sixty-page report that came out on the side of regulation in the interests of safety and the public good, the *Quarterly Review* surveyed the flood of railway bills and noted approvingly that, besides punctuality, comfort, and efficiency, the railways had brought about the mixing of classes. They were breaking down social barriers, emancipating middle- and upper-class women who had hitherto been unable to travel alone, and were increasing the "circulation ... of the current coin of the intellect"—the mental and cultural counterpart to the metaphor of the healthy body. The improvement in circulation was, moreover, promoting a civility and frankness in social intercourse quite "new in the English character."[27]

Others perceived an unnatural "iron network" sweeping away familiar landscapes. Traditional values were being lost in the new familiarity between classes, dialects, and the sexes, between town and country.[28] However, despite the "parliamentaries" which allowed the lower classes expanded mobility, on the whole the railway preserved social exclusion and stratification. The compartments of a passenger train departmentalized the passengers into classes and social rank (though it was difficult to prevent gentlemen from entering lower class compartments to save money) and often segregated them into genders, at the risk of trapping them without communication in case of emergency.[29]

When trade moved with the railway to London and the big cities, the relations of center and periphery, so important to class distinction, became unstable and unrecognizable. Carlyle complained, in "Hudson's Statue" (1851), that the map of the nation was no longer legible:

> Much as we love railways, there is one thing undeniable: Railways are shifting all Towns of Britain into new places: no Town will stand where it did, and nobody can tell for a long while yet where it will stand. This is an unexpected and indeed most disastrous result. I perceive, railways have set all the Towns of Britain a-dancing. Reading is coming

up to London, Basingstoke is going down to Gosport or Southampton, Dumfries to Liverpool and Glasgow; while at Crewe, and other points, I see new ganglions of human population establishing themselves, and the prophecy of metallurgic cities which were not heard of before. Reading, Basingstoke and the rest, the unfortunate Towns, subscribed money to get railways; and it proves to be for cutting their own throats. Their business has gone elsewhither; and they—cannot stay behind their business! They are set a-dancing, as I said; confusedly waltzing, in a state of progressive dissolution, towards the four winds; and know not where the end of the death-dance will be for them, in what point of space they will be allowed to rebuild themselves. That is their sad case. (20: 265–66)

The railway also brought the British capital closer to the provinces and the colonies. As the *Quarterly Review* noted in 1839, a national railway network would bring London nearer to every home, and as "distances were thus annihilated, the surface of our country would, as it were, shrivel in size until it became not much bigger than one immense city."[30] This observer of the phenomenal growth of the railways and their colonization of time and space could not have foreseen how much high-speed travel would contribute to the coming of the global metropolis and the obliteration of rural space in a culture of simulacra and commodities. But to speak of the machine age as a "mighty river" that flowed irresistibly was to naturalize the spread of the railways as a vehicle of universal improvement which, together with the factory, was conquering Nature. It was a rhetorical strategy frequently used to justify the amorality of companies as sovereign bodies answerable only to their board and shareholders and, prior to legislation for limited liability, operating without much restraint in the name of profit and gain. The railway company was an empire to itself and did not generally recognize responsibility for the bodies and property of its passengers, unless forced to do so by government intervention.

The railway was a product of the Industrial Revolution, a development of the improved steam engine used for pumping and for hauling coal in the mines. It was thus an agent of "Abbau" in the literal sense. Only when the Stockton and Darlington railway opened in 1825 was it adapted to passenger transportation. The railway disrupts representation as it mercilessly cuts through the landscape because it exposes what the landscape would otherwise have hidden. In *Hard Times*, the railway and the mining that feeds the industrial city both reveal this aspect of "Abbau": the railway strides "on many arches over a wild country, undermined by deserted coal-shafts, and spotted at night by fires and black shapes of stationary engines at pits' mouths" (HT vii; 196). Traveling by train through the industrial Midlands, Dickens had frightful thoughts of being swallowed up by this "undermined country" of coal-forests and deserted shafts ("Fire and Snow," *Household Words*, 21 January 1854; DJ 3: 192). However much Dickens admired the magnificent railway "striding on many arches," he reserves criticism for what the railway exposes as it mercilessly and indiscriminately cuts through town and country.

The railway exposes to view the invisible city, as in Doré's sketch of lower-class London homes beneath railway arches (fig. 6). Frederick Chichester, in his *Masters and Workmen* (1851), declared the railway had "rent asunder" the worst "plague spots" of the cities and aroused a sense of moral duty and outrage at what lay behind the façades of "plaster palaces and flaunting gin-shops."[31] Engels too was appalled at previously concealed slums exposed to the public gaze by the railway in Manchester.[32] In *Dombey and Son*, the railway lays bare "dark pools of water, muddy lanes, and miserable habitations far below. There are jagged walls and falling houses close at hand, and through the battered roofs and broken windows, wretched rooms are seen, where want and fever hide themselves in many wretched shapes, while smoke, and crowded gables, and distorted chimneys, and deformity of brick and mortar penning up deformity of mind and body, choke the murky distance" (D&S xx; 276–77). Dombey does not associate these deformations of both the landscape and the body with the monster-engine (which does not make or cause these things), nor does he make any connection between the prosperity which the railway has brought him and the poverty exposed by it, between his journey's end and the "ruinous and dreary" end of everything. Yet this is a view all the same of the Two Nations in the Condition of England debate.

Fig. 6: Gustave Doré, "Over London—By Rail" (1872)

Dombey, indeed, makes no connection between the private and the public. The powerful magnate reads into the landscape not a "rich and varied country" rushing past his carriage window but "a wilderness of blighted plans and gnawing jealousies" because he is driven in his pride by the fixed idea that he has competitors for his private feelings for his dead son. Such a competitor is Toodles, who has presumptuously shed a tear for the dead child. The genial Toodles, in fact, is far from the stereotype of the uncouth and obscene railway worker, but the "presumptuous raker" has imposed on Dombey's mourning and is stoking the engine ahead of him: "The very speed at which the train was whirled along, mocked the swift course of the young life that had been borne away so steadily and so inexorably to its foredoomed end. The power that forced itself upon its iron way—its own—defiant of all paths and roads, piercing through the heart of every obstacle, and dragging living creatures of all classes, ages, and degrees behind it, was a type of the triumphant monster Death" (D&S xx; 275). These obsessive thoughts color Dombey's reading of the landscape, yet we can hardly fail to notice in the personification of the monster-engine a symbol that contrasts with the light of progress rushing along in a healthy circulation of capital.[33] The iron machine, pursuant to Newtonian laws, meets no resistance to its forward motion, but mechanically pierces "the heart of every obstacle." It is an inhuman machine "dragging living creatures of all classes, ages, and degrees behind it" that had neither feeling nor judgment, unlike the angelic Death depicted in the scenes of Mrs. Dombey's passing away and the demise of little Paul.

Four of the following five paragraphs end with the "monster Death!" and the "remorseless monster" destroys all that lies before it and robs the traveler even of the objects whizzing past, of distance itself. It leaves behind no trace of its passage or its presence except "dust and vapor."

> Away, with a shriek, and a roar, and a rattle, from the town, burrowing among the dwellings of men and making the streets hum, flashing out into the meadows for a moment, mining in through the damp earth, booming on in darkness and heavy air, bursting out again into the sunny day so bright and wide; away, with a shriek, and a roar, and a rattle, through the fields, through woods, through the corn, through the hay, through the chalk, through the mould, through the clay, through the rock, among objects close at hand and almost in the grasp, ever flying from the traveller, and a deceitful distance ever moving slowly with him: like as in the track of the remorseless monster, Death! (D&S xx; 275–76)

"Away"—this is a landscape that can no longer be seen and enjoyed, but is being constantly and remorselessly lost, no longer familiar or legible, always receding as "glimpses of cottage-homes, of houses, mansions, rich estates, of husbandry and handicraft, of people, of old roads and paths, that look deserted, small and insignificant as they are left behind" (D&S xx; 276). They are insignificant because they can only be glimpsed, while the country rushing past prevents any stable relation to objects. The bridges above fall "like a beam of shadow" on the eye, and the senses are assailed by rattling, shrieking, and roaring, with the hiss of steam, the darkness of the tunnel, and the smoky soot of the coke-fired locomotive.

Dickens's description of Dombey's train journey brilliantly mimics the onomatopoeic rhythm of the powerful machine rushing through time and space, quite new sensations in a culture that was used to measuring time and space in stagecoaches and distances between inns. The landscape flashes past in a way that changes perspective and perception. The prime example of that change is Turner's painting, *Rain, Steam, and Speed—The Great Western Railway* (exhibited at the Royal Academy in 1844), which would have been in the public mind when the first numbers of *Dombey and Son* appeared.[34] Amid a burst of energetic color, the stark outline of the black steam engine emerges out of the stormy elements against a barely discernible landscape and rushes resolutely towards us across Brunel's bridge over the Thames at Maidenhead, outracing a hare, which dashes for cover. The painting's mode of realism juxtaposes the mechanical with the natural, the speed and power of the new Age of Steam with the ploughman and the boaters, who are static and less visible. The hazy background and distorted details make an ambiguous statement about the uncompromising force of steam which has usurped Nature. To be consistent with Ruskin's championing of Turner, we might say that sublime Nature has itself been harnessed by technology. Read alternatively, steam has outpaced and outdated a pastoral tranquility represented by the peaceful river—the painting was exhibited alongside marine views and Venetian scenes.[35] In Turner's *The Fighting "Téméraire"* (1838), the fire belching out of the iron steam tugboat makes a similar aesthetic and historical statement in its contrast with the ghostly obsolescence of the wooden sailing ship under a fiery sunset. These are not the tranquil, naturally ordered landscapes of Constable with their time-honored scenes of English village life and their quiet mimesis of untidy hedgerows. The German scholar Wolfgang Schivelbusch has speculated that there is here a fundamental shift in realism, not unconnected with the replacement of the diorama by the camera.[36] The shutter glimpses one moment in a view in which the viewer is absent, remote, already departed. Landscape has almost been abolished beyond the streaks of color as the train flashes by, collapsing space into time. As in Turner's painting, Dombey's train is described as "working on in such a storm of energy and perseverance, that amidst the darkness and whirlwind the motion seems reversed, and to tend furiously backward, until a ray of light upon the wet wall shows its surface flying past like a fierce stream" (D&S xx; 276).

Looking forward almost prophetically to the introduction of cross-Channel air travel in an 1851 sketch, "A Flight," Dickens described the weird sensation of traveling in an express train as flying. The sense of direction and of place was lost, and Dickens surrendered to a "dreamy pleasure" which left him not caring where exactly he was: "After long darkness, pale fitful streaks of light appear. I am flying on for Folkestone. The streaks grow stronger — become continuous — become the ghost of day — become the living day — become I mean — the tunnel is miles and miles away, and here I fly through sunlight, all among the harvest and the Kentish hops" (*Household Words*, 30 August 1851; DJ 3: 29). Speed does not permit contemplation and only in a hot Paris bath can Dickens begin to wonder where he came from and how many years ago he left London. Hugo described much the same disorienting blurring of vision in his view from a train window in a letter of 22 August 1837: "The flowers by the side of the road are no longer flowers but flecks, or rather streaks, of red or white ... the towns, the steeples, and the trees perform a crazy mingling dance on the horizon."[37] The annihilation of space in temporal experience challenged modes of realism and is reflected in the "onrushing impressions" Georg Simmel saw in urban ways of life. The effects of a fast-changing scene on the perspective of an observer on a moving train impress, almost violently, on the passenger the contrasting realities of England which cannot be contained within conventional representation, a totally new experience of the thrill and wonder of driving through different rocks and soil, town and country, fields and slums.

Landscape is no longer a familiar journey across a panoramic view but a temporal experience of being in motion between two locations untouched, as Ruskin complained, by the landscape of the places through which one is only passing. But then Ruskin thought perception diminished in proportion to velocity, and a quiet walk in a country lane was all he considered an artist needed for his canvas. The train is a place that is nowhere. The perspective from the train, much more than from Nicholas Nickleby's coach, is of a passing scene, of an incomprehensible series of images in such profusion that narrative coherence almost breaks down. Today that disorientation has been swallowed up in nostalgia for the steam age and for a different England of enterprise and national greatness, an invention of the past but also a reaction in the 1960s to Dr. Beeching's ax, whereas in America the Iron Horse is remembered as the conqueror of the Wild West, which opened up the wilderness to civilization, and a means of socialization in the long cars, rather different from the English railway compartments (as Dickens comments in *American Notes*).[38]

Bearing Dombey onwards toward Leamington, that false Arcadia south of Birmingham, on the edge of the industrialized Black Country itself, the train speeds into no future of factories and industry, prosperity, and progress, but "Louder and louder yet, it shrieks and cries as it comes tearing on resistless to the goal" (D&S xx; 276), on its way, strewn with ashes and blackened everywhere, which is like the way of Death. The monotony of Dombey's thoughts of death is turning into another kind of threat, the deadening inertia of atrophied thought and cold hearts. It is the cold calculation of an empire ruled by the will of one man. What mattered was efficiency of traction, profit and loss. No wonder railway passengers complained of being treated like a parcel in freight, carried on purely commercial principles of conveyance of goods between stations; Dickens later complained of his treatment as baggage carried without liability ("Dullborough Town," *All the Year Round*, 30 June 1860). Rail, train, and passenger were integrated into a circulatory railway network. The principle of systemization and rationalization is awesome in the enormous scale of the engineering project, and its extreme application of a dehumanizing utilitarianism returns us to the opposition of the organic to the mechanical in the writings of the Romantics.[39]

It was nevertheless the railway which speeded the prosperity and accelerated the changes resulting from the Industrial Revolution, in particular urbanization. Mobility and commuting further uprooted the individual from the natural environment and removed any sense of belonging to a place or a rootedness in Nature. The railway mania of the mid-forties excited doomsday visions of the railway eliminating the stagecoach and the country inn, as in Wilkie Collins's early sketch "The Last Stage Coachman" (1843). As a coachman, Sam Weller's father has strong views on the subject in *Master Humphrey's Clock*:

> "I con-sider," said Mr. Weller, "that the rail is unconstitootional and an inwaser o' priwileges, and I should wery much like to know what that 'ere old Carter as once stood up for our liberties and wun 'em too,— I should like to know wot he vould say, if he wos alive now, to Englishmen being locked up vith widders, or with anybody again their wills. Wot a old Carter would have said, a old Coachman may say, and I as-sert that in that pint o' view alone, the rail is an inwaser." (MHC iii; 278)

Gone are the sensation of the effort of the horses and the conviviality of fellow-passengers and inns. The engine runs on smooth rails, conquering space at breakneck speed, a "projectile" as it was often called and just as lethal. "Bang," joked Dickens in "A Flight." "We have let another Station off, and fly away regardless.... Bang, bang! A double-barrelled Station!" (DJ 3: 29). Yet Dickens himself scarcely misses "all the horrible little villages we used to pass through, in the *Diligence*," the summer dust and winter mud, the beggars looking in at coach-windows, the discomfort of lengthy journeys and the Frenchman "snoring onions" (DJ 3: 33–34). All this has simply disappeared, leaving the sheer marvel of "flying" to Paris in eleven hours by the South-Eastern Railway. And there is no mistaking the thrill at the strange sensation of fast travel and the wonder of modernity. Indeed, for all the nostalgia for rural rhythms, Dickens was not only firmly on the side of the Corn Law repealers, but the *Daily News*, with which Dickens was closely associated and which for a short time he edited, was backed and financed by the railway interest; it was the first national newspaper distributed by rail and demonstrated the impact of speedy production and delivery. The railway tycoon George Hudson supplied a special train to make sure the newspaper's first number hit the stands on 21 January 1846 with the report of an anti-Corn Law meeting (letter to Joseph Paxton 16 January 1846, *Letters* 4: 472).

Modernity is brought above all by the railway. In the middle of the nineteenth century the steam engine was the ultimate catchphrase for the speed of change. There was little opposition to Gladstone's Regulation of Railways Bill in 1844, and those few villages that rejected the approach of the railway repented after they were bypassed and became an isolated backwater. The speeding up of the postal service, the easing of communications, and more efficient use of natural resources were among the undeniable advantages which brought benefit to everyone. The railway was also responsible for the transformation of the city. Railway construction was one of the major occasions of the rebuilding of London, for example the demolition of Hungerford Market just thirty years after it was built to make way for Charing Cross station, or the building of the world's first underground railway, opened in 1863, whose shafts and covered tracks (unlike later tunnel construction) exposed cross-sections of London's archeological past, as well as homes of the poor, to the gaze of passing pedestrians. Readers of the illustrated periodical press delighted in these spectacular feats of engineering which offered representations of the modernization of the city.[40] Dickens was, to the end of his life, impressed by the shifting scene. The retrospective remarks in the prefaces to his novels and his correspondence cast no doubt on his approval of what was called "improvement." However, Dickens often attacks incompetence and irresponsibility in carrying it out. In a speech in Birmingham, the heart of the Black Country in the crucible of the Industrial Revolution, on 28 February 1844, Dickens pointed up with controlled irony the double standards of the opponents of "new-fangled" ideas by relating his encounter with a gentleman on the train who deplored the passing of the stagecoach and the ruinous effects of high-speed locomotives, but complained of the slightest delay whenever the train stood in a station (*Speeches* 62).

The implications of the building of the railway for writing and reading may be gauged by the oft-quoted description in *Dombey and Son* of Stagg's Gardens. This description of the coming to a North London suburb of the London and Birmingham railway in 1837–38 reflects an ambivalent state of affairs that cannot be described as either construction or destruction. There is none of the sublime that we find in Thomas Talbot Bury's drawings (1838–39) which accommodate the picturesque to the grand design of progress. And while the monumental clearance in John Cooke Bourne's lithograph (fig. 7) apparently corroborates Dickens's description and gives an idea of the mammoth earth-works—the "railway mounds" that Ruskin measured at the end of his essay "Traffic," "vaster than the walls of Babylon"—it does not quite give its sense of catastrophe:

> The first shock of a great earthquake had, just at that period, rent the whole neighborhood to its centre. Traces of its course were visible on every side. Houses were knocked down; streets broken through and stopped; deep pits and trenches dug in the ground; enormous heaps of earth and clay thrown up; buildings that were undermined and shaking, propped by great beams of wood. (D&S vi; 65)

The metaphor of an earthquake sums up the disastrous effect on the landscape of "Abbau" as buildings are thrown up, cuttings are excavated and tunnels are dug ("mining in through the damp earth"). The undermining of the city, moreover, defies any natural growth or constructive plan. Even as a Tower of Babel, this construction is a failure, lending sarcasm to the words that sum it all up: "In short, the yet unfinished and unopened Railroad was in progress; and, from the very core of all this dire disorder, trailed smoothly away, upon its mighty course of civilization and improvement" (ibid.). Critics have seized upon the irony of "in progress" (which suggests unfinished and under construction rather than going forward) and attribute to Dickens a middle-class ambivalence caught between admiration for industrial progress and fear of its disruptive effects,[41] in an unresolved debate over the price of progress between national prosperity and personal loss or displacement.[42] This misses the point that the earthquake has undermined a landscape that happens to be neither pretty nor picturesque and that the shock waves are rocking the epistemology behind Dombeyism.

Fig. 7: John Cooke Bourne, "Early Stages of the
Excavations toward Euston" (1836–37)

The threat, however, comes not from the railways as such but from unscrupulous speculators and the builders of the Babel towers. Dickens's voice of protest was echoed in Carlyle's attack in "Hudson's Statue" on the unbridled greed of wealthy magnates of the sort later portrayed in the figure of Melmotte in Anthony Trollope's *The Way We Live Now*, who got rich at the expense of public morals and the public interest. Carlyle mocked hero-worship of the Railway King, George Hudson, whose contribution to the rapid construction of the railway system fed on the speculative mania of 1844–46 but left the unenfranchised poor no better off and open to the agitation of the Chartists. Dividends are the enemy in *Dombey and Son*, not steam, and the anthropomorphized engine stresses the inhuman character of the whole enterprise, much as the investment fever in *Little Dorrit* ruins Arthur and, in the spirit of Carlyle's essay, shows Merdle to be a monstrous fraud set up for the idol of mankind. Nonetheless, John Francis defended Hudson against his detractors as a model captain of industry who had made the mistake of some questionable practices, referring to the Merdle-like fraud which brought him down.[43] It was the Hudson case and others like it which strengthened support for governmental regulation and inspection of railways, and Dickens's portrayal of Merdle (inspired by the suicide on Hampstead Heath in 1856 of John Sadleir, implicated in banking frauds and the issue of fictitious Swedish railway shares) highlighted the scandalous involvement of members of Parliament and the urgent need for regulation of the institutions of financing.

It is not progress that is wrong, but the machine that has gone out of control when driven by the greedy scramble to build Babel towers and by the "insolence" of Dombey's wealth, identified with the colonialist West India interest rather than railway investment. The name of Stagg's Gardens is in fact, as Michael Steig has explained,[44] derived from the popular use of the hunting term "stag" for the speculators who bought up railway stocks for a quick return and precipitated the financial panic of 1845. The phenomenal growth of the railways inflated the capital being raised to over seventy million pounds. The number of new railway companies ran into the hundreds. When the bubble burst many investors were ruined, and the railway locomotive was caricatured by *Punch* as a monstrous Moloch, eating up families and ruining the country. The monster was worshipped as a Juggernaut (associations of being crushed under a pagan monster), but also as a Dragon (associations of evil combat with England's patron saint). In *George Cruikshank's Table Book* (1845), the steam dragon played havoc with John Bull's stags and gobbled up their families. This symbol of technological conquest and scientific progress, vaunted in the naming of locomotives,[45] constituted a double assault on English values of hearth and property (fig. 8).

In the second description of Stagg's Gardens, it has simply vanished: "There was no such place as Stagg's Gardens. It had vanished from the earth" (D&S xv; 217). "Stagg's Gardens had been cut up root and branch. Oh woe the day! when 'not a rood of English ground'—laid out in Stagg's Gardens is secure!" (D&S xv; 218–19). It is a world that for good or bad has been "cut up root and branch," a misquotation of Wordsworth's 1844 sonnet on the proposed Kendal and Windermere Railway, "Is there no nook of English ground secure / From rash assault?" In two letters to the *Morning Post* in December 1844, Wordsworth pleaded that the railway not be allowed to intrude into the seclusion and retirement of the Lake District, as if its virgin beauty had not already been sufficiently "violated" by tourists in search of the picturesque (especially during the blockade years of the Napoleonic Wars). Wordsworth felt the picturesque was not a taste that could be easily acquired by the uncultivated hordes who would arrive en masse by excursion train, and feared that the aesthetic and emotional power of the inaccessible mountains would be lost; man, he declared, did not live by Political Economy alone. Apart from its class prejudice, this resistance to the intrusion of financial power and quick profits into an elitist culture reflects the widespread fear that the railway would disfigure the natural landscape and its sacred ruins in ways it had not succeeded in doing in the rest of Britain, where the worst excesses were limited to Princes Street Gardens in Edinburgh and Conway Castle.[46] Yet, despite the threat to an England rooted in Nature, the sacrifice of Stagg's Gardens results in neither the loss of a rural picturesque landscape nor an expression of regret at progress. The reader must be baffled,[47] unless this description is taken as double-voiced irony directed at false nostalgia that fails to see the advantages of the new, while lamenting the passing of the "old fashioned," represented by Paul Dombey. It is Paul's dying wish to see Polly, his lost natural fountain, which leads to Walter's and Susan's discovery that Stagg's Gardens has disappeared. Susan's Freudian slip when she refers hysterically to "Polly's Gardens" might hint at loss of maternal love and the secret desire to return to the womb. Paul dies in the following chapter, thus providing a dialogic context for the railway craze that has taken over Camden Town. "Old-fashioned," as Miss Cornelia Blimber explains, means being odd. It means staring out of the window at the sea and tracing miniature lions and tigers in the "arabesque work" of Fancy. This is, however, hardly a protest against steam engines.[48]

The identification of Camden Town with Stagg's Gardens is connected with a sense of loss which has to do with two dislocations. One is a dislocation in Dickens's childhood memory, first moving to the city, then being moved from home after his father's imprisonment for debt. The other is a dislocation within the city, which disrupts the familiar landscape and the mental map that navigates it. Both threaten the sense of a past and the link with maternal nurturing and childhood memory. One of the most jarring dislocations of memory and personality characteristic of the Victorian era is the disappearance of familiar landscapes and their displacement by the mechanical monuments of modernity: the iron bridge, the factory, and the railway. When Dickens revisited the Wellington Academy in Hampstead Road, where he had gone to school, he found "the Railway had cut it up root and branch. A great trunk-line had swallowed the playground, sliced away the schoolroom, and pared off the corner of the house" ("Our School," *Household Words*, 11 October 1851; DJ 3: 36). Such is the fate of childhood memories, like his Chatham Prep School, pulled down many years previously to make way for wider streets. However, like the disappearance of Stagg's Gardens, the denaturing violence of the description and the mechanized image of the remaining building draws our attention to a forcible uprooting rather than a fanciful nostalgia. To speak of the railway cutting up Dickens's childhood "root and branch" is a further example of Dickens's neo-Wordsworthian construction of Nature and nation, in contrast to the railway's naturalizing metaphor of "branch lines" and trunk routes, or the merciless machinations of railway speculators who instruct Veneering how he must maneuver across the valley and cut off his conservatory in order to "cut up the opposition root and branch at the window curtains" (OMF III, xvii; 690).

Fig. 8: George Cruikshank, "The Railway Dragon" (1845)

The coming of the railway craze to Camden Town in *Dombey and Son* is nevertheless depicted with distinct ambivalence. "There were railway patterns in its drapers' shops, and railway journals in the windows of its newsmen. There were railway hotels, coffee-houses, lodging houses, boarding-houses; railway plans, maps, views, wrappers, bottles, sandwich boxes, and time-tables; railway hackney-coach and cab-stands; railway-omnibuses, railway streets and buildings, railway hangers-on and parasites, and flatterers of all calculation" (D&S xv; 218). This is humorous, but not objectionable, apart from a commercialization resulting from the fierce competition between the railway companies driving their lines from the North through London's outskirts into St. Pancras, Euston, and King's Cross. The railway has brought only prosperity to the master sweeper and, despite the initial opposition in the railway's "struggling days," the neighborhood "now boasted of its powerful and prosperous relation." On the conquered and vanquished "frowzy" wastelands of Stagg's Gardens the railway has constructed a monumental landscape of busy streets:

> Where the old rotten summer-houses once had stood, palaces now reared their heads, and granite columns of gigantic girth opened a vista to the Railway world and beyond. The miserable waste ground, where the refuse-matter had been heaped of yore, was swallowed up and gone; and in its frowzy stead were tiers of warehouses, crammed with rich goods and costly merchandise. The old by-streets now swarmed with passengers and vehicles of every kind; the new streets that had stopped disheartened in the mud and waggon-ruts, formed towns within themselves, originating wholesome comforts and conveniences belonging to themselves, and never tried or thought of until they sprung into existence. Bridges that had led to nothing, led to villas, gardens, churches, healthy public walks. (D&S xv; 218)

This sounds like approval of the new, except that it continues, "The carcasses of houses, and beginnings of new thoroughfares, had started off upon the line at steam's own speed and shot away into the country in a monster train." The agency of change would appear to be suspect, for it is a monstrous machine that is liable, like Frankenstein, to run off beyond human control "at steam's own speed." Moreover, all this hurried building and urban expansion has, in the contemporary idiom of the locomotive projectile, "shot away into the country in a monster train," which hints at an urban menace to invade and obliterate the countryside, in the Romantic spirit of Dickens's reading of Wordsworth.

The ambiguity is deepened when Dickens co-opts the city-body trope. The new railway world is described as a smooth-running machine that throbs with the healthy circulation of life-blood in a living body: "To and from the heart of this great change, all day and night, throbbing currents rushed and returned incessantly like its life's blood. Crowds of people and mountains of goods, departing and arriving scores upon scores of times in every four-and-twenty hours, produced a fermentation in the place that was always in action" (D&S xv; 218). Perhaps the problem is just this, that the blood is that of the monster and not, in the common trope of healthy circulation, the beneficial economic blood-flow of commerce circulating in the railway arteries of the nation. The smooth running of the machine is a senseless motion that uproots people and homes, and the "carcasses of ragged tenements" emphasize the dead as against the healthy body. The following sentence picks up the ambivalence of motion and mobility, "The very houses seemed disposed to pack up and take trips" (D&S xv; 218). The latent power of the city's body, as in Wordsworth's sonnet "Composed upon Westminster Bridge," is here morally ambivalent because it suggests not tranquil lethargy but a restless motion directed at unspecified but well understood and as yet unachieved purposes:

> Night and day the conquering engines rumbled at their distant work, or, advancing smoothly to their journey's end, and gliding like tame dragons

into the allotted corners grooved out to the inch for their reception, stood bubbling and trembling there, making the walls quake, as if they were dilating with the secret knowledge of great powers yet unsuspected in them, and strong purposes not yet achieved. (D&S xv; 218–19)

The quake and rumble of the trains again point to a seismic tremor of unnatural power. The railway has won over political representation to its cause, for whereas Parliament had been rough in its cross-examination of "the wild railroad theories of engineers" little more than two decades before (with the opening of the first railway lines), now the same members of Parliament went North "with their watches in their hands, and sent messages before by the electric telegraph, to say they were coming" (ibid.). The new technology ensures that parliamentary representation keeps time with the interests of the railway companies (who numbered among their directors a number of M.P.s and well-connected figures). Wealth and luxury are piling up, and the streets are filling with crowds, but, true to Gray's and Goldsmith's condemnation of the modern Babylon, something vital, as yet unnamed, is being lost with Stagg's Gardens. The "tame dragons" (a domesticated species of the mythical demon fighting England's patron saint) that glide "into the allotted corners grooved out to the inch" (perhaps echoing Tennyson's "ringing grooves of change" with the ironic overtone of planned precision and inflexibility) are achieving a victory of the "conquering engines," of the mechanical at the expense of the organic, which serves the mercantile interests of the Dombeys.

The victory is clear and only deluded diehards could ignore it. Yet the victory of the mechanical has not quashed all that is human. Stoking himself with bread and butter, Toodles is a paragon of lower-class domesticity, who muses on the lines and branches of life or on the mind as a railway junction and who dispenses an instinctive morality by inveighing against any secret doings in tunnels. He manages to transfer any pent-up aggression and anger into the engine that tears up and down the line. Perhaps, after all, the dreaminess of old-fashioned Paul might not be totally out of place on the railway. Railway travel gave Dickens much cause for dreaming: "I am never sure of time or place upon a Railroad. I can't read, I can't think, I can't sleep—I can only dream" ("Railway Dreaming," *Household Words,* 10 May 1856; DJ 3: 370). Dickens sees distinct advantages in railway traveling. The collapsed perception of time and space affords the "luxurious confusion" of imagining Paris from an estranged lunar perspective, while both the novel and the railway bring us from place to place in a twinkling, so that the efficiency of Paris stands in immediate contrast to the slowness of London, Centralization to Circumlocution (DJ 3: 376).

Improved transportation jolts us out of our sense of time and space into an urban world of speed and confusion, as bewildering as Pickwick's flight to London, which is backdated some years before *Pickwick Papers* appeared in 1836, the year of the opening of London's first railway station at London Bridge.[49] The disorientation is intensified by the institution of Railway Time. "There was even railway time observed in the clocks, as if the sun itself had given in" (D&S xv;

218). Traditional conventions of time-marking and natural rhythms had been superseded by the timetable and the imposition on the local or rural community of machine-time according to the arrival and departure of trains. In the delirium of his flight from Dijon and Paris, Carker loses track of time; his watch is unwound and he doesn't recall which day it is. Riding at dizzying speed to Paris, in "A Flight," Dickens loses all notion of place, direction, and time, the more so for the guard's repeated assurance that there was no hurry. In "A Narrative of Extraordinary Suffering," Mr. Lost loses his sanity to Bradshaw's representation of time and place in the British Isles and gives up going where he wanted (*Household Words*, 12 July 1851; DJ 3: 8–9). Since clocks differed from one region to another, trains carried their time with them in the early days of the railway, as ships did, until Greenwich Mean Time, the zero median of imperial space, was adopted as standard railway time in 1842. The "annihilation of space by time," a phrase later adopted by Marx in his analysis of capital,[50] further eroded the local sense of place and belonging, as well as the natural cycles of agriculture and the seasons, which had marked time before the factory bell replaced the church bell in regulation of the day. In a Carlylean opposition of mechanical and organic, steam-age time runs in this novel and in *Hard Times* as smoothly grooved as the dragon trains. The mechanical tick of Dombey's watch fixes her father in Florence's mind at the beginning of the novel, and the clock in Blimber's study disturbs Paul because it seems to mechanically mimic Dr. Blimber's monosyllabic "how, is, my, lit, tle, friend."

Stagg's Gardens is an area condensed into Camden Town by the Stranger's Map of London, which is printed for convenience on a handkerchief. This is appropriate because the visibility of the city has been disrupted beyond recognition by the coming of the railway, and the map's representation does not help to read the city. A good example of this is given by T. M. Thomas in an account of a businessman's coming down to a London suburb to find a residence near the new railway only to find that his large-scale map with its comforting constructions of Church and Nation bears no relation to the labyrinthine anti-Eden of squalor and filth ("A Suburban Connemara," *Household Words*, 8 March 1851). The text of a handkerchief might offer as much legibility as any other.

Gender relations are also in tension in the new configuration of time and space brought about by the railway's shrinking of the map. However uncertain are its pastoral origins, Polly's home is a comically "sacred grove," from which Dombey has ordered that his son be protected because the wet nurse was stereotypically seen as socially and sexually dangerous—it was feared that sexually active wet nurses might corrupt their charges.[51] Polly is punished for that contamination when Dombey cuts the child off from her fountain, which contextualizes this episode in the old-fashioned natural values of tenderness and maternity barred from the world of Dombey. Polly is another hired body, regulated as a matter of wages (a "bargain") and socially as well as sexually distanced by having her name changed to the impersonal "Richards" of formal master–servant relations. But she is quite untouched by Dombey's commodification of her breasts, just as she is immune to class constructions of her as diseased or contagious; in fact, Miss Tox attests to both the cleanliness and the exemplary domesticity of the family home, where she later enjoys tea, coziness, and a lesson in moral reformation.

Fig. 9: H. K. Browne, frontispiece to the first edition of *Dombey and Son* (1848)

Quite unenvious of Dombey's wealth, Polly demonstratively does not attempt a "King and Pauper" exchange of babies, and, in a final irony, Polly comes to nurse Dombey in his despair after his ruin. Polly will not turn into a steam engine and turn out the mechanical stitching that ruins the health of the poor seamstress in Thomas Hood's "The Song of the Shirt" (1843). Her nurturing sets her off from the speculative investment and transportation of goods that drive the iron maidens of the railroad converging on the great city which provide the sustenance of Paul's wealth. The wet nurse in this novel has something in common with the nursing mothers of Dutch genre interiors, as well as Dickens's buxom women who embody healthy family values of love and compassion that are nurtured in the rosy-cheeked, apple-faced Toodles. She shares the femininity of the chaste maidens and naked nymphs of the frontispiece of Dickens's novel (fig. 9) domesticated in a neoclassic and post-Rousseauesque style. For her part, Florence, like Little Dorrit, is a lactating Euphrasia whose breast is spurned by a father,[52] but despite her bruises, she offers her nurturing breast to heal the middle-class home shattered by domestic violence.[53] She withstands maternal deprivation and preserves the power of love against all odds. Though sentimentalized, Florence stands for the infantile pleasures of the breast against Dombey's reality principle of heartless exploitation and control of desire, for fertile reproduction against Malthusian principles of population control. The disappearance of Stagg's Gardens thus has clearly to do with deprivation of maternal love and nurturing. It finds a parallel in the disappearance of Florence's home following her return from the Skettles' and her disturbing discovery of Carker's knowledge and power over her. Dombey's house has disappeared beneath a "labyrinth" of scaffolding and "alteration," and the hammering of the Babel-builders breaks into the enchantment of Florence's solitude. Her mother's portrait has been replaced by chalked instructions for decor, and she is barred from any privacy in her own room; it is from her emotional refuge in Paul's room that Florence is summoned to meet her new Mama.

THE RAILWAY, THE NOVEL, AND THE RAILWAY-NOVEL

> But it is evident that if we want a railway to be made, or its
> affairs to be managed, this man of wide views and narrow
> observation will not serve our purpose.
> —George Eliot, "The Natural History of German Life" (1856)

Along with other novelists, Dickens became a frequent travel companion as circulating libraries opened at many railway stations. Reading killed the monotony and isolation of the railway carriage, which gave no scope for gazing at passersby or window-shopping. Railway newsstands and station lending-libraries catered for predominantly urban tastes with good-quality literature by authors such as Dickens (the second on Tauschnitz's list of special railway editions) or essays by Macaulay. Now a middle-class reader was coming into the book and magazine market, and the more efficient distribution and transportation brought about by the railways broadened the scope of the serial novel and demand for it. *Dombey and Son* itself had to compete with the cheap melodramatic fare of the "railway novel."

When W. H. Smith opened its first railway bookstall in 1849, "railway literature" boomed to include not only Bradshaw, "blue books," and railway newspapers, but a wide range of popular novels, including reprints, translations, and well-known authors. This made for a "cheap" literature both in terms of price and undifferentiated "taste." The book was read instead of the landscape, and often replaced conversation, since the etiquette of a British railway carriage did not encourage striking up friendships with casual strangers (as might happen on long stage-coach journeys). Reading time became railway time, not just time passed on the railway.[54] Railway reading could lift the imagination above the dreary scenery of factories and wet umbrellas: Dickens introduced the fairy scene of glass manufacture with a railway reading of Johnson and Defoe (with W. H. Wills, "Plate Glass," *Household Words*, 1 February 1851). Reading Leigh Hunt and the *Arabian Nights* on the railway carried another *Household Words* contributor,

Henry Morley, away to a romance of long-past chivalry and fantasy. But this is more an escapist fantasy than the mediation of steam and science through Fancy, to which we will return in another chapter.

Ruskin, who detested the railways because he thought they ruined the landscape and eradicated social distance,[55] later complained in "Fiction, Fair and Foul" (1881) about the "railway novel," which traded in the "low" realism of ugly types, warts and all, worth no more human interest than the "sweepings out of a Pentonville omnibus." For the same reason, earlier in his essay Ruskin condemned the morbid "statistics" of death in *Bleak House*, which stank of the inanity and monotony of the city, London's artificial environment, and the steam age that deprived the artist of the natural inspiration of the rural agricultural cycle. Ruskin's wholesale critique of the "Cockney school" for their characters picked up from the gutter and their landscape "by excursion train to Gravesend, with return ticket for City-road" sounds a belated High Tory lament for the prerailway past and for old-fashioned morality. Ruskin had accused Dickens of being the leader of a steam-whistle party, yet it was *Dombey and Son* which was resisting the moral influence of the locomotive and which was in competition with the penny dreadfuls that proliferated with the railways.

Dickens's vivid and innovative recreation of the train speeding across and through the countryside shows an extraordinary awareness of a totally new experience which posed an artistic challenge, while the moral impulse and design of *Dombey and Son* show an understanding of both the global overview of the system and the minute workings at ground level (which Eliot in her essay "The Natural History of German Life" presents as a test of social realism). In a letter I have already quoted to Forster from Switzerland of 30 August 1846, where he was working on *Dombey and Son*, Dickens declared how much effort he put into "getting on FAST" and made his now famous complaint about how difficult it was to write without his "magic lantern" of London streets (*Letters* 4: 612). This is usually taken as an index of Dickens's mimetic dependence on the crowds of his native city and his nighttime walks in its streets, as if a comic novel could not be allowed to flag for a moment and Dickens's imagination might falter in the tranquil pace of a small Swiss town, though Kate Flint has related the trope to the etching of vivid memory tinged with violence in *Pictures from Italy*.[56] However, we should recall that the magic lantern was, besides a popular form of entertainment, a mechanical means of reproduction which nevertheless conveyed the illusion of the real necessary to the imagination.[57] Far from a fallacious mimesis, this points to a deeper relation of speed and novel writing.

The speed of the new means of transportation somehow expresses Dickens's constant need to keep up steam (a current metaphor for the speed of modernity), and he often traveled by train on his reading tours, rather than by the slower and less convenient coaches which would have brought him into closer contact with people and provided him with the kind of characters and stories we meet on Pickwick's tour. On the other hand, the railway expanded Dickens's imaginary landscape, making easier the foreign travel which gave him the distanced perspective on the city and on England, and this, according to Harry Stone, explains the new mastery of form in this novel, as well as the broader imaginative sweep and experimentation.[58]

It is because fast travel by rail shrivels up time and distance that the novelist sees every detail of the characters and places of his imagined London from the tranquility of Lake Geneva and the dark streets of Paris, where he moved to draw on the "life and crowd of that extraordinary place" for a particular stage of writing the novel (letter to Forster, June 1846, *Letters* 4: 569). In the 1858 Preface to *Dombey and Son*, Dickens confessed that he could not remember the landscape in which he had written the novel without imagining Cuttle running away from Mrs. MacStinger across Swiss mountains. Nor could he help recalling the Paris streets along which he wandered at night in the depth of winter when he wrote the chapter in which he parted from little Paul. It is as if writing is walking and getting on. This has been taken as evidence of Dickens's awareness of the limitations of representation, of an inability to make whole the fragmentary experience of landscape.[59] It seems to me that, to the contrary, the altered perception of time and space enables the author to adapt to the pace of the insomniac fever of his imagination, to imagine fleeing with Carker from Dijon, then by train from Paris to England, in a disturbing, disorienting nightmare so different from Dickens's more comfortable Railway Dreaming. The sensation of speed simulates the dissolving self threatened by the total reification represented in Dombeyism and in the locomotive. These new gods neuter any spirituality or sexuality and serve a colonizing, enslaving body. In order that the novel does not become another commodity (like Edith and her art), subjectivity must be saved from merging completely with the railroad (as it does in Dombey's contemplation of Death on the ride to Leamington).

There is another sense, moreover, in which novel-writing is implicated in the railway line. The novel's planned lines and branches are commonplace metaphors applied by Dickens in disclosing the plans for the novel to Forster, and they tend to an end that cannot be foreseen in Dombey's blind representation of the future, symbolized on the wrappers by the stopped-up telescope in the foreground. The lines and branches of the railway are blind to the time of Providence, which watches over Paul (in the opening of chapter 8) like another Major, whose voyeuristic peeping is as blind as other mortal views in the novel. Providence, however, rules over more than the plot of the novel. When Dickens found himself suspended, together with the manuscript characters of *Our Mutual Friend*, over an embankment in the accident of 9 June 1865, described in the postscript of that novel, he had the presence of mind, after helping whomever he could, to clamber in and rescue them.[60] An engraving in the *Penny Illustrated Paper* of 24 June 1865 depicted Dickens relieving a supine maiden in distress with a hat full of water, but his "constitutional" presence of mind nevertheless does not mitigate the traumatic recollection of the shock which, in a flurry of letters to friends, he associates with the scenes of dead and dying. Although he claims to have come out unscathed, his hand shakes as he writes (*Letters* 11: 49–62). For years afterwards, this experience of a rail crash affected his nerves. "I cannot," he admitted to Forster later that month, "bear railway travelling yet. A perfect conviction, against the senses, that the carriage is down on one side (and generally that is the left, and not the side on which the carriage in the accident really went over), comes upon me" (*Letters* 11: 65). Making the same complaint to Pauline Viardot, Dickens noted that his sense of time itself had been put out—his watch, a chronometer, was slow for some weeks (16 August 1865, *Letters* 11: 83)—and joked that he could not reason his watch out of this absurd behavior (to Shirley Brooks, 9 January 1866, *Letters* 11: 134). The railway had, so it seemed to Dickens, battered time as well as his nerves in dragging him to the edge of an unnatural death by machinery, an industrial mutilation of the human body (medical literature paid attention to the neurotic effects of railway traveling only from the 1860s).[61]

A scene in *Our Mutual Friend* describes the hurtling train which carries Bella Wilfer across the Thames toward the dying Eugene Wrayburn and her own destiny:

> Then, the train rattled among the house-tops, and among the ragged sides of houses torn down to make way for it, and over the swarming streets, and under the fruitful earth, until it shot across the river: bursting over the quiet surface like a bomb-shell, and gone again as if it had exploded in the rush of smoke and steam and glare. A little more, and again it roared across the river, a great rocket: spurning the watery turnings and doublings with ineffable contempt, and going straight to its end, as Father Time goes to his. (821–22)

The insistence on the attraction of the "loadstone of Eternity," which determines the end of all mortals, while the rocket-like locomotive hurtles on in utter contempt for the "solemn river," like Dombey's train, points to the mutual benevolence so lacking in the money economy of the city's necropolis, a benevolence which moves Dickens to help his fellow-passengers and recognize the workings of Providence in life and the novel. In noting the metafictional irony that the train accident had almost put an end to the writing of *Our Mutual Friend* and to the novelist's life he discreetly erases from the scene the mistress who was accompanying him, Ellen Ternan, leaving the author to immortality at the end of the novel, unscathed morally or physically.

BETWEEN THE CITY AND THE DEEP BLUE SEA

> ... in a season of calm weather
> Though inland far we be,
> Our souls have sight of that immortal sea
> Which brought us hither,
> Can in a moment travel thither,
> And see the children sport upon the shore,
> And hear the mighty waters rolling evermore.
> —William Wordsworth, "Ode: Intimations of Immortality"

The two systems of time, the linear measurement of progress and a more imaginative, abstract, and metaphysical scheme, confront each other dialogically in *Dombey and Son*. In a Shakespearean "amplified metaphor," which Ermath relates to the tension between providential and secular constructions of history in this novel,[62] the sea's natural order encompasses an eternity in which redemption can be envisioned. This quasireligious chronotope overrides Dombey's commercial sense of a narrow here-and-now ruled by the economic principles of *The Wealth of Nations* and the only too human unnaturalness of Dombey's "master-vice." When the dying Fanny drifts out "upon the dark and unknown sea that rolls round all the world" (D&S I; 11), however fast the doctor's watch may tick, there is no withstanding the timescale of eternity imaged in the sea. Polly's tale of the resurrected seed is meant to comfort Florence, but in its sentimental reference to the well-known gospel parable it points up the difference between the time of judgment and resurrection ("Time"), on the one hand, and the hurtling steam-powered timetable of the machine, on the other.

That old, old man, little Paul looks out to sea at Brighton at the far shore of the otherworldly in search of his deceased mother. His old fashion (not according to the Blimber definition) is the death of innocent angels, as he too, no more impeded by doctors' watches than his mother, flows out to sea, carried by the golden ebb of the river in his bedroom. An older fashion yet is Immortality, "And look upon us, angels of young children, with regards not estranged, when the swift river bears us to the ocean!" (D&S XVI; 225). The romanticized siting of salvation in the hereafter proves stronger than the much-vaunted recuperative effects of Brighton's sea water, but it is left to Florence to take up the otherworldly flow in the present reality of the city. In later chapters we will question whether this can be a sustaining vision of redemption in the city.

The Romantic vision of natural values and eternity represented by the ocean and Paul's old-fashioned ways is juxtaposed, in the opening of chapter IV, with Dombeyism, whose center of world commerce and finance is dead, while the ships which go out daily to trade with the colonies, all the exotica of East India House, are nothing against the antiquated objects in the thoroughly ship-shape, "sea-going" shop of curiosities belonging to the Ships' Instrument Maker, Solomon Gill. These precise instruments of navigation, whose invention or improvement had determined the time and space of Britain's naval empire since the seventeenth century, are nevertheless unsellable and remain the quaint, anachronistic stuff of dream, of individual enterprise outdated by steam and corporate business. Solomon Gill understands nothing of the new age and is so far behind the times that the wooden "Midshipman" falls into the hands of the broker. Yet his obsolescence is of a very different order than Mrs. Skewton's, an archeological relic whose polite, if eccentric conversation is filled with laments that the age has no heart. Carrying his chronometer with him, Gill proves in the end to be ahead of the times, for his prudent investments have brought him profit, while Dombey, deaf to all advice and warnings, has been ruined.

This sounds not dissimilar to the moral principles which Robinson Crusoe learns on his island, and no less commercially prudent than Defoe believed them to be in his day (though he was not so successful in his own pursuit of trade). It is very different from the ruthless business ethics that colonize the world in the name of progress and profits. Science versus commerce might seem a false contrast between two mechanizing systems, except that here science is fired by the "spice" of imagination in an old-fashioned retail trade. The shipwrecks in the tales of heroic death at sea related with such enthusiasm by Walter, which hint at the future turn in his own destiny, and the unchartable course of the aptly (perhaps too obviously) named *Son and Heir* do not follow the planned career, as straight as a railway line, of a Dombey, who, we are told, deals in hides and not hearts. Dombey & Son, Carker advises Edith, "know neither time, nor place, nor season, but beat them all down" (D&S xxxvii; 506). The arrogance of Dombey's imperialism, for which Edward Said has not entirely excused Dickens,[63] is condemned because, well before Conrad, it exposes the barbarism that it uncovered at the heart of civilization. Dombey's heartlessness, like Mrs. Jellyby's, starts at home.

Notes

1 David Masson, *British Novelists and their Styles* (Cambridge: Macmillan, 1859), 238–39.

2 James Winter, *London's Teeming Streets, 1830–1914* (London: Routledge, 1993), 1–15.

3 David Trotter, *Circulation: Defoe, Dickens, and the Economies of the Novel* (New York: St. Martin's, 1988), 61–64.

4 See Jonathan Arac, *Commissioned Spirits: The Shaping of Social Motion in Dickens, Carlyle, Melville, and Hawthorne* (New Brunswick: Rutgers University Press, 1970), 182–83. The American use of "corporation" to refer to proprietors of large industrial conglomerates differs from the English tradition of chartered bodies of political representation, as Dickens noted in chapter 4 of *American Notes*. The ironic associations of the British usage will be apparent in this chapter.

5 Lawrence Frank, *Charles Dickens and the Romantic Self* (Lincoln: University of Nebraska Press, 1984), 58.

6 Roger B. Henkle, "The Crisis of Representation in *Dombey and Son*," in *Critical Reconstructions: The Relationship of Fiction and Life*, ed. Robert M. Polhemus and Roger B. Henkle (Stanford: Stanford University Press, 1994), 90–91.

7 Despite the feminine pronoun usually used for locomotives and ships, Dickens genders the locomotive as masculine, appropriately for its phallic symbolism ("Chips: The Individuality of Locomotives," *Household Words*, 21 September 1850; DJ 2: 283–84). In this note Dickens draws a moral from the differing needs and performance of each machine for the tendency of government to treat humans without regard for their individuality.

8 In Henkle's Freudian interpretation, the train in this novel is a phallic symbol thrusting forward, like Dombey, in an abstraction of the masculine power that has become detached from desire and thus from subjectivity; the locomotive that crushes Carker is similarly a Dionysian body which crushes sexuality by dismembering and devouring its victim's body ("The Crisis of Representation in *Dombey and Son*," 100–101).

9 On the underlying causes for this perception see Gareth Stedman Jones, *Outcast London: A Study in the Relationship Between Classes in Victorian Society* (Oxford: Clarendon Press, 1971).

10   See Gallagher's comparison of Malthus's *Essay on the Principles of Population* with Henry Mayhew's *London Labour and the London Poor* in her "The Body Versus the Social Body in the Work of Thomas Malthus and Henry Mayhew," in *The Making of the Modern Body: Sexuality and Society in the Nineteenth Century*, ed. Catherine Gallagher and Thomas Lacqueur (Berkeley: University of California Press, 1987), 83–106.

11   Graeme Davison, "The City as a Natural System: Theories of Urban Society in Early Nineteenth-Century Britain," in *The Pursuit of Urban History*, ed. Derek Fraser and Anthony Sutcliffe (London: Edward Arnold, 1983), 249.

12   *Lectures on Social Science and the Organization of Labour* (1851), quoted in Davison, "The City as a Natural System," 367.

13   See especially Mary Poovey's comments on the faultlines in these different definitions, *Making a Social Body: British Cultural Formation, 1830–1864* (Chicago: University of Chicago Press, 1995), 17–19.

14   See Jack Simmons, *The Railway in England and Wales, 1830–1914: Vol. 1, The System and Its Working*. Leicester: Leicester University Press, 1978), 39–60.

15   For example, Henry Morley, "Need Railway Travellers Be Smashed?" *Household Words*, 29 November 1851.

16   See Yi-Fu Tuan, *Topophilia: A Study of Environmental Perception, Attitudes, and Values* (Englewood Cliffs, NJ: Prentice-Hall, 1974), 148–49.

17   See John Romano's comparison of *Dombey and Son* with *Madame Bovary* in his *Dickens and Reality* (New York: Columbia University Press, 1978), 166.

18   See Poovey, *Making a Social Body*, for a discussion of the epistemology of the social body in this period and the way it affected constructions of the poor or gender difference in the writings of Chadwick or Mayhew. For a different reading of *Dombey and Son* and *Little Dorrit* as novels that capitalize on the reduction of women's bodies to enslaved property, see Jeff Nunokawa, *The Afterlife of Property: Domestic Security and the Victorian Novel* (Princeton: Princeton University Press, 1994), 3–15.

19   Mikhail Bakhtin, *Rabelais and His World*, trans. Helen Iswolsky (Bloomington: Indiana University Press, 1984), 23–29.

20   Graham Pechey, "The London Motif in Some Eighteenth-Century Contexts: A Semiotic Study," *Literature and History* 4 (1976): 2–29.

21   For a convincing reading of the wrapper design as allegorical of the novel's theme of Pride and Fall, see John Butt and Kathleen Tillotson, *Dickens at Work* (London: Methuen, 1957), 91–96.

22   See examples from *Pickwick Papers, Martin Chuzzlewit, Bleak House*, and *Our Mutual Friend* in Richard D. Altick, *The Presence of the Present: Topics of the Day in the Victorian Novel* (Columbus: Ohio State University Press, 1991), 64–67. On advertising in serial publication of *Bleak House*, see Emily Steinlight, "'Anti-Bleak House': Advertising and the Victorian Novel," *Narrative* 14 (1996):132–62.

23   On fetishism and its implications for the imagination in *Dombey and Son*, see David Simpson, *Fetishism and Imagination: Dickens, Melville, Conrad* (Baltimore: Johns Hopkins University Press, 1982), 39–68.

24   Wolfgang Schivelbusch, *The Railway Journey: The Industrialization of Time and Space in the Nineteenth Century* (Berkeley: University of California Press, 1986), 41–42. In what follows I have drawn on Schivelbusch's brilliant analysis of the railway in terms of the industrialization of time and space and Michael Robbins's fascinating study of the social impact of the railway, *The Railway Age in Britain and its Impact on the World* (Harmondsworth: Penguin Books, 1965), as well as Michael Freeman, *Railways and the Victorian Imagination* (New Haven: Yale University Press, 1999).

25   *Simmel on Culture: Selected Writings*, ed. David Frisby and Mike Featherstone (London: Sage, 1997), 176.

26   See on the derivation of this episode from Carlyle, Michael Goldberg, *Dickens and Carlyle* (Athens, GA: University of Georgia Press, 1972), 47–56. Harry Stone has commented that this theme of "money cannot buy love" was much imitated in the nineteenth century ("The Novel as Fairy-Tale: Dickens's *Dombey and Son*," in *Charles Dickens: New Perspectives*, ed. Wendall S. Johnson [Englewood Cliffs, NJ: Prentice-Hall, 1982], 53).

27   "Railway Legislation," *Quarterly Review* 74 (1844): 250–51 n.

28   See Myron F. Brightfield, "The Coming of the Railroad to Early Victorian England, as Viewed by Novels of the Period (1840–1870)," *Technology and Culture* 3.1 (1962): 45–72.

29   "Railway Legislation," 259–60. *Punch* joked that "ladies only" compartments were necessary to protect gentlemen from compromising situations, a fear echoed by Tony Weller (resurrected in *Master Humphrey's Clock*) after being locked in a railway compartment with a screaming widow whom he suspects of having marital intentions!

30   Quoted in Schivelbusch, *The Railway Journey*, 34.

31   Excerpt in Brightfield, "The Coming of the Railroad," 48.

32   Friedrich Engels, *The Condition of the Working Class in England*, trans. W. O. Henderson and W. H. Chaloner (Oxford: Blackwell, 1972), 61.

33   See Herbert L. Sussman, *Victorians and the Machine: The Literary Response to Technology* (Cambridge, MA: Harvard University Press, 1968), 53–56. Jonathan Arac faults Dickens for not clarifying the connection of Dombey with the "symbol" of the railway or integrating it into a larger perspective (*Commissioned Spirits: The Shaping of Social Motion in Dickens, Carlyle, Melville, and Hawthorne* [New Brunswick: Rutgers University Press, 1970], 108–09).

34   Richard D. Altick conjectures that readers would have superimposed Turner's image on Dickens's hitherto incomparable description of the novel sensations of railway traveling (*The Presence of the Present*, 191).

35   Simon Schama offers an iconoclastic reading of Turner's painting (*Landscape and Memory* [New York: Knopf, 1995], 362–63).

36   Schivelbusch, *The Railway Journey*, 62.

37   Quoted in Schivelbusch, *The Railway Journey*, 55–56.

38   See Ronald J. Zboray, *A Fictive People: Antebellum Economic Development and the American Reading Public* (New York: Oxford University Press, 1993), 68–82.

39   See Sussman, *Victorians and the Machine*, 3–8.

40   See Lynda Nead, *Victorian Babylon: People, Streets and Images in Nineteenth-Century London* (New Haven: Yale University Press, 2000), 27–56.

41   Eagleton cited in Rosalind Williams, *Notes on the Underground: An Essay on Technology, Society, and the Imagination* (Cambridge, MA: MIT Press, 1990), 64. See Sussman, *Victorians and the Machine*, 43–44.

42   Rosalind Williams, *Notes on the Underground*, 64–65.

43   John Francis, *A History of the English Railway: Its Social Relations and Revelations, 1820–1845* (London: Longman, Brown, Green, and Longmans, 1851), 198–241.

44   Steig, "*Dombey and Son* and the Railway Panic of 1845," *The Dickensian* 67 (1971): 145–48.

45   See Freeman, *Railways and the Victorian Imagination*, 13.

46   Robbins points out that the railways actually fitted in quite well with the rural landscape of hedgerows and enclosed fields (*The Railway Age in Britain*, 57–59). See also Humphrey House, *The Dickens World*, 2nd ed. (Oxford: Oxford University Press, 1942), 39–46.

47   Malcolm Andrews, *Dickens on England and the English* (Hassocks, Sussex: Harvester, 1979), 62. See Harland S. Nelson, "Stagg's Gardens: The Railway through Dickens's World," *Dickens Studies Annual* 3 (1974): 41–53.

48   See on the place of *Dombey and Son* in the railway culture of Victorian Britain, Murray Baumgarten, "Railway/Reading/Time: *Dombey and Son* and the Industrial World," *Dickens Studies Annual* 19 (1990): 65–89.

49   Andrews, *Dickens on England and the English*, 56.

50   See Freeman, *Railways and the Victorian Imagination*, 78.

51   Ruth Perry, "Colonizing the Breast: Sexuality and Maternity in Eighteenth-Century England," in *British Literature, 1640–1789*, ed. Robert DeMaria Jr. (Oxford: Blackwell, 1999), 320. Laura Berry's claim that class stereotypes in medical opinion prop up bourgeois colonization of the working-class body ignores the novel's resistance to the dehumanizing effect of exploitation by Dombey's empire ("In the Bosom of the Family: The Wet-Nurse, the Railroad, and *Dombey and Son*," *Dickens Studies Annual* 25 [1996]: 1–28). See also Melisa Klimaszewski, "Examining the Wet Nurse: Breasts, Power, and Penetration in Victorian England," *Women's Studies* 35.4 (2006): 323–46.

52   The myth is in fact subverted and stripped of incestuous implications, because the father is refusing the breast and his daughter's love, though the chains of the father in French sculptor Jean Goujon's version are appropriate to Dorrit's imprisonment and to the "mind-enslav'd" manacles of both Dombey and Dorrit.

53   Lisa Surridge, *Bleak Houses: Marital Violence in Victorian Fiction* (Athens, OH: Ohio University Press, 2005), 69.

54   See Schivelbusch, *The Railway Journey*, 65–68; Zboray, *A Fictive People*, 68–82.

55   On the attitude to the railway in Ruskin's aesthetics see Joseph Bizup, "Architecture, Railroads, and Ruskin's Rhetoric of Bodily Form," *Prose Studies* 21.1 (1998): 74–94.

56   *The Victorians and the Visual Imagination* (Cambridge: Cambridge University Press, 2000), 145–50. See p. 35 above. On the "magic lantern" as both trope and technique of reproduction, see Maria Cristina Paganoni, *The Magic Lantern: Representation of the Double in Dickens* (New York: Routledge, 2008).

57   On Dickens's use of the magic lantern as a technique in his writing see Joss Marsh, "Dickensian 'Dissolving Views': The Magic Lantern, Visual Story-Telling, and the Victorian Technological Imagination," *Comparative Critical Studies* 6.3 (2009): 333–46.

58   "The Novel as Fairy-Tale," 52.

59   For example, Romano, *Dickens and Reality*, 155–56.

60   See Edgar Johnson, *Charles Dickens: His Tragedy and Triumph*. Two vols. (London: Gollancz, 1953), 2: 1018–21.

61   See Nicholas Daly, "Railway Novels, Sensation Fiction and the Modernization of the Senses," *ELH* 66 (1999): 461–87.

62   Elizabeth Deeds Ermath, *The English Novel in History, 1840–1895* (London: Routledge, 1997), 32–37.

63   Edward Said, *Culture and Imperialism* (New York: Knopf, 1994), 13–14. While acknowledging that Dombey is not Dickens, Said nevertheless claims that the representation of Dombey's imperialism is permeated by an unpardonable Anglocentric view that subscribes to Europe's colonization of the world. Nunokawa, too, has applied Said's analysis of orientalism to the colonization of the body in this novel (*The Afterlife of Property*, 40–76).

3

House and Home: *Bleak House*

THE ARCHI-TEXTURE OF THE NOVEL

> The events of human life, whether public or private, are so
> intimately linked to architecture that most observers can
> reconstruct nations or individuals in all the truth of their
> habits from the remains of their public monuments or from
> their domestic relics.
>
> —Balzac, *The Search for the Absolute*

Both architecture and the novel construct an ideology of urban space (space
as designed and perceived, as distinct from lived). In the city, architecture
topographically represents a microcosm, as well as making a political statement
about the subjection to sociopolitical domination and disciplinary control by
one class.[1] *Bleak House* tests the analogy of architecture and plot design, but
also questions the ideology behind them. In imagining the social landscape as
concentric circles of fog and muddle,[2] Dickens is asking whether conventional
forms are stable or meaningful. In the problematic form of *Bleak House*, analogies
of design and form question the legibility of representation of the city; they
deconstruct the privileging of narrative over monumental form in what Julian
Wolfrey sees as the instability and ultimate elusiveness of the meaning of the
city, though not quite in his sense of "architexture" as traces of architecture in the
writing of the city.[3]

Bleak House is a novel which mediates between the private space of the
home and the public, while questioning domestic ideology and accommodating
homelessness in a domesticated structure against the background of fierce
debates over housing as an urban problem. It is a novel that is not quite at home
in the form which houses it. These feelings of unease in the novel form are not
unique. Queen Victoria had occasion, on finishing *Eugene Aram* while her "hair
was doing," to comment that she could "never feel quite at ease or at home when
reading a Novel."[4] D. A. Miller relates Queen Victoria's feelings of unease to the
reader's anxiety in the novel and the form of *Bleak House*:

> For in an age in which productivity is valued at least as much as the
> product, the novel must claim no less the inadequacy than the necessity
> of closure. This inadequacy can now be understood ... in the broader
> context of institutional requirements and cultural needs, as the novel's own
> "work ethic," its imposing refusal of rest and enjoyment. Certainly, when
> reading this novel, though in the reasons of the hearth it finds its own
> reason for being, one never feels quite at home; perhaps, having finished

it, one knows why one never can feel at home. For what now is home—not securely possessed in perpetuity, but only leased from day to day on payment of continual exertions—but a House? And what is this House—neither wholly blackened by the institutions that make use of its cover, nor wholly bleached of their stain—but (in the full etymological ambiguity of the word) irresolvably Bleak?[5]

My reservation is that the identification of closure of novel with the closure imposed by the family does not match the novel's social and moral revision of the home as national and private institution, nor does it account for the displacement of systems of representation. This is a bildungsroman in which Esther realizes herself as subject by gaining control over domesticity, first as housekeeper and then as wife, so that, far from maintaining the panoptical reading of domesticity, this novel actually resists it.[6] The narrational dissonance and the irresolution of narrative voice, not least in the final ellipsis, may have something to do with Dickens's experimentation between *David Copperfield* and *Great Expectations* with autobiographical form. But to deny closure in *Bleak House* is, in my view, to miss the restructuring of moral priorities and ignore the remapping of social hierarchies.

Architecture and the novel both represent—not just describe—and their design of living space reflects aspirations, social and family relations, and changing moral values. Especially in England at the time of the rise of the novel, one's house defined one's "place." *Mansfield Park*, *Wuthering Heights*, *The Mill on the Floss*, and *Bleak House* itself are all novels whose titles and imagined houses imply differing forms of social standing and destiny, from the stately country estate of nobility and aristocracy to the house of untitled landowners and gentrified middle class. The family home was a characteristic chronotope of the eighteenth- and nineteenth-century novel, and Bakhtin suggests Dickens is working in the tradition of *Tom Jones* and *Peregrine Pickle* in his perfection of the European family novel, though in Bakhtin's second schema the stability of the family idyll is disrupted by the intrusion of a destructive or alien force, as in Richardson,[7] something we will also see in Dickens.

The Victorian home-and-garden was thought quintessentially English, because it represented social status, home ownership, privacy, and family values in an urban society where these were a fragile means to survival and enrichment amid social strife and economic instability. The interior design of the Victorian home made visual the social, functional, and sexual segregation of gender and class, delineating seclusion and exclusion. The subjection of the female body to domestication, Nancy Armstrong has argued, was a means of containment of social disorder and violence in the conduct books and domestic novels between Richardson and the Brontës through their channeling of desire to socialized goals: "In the hands of Mrs. Gaskell and Dickens in particular, domestic fiction carried the process of suppressing political resistance into the domain of popular literature, where it charted new domains of aberration requiring domestication."[8] The figure of the woman as angel of the house, however, must be contextualized in the question of what I shall be showing to be a subversion of domestic ideology. I will be questioning whether for Dickens the home is a space for control and repression or whether it can be a site of resistance against a capitalist economy of profit and loss by means of a domestic economy of feelings ruled by a woman. Houses are a synecdoche for the larger decay and ruin, but the ideal home served as a flood-barrier of urban society. In particular, I will be looking at ways in which the inversion of conventional modes of representation constructs an ideal home on the foundations of an alternate political and ethical agenda. Such an agenda may redraw gender as well as generic definitions in the safe boundaries of an ideal home that responds to the dangers of the city but can no longer shelter, let alone call itself home.

ANGELS IN THE HOUSE

> The saying is, that home is home, be it never so homely. If it hold good in the opposite contingency, and home is home be it never so stately, what an altar to the Household Gods is raised up here.
>
> —*Dombey and Son* (xxxv; 478)

One of the best known expressions of the home in the Victorian imagination is John Ruskin's paean to the Woman of Valor in his essay on the woman question, "Of Queens' Gardens" (1865):

> This is the true nature of home—it is the place of Peace; the shelter, not only from all injury, but from all terror, doubt, and division. In so far as it is not this, it is not home; so far as the anxieties of the outer life penetrate into it, and the inconsistently-minded, unknown, unloved, or hostile society of the outer world is allowed by either husband or wife to cross the threshold, it ceases to be home; it is then only a part of that outer world which you have roofed over, and lighted fire in. But so far as it is a sacred place, a vestal temple, a temple of the hearth watched over by Household Gods, before whose faces none may come but those whom they can receive with love,—so far as it is this, and roof and fire are types only of a nobler shade and light,—shade as of rock in a weary land, and light as of the Pharos in the stormy sea;—so far it vindicates the name, and fulfills the praise, of Home.[9]

This *topos classicus* is often quoted, sometimes in conjunction with the name of Dickens,[10] to show the Victorian patriarchal subjugation of woman as Angel of the House, managing domestic space and keeping out the ugly, the uncivilized, and the commercial. Kate Flint's feminist reading of Ruskin suggests representation is both exposure and exposé of the domestic sphere ideology celebrated in Coventry Patmore's *The Angel in the House*.[11] That poem was published after *Bleak House* appeared and was immensely popular among Dickens's contemporaries, but since Virginia Woolf it has been read as prima facie evidence of the oppression of women throughout the Victorian period. Yet despite Ruskin's approval of Patmore's poem, he recognizes in woman a force of moral power and aesthetic beauty, an ideological housekeeper who was queen of the home, matching the kingship of the intellectual male in *Sesame and Lilies*, who participated with her husband in the maintenance of home as a social power base, as well as in the domestic management of political and class control.[12] As a private domain which borders on public space, the home reflects in the representation of its conflict zones the social tensions at large, as well as the personal crises within, which resulted from the reorganization of space and the division of work from home as urbanization and industrialization changed the relationship of public and private in mid-Victorian Britain, with all the consequent shifts in demographic, class, and gender relations. The public domain increasingly encroached on the private. A similar tendency of the Haussmannization of Paris moved the Goncourts to record in their 1860 journal that "the interior is passing away—life turns back to become public."[13]

"Home" in *Bleak House* responds to the crisis by juxtaposing order to chaos, inside to outside. In this binary opposition, the two operative markers are the fire and the lock. The fire is central to the construction of Victorian domesticity, as in Ruskin's evocation of the hearth, and it can indicate domestic as well as spiritual warmth, as opposed to the coldness of an extinguished flame, a hearth of ashes. The lock marks the threshold that forms the semiotic boundary of conflict areas dividing inside from outside, safety from danger. The lock can test effective security depending on the ease with which it can be mastered and opened or closed. As such it defines the parameters of individuality in the English novel which, as Ian Watt has remarked, excludes the multiplicity of the city and guarantees privacy.[14] Besides its sociological and psychological symbolism, the lock also serves as a narrative device to guard the secrets and mysteries that resist penetration. This is an epistemological holdout against violation by the outside forces of public amorality which protects the intimate writing space of, for example, Esther's diary-writing.

Resistance to the official representation of "home" can be measured in terms of personal, economic, social, and sexual security in the fire and lock images which organize fictional space. At Mrs. Jellyby's, for example, Esther adds in parenthesis "(the fire had gone out, and there was nothing in the grate but ashes, a bundle of wood and a poker)" (BH iv; 85). The parenthesis is anything but tangential. The fire smokes and chokes. Attempts to warm up by the fire are futile. The lock of Esther's room at Mrs. Jellyby's proves ineffective, and it is impossible to shut the door. Mrs. Jellyby, who spends much of her time corresponding with Africa, is a model of disorder and an absentee mother. Her house is no home, but a chaos in which objects are comically misplaced, the people are out of sorts, and time is out of order. Mealtimes, a measure of domestic regularity, are out of sync. When Esther and Caddy try to restore order and some semblance of cleanliness,

> such wonderful things came tumbling out of the closets when they were opened—bits of mouldy pie, sour bottles, Mrs. Jellyby's caps, letters, tea, forks, odd boots and shoes of children, firewood, wafers, saucepan-lids,

damp sugar in odds and ends of paper bags, footstools, blacklead brushes, bread, Mrs. Jellyby's bonnets, books with butter sticking to the binding, guttered candle-ends put out by being turned upside down in broken candlesticks, nutshells, heads and tail of shrimps, dinner-mats, gloves, coffee-grounds, umbrellas. (BH XXX; 476)

In this comic listing of incongruous objects, there is a sneaking delight in grotesque confusion, but the devaluation of food as nourishment speaks for a more serious parental neglect and points to denial of maternal love. Mrs. Jellyby's disregard for her family, moreover, suggests an analogy with what Barbara Hardy once called "the bleak housekeeping of England."[15] According to the same analogy, the thin workhouse gruel in *Oliver Twist* is meant to taste of a bitter indictment of England's housekeeping when measured up to Mrs. Bedwin's broth (equivalent to 350 pauper rations!). Mrs. Jellyby's colonialist project is resisted by Esther's economy of feelings. As Ada says, it is maternal love that Esther has brought to the Jellybys (her first moral test), just as it is a spontaneous overflow of compassion which Esther brings into the brickmaker's hovel (another non-home). A further example is that of the orphans locked in a cold room with no fire; it is to Esther that Mrs. Blinder gives the keys. Summery Miss Summerson, the sentimental story goes, brings the sunshine into everybody's life.

When we first view it, it seems as if the incessant rain will prevent the sun from ever shining on Chesney Wold. The rain has sapped away at the bridge in the park, cutting off the last link to signification for Lady Dedlock, who looks out of her windows in "alternately a lead-coloured view, and a view in Indian ink" (BH II; 56). The instruments of inscription (lead and ink) have blotted out the water-logged, stagnant social and emotional landscape. The "childless" Lady Dedlock may well envy the domestic family scene denied to her of the keeper's lodge with its "light of a fire" and smoking chimney, while Mrs. Rouncewell holds keys to meaning and to secrets, as well as to the gate.

The locks of the Dedlock estate are dead in several senses. The family are in a legal deadlock, since Lady Dedlock's property is the subject of an interminable Chancery suit, and the litigation with Boythorn over boundaries and property rights is maintained out of principle beyond the end of the novel. The deadlock is also political, against the background of the defeat of Lord Russell.[16] The analogy of domestic and national deadlock makes a strong indictment of the stagnation of politics and justice, indicated in the wasteful dead heritage of the landed aristocracy, the deadness of the Dedlock home and the lack of talent in the House (with reference of course to Parliament). Both Sir Leicester and Mr. Tulkinghorn are described as "rusty," meaning antiquated but also hinting at corroded keys to a larger scheme.

The real victor at Chesney Wold is the cold which no fire can dispel and which Sir Leicester's gout cannot resist.

The blazing fires of faggot and coal—Dedlock timber and antediluvian forest—that blaze upon the broad wide hearths, and wink in the twilight on the frowning woods, sullen to see how trees are sacrificed, do not exclude the enemy. The hot-water pipes that trail themselves all over the house, the cushioned doors and windows, and the screens and curtains, fail to supply the fire's deficiencies, and to satisfy Sir Leicester's need. (BH XXVIII; 445)

By contrast the first impressions of Bleak House are of a beaming light in the darkness. John Jarndyce dispels the emotional confusion and anxiety by inviting Richard to warm himself. The radiant light and fire shine on the passion of Ada and Richard here and at several points in the book. The cheerfully blazing fire in Esther's room declares the wealth of provision and the warmth of the domestic hearth in the house and points to a transformation of mind and body that runs counter to the bleakness of the house's curious name, a name which would seem more suited to other domestic spaces in the novel where such transformation is lacking.

Unaware of any title to be a lady of leisure, Esther cheerfully takes up her role of Bleak House's moral housekeeper who must dispel the cobwebs and emotional distress so that Mr. Jarndyce's Growlery may be closed up. That domestic occupation of housekeeper (a *lieu-tenant* of the master of house in Lacanian terms, a placeholder for the absent father) may inscribe a contradictory ideology of domesticity,[17] and it enables a becoming of self, both in the literal search for her name and in the psychological construction of her relations with the world around her, as well as a formation of femininity in Dickens's understanding of the woman's formative emotional influence in the home. The spring lock in the window seat might have Freudian connections with the confusion of Jarndyce's roles as father and bridegroom[18] and the need to keep the room-womb under control. Yet Esther's fantasy that three Adas might get lost in it is surely one of several projections of the desire to inhabit the house and possess it in mind as well as in body, though it also betrays a fear of being trapped inside, of losing identity in the larger unit of matrimony and community. So confused are her roles, that Esther jokes she almost lost her name to the mythic Dame Durden. Esther is surprised at being entrusted so soon with the keys to the house and when she has to master her emotions she gives the keys a shake to remind herself of Duty, her altruistic usefulness to others which does not so much as cancel out self, in the sense of the shame she was supposed to feel at her birth, as construct a femininity that resists her reduction to a sexualized commodity. The resulting self-empowerment enables both moral agency and authorship of her story.

In his study of symbolization in Dickens and Victorian art, Chris Brooks understands the key to be an unequivocal symbol of imprisonment, but this is to read Esther's point of view as limited and nonautonomous and to interpret Bleak House as another prison of which Esther is the warder, from which she sorties on missions of moral colonialism.[19] Nor do I agree with Elizabeth Langland[20] that Esther's house visits among the poor are not so different from Mrs. Pardiggle's aggressive philanthropy, a moral policing of middle-class domestic virtue which might be comparable with Margaret Hale's visits to the Higgins family in *North and South*. We are shown that there is little chance the brick-maker will leave off beating his wife or mend his irreligious ways. Rather, the construction of home is working in two contrary directions—to confirm the social aspirations of middle-class domesticity while deconstructing its values in a subversive architecture.

The homeliness of Bleak House is unmistakable. Chapter 6 is entitled "Quite At Home." Yet it is one of those houses that are "delightfully irregular" (BH vi; 115). Unlike Skimpole's Polygon, this is irregularity under control, and the innumerable doors open up to an imaginative space that allows growth of moral personality and subverts the discourse of Victorian domesticity.[21] The quaint variety and profusion of household objects in Bleak House, for example, resist commodification of property as acquisition, which leads to obsession with money and to ruin. Unlike the foggy labyrinth of London or the stagnant deadness of Chesney Wold, the odd assortment of furniture and paintings betokens "light and warmth, and comfort" (BH vi; 117). The interiors and furnishings of the houses in *Bleak House*, like other interiors in Dickens's novels, reflect the ambience and personality of the inhabitants, expressing their vitality or their deadness, and exteriorize character, in the manner of Poe's physiology of furniture. Esther's room is warm and bright, while Richard's, seen through Esther's eyes, is unstructured.[22] Smallweed's tomb of a room is explicitly presented as an allegory on this theme. The Dombey house is likewise furnished in frozen mourning, in chapter 3 of that novel. In *Little Dorrit*, too, the crooked furniture resembles the crooked, antiquated, and decrepit form of the Clennam house.

Bleak House is a construction of moral space, not just a description of place. The illegitimate orphan Esther has to prove that she is not merely an idealized angel on the hearth, a Ruth Pinch jingling her keys in delight at being Tom's housekeeper, nor another idealized angelic Nell who has restored the hearth to ancient English village dwellings, but that she is worthy of a higher ideal of home. Despite her (excised) dream of anxiety that the keys would not fit, "Every part of the house was in such order," Esther tells us, "that I had no trouble with my two bunches of keys" (BH viii; 142). When she is away convalescing at Boythorn's, nobody else can "manage the keys" (BH xxxvi; 571). Esther forms a stark contrast to Dora, David Copperfield's "child wife" who jingles her basket of keys in a useless make-belief of housekeeping (DC xliv; 715), and is more like Agnes who jingles her basket of keys in remembrance of her love for David and her moral responsibilities (DC lx; 913).

Feminine subjecthood and moral agency complement the parallel masculine voice in *Bleak House* which indicts society for its treatment of the homeless. It is Esther who supplies the missing social responsibility through her making of home and of self which is implicit in that indictment and which is so lacking in the legal system. Esther is an angelic projection of Dickens's ideal woman, in fact a projection of the "little housekeeper" he saw in Georgina Hogarth,[23] who was everything that Catherine Dickens was not,[24] but in many ways Esther is also an idealized alter ego who succeeds where Dickens believed the missionaries and utilitarians had failed.

A Bleak Vision

> As a people we deserve to be visited with pestilence, if we
> neglect the great social duties which we owe to the poorer
> classes congregated in our towns.
> —Hector Gavin, *Sanitary Ramblings*

> The true wealth of a nation is the health of her masses.
> —Charles Kingsley, "Great Cities and
> Their Influence for Good and Evil"

Moral regeneration was very much in Dickens's mind when writing *Bleak House* against the background of the cholera outbreak of 1850.[25] Henry Mayhew's investigative journalism in the *Morning Chronicle* in 1849 had drawn public attention to the scandalous neglect of public health in London and other cities. Doctors and missionaries recognized that the inherent social as well as political dangers made it essential to gain "knowledge" of the city, but their diagnosis of the diseased social body was an ideologized representation which sought to regulate the lower classes. In his Malthusian survey of the capital, *London as It Is* (1837), John Hogg, a medical doctor of the Edinburgh school, blamed disease on lack of urban planning and London's polluted air. The problem of disease could not be understood without examining housing conditions and measuring them against middle-class values of domesticity. The theory, repeated by the second report of the Commissioners of the Health of Towns (1845) and by Charles Kingsley in a lecture of 1857, that pollution deprived the lungs of air, thereby causing depression of nervous energy and leading to deviant behavior (alcoholism and promiscuity), used medical and theological arguments to segregate the classes and preserve moral purity from contamination by the diseased and corrupt masses.

There was a general recognition after Edwin Chadwick's report on *The Sanitary Condition of the Labouring Population of Great Britain* (1842) that unsanitary and overcrowded housing spread disease. According to the prevalent miasmic theory, disease spread by inhalation of harmful odors and poisonous gases (the role of bacilli was not yet identified in contaminated drinking water).[26] Apart from disease, accommodation of several families in one room, alongside thieves and prostitutes, without privacy, or adequate clothing and food, encouraged immorality and crime. But the blame for this moral disease was not infrequently placed on the side effects of the free market (such as rack-renting petty landlords) or the poor themselves. In *The Moral and Physical Condition of the Working Classes Employed in the Cotton Manufacture in Manchester* (1832), James Kay typically considered the houses of the laboring poor to be devoid of the middle-class standards of respectability. Disease was rife because these were not decent homes and nothing resembling domesticity existed there: women and children were sent to work; men were demoralized by exhausting labor in factories; the diet was unhealthy and morals lax.

Other observers had some difficulty in making their descriptions of the most disgusting inhuman conditions credible to their readers. They often preferred to rely on official statistics and police reports for evidence of the reality immediately behind the smart New Oxford Street (recently erected in 1847), which effectively removed from sight the rookeries of St. Giles'. Such "improvements" tended to worsen overcrowding because tenants evicted by slum clearance had nowhere to go. George Godwin, editor of *The Builder*, argued in *Town Swamps and Social Bridges* (1859) that homes represented national health, and poor housing "bred" crime and prostitution. This linking of architectural design with morality and disease was commonplace. The preacher Thomas Beames, in *The Rookeries of London* (2nd ed., 1852), castigates London slums as "beds of pestilence" and "rendezvous of vice." Beames resorts to the metaphors of breeding and infection in his prediction that a monstrous generation of the criminal poor "hatched from the viper's egg" will turn London into a penal colony. If another Wat Tyler rebellion is to be averted, he declared, this human problem of capitalism must be dealt with.

Similarly, the Manchester preacher John Knox thundered in *The Masses Without* (1857) against the immorality that arose from the unsanitary conditions of the poor in London and other big cities. Mary Bayly, in *Ragged Homes and How to Mend Them* (1860), recommended religious instruction and cheap soup recipes to win over the poor, while Charles Bosanquet, in *London: Some Account of Its Growth* (1868), guided lay professionals in parochial work among the urban poor. Several writers, however, attacked the "false charity" of Ragged Schools and soup kitchens and recommended Malthusian solutions such as curbing reproduction among the lower classes They had little patience for romantic compassion: John Hollingshead, in *Ragged London in 1861*, castigates Dickens's "fanciful representation" of the poor in *Oliver Twist*. Others proposed emigration of "unwilled" paupers to the colonies (as did James Greenwood in *The Seven Curses of London*, 1869). Public health inspectors in midcentury, however, pointed to the connection between overcrowding and disease, and realized that sanitary reform alone would not prevent the spread of epidemics.[27]

About the facts there could be little dispute. Investigators of housing conditions in the big cities could barely restrain themselves from retching and vomiting after visiting the homes of the poor; the popular author Thomas Miller, in *Picturesque Sketches of London, Past and Present* (1853), has to retreat from the stench, which is not dispelled by his cigar. Yet a cold statistical report could never move the wealthy and powerful to action as much as scenes such as this one in chapter 8 of Kingsley's *Alton Locke*:

> Blood and sewer-water crawled from under doors and out of spouts, and reeked down the gutters among offal, animal and vegetable, in every stage of putrefaction. Foul vapours rose from cow-sheds and slaughter-houses, and the doorways of undrained alleys, where the inhabitants carried the filth out on their shoes from the backyard into the court, and from the court up into the main street; while above, hanging like cliffs over the streets—those narrow, brawling torrents of filth, and poverty, and sin—the houses

with their teeming load of life were piled up into the dingy, choking night.
A ghastly, deafening, sickening sight it was.[28]

The common equation of poverty with filth and sin appears in the "phalansteries"
of vice in the common staircase of a tenement slum, but it is soon corrected by
the compassionate Scottish clergyman who identifies with the angelic figure
languishing in the clean and tidy bare room occupied by women who have
been unable to find firewood to heat the hearth, neither by honest labor nor
prostitution. Similarly, it is by imaginative compassion that the reader is led down
into Davenport's cellar in Mrs. Gaskell's *Mary Barton*, into the nauseating stench
and pitch darkness where his wife is crying by the empty hearth.

Jacob's Island, a refuge of the desperate and the destitute, was another
notorious slum district and one of London's several invisible cities hidden in a
maze of muddy streets, "the filthiest, the strangest, the most extraordinary of the
many localities that are hidden in London, wholly unknown, even by name, to the
great mass of its inhabitants" (OT L; 442). Its description in *Oliver Twist* anticipates
the social collapse portended in the falling houses of Tom-All-Alone's,[29] and the
connection between housing conditions and disease makes an urgent plea for
something to be done. The filth is rendered even more obscene by the appalling
scene of the inhabitants drinking water polluted by feces:

> in the Borough of Southwark, stands Jacob's Island, surrounded by a muddy
> ditch, six or eight feet deep and fifteen or twenty wide when the tide is in,
> once called Mill Pond, but known in the days of this story as Folly Ditch. It
> is a creek or inlet from the Thames, and can always be filled at high water by
> opening the sluices at the Lead Mills from which it took its old name. At such
> times, a stranger, looking from one of the wooden bridges thrown across it
> at Mill Lane, will see the inhabitants of the houses on either side lowering
> from their back doors and windows, buckets, pails, domestic utensils of all
> kinds, in which to haul the water up; and when his eye is turned from these
> operations to the houses themselves, his utmost astonishment will be excited
> by the scene before him. Crazy wooden galleries common to the backs of
> half a dozen houses, with holes from which to look upon the slime beneath;
> windows, broken and patched, with poles thrust out, on which to dry the linen
> that is never there; rooms so small, so filthy, so confined, that the air would
> seem too tainted even for the dirt and squalor which they shelter; wooden
> chambers thrusting themselves out above the mud, and threatening to fall
> into it—as some have done; dirt-besmeared walls and decaying foundations;
> every repulsive lineament of poverty, every loathsome indication of filth, rot,
> and garbage; all these ornament the banks of Folly Ditch. (OT L; 443)

As Gareth Stedman Jones tells us in *Outcast London*, it was Dickens's descriptions
of Saffron Hill and Jacob's Island in *Oliver Twist*, as well as novels by Ainsworth,
Bulwer-Lytton, and Reynolds, that fed the connection in the public imagination
of morality with the free circulation of air and exposure to the public gaze of
London's slums.[30]

Conventionally, as H. M. Daleski has commented, the criminals are classified in *Oliver Twist* with the homeless paupers as outcasts and outlaws who inhabit the dilapidated and labyrinthine ruins: "To be out in the streets, moreover, is to move through the darkness of a hell on earth."[31] In *Oliver Twist*, however, these are "our bare streets," a metonym of the larger social structure for which there is implied a collective responsibility. The winter night out on the streets is "bleak, dark, and piercing cold, it was a night for the well-housed and fed to draw round the bright fire and thank God they were at home; and for the homeless, starving wretch to lay him down and die" (OT xxIII; 215). In later novels the bleakness of the streets, which threatens social stability and endangers life and health, overshadows the inner sanctity of the domestic hearth. In the 1850 preface to *Oliver Twist*, Dickens drew attention to what he saw as the root of the problem: he was convinced that "nothing effectual can be done for the elevation of the poor in England, until their dwelling-places are made decent and wholesome."[32]

Dickens believed the key to all reform lay in rethinking housing policy and acknowledging public responsibility for the appalling living conditions of the laboring poor. This was something accepted by utilitarian reformers like Chadwick, who argued in his 1842 report that epidemic disease was not income-related, that high employment and prosperity, as he put it, "afforded to the laboring classes no exemptions" from it.[33] Chadwick showed that incidence of disease was related to bad housing and insanitary conditions, a departure from middle-class attitudes which blamed the living conditions of the poor entirely on their moral depravity, ignorance, and filthy habits. Chadwick nevertheless incorporated such attitudes in his appeal to High Tory and government circles who conceded the need for correction of admitted evils and existing abuses. Appealing to the ideal of middle-class domesticity as a moral and economic model of decent homes,[34] Chadwick rejected existing methods of representation of poverty which had no standard criteria, such as insurance evaluations of life expectancy. Instead, Chadwick remapped the topography of disease (in maps of Aberdeen and elsewhere) to represent the relation of incidence of disease to sanitation and disconnect it from occupation.

In his lectures on public health, *The Unhealthiness of London, and the Necessity of Remedial Measures* (1847), *The Habitation of the Industrial Classes* (1850), and his detailed description of the slums of East London's Bethnal Green, *Sanitary Ramblings* (1848), Hector Gavin, a specialist in forensic medicine at Charing Cross Hospital, also connected the high mortality rates with bad or inadequate sewage, pollution, filth, and inferior housing, and thus showed it was not a class problem but a case for government intervention. Only legislation, he believed, could overcome the resistance by the working classes (on the unreasonable grounds that it let in the cold) to ventilation of their dwellings and introduce certification of healthy homes, though Dickens and others despaired of any effective parliamentary action. The 1868 municipal reforms which set up a modern sewage and drainage system for London nevertheless recognized the connection between sanitation and disease.

Disease and contamination could no longer be eliminated simply by the exclusion prevalent in the class concept of home.

In *Bleak House* the contagion of disease connects all classes and therefore none are immune from social responsibility; the miasmic theory, by contrast, which was gaining ground in the public debate over legislation on infectious diseases, localized disease in low-class areas (germ theory was as yet unknown).[35] That connection was one claimed by Carlyle's Irish widow who proved her sisterhood by dying and infecting others with her typhus fever and who will, like Jo, wreak her retribution on a diseased, morally bankrupt society in *Past and Present* (10: 149). Jo communicates his disease (no doubt a case of smallpox) to Charley and Esther, so that Jo's homelessness literally touches Esther, as does the contact with the contagion of the burial ground, which in Jo's delirium connects Esther with her mother and the corpse that carries the secret of her identity. The scandalous state of overcrowded burial grounds, which was meticulously investigated in Chadwick's *Report on Interment in Towns* (1843), gives Dickens occasion for an impassioned protest in his description of the burial place of Nemo. Locked in on purpose, Nemo ("no one" in English) is also an everyman or typical nobody of Victorian society. Sown in corruption, he is "to be raised in corruption: an avenging ghost at many a sick-bedside: a shameful testimony to future ages, how civilization and barbarism walked this boastful island together" (BH xi; 202). Jarndyce's cynicism about an institutional solution barely hides the authorial irony toward the treatment of the homeless sick crossing sweeper who has been moved on as a public nuisance. It is Skimpole's opinion, as a former medical man, that Jo would be better treated by society if he were a criminal, and his mysterious removal is indeed a police matter.

As in *Hard Times* and *Our Mutual Friend*, Dickens was (like Carlyle) skeptical that the evils of industrial capitalism could regulate themselves. All his life he remained convinced that government was morally blind to the realities of city streets, a blindness which would eventually work against the self-interest and freedom on which the economic order stood. In a speech to the Metropolitan Sanitary Association on 10 May 1851, Dickens claimed that the investigations of Chadwick and Southwood Smith, as well as the evidence of his eyes, or rather his nose, had convinced him that sanitation had to precede any social reform and that education and religion could do nothing without it. Dickens insisted that the moral and physical effects of disease were connected and affected all classes: "That no one can estimate the amount of mischief which is grown in dirt; that no one can say, here it stops or there it stops, either in its physical or moral results, when both begin in the cradle and are not at rest in the obscene grave, is now as certain as it is that the air from Gin Lane will be carried, when the wind is Easterly, into May Fair, and that if you once have a vigourous pestilence raging furiously in St. Giles', no mortal list of Lady Patronesses can keep it out of Almack's" (*Speeches* 128). Dickens then went on to deride the kind of missionary he satirized in the Reverend Chadband (whose name happens to chime with that of the no less zealous utilitarian reformer) because there could be no spirituality where the living conditions did not permit the sanctity of either life or death (*Speeches* 129). In chapter 38 of *The Old Curiosity Shop*, Dickens had castigated the nation's property-owning rulers for not realizing that without decent living conditions there could be no love of home or love of country; true patriotism, he concluded, was to be found in the unenfranchised who truly loved home but had no home of which to boast (OCS xxxviii; 363–64).

This echoes George Godwin's plea for decent homes for the poor as the social bridge which would prevent London sinking into a bestial swamp of crime and alcoholism, and it was a message Dickens drummed into his readers in his novels, using his fiction to show "the preventable wretchedness and misery in which the mass of the people dwell, and of expressing again and again the conviction, founded upon observation, that the reform of their habitations must precede all other reforms; and that without it, all other reforms must fail. Neither Religion nor Education will make any way, in this nineteenth century of Christianity, until a Christian government shall have discharged its first obligation, and secured to the people Homes, instead of polluted dens" ("To Working Men," *Household Words*, 7 October 1854; DJ 3: 227). Despairing of the ruling classes, who could only make jokes during a plague, Dickens called on the proletariat to join forces with the middle classes and force out of office a government that had lost touch with reality and was bound up with red tape.

This is no call to arms, and in putting on the working classes the onus of taking action Dickens seems to be rather idealistically hoping that a moral awakening could restore a sense of responsibility and counter both radicalism and indifference. There is, however, another dire warning in the words of the 1850 preface to *Oliver Twist* that the desperate misery of the rapidly breeding poor bore "the certain seeds of ruin to the whole community."[36] This is a warning that contains a note of anxiety about middle-class security, a fear akin to Carlyle's in *Past and Present* of the consequences of laissez-faire. That fear seemed to be borne out by the events of 1848 in Europe.

Disease, both contagious and moral, is shown in *Bleak House* to penetrate all domestic boundaries, including Bleak House. Disease is both literal and metaphorical, a social contagion that connects different classes and levels of meaning that are usually represented as impervious. Tom-All-Alone's gives angry expression to Dickens's outrage at London's slums:

> As, on the ruined human wretch, vermin parasites appear, so these ruined shelters have bred a crowd of foul existence that crawls in and out of gaps in walls and boards; and coils itself to sleep, in maggot numbers, where the rain drips in; and comes and goes, fetching and carrying fever, and sowing more evil in its every footprint than Lord Coodle, and Sir Thomas Doodle, and the Duke of Foodle, and all the fine gentlemen in the office, down to Zoodle, shall set right in five hundred years—though born expressly to do it. (BH xvi; 272–73)

Tom-All-Alone's is a version of Bleak House, and is connected to Chesney Wold by infectious as well as illicit relations. Drawing inconsistently on theories of infection, the narrator declares its "pestilential gas" and "contagion" will wreak their brutal revenge. The bleakness of the house in the novel's title pervades more than one house in the novel, and while Dickens uses the synecdoche of these houses to allegorize the social hierarchy, he also challenges the ideological assumptions of the discourse of domesticity and warns of imminent social collapse.

Bleak House was originally called The Peaks but turned Bleak when inhabited by Tom Jarndyce's misery. The London counterpart to the former Bleak House is described by John Jarndyce as

> a street of perishing blind houses, with their eyes stoned out; without a pane of glass, without so much as a window-frame, with the bare blank shutters tumbling from their hinges and falling asunder; the iron rail peeling away in flakes of rust; the chimneys sinking in; the stone steps to every door (and every door might be Death's Door) turning stagnant green; the very crutches on which the ruins are propped, decaying. Although Bleak House was not in Chancery, its master was, and it was stamped with the same seal. These are the Great Seal's impressions, my dear, all over England—the children know them! (BH VIII; 147)

The imagery of national decay and death creates an obvious corollary with the diseased body of the city: the "London" of the novel's opening is both toponym and trope for the fog of Chancery and the larger social perspective. The anthropomorphic metaphor of blindness and vision links the seeing eyes of houses in Tom-All-Alone's and the Dedlock estate with the blindness of Chancery and of the aristocracy.

As a piece of landed property, the country house represents the interests of the ruling classes and the ethos of social order. Chesney Wold, like Satis House, has outlived its time, and in both cases the plot hinges on an inheritance which is proven worthless, as is the education in self-hatred of Esther or in the hard-heartedness of Estella. Dickens voices his indignation at the social irresponsibility of the upper classes, although he does not spurn their legacy outright and in fact reserves some respect for Lady Dedlock's coolness and willful independence.

The Lord Chancellor's Seal is a literal mark of the Condition of England. It seals the fate of the nation, and Miss Flite has already forewarned us of the Sixth Seal in Revelation. The allegory can be followed only too easily by readers versed in the Christian scriptures,[37] allowing us to read an apocalyptic interpretation into the construction of home in the novel. Yet Jarndyce's fantastic turn of phrase, like much eccentric speech in the novel, suggests much more and questions its hermeneutics. Although there is no doubt it is in Chancery, uncertainty undermines the structure of Tom-All-Alone's as much as its collapsing walls, and its identity with Tom Jarndyce's London slum is uncertain. Uncertainty is the state of mind of Jo the crossing sweeper, and uncertainty seems to seep into the implied eschatology of the allegory, but also into conventional deciphering of the text of the city.

Incoherence implies there cannot be organized or systematic change in the city because it cannot be perceived meaningfully as "useful knowledge." In *Bleak*

House, London fog enshrouds everything in impenetrable mystery and death, and it brings on at first glance what J. Hillis Miller has termed "hallucinatory incoherence."[38] Yet there is a growing vision here, developed further in *Little Dorrit* and *Our Mutual Friend*, that penetrates and transcends the walls of Law. The fog is densest where Chancery sits, the "most pestilent of hoary sinners" (BH 1; 50). The Lord Chancellor can see nothing but fog, while the members of his court are "mistily engaged in one of the ten thousand stages of an endless cause, tripping one another up on slippery precedents, groping knee-deep in technicalities, running their goat-hair and horsehair warded heads against walls of word; and making a pretence of equity with serious faces, as players might" (BH 1; 50). In a Carlylean metaphor for the Condition of England, pestilence, mist, and blindness emerge out of the slippery mud, like a miasma out of the noxious gases on the river. This gives the impression that the practice of Equity is a game in a hopeless mire of words, but one inextricably linked with the issues of life and death in the novel, as well as with the health of the nation. Krook's chancery is a smaller model of the no less crooked larger one, just as Jaggers's Little Britain forms a microcosm in *Great Expectations* of the national scale of criminality of a legal system contaminated by the proximity of cattle slaughter in Smithfield, while the forge and Satis House offer contrasting sites of national and social identity.

Literacy does not necessarily bring legibility, a crucial point in a novel whose plot hinges on the reading of legal texts. Equally unreadable are the "dead letter" of the legal vocabulary and the slurred aristocratic discourse of Dedlock's senile cousin. With a few notable exceptions, the crossing sweeps interviewed in Henry Mayhew's *London Labour and the London Poor* are illiterate, but their honest work is useful for keeping streets passable and entrances free from mud. The children among them are sent out by their parents or work in gangs, and, in contrast to Jo, they are picked up by the police, presumably on the lookout for beggars, only when they are found with money on them, given to them by wealthy ladies and gentlemen for sweeping the mud on rainy days or as a reward for tumbling or for bringing cabs after the opera.[39] Neither Dickens nor Mayhew automatically make the widespread equation of illiteracy and poverty with crime, though both regard illiteracy as a social ill that is a bar to productive labor. Mayhew is often appalled at the ignorance among his informants of basic current affairs or religious belief. The signs in city streets are meaningless to Jo and therefore the world is *different*, but no less strange and real. Jo's illiteracy lends the reading of the city a dissonance which grants the outcast a legitimacy that undoes the usual sanitization in *Punch* and the *Illustrated London News* of the homeless into either comic or picturesque figures on the margins of the city. These stereotypes lack the humanity we do find in the figure of the waif on a dust-heap on a polluted city street in the *Pictorial Times* (fig. 10), a glimpse of flesh-creeping horror on the banks of the Thames between Lambeth Palace and Vauxhall Gardens that might be easily missed by the gentleman about town.[40]

Fig. 10: "Condition of the Poor" (1846)

The significant errors of Jo's idiolect deconstruct standard semantics and give unexpected new meaning to the confusing profusion of the city's signs beyond the mere recording of language abuse we get in "Seven Dials." Dickens's whimsical love of malapropisms, such as "inkwhich," playfully suggests that the inscription of legal testimony and the inscription of the Foreign Bible Society, whose steps are so respectfully swept by Jo, are arbitrary signifiers detached from any meaning or knowledge as far as they concern Jo. Certainly, their ink brings him no enlightenment, and their linguistic and ideological colonialism does not help dispel the novel's mystery about Esther's identity, which causes such confusion in Jo's mind. In keeping with Jo's idiolect, ideology is undone when Snagsby describes his experience of being moved on as "Joful and woful" (BH XIX; 320). The appeal at the close of chapter XLVII, punningly entitled "Jo's Will," to Queen and nobility, to clergy and compassionate men and women, makes Jo representative of all Jos who are constantly being moved on and "dying thus around us every day" (BH XLVII; 705). Jo's request for someone to write down his "Will" gives voice and agency (legacy and will) to England's mute unrepresented population in a novel which places destitution on the literary and linguistic map, just as Chadwick and Gavin were drawing disease on the social and urban map.

The subversive voice of Jo's idiolect underscores the tension between his mapping of the city and the official toponymy, between signified and signifier, so that the ironies of naming, misnaming, and unnaming are never resolved. The dead legal hand that attaches property to patrimony deepens rather than solves mysteries of identity in so far as they are determined linguistically. After almost losing her identity in the confusion of names she is given, Esther eventually acquires a new identity—both figuratively and literally a new face—at the end of the novel, but she does not do this by subscribing to the legal or linguistic system of patrimonial lineage.

Reading once more serves as a playful test of the *lisibilité* of the city, and, by analogy, of the novel, situated at the generic juncture of the inheritance plot and the detective story. Esther finds the books and newspapers at Kenge and Carboy's illegible (BH III; 76–77), while Krook, an illiterate hoarder of other people's ruined lives, tries unsuccessfully to penetrate the secrets contained in the discarded legal parchments which are the texts of their lives converted to ink (like Mrs. Jellyby's daily conversion to ink of her daughter Caddy). Krook's name suggests moral and linear irregularity and his mark is crooked when he spells out in the writing on the wall, in a backward, illiterate, and legal hand, Bleak House and Jarndyce. The fact that the decisive copy of the Jarndyce will is found among the property left by Krook anticipates the stronger hint of moral salvation in the motif of salvage in a later novel, *Our Mutual Friend*. It is also the copyist's "legal hand" of the document in the Jarndyce case shown by Tulkinghorn to Lady Dedlock at the beginning of the novel which makes Lady Dedlock's mysterious secret legible to Tulkinghorn and which sets in motion Tulkinghorn's machinations. Esther then learns the secret— which is the secret of her own identity—in a letter from her "natural" mother that must be destroyed (made illegible) for that natural love to be maintained. Not only does Dickens name Esther after a real-life orphan, Esther Elton, but he christens Esther's handmaid with his own name and has her teach Charley to read, none too successfully. Perhaps such naming playfully signs Dickens's own story of poverty (Charley's father works for a broker who secures furniture and other property against debts) and identifies the author with an ideal housekeeper.[41] Esther herself is orphaned from an impoverished scribe whose illegible and anonymous inscription in the graveyard must be recovered from anonymity and annulment (Nemo is no one but also a morbid Nemesis), deciphered before she can finally establish her biological and moral identity.

The difficulty of reading in these examples matches the reader's difficulty in reading the novel's mystery plot. J. Hillis Miller has justly characterized this novel as "a document about the interpretation of documents"[42] because of its foregrounding of documents which puts stress on hermeneutics and epistemology. Dickens had had experience of parliamentary reporting and stenography in legal courts (parodied by David Copperfield's illegible attempts at shorthand), and his satirical descriptions in *Sketches by Boz* made fun of antiquated ecclesiastical legislation or the obscure inscriptions of legal wills by which the dead inflict their passions on the living ("Doctors' Commons"), as well as the Babel of language in Parliament ("A Parliamentary Sketch"). So there may well be conscious irony in a text that tests the limits of artistic and legal modes of interpretation. Not for nothing does Esther declare she is "not clever" and complain about the difficulty of narrating. I believe, however, this is because legibility is an issue in Dickens's representation of the city, not because Esther's reading is "unreliable" or because of indecision about the possibilities of interpretation. The novel is constructed out of language, but the represented discourses are often opaque. What cements the novel if anything must therefore be a metalanguage which rereads other discourses.

Gothic Houses and Uncanny Homes

> ... vast machines, more or less Italianate or more or less
> Gothic, without any clear-cut character.... They are the houses
> of rich people who like their comforts and know how to get
> them and who, sometimes and often enough unfortunately,
> have indulged in architectural whims. Many of their stylish
> cottages, topped or overburdened with gables, look like toys
> made of painted cardboard. All their imagination, all their
> native inventiveness has gone into their parks.
>
> —Taine, *Notes on England* (1872)

Bleak House has been classified more than once as "Urban Gothic,"[43] and it is hard to
think of the bleakness in the title without the associations of a Gothic atmosphere. The
ghost at Chesney Wold will walk when the house is visited by disgrace or calamity, and
it steps with the ambiguous patter of rain on the pavement when Lady Dedlock visits
Nemo's grave. Mrs. Rouncewell hears the ghost walk louder prior to Lady Dedlock's
flight. The Jarndyce and Jarndyce case is the family curse and it has taken possession
of Richard's mind and soul. It is reflected in the "funereal panel" at his apartment, a
strange refuge and a "cruel place" into which Esther voyeuristically peeps on her secret
visit to Richard and Ada's marital home. As Robert Mighall has demonstrated, the
Gothic atmosphere of Chesney Wold is in fact a transformation of the urban horrors
of city slums, of the stagnant and anachronistic legal labyrinth that entangles everyone
and everything, as well as an emanation of the decrepit and decaying aristocracy
which holds the nation in its ghastly grip.[44] As such, it projects middle-class anxieties
about miscegenation and contagion; by showing the horrific correspondences across
classes of disease and homelessness, Dickens disabuses his readers of the illusion of
comfortable safety in the domestic ideology of the Victorian home.

Krook's house, too, is haunted by evil, by his madness, and by his fiendish
cat Lady Jane. Krook's "Rag and Bottle Warehouse" is a fanciful graveyard of the
legal world, which like the larger Chancery, transforms people into objects of dead
storage value. The old man fondles Ada's tresses covetously in a suggestively erotic
gesture reminiscent of Quilp's ghoulish desire for Nell, though Krook proves not to
be a fireproof salamander like Quilp (which doesn't save Quilp from drowning).[45]
Krook is obsessed with being "possessed of documents," while the shutters' eyes in
Nemo's old room are watchful and the air stinks of the putrid atmosphere as Guppy
and Jobling (a.k.a. Weevle) nerve out their midnight vigil. Yet the Gothic cannot
be taken too seriously. Krook's death by "internal combustion" is too much of an
anticlimax, and the contagion in the air smells more of the moral evil of Chancery.
Following Carlyle's invocation of a conflagration that would burn up the "worn-
out rags" of the world in *The Latter-Day Pamphlets* and perhaps thinking of the
1834 fire which destroyed the Houses of Parliament, Dickens seems to be looking
to a purging fire (like the one in *Sartor Resartus*) as more effective than legislation
in curing social ills, though the classical allusion to the Mephitic vapors of Hades
only mildly suggests a regenerative apocalypse.[46]

The Gothic was, by the time Dickens wrote *Bleak House*, somewhat the worse for wear, especially since its parody in Poe's artful demolition of the House of Usher. Indeed, it was Dickens who had, according to the rejection note received by Poe from the editors of *The Southern Messenger*, "given the final death-blow to writings of that description."[47] That, incidentally, does not seem to have deterred Dickens from reworking the Gothic more than once. Apart from Satis House, the Clennams' house in *Little Dorrit* is a house of the dead, "dull and dark," "crooked" and heavy with a lethargic atmosphere, a skeleton, a commercial House "in decline" that falls at the climax of the novel, as in Poe's "Fall of the House of Usher." Collapse of houses mocks the fall of a dynasty in such Gothic tales as *The Castle of Otranto*, whose influence is weakly echoed in the fall of the House of Dombey. There is, in fact, a similar play on the associations of decease and disease in Poe's story and *Bleak House*. The descent of the Dedlocks declines to its end, like that of the Ushers, and Sir Leicester literally falls in chapter LVI. The House of the Dedlocks is left a body without life as the shadow falls over Lady Deadlock's portrait following the discovery of Esther's identity. The fire symbolically goes out in the chapter significantly entitled "National and Domestic," which suggests a political as well as spiritual crisis in the allegory of the Fall. Such Gothic treatment of a social, or apocalyptic vision is, of course, quite foreign to any of Poe's designs.

Eventually Esther comes to the eerie realization that she is the ghost walking the pavement at Chesney Wold and runs away from herself. Yet, whatever dread it holds for her after she decides she must avoid meeting her mother, the atmosphere does not reach truly Gothic terror. For Ada and Esther the "pervading influence" of Chesney Wold is "undisturbed repose."

> It was a picturesque old house, in a fine park richly wooded…. O, the solemn woods over which the light and shadow travelled swiftly, as if Heavenly wings were sweeping on benignant errands, through the summer air; the smooth green slopes, the glittering water, the garden where the flowers were so symmetrically arranged in clusters of the richest colours, how beautiful they looked! The house, with gable and chimney, and tower, and turret, and dark doorway, and broad terrace—walk, twining among the balustrades of which, and lying heaped on the vases, there was one great flush of roses, seemed scarcely real in its light solidity, and in the serene and peaceful hush that rested on all around it. (BH XVIII; 300)

Repose here is delusive and menacing, and the note of nostalgia in the topos of the English country house might contain personal associations of Rockingham Castle, an Elizabethan mansion where Dickens stayed with friends of his. This touch of envy at the houses of the great[48] might also express the wish to own the landscape by commanding its prospect.

As we approach the revelation of Esther's identity, the wind howls, the gardener cannot sweep up all the fallen leaves, and the smell of ghostly stagnation creeps in. Secret memories give grounds for Robert Newsom's Freudian explanation for the haunting of houses in this novel when repression turns the homely into the uncanny.[49] The "romantic side of familiar things" (BH 43) is one aspect of Dickens's "attraction of repulsion" and points to the deep connection between the *heimlich* and the *unheimlich* in Freud's essay on "The 'Uncanny.'" The *unheimlich* is something secretly familiar *(heimlich)* which has been repressed; the very concept of homesickness can be interpreted as a compulsive return to that secret home in the mother's womb.[50]

The home, then, is a source of an uncanny knowledge, and commentators on Freud's essay have shown it to feminize the home as source of shameful and secret knowledge of the womb, origin and threat in male neuroses, that explains the lure of nostalgia and its repression.[51] In the "haunted" house, coziness slides into dread, an anxiety particularly associated with the modern urban experience of crowds and homelessness, as well as with the traumatic effects of the First World War, at the time Freud was writing.[52] It may also account for the nostalgic homesickness Lukács discerned in the Romantic concept of a primal loss in the disparity of the novel's form from lived experience, its inability to embrace the empirical totality of the represented world.

Nevertheless, Freud's careful distinction between real-life cases and literature frees fictional modes of representation from reality-testing, and the material may be modified or altered by poetic license,[53] as in Freud's example of E. T. A. Hoffmann's "The Sandman." However, in Freud's account of his own wandering in the red-light district of an Italian town one hot summer which indicates a compulsive return to the shameful site of repressed sexual knowledge, as in Hoffmann, the "uncanny" is sited in the home, and the fear of castration results in an estrangement of vision from the perspective of the outcast or wanderer on the city street.[54] In modernist portrayals of the flâneur in fin de siècle Vienna in Hofmannsthal, Schnitzler, or Musil, such a figure becomes a powerless castrated Other robbed of subjecthood, who is reduced to the object of the public gaze described in Lacan's "Four Principles of Psychoanalysis,"[55] yet enabled with a different view of the world. This modern urban experience of the uncanny was described by Dickens in the return of John Harmon/Rokesmith/Handford to the scene of his "murder," a literal disembodiment of self in his homeless wandering in London's Limehouse district of drug-dens and brothels:

> He tried a new direction, but made nothing of it; walls, dark doorways, flights of stairs and rooms, were too abundant. And, like most people so puzzled, he again and again described a circle, and found himself at the point from which he had begun. "This is like what I have read in narratives of escape from prison," said he, "where the little track of the fugitives in the night always seems to take the shape of the great round world, on which they wander; as if it were a secret law." (OMF II, xiii; 421–22)

In this repetition compulsion, the drowned man must circle around the point of his demise/origin in an estranged state of self-alienation until he finds his true self again in the imprisoning labyrinth of the city.

In *Bleak House*, Esther's narrative of her repressed family romance is a similar attempt to reconstruct subjecthood and control the gaze (symbolically through veiling and unveiling the face). At the same time, the repression is shown to derive from an illness of the social body caused by psychological, social, and political forces outside, as much as from the anxiety within the home traceable to infant trauma and Esther's desire to return to her mother's womb. Closed up, Chesney Wold is a "body without life," a palpable gap in the body politic in need of new habitation. The town house, too, though not usually in the "same mind" as the place in the country, reads like an auctioneer's catalog. As Jonathan Arac has said of *Dombey and Son*, "the question the '*un-heimlich*' asks is when is a home not a home, and the answer here is, when no one is living there, when the life is all in the things, only latent in the people, like springs under stone."[56] Esther's homemaking would then be an attempt to undo the kind of repression of subjecthood and sexuality which we saw in Dombey's commercial house and family home.

In another sense, the fictional plot structure serves as a metonym of other representations of knowledge, such as portraits which figure in significant moments of recognition paralleled by incomplete or nonmatching series of pictures in *Bleak House*.[57] It is, significantly, the defacement of the family portraits by strangers which upsets Sir Leicester when the police invade Chesney Wold. Similarly, the defacement of Esther is an essential phase in the re-formation of her moral personality which resists social determinism: she must reopen her eyes to reread the moral landscape after being temporarily blinded by disease. As Valentine Cunningham suggests, Esther's veiling and unveiling after her disfiguring disease exemplifies the "persistent doubling of vision and knowledge, a version of the famous Pauline seeing, through a mirror, but still in an enigma (*per specula in aenigmate*)."[58] So penetration of the text and textile, as Valentine Cunningham would have it, must result in a rereading of identities and reinterpetration of meaning in a "teetotum" of signification, like the Apple Pie alphabet describing the nonsensical hermeneutics of Law in Jarndyce's explanation in chapter 8.[59]

The mystery plot of *Bleak House* relies on concealment and revelation, which generically links it to the detective story and combines the inheritance novel with the search for identity in the city (as in *Our Mutual Friend*, this is the mystery of the missing body of the inheritor). The structure of *Bleak House*, however, might count as one of Henry James's "baggy monsters" in the preface to *The Tragic Muse*, and many readers find the novel's bagginess unsatisfactory. Esther's narrative is neither fully woven into the fabric of the novel nor sufficiently autonomous from the authorial voice. Yet H. M. Daleski finds a "pre-Jamesian innocence" in the dual narration,[60] and other commentators, too, find the development of Esther's personality convincing. Steven Marcus, on the other hand, senses a homelessness in the absence of a stable or settled narrative perspective,[61] while the multiple split in narration has prompted Adam Zachary Newton to liken the novel to a haunted house for the reason that it conceals instead of confessing secrets.[62]

What Dickens has to achieve is what Poe termed, in his "Philosophy of Composition," unity of effect in order to recover form and meaning from disintegration and collapse, just as "The Fall of the House of Usher" builds the carefully worked effect of a metafictional house of cards which collapses like the house of cards in the wrapper illustration of *Dombey and Son*. When Esther speaks of "passages of my narrative" (BH LX; 869), the architectural correspondence suggests concealed beginnings and endings, and seemingly exitless interconnecting passages. The Gothic form of *Bleak House* matches the irregular shape of the plot: one room leads into another, just as one mystery leads into another.[63] The novel's allegory of its own reading (like the one on Tulkinghorn's ceiling) is a performance of a text which must grow skin and sinews, must give illusion of a reality, while remaining playfully aware of its fictionality. The self-reflexive discourse of the novel draws our attention to its ontology as a fictional home at the same time as the feeling of uneasiness and insecurity emanates from the form of the novel itself, as if it were bent on self-destruction.

The collapsing buildings in *Bleak House*, *Little Dorrit*, and *Great Expectations* offer an image of London that was common enough in warnings of the fate of civilization if Britain did not reform its institutions and look to the decay of its moral fabric. It is found in anti-Papist propaganda, prior to the removal of Catholic civil disabilities in 1829, or in the apocalyptic visions of the ruined city employed by Macaulay in 1824 (in a review of Mitford's *Greece*) and repeated in his review of Mill's *Essay on Government* in 1829, which contrasted the immortality of the heritage of Athens with its destruction and oblivion. In this doomsday forecast of the end of Britain's glorious Augustan age, Macaulay prophesied the New Zealander tourist finding naked fishermen amid the city's ruins. The British seemed doomed to follow the fate of the Roman Empire; it was, after all, on the steps of the ruined Capitol in 1764 that Gibbon thought of writing "the decline and fall of the city" (as he put it in his autobiography). But then ruins and destruction also have their Romantic charm and Gothic theatricality. However, it was the modernization of London with its demolition of old buildings that accentuated the lessons of the past for the future as the process of what Lewis Mumford called "Abbau" revealed a fantastic vision of half-built ruins. Doré later imagined the apocalyptic relapse into barbarism as the concluding tableau of *London: A Pilgrimage* (1870) (frontispiece), a visual and textual tour of the capital co-authored with Blanchard Jerrold, which fed on urban mythologies, as well as literary tropes and citations. While the pilgrimage began, conventionally, with the Thames and the entry into the world's commercial highway, the contrasts of work and leisure close with a reversal of civilization and savagery as the aborigine tourist sketches the ruins of St. Paul's one hundred and fifty years hence. As Lynda Nead comments on Doré's apocalyptic vision, "Ruin is the resolution of the contradictory impulses of modernity."[64]

The regressive view of civilization's primeval slime and collapsing houses in *Bleak House* clearly draws on these common images of the fall of empire and the inevitable ruin of the Victorian Babylon. Breakdown of structure and of signification is the condition of the world of Chancery. Yet if fragmentation reflects a disintegration of the alienated personality in the urban wasteland, it is a fragmentation that implies by negation signification and structure in the chaos of modernity, a vision of the city that seems to anticipate the modernism of T. S. Eliot's "fragments ... shored against my ruins."[65] In fact, in his 1927 essay "Wilkie Collins and Dickens," T. S. Eliot was so far from thinking that a fragmented vision meant a disintegration of form that he hailed *Bleak House* as "Dickens's finest piece of construction."[66] Fragmentation of vision in Dickens has been recognized as evidence for stylistic complexity,[67] and there is an overriding perception in the novel of a larger wholeness and unity: the dilapidated houses of Skimpole and Jellyby, as well as the rotting mat on Nemo's hearth, are indicative of a process of decomposition, of decay into collapse and breakdown, that makes up a whole vision.[68] Dickens's novel breaks open the closed hermeneutics of Chancery, whose meaning will ever be indeterminable. Instead, the novel offers recognition of otherness in regeneration of moral relations, without which there can be no identity of self.

THROUGH GLASS DARKLY

> A Palace as for fairy Prince,
> A rare pavilion, such as man
> Saw never since mankind began
>   And built and glazed!
> —Thackeray, "May-Day Ode," *The Times*, 1 May 1851

The bleak vision of England in Dickens's novel is strangely out of tune with the official view of 1851 as the year of prosperity and the triumph of the machine age, the year of the Crystal Palace. The Crystal Palace is not mentioned in *Bleak House*, but it is an unspoken presence implicitly negated by the architecture, ideology, and narrative form represented in the novel.[69] The very design of the furniture on display at the Great Exhibition of 1851 speaks for a comfort absent from the slums of Tom-All-Alone's and for a conformity with Victorian taste that doesn't match the delightful irregularity of Jarndyce's Bleak House.

A symbol of domesticity and a highly visible monument to the spirit of the age, London's most talked about public building was six times larger than St. Paul's Cathedral and took a fraction of the time to build. Opened only a few months before the appearance of the first installments of *Bleak House*, the Crystal Palace represented the economic optimism and victorious imperialism of midcentury, the celebration of utility, the ethics of work, and universal peace. The Crystal Palace both housed and represented the Great Exhibition, an exhibition of art and design, as well as its own industrialized construction. It was regarded by many as the epitome of "Victorianism," though in view of the government crisis and other troubles at home and abroad (such as Louis Bonaparte's *coup d'état*) some have doubted whether it offered a vision of "an abiding city."[70] Perhaps it was no coincidence that the bestseller at the time was the poet laureate Tennyson's *In Memoriam*. Certainly, it was a representation of Victorian Britain as an industrial nation that contained contradictions and tensions between the competing constructions of nation, class, and gender, between provinces and metropolis, between public and private (for example, between laissez-faire capitalism and public initiative or funding).[71] The model cottages displayed in the exhibition grounds promoting decency and ventilation contrasted with the grim realities at the other end of town, where thousands had little that could be called house or home and had nothing to look forward to except disease and death.

The ultimate city of indoor streets, a glass arcade of manufactured goods and global commerce, the Crystal Palace's organization and representation of science and trade inspired the young William Whitely to think of the department store. It was an emporium of the world metropolis which displayed goods that were not supposed to be for sale (though many products were purchasable in London shops), and so a step was taken toward the consumer market in which desire is divorced from consumption, creating a fetishized commodity culture in which Esther's domestic economy offers a futile vanguard resistance.[72] In fact, the Exhibition accurately reflected middle-class domestic comfort; for all the emphasis on manufacture and science, it was still a nation of shopkeepers and domestic servants.[73] The unenfranchised and commercially powerless classes were segregated, and obstruction by the commissioners led to the dissolution of a committee, to which Dickens was appointed, charged with overseeing access to the Great Exhibition by the laboring classes. These, after all, were the target audience of the Exhibition's educational aim to inculcate industry in its then current meaning of hard work, diligence, and duty.[74] Radical artisans saw an educational opportunity in the Exhibition, but it was radicalism that was feared by the proponents of the Exhibition's aim of social harmony, and there was an obvious aristocratic privilege involved in the running of the Exhibition. But then the emphasis on artifacts and artifice would not have appealed to the plebeian pocket despite the cheap excursion rates, and one wonders what working-class visitors would have made of statues of naked nymphs or Greek women in chains.

In *The Crystal Palace Illustrated Catalogue* published by the *Art Journal*, the leading art critic Ralph Wornum complained of uneducated and imitative style in the gaudy, vulgar domestic utensils on display, which were more decorative than practical, though they were meant to transform the very concept of design by applying art and science to industry, an aim associated above all with the *Journal of Design* and the name of Henry Cole, one of the principal organizers of the Exhibition and an indefatigable proponent of innovative schemes and reforms. As Superintendent of the Department of Practical Art, Cole was (as will be seen in the next chapter) the butt of Dickens's satire of utilitarian art in *Hard Times*, perhaps rather unfairly considering Cole's success in combining decorative style with utility in his prizewinning tea service of 1845 and his efforts to wed production and design.[75]

Dickens could barely contain his unease with the overabundance and all-inclusivity of the Exhibition: "I find," he wrote to Lavinia Watson on 11 July 1851,

"I am 'used up' by the Exhibition. I don't say 'there's nothing in it'—there's too much. I have only been twice. So many things bewildered me. I have a natural horror of sights, and the fusion of so many sights in one has not decreased it" (*Letters* 4: 428). Dickens confessed he had actually only seen the Crystal Fountain and "perhaps" the Amazon, though he politely lied whenever asked if he'd seen something in order to be spared the inevitably unbearable explanation. In the same letter, Dickens deflates the grandiose monumentality of the Crystal Palace when he gleefully describes the visit of a group of one hundred children from Angela Burdett-Coutts's schools who could not keep their sticky fingers off the exhibits; he concludes with the story of one schoolboy who went missing and who believed the police station and Hammersmith workhouse (where he spent the night) were all part of the Exhibition: "It was a Great Exhibition, he said, but he thought it long" (*Letters* 6: 429). Dickens had an "instinctive feeling against the Exhibition," and predicted that the bewildering effect of the Exhibition's overwhelming display of fact and artifacts would result in the "boredom and lassitude" of the public, who would be poorer in pocket for the experience instead of being invigorated or impressed (letter to W. H. Wills, 27 July 1851, *Letters* 6: 448–49).

There seems little appreciation in this response of the Crystal Palace's ideological statement of power, in particular its construction of nation, class, and gender, which stressed the superiority of the English in the various representative "departments" of the exhibition. It was both a representation of an industrial nation and a producer of representations in the statistical accounts of the enormous quantities of goods shipped by the new railways, catalogues, architectural models, and dioramas of cities.[76] An ideological and class skew was given to knowledge in the Exhibition's innovative classification into raw materials, machinery, manufacture, and fine arts, progressing, as it were, from the "raw" to the "cooked," from the resources of the new mineral-based economy to finished products,[77] a classification which Mayhew, in his "natural history of labour" in the introduction to volume 4 of *London Labour and the London Poor*, thought worse than useless. The machinery section was, of course, the most popular, with its attraction of steam engines, railway locomotives, bridges, and all kinds of weird and wonderful inventions that demonstrated applied (though not always practical) science, but profusion and confusion vied with the awe which the untouchable wonders exerted over the viewers of the spectacle.

It would be wrong to underestimate the unprecedented vastness of an engineering project involving calculation and rationality on a scale, with its thousands of standardized prefabricated parts, much grander than Gradgrind's storehouse of facts. The origins of the Crystal Palace, however, throw light on its contradictory ideological claims and the confused aesthetics of the Exhibition. Joseph Paxton, the designer of the Crystal Palace, was an engineer and investor in the railways that were responsible for the expansion of trade and development of industry, and the chief engineers responsible for the construction were railway builders who brought with them the techniques and concepts of the steam age. Yet the model was the conservatory Paxton had built on the Duke of Devonshire's estate at Chatsworth, a huge indoor heated subtropical garden. This was a typically Victorian attempt to harness technology to the domestication of Paradise under glass, as well as representing theories of natural history, like the botanical collection in the Palm House at Kew Gardens or the display of predators at feeding-time in London Zoo which so disgusted Dickens.[78] The origins of Paxton's design in a conservatory links the Crystal Palace with the pastoral tradition of a terrestrial Eden, symbolized by the gigantic crystal fountain, which looks to a new earthly paradise, while the 1848-foot nave emphasizes the ecclesiastical revivalism of this temple of science.[79] Modernity promises here, however, not a return to Nature, but the greening of the city, in the literal sense that the Crystal Palace enclosed the elms of Hyde Park.

Household Words carried a leading article by W. H. Wills, "The Private History of the Palace of Glass" (18 January 1851), devoted to Paxton's Crystal Palace, which told how Paxton's design for the Crystal Palace had been born on blotting paper at a railway company board meeting and rushed to London to displace the competing tenders for the Great Exhibition, a radical solution effected by suitably modern means of engineering and communication. Wills stressed Paxton's concept of a glass prefabricated structure and the scientific control of climate and temperature, drainage, and ventilation. To see the ideological construction behind such design it is enough to recall Paxton's previous experience in urban planning, a public park at the Liverpool suburb of Birkenhead that followed the principles of Edwin Chadwick's recommendations for circulation and ventilation in the regulation of the masses' recreation (which would also divert them from political agitation),[80] while his proposal for the Great Victorian Way in 1855 linked London's railway stations on an east-west axis with a rapid transit communication that was glassed in with arcades and heated in winter, combining circulation and control with a shopping emporium. The Crystal Palace thus connected landscaping in the country houses of the landowning classes with design of the glass-roofed arcades and railway termini of the industrial city, which superseded them. Time and space were contained under one roof in a prefabricated state-of-the-art construction of glass and steel, an immense structure made feasible by the recent abolition of taxation on glass windows.

In Pugin's Gothic hall, the medieval was welded with modern machinery, much as a Gothic hotel fronted a huge engine-shed in St. Pancras Station. Queen Victoria banqueted in historical style in Pugin's hall, and celebration of the medieval past was far from being incompatible with middle-class aspirations for enrichment from free trade and competition. The universalism of fair and brotherly competition was presented as a Christian mission of world peace under British leadership by Prince Albert in his programmatic speech at Mansion House, 21 March 1850, when he declared that this "period of most wonderful transition" tended to the providentially and historically ordained "great end" of the "unity of mankind"—to be achieved by global trade and the division of labor in the factory system. Yet, notwithstanding some pious sermons on model housing for the poor and (with foreign visitors in mind) the superiority of the British constitution, radicalism simmered, and the laborers were clearly not to be appeased by bread and circuses (or in this case scientific wonders and pyrotechnics).[81]

The evanescence of the Crystal Palace, which dissolves time and space into transparency, is the mark of its modernity. The Crystal Palace can be compared with another glass city, Fourier's utopian *phalanstère*, which Walter Benjamin hailed as the ultimate "city of arcades" that expressed the scientific impulse of the machine age to perfect social production welded to the iron of the railway and the factory.[82] It was, indeed, a landmark of modernity before Baudelaire sauntered along Haussmann's boulevards and, as a center of urban capitalism, London preceded and in some ways surpassed the modernity of Paris.[83] Yet for all the innovation of its materials and prefabricated construction, the Crystal Palace influenced steel-and-glass architecture only with Siegfried Giedion and the American skyscraper in the next century, though Ebenezer Howard included a Crystal Palace in his model factory town in his *Garden Cities of Tomorrow* (first published as *Tomorrow: A Peaceful Path to Reform* in 1898). This was an indoor pleasure garden and commercial arcade, as well as permanent exhibition, at the center of a strictly controlled ecosphere. The sanitation problems of Dickens's day have been solved, and a balance has been achieved between public and private, work and leisure, a utopian vision that was to influence twentieth-century urban planning and the garden city movement. Nonetheless, like previous ideal cities, the concentric design places public institutions at the center of its control and representation, including the repository of knowledge, the library, and the Crystal Palace, a place of entertainment which exhibits aesthetic taste and industrial design.

The Russian radical Nikolai Chernyshevsky lauded the Crystal Palace in the leading Russian journal *Notes of the Fatherland*, but Fyodor Dostoevsky responded with horror to the utopian *phalanstères* of Chernyshevsky's novel *What Is to Be Done?* (1861), of which the Crystal Palace (in Vera Pavlovna's fourth dream) is a pale prophecy. Dostoevsky abhorred the instrumentality and finality of what his Underground Man derides as an ant-hill and a chicken-coop because it reduced humankind to cogs in a machine, a nightmare of the utilitarian means becoming the end—the absolute rule of reason. What particularly horrified Dostoevsky in *Winter Notes of Summer Impressions* (1863) was the utopian claim to have herded together all of mankind into one flock, which he discerned in the Crystal Palace's programmatic universalism. By the time Dostoevsky saw it, the Crystal Palace had been removed to Sydenham Hill, where it was transformed into an Aladdin's cave of art and science, above all as a lower-class Arcadia, which Hippolyte Taine succinctly described as a monstrous pantheon not to taste but to power.[84]

The ideology behind the Crystal Palace always remained an object of critique in Dickens's writings. The Crystal Palace represented in its architecture and its exhibits the discipline of work and the social goal of Progress, but its glass walls enclosed a visibility of the kind of Benthamite surveillance that Foucault describes in the similar prison-machine of Fourier's *phalanstère*.[85] Beneath the universalist dream lay the transparency of the public gaze where everyone sees everyone. It is surely no coincidence that Jeremy Bentham also modeled his "Panopticon" on an English conservatory and that it answered the need for supervision in the new factories, where (as in the panorama) the gazing eye commanded an all-inclusive view.[86]

Dickens nevertheless admired such "self-made men" as Paxton, a promoter of the railway interest, with whom he had worked in the launching of the *Daily News* and whom he called in to design the set for Bulwer-Lytton's *Not So Bad as We Seem*, performed at Devonshire House in March 1851.[87] Himself also a protégé of the Duke of Devonshire, Dickens scoffed at cynics who doubted the feasibility of the Crystal Palace and he lauded its builder as "a great natural genius, self-improved," a "worthy type of industry and ingenuity and industry triumphant" ("The Last Words of the Old Year," *Household Words*, 4 January 1851; DJ 2: 313). In a speech of 9 June 1851 he attributed Paxton's spectacular rise up the social ladder to his "genius and good sense" (*Speeches* 135). Thrift and the discipline of hard work, so beloved of Samuel Smiles, were the watchwords of Charles Dickens's own success; the literary example in *Self-Help* was Edward Bulwer-Lytton, Dickens's mentor. Paxton's name became synonymous with the Victorian work ethic embossed on the Exhibition medals, *Pulcher et ille labor palma decorare laborem* (as well as, in an unintended pun, with the *Pax Britannica* which the Exhibition celebrated), despite the fact that, as *Punch* made clear, the laborers doing the work were not to be seen.[88]

Dickens wished for "a great display of England's sins and negligences" (DJ 2: 313), and in that sense *Bleak House* is a counterexhibition of misery and injustice.[89] If *Dombey and Son* criticized the inhuman drive for wealth behind the steam engine, it is not surprising that Dickens should be less than enthusiastic about the Crystal Palace, which he mocked as "the-great-exhibition-of-the-works-of-industry-of-all-nations" ("The Amusements of the People," *Household Words*, 30 March 1850; DJ 2: 181). The greatest show of all times, he complained, failed in its utilitarian zeal to appease the imagination and left no room for the moral appeal of art. This attack on utilitarianism, which we shall take up in the next chapter, is in line with Ruskin's dismissal of the Crystal Palace (in *The Two Paths*, 1858–59) as an overlarge greenhouse devoid of imagination or durability which, together with "some very ordinary algebra," was "all that glass can represent to human intellect."[90]

However, in his piece on the Crystal Palace (written with R. H. Horne, "The Great Exhibition and the Little One," *Household Words*, 5 July 1851), Dickens contrasted the "Progress" of the West, in the Great Exhibition, with the "Stoppage" of the East, in the Chinese Gallery at Hyde Park Place, where an American traveler exhibited his collection from 1841. The liberalism of a society regulated by police, he writes, is at infinite advantage over a backward, primitive culture of perfect Toryism (UW 1: 322). China was seen through the prevailing Orientalism and was associated with a threatening heathen sexuality and cruelty that had to be controlled. These stereotypes served to define the self-image of the British through perceptions of the Other and the exaggerated fears of foreign infiltration during the Exhibition. In the context of the Oriental question and the Opium Wars looming in the contemporary press, Dickens's article would at first sight fit in with the stereotype of the barbarian warriors futilely resisting the advance of the winged locomotive of Progress (fig. 11), if not for Dickens's send-up of such racial stereotypes in his piece on the Chinese boat moored on the Thames ("The Chinese Junk," *The Examiner*, 24 June 1848; DJ 2: 100–102). This is a parable of absolute Toryism that refuses to see that forms must be sacrificed to ends in a civilization of industry and railways. To read it as approval of power and control (in quite Foucauldian terms, typical of Western colonial views) is to ignore Dickens's characteristic concern with matters nearer home, particularly the repeal of the Corn Laws and Free Trade, which the Great Exhibition showed to be irreversible.[91] Paradoxically, it was government bureaucracy and opposition to innovation—"do-nothing-ism"—which almost scuttled the Great Exhibition before it got off the ground.

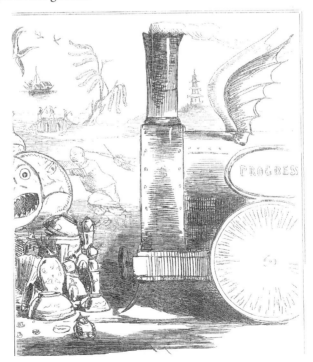

Fig. 11: "The Great Barbarian Dragon" (detail) (*Punch*, 3 September 1853)

The opening image in *Bleak House* of London caught up in the tenacious mud of an antediluvian primitivism exposes the chaos of what Carlyle showed in *Past and Present* and *Latter-Day Pamphlets* to be a moribund society where no change seemed possible, where, together with the fog, mud blocked the healthy circulation of traffic and of ideas. It is an image that suggests obstruction of any circulation of health and wealth exhibited in the Crystal Palace. In the common medical analogy of urban society, Progress depended on circulation, and David Trotter has shown Stoppage to be opposed to Circulation—of trade, of ideas, and of the progress of the plot—at several levels of *Bleak House*.[92] Circulation of meaning is also a struggle for control of hermeneutics, without which there can be no social process. Dickens's impatience for any Stoppage is a continual bee in his bonnet, as in his address to the Metropolitan Sanitary Association when he pleaded that no "Stoppage" should impede the improvement of circulation of air and water, which according to the miasmic theory was essential to prevent disease (*Speeches* 131–32). The imaginary Megalosaurus waddling up Holborn Hill neatly reverses the progressive timescale of Victorian ideology and natural history.

Dickens was not alone in his skepticism. Gustave Doré's etching of Ludgate Hill clogged with horse-drawn traffic makes an effective contrast with the locomotive speeding along the viaduct overhead, a progress signposted also in the partly covered inscription "Crystal Palace" (fig. 12). The mass excursion by train of laborers and their families to see the Exhibition resulted in mobs descending on London and exacerbating the lodgings crisis. London was displayed to the visitors from the North as a very different kind of exhibition, one Henry Mayhew satirized in *1851 or, The Adventures of Mr. and Mrs. Sandboys and Family Who Came Up to London to See the Great Exhibition* (1851).

Cruikshank's cartoon illustrating Mayhew's text shows a blocked Regent's Circus jammed with traffic unable to progress to the Crystal Palace—one of a pair contrasting the emptied streets of Manchester (fig. 13). This gives a graphic illustration of Dickens's own impatience with anything that impeded Circulation, whether it be the incompetent bureaucracy of the Crimean War or the Circumlocution Office's obstruction of the inventor Doyce in *Little Dorrit*. Such impatience, which tempers Dickens's general approval of progress, provides a further reason why Dickens fled London at this time, in addition to the "grave family sorrows," which made him want to get away from the crowds and excitement of the Great Exhibition when he "ran away" from London in summer 1851.[93]

If Bucket investigates the intimate secrets of the dead aristocracy, Inspector Field (who likewise inspects dead relics of the past, the dinosaurs and classical treasures in the British Museum) offers a rather different representation of the greatest nation on earth, in the rookeries of London, where his "bull's eye" lantern keeps society's moral sewage under surveillance ("On Duty with Inspector Field," *Household Words*, 14 June 1851). By day, the police sergeant translates for foreign visitors to the Great Exhibition, but at night he joins Inspector Field for a tour of a counterexhibition that reforms

Fig. 12: Doré, "Ludgate Hill—A Block in the Street" (1872)

3 13: Cruikshank, "London Crammed and Manchester Deserted" (1851)

blocked by red tape and vested interests: "Thus, we make our New Oxford Streets, and our other new streets, never heeding, never asking, where the wretches whom we clear out, crowd. With such scenes at our doors, with all the plagues of Egypt tied up with bits of cobweb in kennels so near our homes, we timourously make our Nuisance Bills and Boards of Health, nonentities, and think to keep away the Wolves of Crime and Filth, by our electioneering ducking to little vestry-men, and our gentlemanly handling of Red Tape!" (DJ 2: 363). Similar sentiments are voiced in "The Metropolitan Protectives" (written with W. H. Wills, *Household Words*, 26 April 1851), which makes fun of the xenophobic fears of foreign spies or agents-provocateurs invading London for the Great Exhibition and suggests destitution on London's streets should be of more concern than middle-class anxieties about the security of their domestic castles (UW 1: 273). Stoppage is equally caused by the antediluvian fog of Chancery whose endless running up against "walls of words" (institutionalized in the "Circumlocution Office" in *Little Dorrit*) contrasts with the Crystal Palace. The novel thus represents itself both as artifact and as a legal claim (Dickens was plaintiff in Chancery in 1844 in successful injunctions to protect copyright on his work and knew what it was like to see his expenses lost). In doing so, it resists the illegible discourse of Chancery by offering a different working-out of social destiny in the plot.

NOTES

1   See Simon Varey, *Space and the Eighteenth-Century Novel* (Cambridge: Cambridge University Press, 1990); John B. Bender, *Imagining the Penitentiary: Fiction and the Architecture of Mind in Eighteenth-Century England* (Chicago: University of Chicago).

2   Robert Newsom, *Dickens on the Romantic Side of Familiar Things: Bleak House and the Novel Tradition* (New York: Columbia University Press, 1977), 11–45.

3   Julian Wolfreys, *Writing London: The Trace of the Urban Text from Blake to Dickens* (London: Macmillan, and New York: St. Martin's Press, 1998), 124–26, 143–49.

4   Diary for 23 December 1838, reprinted in *Dickens: The Critical Heritage*, ed. Philip Collins (London: Routledge, 1971), 44.

5   D. A. Miller, *The Novel and the Police* (Berkeley: University of California Press, 1988), 106. See Dominick LaCapra's criticism of this analysis, "Ideology and Critique in Dickens's *Bleak House*," *Representations* 6 (1984): 116–23; see also John Reed, "Authorized Punishment in Dickens's Fiction," *Studies in the Novel* 24.2 (1992): 112–30.

6   As Kevin McLaughlin argues in a Hegelian reading of *Bleak House*, "Losing One's Place: Displacement and Domesticity in Dickens's *Bleak House*," *Modern Language Notes* 108.5 (1993): 875–90.

7   Mikhail Bakhtin, *The Dialogic Imagination: Four Essays*, trans. Caryl Emerson and Michael Holquist (Austin: University of Texas Press, 1981), 232.

8   Nancy Armstrong, *Desire and Domestic Fiction: A Political History of the Novel* (Oxford: Oxford University Press, 1987), 163.

9   Ruskin, *Sesame and Lilies* (London: George Allen, 1903), 108–09. Welsh points to the source of the phrase "shade as of rock in a weary land" in Isaiah 32.2, which adds an apocalyptic dimension to a ritual repetition of pious phrases about household gods

and sacrifice, as Welsh reads this (*The City of Dickens* [Oxford: Oxford University Press, 1971], 161).

10   For example, Jenni Calder, *The Victorian Home* (London: B. T. Batsford, 1977), 11–14; Monica Cohen, *Professional Domesticity in the Victorian Novel: Women, Work, and Home* (Cambridge: Cambridge University Press, 1998), 70.

11   Flint, *Dickens* (Atlantic Highlands NJ: Humanities Press, 1986), 114–15.

12   Elizabeth Langland, "Nobody's Angels: Domestic Ideology and Middle-Class Women in the Victorian Novel," *PMLA* 97.2 (1992): 297–98.

13   Quoted in Lennard Davis, *Factual Fictions: The Origins of the English Novel* (Philadelphia: University of Pennsylvania Press, 1996), 65.

14   Watt, *The Rise of the Novel: Studies in Defoe, Richardson, Fielding* (London: Chatto & Windus, 1957), 192–96.

15   Hardy, *The Moral Art of Dickens* (London: Athlone Press, 1970), 139.

16   John Butt and Kathleen Tillotson, *Dickens at Work* (London: Methuen, 1957), 187–89.

17   See Martin A. Danahay, "Housekeeping and Hegemony in Dickens' *Bleak House*," in *Keeping the Victorian House: A Collection of Essays*, ed. Vanessa D. Dickerson (New York: Garland, 1998), 6.

18   See Steven Cohan, "'They Are All Secret': The Fantasy Content of *Bleak House*," *Literature and Psychology* 26 (1976): 88.

19   Chris Brooks, *Signs for the Times: Symbolic Realism in the Mid-Victorian World* (London: Allen & Unwin, 1984), 60–61.

20   Langland, "Nobody's Angels," 297.

21   See Frances Armstrong, *Dickens and the Concept of Home* (Ann Arbor: UMI Research Press, 1990), 96–97. The Polygon, where Skimpole's house is situated and where the Dickens family lived for a brief period, is named for its multiple angles which emphasize disorder and irregularity. The autobiographical location would identify Skimpole's carelessness with the financial irresponsibility of Dickens's father, but also alludes to the moral carelessness of the domestic affairs of the poet Leigh Hunt.

22   Alice van Buren Kelley, "The Bleak Houses of *Bleak House*," *Nineteenth-Century Fiction* 25 (1970): 266–67.

23   Doris Alexander, *Creating Characters with Charles Dickens* (University Park: Penn State University Press, 1991), 69–76.

24   Fred Kaplan, *Dickens: A Biography* (New York: William Morrow, 1988), 302.

25   See Angus Wilson, *The World of Charles Dickens* (London: Secker & Warburg, 1970), 226.

26   On the development of medical opinion on communicable disease and the debate between "miasmatists" and "contagionists," see George Rosen, "Disease, Debility, and Death," in *The Victorian City: Images and Realities*, ed. H. J. Dyos and Michael Wolff (London: Routledge, 1973), 2: 625–67. See Pamela K. Gilbert, *Mapping the Victorian Social Body* (Albany: State University of New York Press, 2004); Gilbert, *The Citizen's Body: Desire, Health, and the Social in Victorian England*. (Columbus: Ohio State University Press, 2007), 141–51.

27   Anthony S. Wohl, "Unfit for Human Habitation," in Dyos and Wolff, eds., *The Victorian City*, 2: 611–12.

28   *Alton Locke, Tailor and Poet: An Autobiography* [1831] (London: Macmillan, 1890), 32.

29   H. M. Daleski, *Dickens and the Art of Analogy* (London: Faber and Faber, 1970), 64–65.

30   Gareth Stedman Jones, *Outcast London: A Study in the Relationship Between Classes in Victorian Society* (Oxford: Clarendon Press, 1971), 180.

31   Daleski, *Dickens and the Art of Analogy*, 50. That it is not only a problem of the big cities may be seen in chapter xxxviii of *Oliver Twist*, prior to the melodramatic meeting

between the epileptic Monks and Mr. and Mrs. Bumble, where the ruinous houses on the margins of the parish spawn crime.

32   *The Adventures of Oliver Twist*, ed. Steven Connor (London: Dent, 1994), xli.

33   Edwin Chadwick, *The Sanitary Condition of the Labouring Population of Great Britain*, ed. M. W. Flinn (Edinburgh: Edinburgh University Press, 1965), 422; see also 212–14.

34   Mary Poovey claims *The Sanitary Condition* erases or marginalizes outcasts and women in its patriarchal ideal of home in a bid for political control (*Making a Social Body: British Cultural Formation, 1830–1864* [Chicago: University of Chicago Press, 1995], 118).

35   On the trope of "contagion" in social and literary discourse in the 1850s and 1860s see Allan Conrad Christensen, *Nineteenth-Century Narratives of Contagion: "Our Feverish Contact"* (London and New York: Routledge 2005).

36   *The Adventures of Oliver Twist*, xlii.

37   See Jane Vogel, *Allegory in Dickens* (Birmingham, AL: Alabama University Press, 1977), 57–58.

38   *Charles Dickens: The World of His Novels* (Cambridge, MA: Harvard University Press, 1958), 163.

39   *London Labour and the London Poor* [1861–62] (London: Frank Cass, 1967), 2: 494–507.

40   "The Byeways of Life in London," *Pictorial Times*, 10 October 1846, 1–2.

41   Danahay goes further and senses in the similarities between the novelist's labor and Esther's housekeeping a risk of crossing gender lines and of effeminacy ("Housekeeping and Hegemony in Dickens' *Bleak House*," 17–19).

42   *Victorian Subjects* (Hemel Hempstead: Harvester Wheatsheaf, and Durham: Duke University Press, 1991), 179.

43   Allan Pritchard, "The Urban Gothic of *Bleak House*," *Nineteenth-Century Fiction* 45.4 (1991): 432–52; Ann Ronald, "Dickens' Gloomiest Castle," *Dickens Studies Newsletter* 6 (1975): 71–75.

44   *A Geography of Victorian Gothic Fiction: Mapping History's Nightmare* (Oxford: Oxford University Press, 1999), 70–77. See on the spectral effect of representing London as Urban Gothic in *Little Dorrit*, Julian Wolfreys, *Victorian Hauntings: Spectrality, Gothic, the Uncanny, and Literary* (Houndmills: Palgrave Macmillan, 2002), 94–109.

45   George Lewes for one indignantly refuted the scientific possibility of spontaneous combustion, in which Dickens sincerely believed, and Dickens countered with real-life cases to summon the authority of his fiction as a truthful account (preface to the 1st ed., BH 42). See Gordon Haight, "Dickens and Lewes on Spontaneous Combustion," *Nineteenth-Century Fiction* 10 (1955): 53–63.

46   Michael Goldberg, *Dickens and Carlyle* (Athens, GA: University of Georgia Press, 1972), 72–77.

47   Letter from James Heath to Poe, 12 September 1839, quoted in Thomas Woodson, "Introduction," in *Twentieth-Century Interpretations of "The Fall of the House of Usher,"* ed. Thomas Woodson (Englewood Cliffs, NJ: Prentice-Hall, 1969), 9.

48   Philippa Tristram, *Living Space in Fact and Fiction* (London: Routledge, 1989), 31.

49   Newsom, *Dickens on the Romantic Side of Familiar Things*, 57–59; see also Christopher Herbert, "The Occult in *Bleak House*," *Novel* 17.2 (1984): 105; Maria M. Tatar, "The Houses of Fiction: Toward a Definition of the Uncanny," *Comparative Literature* 33.2 (1981): 181.

50   Freud, "The 'Uncanny,'" *The Standard Edition of the Complete Psychological Works of Sigmund Freud* (London: Hogarth, 1951–), 17: 245.

51 The opposition of home and homelessness in Freud's analysis of the uncanny is applied to *David Copperfield* in Michael Greenstein, "Between Curtain and Caul: *David Copperfield's* Shining Transparences," *Dickens Quarterly* 5.2 (1988): 75.

52 Anthony Vidler, *The Architectural Uncanny: Essays in the Modern Unhomely* (Cambridge, MA: MIT Press, 1992), 6–8.

53 Freud, "The 'Uncanny,'" 249.

54 Freud, "The 'Uncanny,'" 236–37.

55 Andreas Huyssen, "The Disturbance of Vision in Vienna Modernism," *Modernism/Modernity* 5.3 (1998): 34–36.

56 Arac, *Commissioned Spirits*, 104. Carlyle's *The French Revolution* and Dickens's *Bleak House* both build on the synecdochal analogy of house and social structure in an analysis of social collapse and moral contagion (*Commissioned Spirits* 123–38).

57 Kelley, "The Bleak Houses of *Bleak House*," 266–67.

58 Valentine Cunningham, *In the Reading Gaol: Postmodernity, Texts, and History* (Oxford: Blackwell, 1994), 89.

59 Cunningham, *In the Reading Gaol*, 292–93.

60 Daleski, *Dickens and the Art of Analogy*, 156.

61 "Homelessness and Dickens," *Social Research* 58.1 (1991): 95.

62 Newton, *Narrative Ethics* (Cambridge, MA: Harvard University Press, 1995), 243–45.

63 Kelley, "The Bleak Houses of *Bleak House*," 266.

64 Nead, *Victorian Babylon: People, Streets and Images in Nineteenth-Century London* (New Haven: Yale University Press, 2000), 214.

65 See J. Hillis Miller, *Charles Dickens: The World of His Novels*, 160–224.

66 T. S. Eliot, *Selected Essays* (London: Faber & Faber, 1950), 462.

67 Harvey P. Sucksmith, *The Narrative Art of Charles Dickens: The Rhetoric of Sympathy and Irony in His Novels* (Oxford: Oxford University Press, 1970), 277.

68 J. Hillis Miller, *Charles Dickens: The World of His Novels*, 190–92; Ian Ousby, "The Broken Glass: Vision and Comprehension in *Bleak House*," *Nineteenth-Century Fiction* 29 (1975): 381–92.

69 As has been noted by a number of scholars; see Emily Heady, "The Polis's Different Voices: Narrating England's Progress in Dickens's *Bleak House*," *Texas Studies in Literature and Language* 48.4 (2006): 312–39.

70 Asa Briggs, *Victorian People* (Harmondsworth: Penguin Books, rev. ed., 1965), 26. See also Briggs, *Iron Bridge to Crystal Palace: Impact and Images of the Industrial Revolution* (London: Thames and Hudson, 1979), 165–67; Briggs, *1851* (London: The Historical Association, 1951; reprinted 1972), 3–4.

71 These tensions are underscored in Jeffrey Auerbach's study of the exhibition, *The Great Exhibition of 1851: A Nation on Display* (New Haven: Yale University Press, 1999). In what follows I have drawn liberally on this study, as well as C. H. Gibbs-Smith, *The Great Exhibition of 1851* (London: HMSO, 1951); John Davis, *The Great Exhibition* (Stroud: Sutton Publishing, 1999); and John McKean, *Crystal Palace: Joseph Paxton and Charles Fox* (London: Phaidon, 1994). See also Hermione Hobhouse, *The Crystal Palace and the Great Exhibition: Art, Science and Productive Industry* (London: Athlone, 2002).

72 See Andrew Miller, *Novels Behind Glass: Commodity Culture and Victorian Narrative* (Cambridge: Cambridge University Press, 1995); Philippe Hamon, *Expositions: Literature and Architecture in Nineteenth-Century France*, trans. Katia Sainson-Frank and Lisa Maguire (Berkeley: University of California Press, 1992); Thomas Richards, *The Commodity Culture of Victorian England: Advertising and Spectacle, 1851–1914* (Stanford: Stanford University

Press, 1990), 17–40; P. H. Hoffenberg, *An Empire on Display: English, Indian, and Autralian Exhibitions from the Crystal Palace to the Great War* (Berkeley: University of California Press, 2001).

73   Asa Briggs, *Victorian People*, 28; see also Calder, *The Victorian Home*, 92.

74   John Davis, *The Great Exhibition*, 189; Helen Small, "A Pulse of 124: Charles Dickens and a Pathology of the Mid-Victorian Reading Public," in *The Practice and Representation of Reading in England*, ed. James Raven, Helen Small, and Naomi Tadmor (Cambridge: Cambridge University Press, 1996), 270; Auerbach, *The Great Exhibition of 1851*, 130–31.

75   See pp. 153–55 below.

76   See on this Andrew Miller, *Novels Behind Glass*, 55.

77   See Christopher Hobhouse, *1851 and the Crystal Palace* (London: John Murray, 1937), 70; Auerbach, *The Great Exhibition of 1851*, 92–94, 98–99.

78   Simon Schama, *Landscape and Memory* (New York: Knopf, 1995), 562–67.

79   Max F. Schulz, *Paradise Preserved* (Cambridge: Cambridge University Press, 1983), 180–94.

80   Chadwick, *The Sanitary Condition*, 337–38.

81   Briggs, *Victorian People*, 47–48.

82   Walter Benjamin, "Paris—Capital of the Nineteenth Century" [1939], *The Arcades Project*, trans. Howard Eiland and Kevin McLaughlin (Cambridge, MA: Harvard University Press, 1999), 16–17.

83   Evan Horowitz, "London: Capital of the Nineteenth Century," *New Literary History* 41 (2010): 111–28.

84   Hippolyte Taine, *Notes on England*, trans. Edward Hyams (London: Thames and Hudson, 1950), 188–89.

85   Michel Foucault, *Surveillir et punir: Naissance de la prison* (Paris: Gallimard, 1975), 226.

86   Hamon, *Expositions*, 70–71; Vidler, "The Scenes of the Street: Transformations in Ideal and Reality," in *On Streets*, ed. Stanford Anderson (Cambridge, MA: MIT Press, 1978), 54, 108 n. 83; Stephan Oettermann, *The Panorama: History of a Mass Medium*, trans. Deborah L. Schneider (New York: Zone Books, 1997), 41–45.

87   On Dickens's attitude to Paxton and the Crystal Palace, see T. W. Hill, "Dickens and the 1851 Exhibition," *The Dickensian* 47 (1951): 119–20.

88   "Specimens from Mr. Punch's Industrial Exhibition of 1850—to Be Improved in 1851," *Punch*, 13 April 1851.

89   Philip Landon, however, concludes that Dickens failed ultimately to counter the panoptic discipline of the Crystal Palace in *Bleak House* ("Great Exhibitions: Representations of the Crystal Palace in Mayhew, Dickens, and Dostoevsky," *Nineteenth-Century Contexts* 20 [1997]: 27–59).

90   On Ruskin's attitude to the Crystal Palace see Martin Wiener, *English Culture and the Decline of the Industrial Spirit, 1850–1980* (Cambridge: Cambridge University Press, 1981), 29; John Davis, *The Great Exhibition*, 194–95.

91   See Auerbach, *The Great Exhibition of 1851*, 173–87. China sent no official delegation to the Exhibition because it did not accept the superiority of the Western notion of progress based on industrialization (Davis, *The Great Exhibition*, 104–05).

92   Trotter, *Circulation: Defoe, Dickens, and the Economies of the Novel* (New York: St. Martin's Press, 1988), 99–123.

93   John Forster, *The Life of Charles Dickens*, rev. ed. (London: Dent, 1969), 2: 57.

4

The Factory:
Fact and Fancy in *Hard Times*

HARD TIMES FOR *HARD TIMES*

> Quantity of pleasure being equal, push-pin is as good as poetry.
> All poetry is misrepresentation.
> —Jeremy Bentham

> Never wonder.
> —Thomas Gradgrind (HT I, VIII; 89)

> ... it is better not to wonder.
> —Mrs. General (LD II, v; 527)

A novel of individual growth and imagination like *Hard Times* (1854) would appear to work against Bentham's felicific calculus which regards society as an aggregate of individuals who determined through their own interest the "happiness of the greatest number." Catherine Gallagher has argued, however, that, ironically, Dickens shared the same premises as the Political Economists whom he mocked, and that he did not differ significantly from the definition of labor in Adam Smith's *Wealth of Nations* or common attitudes to leisure and industriousness. Gallagher sees Dickens's sole industrial novel as a self-legitimizing claim to "amusement" in an inadequate response to the real life problems of industrialization which actually shows the productivity and reproductivity of all characters, including the circus people.[1] Indeed, the caricature of Bentham's philosophy in the novel has encouraged readers to think Fact and Fancy are opposed without realizing that Dickens is presenting a dystopian vision of the industrial city which would eliminate any form of imagination. Rather, Fact and Fancy are two competing metasystems of representation in *Hard Times* which motivate character and plot in the ideational and spatial spheres of each binary model. Spatial metaphor functions as a sustained structuring device which resists the naturalization of abstract space in the Malthusian justification of an economic policy based on unbending and divinely ordained "natural" laws responsible for the cruel realities of the industrial city. Throughout the novel, and most famously in the "keynote" fifth chapter, Dickens is employing Fancy to show what is wrong with the industrial city—not just its ugliness or its cruelty, but what is wrong *fundamentally* with its totalizing, false system of representation.

Little attention, unfortunately, has been paid to the novel's dialogized response to those principles of utilitarianism which contradict the poetics, orientation, ideology, and social function of the novel. The dialogizing of opposing discourses, in Mikhail Bakhtin's analysis of the novel, does not necessarily assume that all or any of the represented views are the author's own: "...the dialogical approach can be applied to any meaningful part of an utterance, even to an individual word, if that word is perceived not as an impersonal word of language, but as the sign of another's semantic position."[2] One scholar who has applied Bakhtin's notion of double-voiced discourse to the nineteenth-century novel concludes that the heteroglossia opened up by this perspective does not occlude the distinction between analysis of narrative devices and the ideological conclusions that may be drawn from the diversity of represented discourses:

> While Dostoevsky may create polyphonic novels that are truly dialogic in the sense that the author in no way presents a final resolution to conflicts between the dominant ideas ("ideologies" in Bakhtin's sense) of the characters, the irreducible mental structures he gives them are nevertheless creations of the author—minds and interrelations so constructed as to be irreducible and beyond external evaluation.[3]

The issue is one of both epistemological and political representation that goes beyond the ancient quarrel between Reason and Imagination. As Bakhtin tells us, because the novel is determined by experience, knowledge, and practice (unlike the epic), when the novel becomes the dominant genre, epistemology becomes the dominant discipline.[4] Modern government could not efficiently manage an urbanized industrialized economy without a statistical representation of the needs of the population and the prosperity of the nation. A poet, however, would have a very different view of what constitutes "knowledge" and "progress." When Macaulay blasts Robert Southey in his 1830 review of the poet laureate's *Sir Thomas More: or, Colloquies on the Progress and Prospects of Society* (1829), we cannot ignore the head-on clash of ideologies and poetics, of aesthetics and historiography, between romantic nostalgia for the past and scientific government, between a lament for the deterioration of society and hard facts showing better standards of living. Southey detested the Iron Bridge and all that stood for modernization and the factory system. In *Letters from England* (1807) he summed up the price Britain paid for its newfound wealth in stereotypes of the debauchery arising from herding together men and women in confined factories and the deprivation caused by child-labor of childhood innocence, sports, fresh air, and education (Letter 38). These are common perceptions found in the discourse of the Industrial Revolution of the threat to the English class hierarchy caused by shifts in social mobility and the distortion of gender and sexual relations, as well as family dysfunction, resulting from female labor in factories.

In her pamphlet *The Factory Controversy* (1855), the journalist and Political Economist Harriet Martineau attacked the author of *Hard Times* precisely for getting his facts wrong about the factory system both in the novel and in *Household Words*. The argument has particular relevance for the novelist's satire of the abuse of statistics: Martineau clears the employers of criminal negligence because "only" twelve out of five thousand accidents annually were fatal! Martineau writes off Dickens's humanitarian attitudes to such "facts" as no less ludicrous than Mrs. Jellyby's compassion for the natives of Borrieboola-Gha. According to Martineau, Dickens, in his novel, and the factory inspector Leonard Horner, in his reports, failed to understand that the employers took seriously their responsibility for the workers' beneficence and that government intervention was an infringement of civil liberty, a "mischievous" meddling with economic considerations by impractical regulations on fencing machinery. Martineau portrayed the editor of *Household Words* as one who had set himself up as the great reformer by venturing out of his sphere into the field of social action. She proclaimed Dickens's views to be dangerous, though she consoled herself with the thought that no worker of any intelligence would be misled by his "misrepresentations" and "mis-statements." However, had this still been the era of Luddites, Dickens would be charged with inciting the burning of factories and the assassination of their owners![5] In her *Autobiography*, written in 1855, Martineau lavishes praise on Dickens the artist, though reserving her disagreement over his representation of English society. She would not try to make of him a Political Economist, but she regrets that he did not teach the suffering lower classes some self-discipline, which she clearly believes it is the novel's task to police.

In her own articles on factories in *Household Words* beginning 18 October 1851, Martineau justifies the employers' position, based on the rational principle of Political Economy, that trade must not be interfered with by meddling legislation and that it was the workers who were at fault for accidents through ignorance or carelessness, as the statistics plainly showed. In his novel and in his response to Martineau, Dickens presented such arguments as mere excuses for saving money at the cost of human lives and called them the "fictions" of Coketown, whose employers avoided compliance with regulations by threatening to "pitch their property into the Atlantic" (HT II I; 145–46)[6] Nothing could be further apart than these assumptions about the workings of society, and the disagreement led to Martineau ending her collaboration in Dickens's journal. E. P. Whipple, writing in 1877, recognized the implications of the attack on Dickens's alleged ignorance of economics and statistics in *Hard Times*, where he let "benevolent passions" get the better of "inexorable laws." Whipple regretted that Ruskin and (of all people) Macaulay had condoned this invasion of science by art (though, to give him his due, Macaulay complained in his journal for 12 August 1854 of the book's "sullen socialism").[7]

The difference of opinion over representation leads not just to a crude and false opposition of "Facts" versus "Fancy," but also to a fundamental difference of opinion over representation of knowledge, and hence representation of the new industrial city. Are knowledge of society and the policies of government to be guided by statistics or inspired by poetry? Must the fields of politics, science, and literature be segregated? Can poetry, as Mrs. Gaskell believed in *Mary Barton* (1848), teach the morality lacking in economic law? Certainly, Chalmers's fundamental principle of Political Economy allowed no place for the benevolence and compassion on which Dickens's urban realism rested. The two representations of society were clearly in collision, and the disagreement concerned not only what reforms were necessary, but how society was to change. We should remember that for Tories reform prior to 1867 was supposed to regulate the existing order so as to conserve it and maintain economic growth (as Peel advocated at the time of the so-called "Great Reform" in 1832), not to uproot something rotten in the system. Macaulay, however, believed the rules of representation had to change with the shift of power to commerce and industry, which were the guarantees of the inevitable march of progress. For poets like Southey, on the other hand, modernity and machinery brought loss of national identity and destruction of Nature. The engagement of *Hard Times* in the discourse of the Industrial Revolution cannot therefore be divorced from its epistemology and poetics. This chapter will examine the representation of Coketown in the context of the medical and social discourse about factories, but also within the debate over representation, a question which Dickens self-consciously treats as an issue of his own novelistic practice.[8]

A.-J. Greimas has proposed an urban semiotics which reads the city as a text with a grammar and syntax. To apply to literary representation of the city the experience and architecture of the urban environment, with its accompanying mythologies embedded in both sender and receiver, is to draw a parallel between an urban epistemology and what happens in the written text. Greimas makes no such parallel, except in as much as both are coded modeling systems of signification[9] that make sense socially and anthropologically. The binary oppositions in Greimas's urban semiotics nevertheless operates on universal principles of functionality. The conception of the city, as distinct from its perception, is determined culturally and socially, and opposes *here* and *elsewhere*, *individual* and *society*, *private* and *public*. These anthropological fields of symbolic meaning are suggested by Lévi-Strauss's study of territorial boundaries in primitive society whose geometric topography reflects a cosmography, often, as Eliade has shown, based on the concentric axis of religious belief systems.[10] Although they evolve over time and in different cultures, such cosmic mappings acquire spatial meaning in the organization of structured hierarchies along horizontal and vertical poles.[11] Yi-Fu Tuan develops Lévi-Strauss's binary oppositions in his structural analysis of primitive societies to show that human sensory behavior organizes our perception of space not just into colors and sounds, but also into semantic fields of cosmographic, geographic, and biosocial symbolism, for example in the geometric and concentric design of ancient cities around sacred space.[12] Center versus periphery is one opposition that constructs community and nation, for example, the centrality of nineteenth-century Manchester as the industrial hub of the earth, or London as the world metropolis and heart of Empire.[13]

Such territorial ordering of differentiation in human geography, particularly the opposition of openness to enclosure, may be found in the boundaries of Dickens's fictional landscape, which correspond to the binary oppositions embedded in cultural constructions of town/country. In common with the strategies of spatial representation in nineteenth-century urban realism, these oppositions operate according to the homologies applied to literary texts by Greimas in *Sémantique structurale*, which manipulate imagery in the structuring of a visualized fictional world.[14]

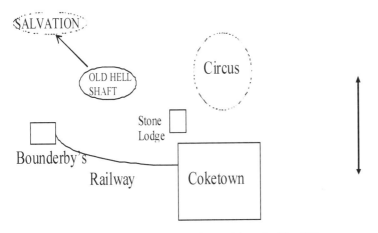

Diagram 1: Binary Oppositions in *Hard Times*

The homologies of natural/not natural and open/closed in *Hard Times*, for example, correspond at the ideational and plot levels to the semantic fields of "Fact" and "Fancy" in a vertical polarity of up/down (see diagram 1). The city is a closed space, a hell, from which escape is possible only through a shaft leading to the Other World of salvation. The plot can only be resolved in a conversion of protagonists from the city of "Fact" to other-worldly "Fancy" or their elimination. Gradgrind is won over to the circus; Bounderby is exposed as a fraudulent self-made man. Bounderby's garden is a false Eden, where Louisa is tempted by the deceitful Harthouse, while Tom is the sinful Adam of the industrial anti-Eden. The set of <town: country> ~ <not natural: not closed> privileges the zone of the natural, and the fact that its space is either open (the circus) or transcendental (the other world) adds a further spatial and temporal dimension to the scheme in which it is opposed to the hell of Coketown. Greimas's putative urban epistemology illustrates Dickens's semiotic modelling of rival ideologies and worldviews. Hence the absurd closure of mind of Gradgrind is underscored by images of coldness, sterility, and enclosure. The alternative is not escape to the country, which is no longer accessible except in death (such as Nell Trent's and Paul Dombey's) or in a transcendental experience (such as Little Dorrit's or Jenny Wren's), but in a conceptualization from within the city of the otherworldly city of the spirit (diagram 2). What Dickens does is to place competing models of society and competing models of representation in binary opposition of *open* to *closed* systems which generate alternately "true" and "false" representations of social space. The spatial metaphor is doubly significant in view of the contemporary attempt to naturalize abstract space into controlled geometric form, an attempt which Mary Poovey traces back to Hobbes's functional equivalence in *Leviathan* of individuals with their calculable monetary value. Modern space was visualized into plans and diagrams, so that geometric form was both mimetic and abstract (as in mathematical formulae); this duality led to commodification, reification, and fetishization because the representation of abstract space obscured the life of individuals as individuals.[15]

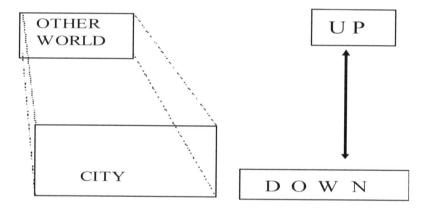

Diagram 2: Spatial Oppositions in Dickens

As in the symbolism of *Dombey and Son* and *Bleak House*, the opposition of open to closed space works analogically to opposition of open to closed systems of ethics and language. The openness of metonymy invalidates the closure of space and of mind in the Gradgrind system and in the industrial landscape of Coketown for which it is responsible. Dickens's sophisticated play of signification and identity satirizes a sign system that insists on the strict one-to-one literalness of the relationship between *signifier* and *referent* and that denies any value but a utilitarian one to the text. The butt of Dickens's satire is a sign system which conceals a void of meaning and which, for all the useful facts stored in Gradgrind's system, serves no useful purpose, except to impose an inhuman uniformity and imprisoning monotony of thought. The absolutist standardization, like the principle of standardized prefabrication in the Crystal Palace, amounts to the absolutist *indifference* of the modern city in which difference and differentiation are impossible.[16]

MINING THE CITY

Did Titus Salt, near Bradford town,
A wondrous pleasure dome decree...?
—(contemporary ditty)

... the workers' dwellings of Manchester are dirty, miserable and wholly lacking in comforts. In such houses only inhuman, degraded and unhealthy creatures would feel at home.
—Friedrich Engels[17]

The semiotic map of the city in *Hard Times* parodies model towns in paternalistic schemes such as Robert Owen's New Lanark, which sought to form moral character through a planned environment (a parallelogram rather than a panopticon) and promised a New Jerusalem for its workers. Sir Titus Salt's Saltaire—designed by the Bradford architects Lockwood and Mawson and built in 1851–53 (fig. 14)—also used architecture to inculcate the merits of industry and temperance. The streets are as monotonous and geometric as Coketown's and similarly represent the idea that social reform can be achieved by forcing conformity and rational calculation.

Fig. 14: Salts Mill, Saltaire (1851–53)

Rather than a representation of Preston or some other real place, Coketown is a dystopian projection of the model factory town in a horrendous vision, not of some antiquated system or dying aristocracy as in *Bleak House*, but of a future England governed by Dombey, Bounderby, Gradgrind, & Co. The modern industrial city is characterized as an unnatural and inhuman space in the "keynote" descriptions of Coketown, the archetypal factory town:

> It was a town of red brick, or of brick that would have been red if the smoke and ashes had allowed it; but as matters stood it was a town of unnatural red and black like the painted face of the savage. It was a town of machinery and tall chimneys, out of which interminable serpents of smoke trailed themselves for ever and ever, and never got uncoiled. It had a black canal in it, and a river that ran purple with ill-smelling dye, and vast piles of building full of windows where there was a rattling and a trembling all day long, and where the piston of the steam-engine worked monotonously up and down, like the head of an elephant in a state of melancholy madness. It contained several large streets all very like one another, and many small streets still more like one another, inhabited by people equally like one another, who all went in and out at the same hours, with the same sound upon the same pavements, to do the same work, and to whom every day was the same as yesterday and tomorrow, and every year the counterpart of the last and the next. (HT I, v; 65)

As in the description of the industrial wasteland in *The Old Curiosity Shop*, the elephantine machine threatens to go out of control. This image of a monstrous body alienated from itself expresses the denaturation of the landscape and the dehumanization of the workers. In a remarkably similar description of Manchester in 1861, the English factory town looks to Hippolyte Taine like a huge hard-labor penal colony.[18] The factory, like the school, is a kind of prison whose disciplinary power, in Foucault's reading in *Discipline and Punish* of Bentham's "Panopticon," controls the individual and individuality through the space of its architecture.[19] The abstraction of space makes every part of the city without exception "severely workful." The schoolroom, the churches and chapels, the factories and the laborers themselves are disciplined to statistical determinism and laws of production.

The "vast piles of building," however, do not suggest some constructive purpose, but instead present a confused horror of "rattling" and "trembling" in Mumford's picture of unplanned urban sprawl.[20] The town has grown "piece-meal, every piece in a violent hurry of some one man's purpose, and the whole an unnatural family, shouldering, and trampling, and pressing one another to death" (HT I, v; 65). The variety of chimneys in the stifling workers' quarters are signs which the houses of Coketown put out to suggest that their inhabitants are similarly stunted and crooked (HT I, x; 102), as if to signify the inhuman and unnatural products of extreme rationalization and conformity by coercion. In this Hobbesian jungle, a prison-house of death, Nature is bricked out as hermetically as poisonous gases are bricked in.

The argument from Nature attacks the underlying Victorian advocacy of competition in the market economy as inevitably ameliorist. Not for nothing does Sissy mistake Natural for National Prosperity, for this is very much the issue at stake in the contest of Macaulay's representation of National Prosperity versus

Southey's Romantic opposition of natural to unnatural beauty. Coketown is an "unnatural" town of red brick, and it is blackened by smoke "like the painted face of a savage" (HT I, v; 65). The simile echoes Carlyle's criticism in *Past and Present* of laissez-faire economics with its jungle law of savagery, as well as De Tocqueville's and Taine's conclusion that the factories had turned civilization into unnatural savagery.[21] The true face of civilization beneath the mask of progress and rationality is exposed in an analogy between colonialism and the treatment of English workers, along the lines of Richard Oastler's comparison earlier in the century of conditions in Bradford worsted mills with colonial plantations, which suggested that native English factory workers were treated worse than slaves.[22]

When the smoke and appalling insanitary conditions of factory towns could not be presented as evidence of energy and progress, it was, as in the 1832 pamphlet by James Kay, *The Moral and Physical Condition of the Working Classes Employed in the Cotton Manufacture in Manchester*, deplored as inevitable side effects of a civilizing factory system, which brought prosperity to the nation and its global empire. On the other hand, Peter Gaskell, in his study of the effects on health of the factory system, *Artisans and Machines* (1836), blames the less enlightened factory owners and in particular the atomization of life in Manchester and other large industrial cities for the sick growth of a degenerate, immoral population, but again the proposed solution is to make the system work more efficiently through education and removal of abuses, a medical remedy which, as will be seen in chapter 6, treats society as a diseased body.

Nature is "undermined," as in Mumford's scheme of "Abbau," because mining literally undermines the environment, but also because meaning is undermined: the closed space of Gradgrindery is as empty and void as the disused collieries, as is the cellarage and vaults in the schoolroom. The city's destruction of the "wild country" is actually reversing the process of civilization, as in *The Old Curiosity Shop*, into pits of hellfire. In the significantly titled chapter "No Way Out," Dickens again strikes the "key-note" for his description of the city.

> The Fairy palaces burst into illumination, before pale morning showed the monstrous serpents of smoke trailing themselves over Coketown. A clattering of clogs upon the pavement; a rapid ringing of bells; and all the melancholy-mad elephants, polished and oiled up for the day's monotony, were at their heavy exercise again. (HT I, xi; 107)

The City of Man mocks Nature and consigns the work of God to oblivion next to that of man. The "fairy palaces" are really monstrous infernos and the "forests" of looms are scaffolds, not picnic-sites. The natural elements themselves engender death, not life, because of the high levels of environmental pollution, for "so does the eye of Heaven itself become an evil eye, when incapable or sordid hands are interposed between it and the things it looks upon to bless" (HT II, i; 147). Following Carlyle's attack on the worship of Mammon and in the spirit of the novel's "inscription" to the author of *Past and Present*, each of the different denominational chapels in the "ugly citadel" is presented as "a pious warehouse," so different from Sleary's equestrian temple. The sacrilegious parody of the new mercantile faith which teaches that all relations and values are based on facts concludes with a hilarious send-up of the Doxology: "and what you couldn't state in figures, or show to be purchaseable in the cheapest market and saleable in the dearest, was not, and never should be, world without end, Amen" (HT I, v; 66).

In order to hammer home the opposition of the unnatural machine-world mentality of Gradgrindery and a more humane, more truthful outlook, the novel sets up juxtapositions of humanity versus inhumanity in accordance with the keynote plan of Coketown's ideological territory. The private world of the individual, the claims of civil liberty, and humanity itself get swallowed up by the demands of the public sphere. The false rhetoric of Bounderby demands that private concerns be of no concern to the public sphere (that is to say, to the interests of those holding economic and political power). Stephen Blackpool walks along the streets of Coketown, chewing a little bread, on his way to see Bounderby, comfortably at lunch on chop and sherry. Stephen's desperate plight cannot touch the great man, who can only see simple causes and self-interest. There is a law for the rich and another for the poor. Stephen cannot afford a divorce, therefore he can have no redress for his personal troubles. His conclusion that "*'tis* a muddle" (HT I, xi; 113; emphasis in the original) explodes the supposed order of a mathematically rational and infallible system of the happiness of the greatest number, which is shown to mean the interests of the manufacturers. This provokes Bounderby's warning to Stephen that the institutions of England, the political and social institutions of representation, are none of his piece-work. If Hands complain, reasons Bounderby, they must be looking for venison and turtle soup with a golden spoon. Bounderby's answer to trade-union militancy is to have agitators transported. Yet Blackpool, given a chance to explain his position in front of his employer and the gentleman from London, James Harthouse, after he has been sent to Coventry for not joining his comrades, warns that laissez-faire policies only perpetuated the evil of the system: "lettin alone will never do't. Let thousands upon thousands alone, aw leading the like lives and aw faw'en into the like muddle, and they will be as one, and yo will be as anoother, wi' a black unpassable world betwixt yo ..." (HT II, v; 182).

In his blue chamber, surrounded by the statistical representation of Blue Books, Gradgrind—as an M.P., an agent of political representation—likewise fails to perceive the "muddle" seen by Stephen.[23] *Bleak House* similarly shows the muddy muddle of the city and of Chancery which can give no coherent sense of progress or rationality in the social order, much to the confusion of Jo in that novel. The exposure of what Carlyle in *Past and Present* called an unilluminated chaos collapses utilitarian and positivist representations of the economy of human relations, such as Henry Buckle's materialist *History of Civilization in England* (1857) which dissected the "moral anatomy" of society. Buckle had read every book there was to read, and Dickens evidently had little patience for this "perfect Gulf of information," whose habit of taking aim before "exploding a mine of knowledge" made him feel he was always on his back with his legs in the air (letter to Frank Stone, 30 May 1854, *Letters* 7: 343)—an image of violent coercion caricatured in Gradgrind's "canon" and the pugilist government official in *Hard Times*.

Like Harriet Martineau's didactic *Illustrations of Political Economy* (1832), those "leaden little books ... showing how the good grown-up baby invariably got to the Savings-bank, and the bad grown-up baby invariably got transported" (HT I, VIII; 90), do not tell the truth. Similarly, Bounderby dismisses workers' grievances because he cannot admit anything that does not support the employers' untrue claims, "the fictions of Coketown." The problem of the laborers is not, after all, reducible to such simple "facts" as alcoholism or narcotics, or other signs of the workers' indolence and depravity, but rather the statistics and Blue Books represent an unnatural false view, that renders invisible the workers' enforced urban condition in their "close rooms," from which they can only escape through death. And—as if to stress the hermetic closure of Coketown—even getting a coffin through the window of the narrow houses is difficult.

Their false visual and political representation underscores the moral blindness of Bounderby and Gradgrind, whose optical powers are on par with Mr. Tickle's display of newly invented spectacles to the Mudfog Association that enabled him to see objects at a great distance in bright colors but rendered him blind to those immediately next to him. Like Oastler's manufacturers, they number among the "large number of most excellent persons and great statesmen [who] could see, with the naked eye, most marvelous horrors on West India plantations, while they could discern nothing whatever in the interior of Manchester cotton mills" (DJ 1: 546).

For all its rational, scientific planning, Coketown remains ever shrouded in haze, an elephantine machine that might one day go out of control. By substituting national for natural growth, by enforcing regulated, closed forms, the Gradgrinds and Bounderbys have turned the model industrial Eden of Coketown into an Inferno. However much the Gradgrinds and Bounderbys claim to dispel the mysteries of life, it is the secrets to which they are blind which must inevitably undo them (presumably they are blinded by the "sick ophthalmia and hallucination" brought on by the motive-grinding and profit-and-loss philosophy derided in *Sartor Resartus*). These secrets are unscientific mysteries penetrated by those who perceive an existence beyond the reality of the city, such as the circus horse-riders who perform their art on the border of, yet beyond, the city. This is a "comprehensive vision" (as F. R. Leavis called it)[24] in the sense of both sight and prophecy.

The choice, however, is not between Town and Country, but between Good and Evil. Tom takes the money and goes to the bad, implicating Stephen in his sinister machinations. Louisa, drawing on her sympathy through imagination, wants to put money to the good: she offers money to Stephen who has resolved to quit town. The key to social change is individual moral regeneration, an attitude that contests a utilitarian understanding of society as governed by economic law and a Benthamite view of an unchanging human nature, motivated by the desire for pleasure while avoiding pain. Stephen, who is tied to a drunken woman by an unfair law, overcomes temptation. He lives up to his naming for a martyr by keeping his oath and suffering for it. Stephen almost incredibly shares with Oliver Twist a "perfect integrity," though he is assisted by his ministering Angel, Rachael.

The morality of the situation defeats its economic logic. Louisa falls for the opportunist Mr. James Harthouse and goes down, lower and lower. Her symbolic descent is observed by Mrs. Sparsit on her fanciful Giant's Staircase, mindful of her own social descent, or her phony representation of it, as well as alluding to political fall on the grand staircase of the Ducal Palace in Venice in Byron's *Marino Faliero*.[25] Yet Louisa is freed at last from her mental and moral servitude to the empire of Bounderby. In the three-dimensional model of the city, descent implies eventual spiritual ascent. Louisa must adjust her spatial relationship to the city and must reread Stephen's behavior which she had earlier misinterpreted according to the Gradgrind representation of things.

The answer is not to be found in an escape to the country, where, following the trend by manufacturers to gentrify themselves (described for example in Mrs. Gaskell's *Mary Barton*), Bounderby has taken a country retreat in a rustic spot. Bounderby brings with him his unnatural city identity, "bullying" the very pictures, which he contemptuously devalues. Horsekeeping is not for him, though he bids Harthouse welcome to bring down horses, for he sees no utility in having more than one horse, in keeping with the utilitarian teaching of the model school. Moreover, the idea insults his self-image of a maggot grown large (HT II, VII; 197).

There is, in fact, "No Way Out." Indeed, when Sissy and Rachael go for a walk in the country, "midway between the town and Mr. Bounderby's retreat," they discover that the "green landscape" is "blotted" by the urban industrial wasteland and the Sunday peace is broken only by nonconformist larks (HT III, VI; 283). It is here that they find the fugitive Stephen Blackpool lying injured in a disused pit called, significantly, the Old Hell Shaft. Stephen is rescued from his descent into Hell, and his innocence is established, largely through the instrument of Louisa and her reformed father. He is then carried in the direction of the star that guides him to eternal salvation "through humility, sorrow, and forgiveness" (HT III, VI; 291–92). We are to suppose that the heavenly city is reached through a descent to hell and a moral reevaluation of the ideal home which he cannot enjoy on this earth. In *Our Mutual Friend* Betty Higden too escapes the cruel degradation of the Poor Laws by posthumous salvation, dying in the arms of Lizzie Hexam, an agent of regeneration through love and the imagination like Sissy. The movement is up and beyond, to a transcendental Other World uncorrupted by the city. The christological plot structure is emphasized by the book titles "Sowing," "Reaping," and "Garnering," as well as the gospel references in the chapter headings, "The One Thing Needful" and "Murdering the Innocents." Coketown is a type of Inferno; its serpents are symbolic of the Fall, the ultimate corrupted Garden that reaps an unnatural harvest in which the seed falls on barren ground.[26] The image of the city as wilderness, which Robert Southey applied to London in the *Colloquies*, thus relates to Coketown's twin image as Babel and Babylon. The lie of a unified sign system (one language) conceals a confusion (Blackpool's "muddle") comparable with the legal Babel of *Bleak House*.

FENCING THE SHAFTS

"For oh," say the children, "we are many,
And we cannot run or leap;
If we cared for any meadows, it were merely
To drop down in them and sleep."
—Elizabeth Barrett Browning, "The Cry of the Children"

We honour the poet, whose heart yearns after the beautiful and true.... But the discoveries of a Newcomen, and a Watt, and the inventions of a Cartwright, a Kay, a Wyatt, and an Arkwright, excite in our minds wonder more intense and admiration more profound.
—Robert Lamb, "The Manufacturing Poor,"
Fraser's Magazine, January 1848

The factory town was an unknown world for the wealthy Londoner addressed by Robert Lamb, but William Cooke Taylor warns us in his *Tour of the Manufacturing Districts of Lancashire* (1842) that outsiders expecting the stereotyped inferno would be disappointed. An inveterate anti-Corn Law Leaguer, Taylor insists that the factory system has wrought an irrevocable and unprecedented revolution, for which there was no precedent that could prepare the observer conceptually or socially. Taylor is writing in the spirit of useful knowledge against the current of anti-urban prejudice and ignorance among English intellectuals intimidated by the emergence of an urban proletariat, whom they regard as an elemental tidal wave which threatens the riot and disorder that accompanied the economic depression of the early forties. This is a force of fire and water that cannot be turned back, for the factory operatives cannot in times of depression be returned to farm labor or the rural parish even if the land could support them.[27]

In keeping with his criticism in his *Natural History of Society* of the artificial division and distrust between the classes, Taylor argues that it is restrictive legislation and ignorance which are largely responsible for a suffering and wretchedness more unjust than the worst cellars of Liverpool or wynds of Edinburgh.[28] Manchester, the self-proclaimed commercial hub of the universe, is, like Coketown, severely workful and strikes the observer as gloomy or frantic according to the state of business in the Exchange. The laborers' districts are poor, hurriedly built, and overcrowded; they are characterized by pollution, class segregation, and destitution. Taylor ascribes these conditions to immigration of unskilled workers, particularly Irish, and to a connection he makes between morality and mortality. Conditions, however, do not seem to be quite as obscene and inhuman as in Kay's earlier investigation of Manchester's laboring poor. In response to opponents of the factory system, it is in small manufacturing towns and semirural districts that Taylor presents evidence for the morality of indigenous mill workers and the benevolence of employers such as the Ashworth brothers, who are motivated by their own interests as much as by philanthropy; they promote mutual understanding in their relations with the workers, particularly through "correct" industrial management and "moral restraint" in insistence on cleanliness, chastity, and decency, which safeguarded the health of a skilled labor force that could not easily be replaced.[29] The machines are not monsters devouring children, accidents being rare, and the toil is neither excessive nor incessant. Factories are benign places of comfort which offered better standards of living and working conditions than farms or mines. The magnitude of the Grants—models for the Cheeryble brothers in *Nicholas Nickleby*—is acknowledged in a public memorial in the ancient forests of Rosendale, now transformed by a prosperous textile industry. The villain of the market forces which have reduced factory workers to subsistence wages or actual starvation is of course the Corn Laws, not the machine or capitalism. Only cynics, Taylor retorts to critics of the first edition of his *Tour*, would say the workers are too fearful of job security to complain or to wreck the employers' property. Taylor's personal investigation of macroeconomic, historical, or social processes is nevertheless no less ideologically biased than the preachers of Political Economy and defenders of child labor or unregulated hours. Such descriptions aim to inculcate in the laborers, as the statistician J. R. McCulloch put it, "the principles that must determine their condition in life," above all the advantage to them of mechanization,[30] and to encourage in the employers what Kay so happily termed "enlightened benevolence."[31]

Discipline to morality and regulation of sexual behavior are also recommended as a remedy for the brutalizing effect of the factory system by Peter Gaskell in his study of the effects of steam-powered machines on the human body, *Artisans and Machinery: The Moral and Physical Condition of the Manufacturing Population Considered with Reference to Mechanical Substitutes for Human Labour* (1836). Indeed, the industrial city and the monstrous steam-engine that powered the factories were often associated in the medical literature with malformation of the human body and deviant sexuality. Gaskell adduced medical evidence to show physiological malformation in bone structure and deterioration in general physique among factory workers in large towns. He claimed the high temperatures in cotton-mills encouraged early puberty and, together with proximity of the sexes for long hours of repetitive mindless working at the machines, led to extramarital intercourse and general demoralization, including loss of family values and domesticity, while "too early sexual excitement" and long hours at the loom allegedly caused female factory workers to become masculine in voice and "unsexual" in appearance.[32] Urban industrialization was producing a "degenerate race."[33]

Dickens had little personal experience of mechanical mass production (his own brief stint in the Blacking Warehouse hardly counts). He is interested as a novelist neither in actual conditions nor in the sound economic principles of the division of labor, but is concerned with the moral effects of industrialization on the human spirit. In *The Old Curiosity Shop* machines have become autonomous monsters, huge weird clanking things that suck life out of the earth and the workers, while in the more insidious merging of worker and machine, the machine seems to operate and stop in Stephen Blackpool's own head (HT I, x; 103). The "attributes of Coketown" cannot after all be separated from the workers' alienation from the products of their labor, the "comforts of life which found their way all over the world" (HT I, v; 65). This is an alienation from both self and environment which Karl Marx would have appreciated, but would have analyzed quite differently. It parodies a failed attempt to naturalize the factory system. The canal is black and polluted by purple dye. The heat is unnatural, confining and asphyxiating. It is unpleasantly hot among the "smoke-serpents." In summer the heat is "stifling" and in autumn it is just as unpleasantly damp and cold on the streets.

Much has been made of Dickens's article "On Strike" (*Household Words*, 11 February 1854) on the textile mill strike of 1853–54 in Preston. The strike was a test of union power after the employers responded to the demand for a ten-percent pay rise with a lockout and the workers had to rely on voluntary contributions in order to survive (the strike collapsed in April 1854). What has been overlooked is the consistency with which Dickens takes neither side in his article because he cannot accept that all questions must be settled according to Political Economy: "Masters right, or men right; masters wrong, or men wrong; both right, or both wrong; there is certain ruin to both in the continuance of or frequent revival of this breach. And from the ever-widening circle of their decay, what drop in the social ocean shall be free!" (DJ 3: 210). The plea for arbitration and for a more truthful view of the workers, who are characterized by a brotherly love and a respect for law and order, may sound to us foolishly idealistic, but it does reflect an underlying message of the novel that the confrontation of men and masters must be reappraised as a human one with rights and wrong on both sides.

Dickens caricatures the employer Mr. Snapper as complaining that the hands want some grinding to bring them to their senses; like that other grinder, Mr. Gradgrind, he cannot see anything other than in stereotyped Political Economic terms. Dickens retorts "that Political Economy was a great and useful science in its own way and in its own place; but that I did not transplant my definition of it from the Common Prayer Book, and make it a great king above all gods" (DJ 3: 198). What Dickens objected to was the making of Political Economy into an absolutist inhuman system applied with coercion. Both masters and workers, he warned, were wrong in persisting with confrontation instead of arbitration, because violence would only lead to mutual bitterness and national decay (another motif carried through from the threat of moral contagion in *Bleak House*). It was the blind subservience to the principles of Political Economy that was wrong; as Dickens wrote to Charles Knight, thanking him for a copy of the latter's *Knowledge is Power* (30 December 1854), it was "those who see figures and averages, and nothing else—the representatives of the wickedest and most enormous vice of this time—the men who ... will do more to damage the real useful truths of political economy, than I could do (if I tried) in my whole life" *(Letters* 8: 492). And Dickens wrote of Mr. Gradgrind that "there is reason and good intention in much that he does—in fact, in all that he does—but that he over-does it. Perhaps by dint of his going his way, and my going mine, we shall meet at last at some halfway house where there are flowers on the carpets, and a little standing-room for Queen Mab's Chariot among the Steam Engines" (letter to Henry Cole, 17 June 1854, *Letters* 7: 354).

Dickens was on record as being opposed to strikes on the grounds that they were a breach of the responsibility workers held toward the employers, who had invested their capital, and toward the public, who entrusted them with their safety ("Railway Strikes," *Household Words*, 11 January 1851), though Dickens had earlier in his career spoken on behalf of the striking journalists on the *Daily News*. Dickens believed the workers to be a decent lot, only they were led astray by demagogues and professional speakers. The quiet order and tolerance of a union meeting in Preston which Dickens attended and described in "On Strike" contrast with the demagoguery in the novel of Slackbridge, who is *slack* in bridging the class divide. Not much faith is shown here in the trade unions to safeguard the individual interests of their members. Stephen's oath might, indeed, reflect a belief that strike action would be counterproductive and that violence was reprehensible.[34] What Dickens complains of in "Railway Strikes" is the sheer waste of energy caused by strikes, which are not going to break the "iron law" of wages but will, by the unemployment they will bring, actually worsen the workers' conditions; the same danger of destructiveness persuades the women to restrain the unemployed mob from violence against the earlier background of Chartism in *The Old Curiosity Shop*. This is no doubt why Dickens could safely appease Mrs. Gaskell whose *North and South* appeared in *Household Words* from September 1854 and who was concerned that there might be overlap in their competing fictions if Dickens intended to have a strike in his: "The monstrous claims at domination made by a certain class of manufacturers, and the extent to which the way is made easy for working men to slide down into discontent under such hands, are within my scheme, but I am not going to strike" (letter of 21 April 1854, *Letters* 8: 320).

Dickens the social reformer is too often seen only as the converter of Scrooge. Yet there is no mistaking Dickens's awareness of the appalling conditions of the laborers and of the blame that lay in the manufacturers' resistance to regulation and reform on the grounds that they interfered with the principle of free trade, an excuse which is spared no irony in *Hard Times*. The factory accidents are in fact alluded to in Stephen's dying speech attacking government unwillingness to do anything about unfenced machinery and mine shafts. His mention of Rachael's sister in book II, chapter xiii, a child victim of a factory accident, was accompanied by a footnote reference in the corrected proofs (later deleted) to Henry Morley's piece "Ground in the Mill" which appeared in the same issue of *Household Words* (22 April 1854) as chapters vii–viii of *Hard Times*. This would have introduced a direct statement on the current industrial dispute that would have been more in keeping with "industrial" novels like Mrs. Gaskell's *Mary Barton* and Disraeli's *Sybil*, or with the reports of commissions of inquiry and medical or social investigators. The suffering of factory children in particular did draw comment in an earlier novel, *Nicholas Nickleby*, in a contrast with sunburnt gypsy girls who are "not crippled by distortions, imposing an unnatural and horrible penance upon their sex," whose "lives are spent, from day to day, at least among the waving trees, and not in the midst of dreadful engines which make young children old before they know what childhood is, and give them the exhaustion and infirmity of age, without, like age, the privilege to die" (NN L; 664).

The deliberate omission of direct and explicit documentation of the horrors of the factory system in *Hard Times* speaks for Dickens's artistic purpose, not at all an attempt to whitewash the employers or ignore abuses of the factory system. A description of Rachael's little sister's horrific mangling to death would have unbalanced the emotional weight of the novel and to make of Stephen what Dickens quite obviously does not want him to be, an ideological vehicle in the propaganda war between masters and men. Stephen is urged by Rachael to let these things be, and he promises to do so (the apparent explanation for his opting out of the union). Readers of the novel would in any case have been well aware of the horrors of the factory system from the public debates over the last two decades around the Factory Bills and the campaign in *Household Words* in 1854–55 for enforcement of safety regulations, including Henry Morley's piece, which sufficiently amplified the point that national prosperity was bought at the price of workers' bodies and lives because the government did not fully implement the law in order to protect the employers' interests and pockets.

Morley's piece, moreover, had pleaded for prosaic facts instead of the romantic image of the death of innocent children in poetry, whereas Dickens was arguing in his novel that it required the imagination of poetry and fiction to understand what was really wrong with a system in which individual destinies are understood only in the aggregate, and the public sphere is of no concern to mere Hands such as Stephen. Sissy's inability to understand that accidents are a matter of statistics and have nothing to do with the grief of bereaved families refutes Martineau's comments on the subject. It is this tension between the public and private to which Macaulay called attention when pleading for the Ten Hours Bill (speaking in the House of Commons, 22 May 1846) on the grounds that health and education were matters that belonged to the public sphere and could be regulated without any restriction of laissez-faire, just as the principles of Adam Smith's *Wealth of Nations* were regulated and policed by the state. It is not hard to see the paradox in the manufacturers' argument for liberty, and it is parodied in the coercion with which facts are to be enforced in the commissioners' millennium envisaged by the government inspector in *Hard Times*. So Martineau's attack on *Hard Times* is very much on target when it comes to how and by whom the national interest is to be represented and what exactly is its relation to the individual. Individuals, she argues, have no voice in what is not their business. Bounderby repeats this advice to Stephen, and elsewhere he insists that any "imaginative qualities" other than his monopoly on truth are mere disguises for demands of turtle soup with a golden spoon (III III, 262).

The question which occupies so many critics—the bearing of the omission of factory accidents on Dickens's real-life political beliefs—can surely be relevant only if the literary text is put in a polarized position of fictional or historical discourse, and if experience is confused with representation. When they compare *Hard Times* to Engels's *Condition of the Working-Class*, Marxist critics often conclude that Dickens suffered from middle-class prejudice and subscribed to the very system he criticized[35] or that he failed to represent the working classes "truthfully."[36] On the contrary, what Dickens is trying to show is that the working classes do not conform to the purely statistical representation of reality projected by Political Economists and would-be reformers who follow the theories of Malthus and Adam Smith, for whom the younger Gradgrinds are named. It is nevertheless true that Dickens describes the laborers hazily, as an outsider, without the sympathy, however sentimental, for their actual conditions that Mrs. Gaskell shows in *North and South*. Dickens holds far less committed a view, and in the long run a far less utopian one, than Mrs. Gaskell's when compared with the interclass cooperation and affirmative action which Margaret brings about through her ethical self-reformation and moral influence.

Reading *Hard Times* in its serialization in Dickens's *Household Words* was inevitably contextual with *North and South* and articles that appeared in the journal which placed it as a "novel of social reform" in the thick of the Condition of England debate. These articles helped shape a newly influential public opinion that pressured government to enforce factory legislation (for example, the safety provisions of the 1844 Factory Act) and they campaigned against an incompetence that was costing lives in both the factories and the Crimea.[37] Some scholars have found contradictions or inconsistencies in the novel when compared with *Household Words*,[38] yet the attempt to resolve the problematic status of *Hard Times* on the borders of fiction and life underestimates the difference between the mode and the aims of representation of, respectively, art and journalism, not to mention the difficulty of establishing an authorial (or editorial) position behind the rhetorical strategies of the various discourses which they construct.

The connection of political and fictional representations has often been made, but usually in an empiricist matching of Dickens's words (in fiction) to his deeds (in his speeches and correspondence).[39] Catherine Gallagher, in *The Industrial Reformation of English Fiction*, contends that the representation of facts and the representation of values were in a relationship of tension, which made the form of the polemical novel itself an object of inquiry and of conflicting claims. The constraint on metaphorical analogies such as that of worker and slave or family and social institutions required a new practice of realism that would resolve the questions of environmental determinism and individual liberty in Coketown's "unnatural family" (I, x; 102). Gallagher reads *Hard Times* as metaphorically discursive, together with Mrs. Gaskell's *North and South*, on the tensions between public and private realms. Insisting on the family-society analogy as the primary organizing principle of the metaphors in this novel, she interprets the novel as a displacement of the generic conventions of the family romance.[40] Gallagher asserts that in both *Hard Times* and in *North and South* their authors "attempted to describe industrial society and present solutions to the problems of class antagonism"; both "ostensibly propose that social cohesion can be achieved by changing the relationship between family and society, by introducing cooperative behavior, presumably preserved in private life, into the public realm." Both, however, realize "contradictions latent in social paternalism and domestic ideology" and "ultimately propose the isolation of families from the larger society."[41] The family model in the biological analogy of society is, nevertheless, not consistent in *Hard Times* since, apart from giving support for spontaneous feeling, neither Stephen nor the circus people offer a practical alternative to Gradgrind's unnatural relations based on calculation or Mrs. Sparsit's calculating housekeeping.

Reading *Hard Times* contextually with Charles Kingsley's *Yeast* (serialized in *Fraser's Magazine* in 1848) and his novel about a London poet-tailor, *Alton Locke*, Mrs. Gaskell's *North and South* and *Mary Barton*, and the writings of Carlyle, one might expect to find some proposal for resolution of the class conflict. However, Carlyle's candidacy in *Past and Present* of the Captains of Industry as social and managerial leaders contrasts with the false Bounderby type who is largely an instrument for the negation of two "popular fictions" (misrepresentations): the self-made man and the unjust claims of some mill-owners in hearings before parliamentary commissions.[42] Rouncewell, the Iron Master in *Bleak House*, is a more ambivalent type of factory owner, who, like Bounderby, is also the banker of a northern town; he would be unsuited for Carlyle's new *aristos* because he has himself adopted the Mammonism and self-interest of the old non-working aristocracy.[43] Doyce, in *Little Dorrit*, is a more sympathetic and honest man, an inventor and not just an entrepreneur, yet his factory is "filled with benches, and vices, and tools, and straps, and wheels; which, when they were in gear with the steam-engine, went tearing round as though they had a suicidal mission to grind the business to dust and tear the factory to pieces" (LD xxiii; 312). Curiously, the end product of all this murderous grinding is unnamed, and while Arthur's business sense is commended for being based on his earnestness and feelings, it would appear to be seriously flawed when the business crashes. Dickens was perhaps being impractically idealistic on this point, but in his satire of banking scandals and an incompetent bureaucracy, he is responsible for some confusion in suggesting that the state obstructed science, when everyone knew that the advancement of applied technology was the priority of reformers, from Prince Albert down, who saw it as furthering laissez-faire and prosperity. Raymond Williams thought Dickens had canceled out any "normal" representation and ended up in an anarchic adolescent confusion about industrial society that did not distinguish between Gradgrindery and the many sincere reformers, like Edwin Chadwick, who were trying to alleviate its evils.[44]

The notion of Fancy in *Hard Times* should tell us that it is a faulty vision which Dickens criticizes and readers who test the historical accuracy or verisimilitude of Dickens's picture of the industrial landscape miss that fundamental aim. As David Lodge notes:

> The reason is not that criteria of empirical truthfulness are wholly irrelevant (they are not); but that in referring from fiction to fact and back again, the critics are ignoring a vitally important stage in the creative process by which narratives are composed, viz. the transformation of the deep structure of the text into its surface structure.... It is in this process that the particular literary identity of a novel, and therefore the range of reader-responses appropriate to it, are determined.[45]

Roger Fowler has reinforced David Lodge's insight in his Bakhtinian reading of *Hard Times* as a polyphonic novel. The lack of linguistic differentiation which Fowler finds in Bakhtin's theory is rectified by applying M. A. K. Halliday's terminology to a discourse analysis of the speech patterns in the text. Taking that approach further in a modal analysis, Jean-Jacques Weber has shown the tensions between the ideological discourses of the fictional worlds in the novel. In Weber's view, the novel emerges as lacking any monological authorial or authoritative discourse because the issues it raises are left open; the covert authorial voice, undiscerned by most critics, simply makes a humanitarian appeal for reason and compassion in maintenance of the status quo. I would argue that Dickens is pleading for moral improvement through a sympathetic portrayal of individuals such as Rachael—an archetypal matriarch—whose forbearance influences Stephen and stays his hand from murdering his wife. Forbearance is not approval or acceptance, but exemplary of a Christian compassion through an imaginative empathy which resists easy classification into class, family, or gender. The siting of salvation in the hereafter and in the spirit does not detract from the conclusion that individuals can bring about change in this world. The city, with its mills and schools, can be put to the Good—just as the mill and the school in *Our Mutual Friend* are not inherently evil. It all depends on a responsive and responsible relationship with environment, in contrast to utilitarian determinism.

THE AESTHETICS OF FANCY

> Then who so will with virtuous deeds assay
> To mount to heaven, on Pegasus must ride,
> And with sweete Poets verse be glorified.
> —Spenser, *The Ruines of Time*

How then does *Hard Times* propose that the chasm between men and masters be bridged? The answer, in my reading of the novel, is in the text's own performance, which shows that the imagination is not idle, as Bounderby would have it, but that what Dickens calls Fancy is doing its work and doing it usefully. Far from merely subscribing to a status quo sugared by compassion, it shows through exemplary stories that a Benthamite rational egoism cannot be a training for life and that there are other elements left out of Bentham's sum of human motivation, foremost among them, as J. S. Mill had also noted, the role of the imagination in formation of moral personality.[46]

Although critics have routinely examined Fancy in *Hard Times*,[47] they have not always noticed the larger implications for the novel of Dickens's often cited article "Fraud on the Fairies" (*Household Words*, 1 October 1853). In that article Dickens blasted George Cruikshank, the illustrator of *Oliver Twist*, for altering fairy tales as a propaganda tool in favor of teetotalism (which was far from being his favorite cause). For one thing, the conscription of innocent children's stories for any agenda was unjustifiable and sounded like the didactic utilitarian literature of the sort Dickens proceeded to satirize in an updated parody of "Cinderella" which distorted the time-honored originals. Among the reports of the Mudfog Association there is a similar satire of utilitarian attacks on children's ignorance of Fact arising from their indulgence in Fancy: the story of Jack and Jill might be laudable if the children were toiling uphill on a domestic errand, but it was inexcusable that Jill should laugh at Jack's disaster (DJ 1: 527). However, this was also an occasion, as Dickens explained to Angela Burdett-Coutts, to launch a plea for "a little more fancy among children and a little less fact" (18 September 1853, *Letters* 7: 148).

> In an utilitarian age, of all other times, it is a matter of grave importance that Fairy Tales should be respected. Our English red tape is too magnificently red to ever be employed in the tying up of such trifles, but every one who has considered the subject knows full well that a nation without fancy, without some romance, never did, never can, never will, hold a great place under the sun. (DJ 3: 168)

This appeal to empire-building is a way of arguing for capitalism with a human face, for only Fancy can introduce "gentleness and mercy" into working lives; it is a defense of literature as a moral agent indispensable to a humane society that abhors tyranny and brute force.

The plea that fantasy should be left inviolate is not just asking for respect for the fairy tales of childhood; it is a plea for imagination in literature and in the workplace. A literature which is neither utilitarian nor instrumental recognizes the true poetry of the "fairy-tales of Science" (to use Tennyson's phrase) by showing that the wonders of Nature can be appreciated only through the imagination and reminding us that if there had been less wondering and wonderment there might have been fewer inventions. James Watt would have been poorer by a penny for his thoughts in that apocryphal tale of his improvement of the steam engine, and Sol Gill would have had no marvelous tales to tell. For Tennyson and Dickens, the discoveries in geology, anthropology, archeology, and evolution theory that had transformed intellectual horizons, as advances in optics and physics had done in the late seventeenth century, opened their eyes to the poetry of science, though not every statistician could see the science in poetry.[48]

"Fancy" was used too diversely and variously for us to seriously relate Dickens's use of it to Coleridge's seminal distinction of "Fancy" and "Imagination" or to allow us to identify in more than general terms a romantic concern with the imagination. Nonetheless, a similar opposition of Fancy and Fact can be found at the core of the culture wars of mid-century. Cardinal Newman's anti-utilitarian theory of education, *The Idea of a University*, argued that knowledge was not confined to the valuation of Utility and that Reason brought not only knowledge, but also an idea of the world perceived with the senses and the imagination. Romantics thought they perceived a tendency of science to reduce the illusion of poetry to what Keats called in "Lamia," a "dull catalogue of common things."[49] Though not at all opposed to science, in "The Preface" to *Lyrical Ballads*, Wordsworth kept his faith in poetry to resist the almost "savage torpor" of the industrial city which, along with the artificial melodrama of the Gothic, blunted the senses. In *England and the English* (1833), Dickens's friend and literary mentor Edward Bulwer-Lytton regretted that such utilitarian writing had ousted the Romantic novels of Scott which taught the principle of benevolence. Despite his respect for intellectuals such as Miss Martineau and his acknowledgment of their benefit to reform, he feared "lest the desire for immediate and palpable utility should stint the capacities of genius to the trite and familiar truths"—a fear that would be diminished when critics recognized the "inexhaustible" power of the imagination.[50] Likewise, George Eliot, who had no great love for dogmatic abstract theory, declared her fictional portrait was not going to conform to statistical findings in chapter 5 of "The Sad Fortunes of the Reverend Amos Barton" (1857), and Mrs. Gaskell defended her ignorance of Political Economy in *Mary Barton*.

For Macaulay, however, in his 1825 essay on Milton (and as we saw in his critique of Southey), the scientific representation of the world was irreconcilable with a poetic description. "Fact" had its proponents, too. The "useful knowledge" disseminated in the cheap literature of the 1830s served as propaganda for the virtues of Political Economy, a kind of economic Protestantism with Adam Smith as its god and Harriet Martineau his prophet.[51] And *Knight's Cyclopedia of the Industry of All Nations* (1851), published the year of the Great Exhibition, showed what happened when knowledge was reduced to an exhibition of useful production (Cambridge, for example, is dismissed as being merely a place of education, and there is no entry for Oxford). The proliferation of scientific investigation and of scientific writing did have an enormous impact on the way Victorians thought about their world and not least on the novel of social reform, which, as Patrick Brantlinger has shown, worked as the equivalent of the blue books (so beloved of Mr. Gradgrind) in spreading knowledge. If Charles Bray could prove statistically in *Philosophy of Necessity* (1841) that marriages were based on economic factors rather than love,[52] then a Gradgrind who could advise Louisa in the same statistical spirit is perhaps not an exaggerated invention. What *Hard Times* shows, however, is that Gradgrind's statistical account of society clearly contradicts the lived life of individuals, which it is the business of fiction to show.

At the end of the "key-note" description of Coketown in book I, chapter v, in the transition to the introduction of the circus people, the narrator wonders whether there was not in the employers' stereotype of the ungrateful laborers and the Political Economists' statistical tables one thing that had been

> deliberately set at nought? That there was any Fancy in them demanding to be brought into healthy existence instead of struggling on in convulsions? That exactly in the ratio as they worked long and monotonously, the craving grew within them for some physical relief—some relaxation, encouraging good humour and good spirits, and giving them a vent—some recognized holiday, though it were but for an honest dance to a stirring band of music—some occasional light pie in which even M'Choakumchild had no finger—which craving must and would be satisfied aright, or must and would inevitably go wrong, until the laws of Creation were repealed? (HT I, v; 67–68)

Immediately following this plea, Gradgrind and Bounderby repair to the Pegasus's Arms, a pub which is appropriate "home" to Sleary's horseriders, since it was Pegasus's kick which brought out of the mountain the soul-inspiring waters of Hippocrene that came to be associated with poetic inspiration. Of course, the winged horse behind the bar displays a low form of entertainment, but that is without doubt a deliberate choice. Pegasus was an emblem inevitably linked with the equestrian circus,[53] yet it is not a matter of circus "philothopy" pitted against Gradgrindery—the circus people have a poor idea of education and are mostly illiterate—but a question of what is wrong with Gradgrind's definition of social function and of precisely what is at fault in urban industrial civilization.

Fancy is here both aim and mode of representation. It is through the imagination that we must accept the urgent necessity of communication between employers and employees, of finding a language of representation that would somehow bring them closer to mutual understanding—when the starlight clears the muddle, the dying Stephen realizes some have "been wantin' in unnerstan'in me better," but he has also been wanting in understanding others better, and "in our judgements, like as in our doins, we mun bear and forbear" (HT III, vi; 290–91). In a passage opening the chapter "Stephen Blackpool" that has apparently nothing to do with the subject, Dickens writes sarcastically: "I entertain a weak idea that the English people are as hard-worked as any people upon whom the sun shines. I acknowledge to this ridiculous idiosyncrasy, as a reason why I would give them a little more play" (HT I, x; 102). As Sleary advises Gradgrind and Bounderby, people must be amused. What Sleary says neatly connects the themes of art, education, and industrial relations in the novel. It is in line with the thinking behind Dickens's 1853 Birmingham speech, in which he lavished praise on the educational institutions of that town for bringing knowledge and literature to the workers whose places of work were palaces of harmony (*Speeches* 154–60). The ring presented to Dickens on that occasion was in his eyes a fairy ring entrusted to him to keep faith to his mission to widen the readership of literature. One might scoff at this populist rhetoric, though there were employers such as the Preston mill-owner John Goodair, who had sufficient belief in the intellect of his workers to propose in his 1854 pamphlet *Preventing Strikes* that informal discussions on current affairs were a way of educating both sides to mutual understanding; other employers provided reading rooms and restrooms. Nonetheless, there is an unstated argument here that popular culture (and the novel) can be useful in bridging the class divide and fostered values felt to be lacking in utilitarian theories. The story of Sissy Jupe and the dog Merrylegs shows "one, that there ith a love in the world, not all Thelf-interetht after all, but thomething very different; t'other, that it hath a way of calculating or not calculating, whith thomehow or another ith at leatht ath hard to give a name to, ath the wayth of the dogth ith!" (HT III, viii; 308). The circus is not a model society, nor is Dickens extolling "circus values" (especially if we are to judge by the traveling entertainers in *The Old Curiosity Shop*). Yet the circus people represent a childlike sincerity, honesty, and spontaneous compassion missing in the calculating language of Gradgrindery—the "one thing needful," like the faith missing in the hedonistic calculus of pleasure of the Motive-Grinders and Profit-and-Loss Philosophers in the Mill of Logic in *Sartor Resartus*.

Dickens is not simply advocating the merits of popular culture. He is pleading for the necessity within the industrial city of art as recreation (in the sense of both leisure and creativity) and for the necessity of a nonutilitarian art which does not substitute model for reality. "People mutht be amuthed. They can't alwayth be a learning, nor yet they can't be alwayth a working, they an't made for it. You *mutht* have uth, Thquire" (HT III, viii; 308). The preaching of this moral imperative in the mouth of a man like Sleary sounds so uncharacteristic that he is surprised at being such a "Cackler." It is in their deeds, as well as in performance, that the circus people must show compassion in order to refute Gradgrindery, which allows for it neither in its arithmetic nor in its speech. The circus art is, moreover, a narrative art[54] and its rhetoric (not to mention livelihood, like Jupe's) depends on art as skill as well as stratagem, like the deft sleight of hand Dickens learned in the Blacking Warehouse.[55] The analogy of novelist as producer and as performer opposes mechanization in the factory of production and of the spirit by making art a craft.

The importance of the circus to represent that argument can be seen in the fact that the most famous Victorian circus, Astley's, figures large in Dickens's writing, for example in *The Old Curiosity Shop*, where the audience is pictured as plebeian in the illustration by "Phiz," unlike Thackeray's Newcomes who sit in a private lodge at Astley's, which did attract the different classes, as Rowlandson and Pugin carefully recorded in their popular engraving, also used in contemporary posters for the circus (fig. 15). For many years one of London's major attractions,

Astley's Amphitheatre purveyed popular entertainment in the tradition of pantomime and indulged in epic presentations of historical battle scenes as well as low comedy. Astley's followed other Victorian theaters in putting on scenes from *Pickwick Papers* and *Oliver Twist*, among the adaptations of popular lore and literature, so that Dickens's novels were performances in more than one sense.[56]

Fig. 15: Augustus Pugin and Thomas Rowlandson, "Astley's Amphitheatre" (1808)

The circus's connection with pantomime is particularly relevant to Dickens's aesthetics. In the "Stray Chapters" Boz wrote for *Bentley's Miscellany* in March 1837, parallel with the serialization of *Oliver Twist* which satirized utilitarian "philosophy," the pantomime was extolled as the "mirror of life" and it was "this very circumstance" that was the "secret cause" of the audience's "amusement and delight" (DJ 1: 501). Joseph Grimaldi, the renowned Italian clown, transformed English pantomime, which adopted several of the personages of the *commedia del'arte*, such as the pantaloon, the harlequin, and the clown. Dickens wrote an introduction to the 1838 edition of Grimaldi's memoirs, and in this putative essay on mimesis and art he takes up the slapstick comedy of the clown as the central, cathartic figure in the representation of the ups-and-down of life, disappointed love, and the buffoonery of politics. What Dickens calls "the representation of life" inverts the relation of stage and life in Shakespeare's "all the world's a stage" (DJ 1: 507) when the clown takes the harlequin's wand and magically transforms the principal actors, so that (true to Romantic poetics) the familiar is estranged into strange truths. The circus, then, conveys Dickens's understanding of how art should ideally capture both the reader's empathy and imagination. When Jupe fails to do that and the audience stops laughing, he is finished as an artist. The figure of the clown introduces into Dickens's novels a Bakhtinian carnivalization of the everyday, which redeems it through an anarchic subversive laughter, another reason why the circus is a threat to Bounderby and Gradgrind.[57] In the performance of the text, Dickens is borrowing the language of the popular theater, as David Lodge has shown, and he is exploiting the mixed media form of the pantomime.[58] By doing so he is in effect defending the legitimacy of his own aesthetics.

Because imagination serves as mode as well as metaphor for the vision of the novel, the novelist can play the role of both entertainer and moralizing educator. Art as play thus belies any contradiction between *homo ludens* and *homo faber* since it is through the production of the novel that the imagination is brought playfully into sympathy. The circus is a performance of that joining of work and play, and is not supposed to represent a real instrument in social change, like soap for public hygiene, though Paul Schlicke's extensive researches on the historical background in this arena spotlight its importance as adult entertainment.[59] The remark following the description of Astley's in *The Old Curiosity Shop*, "We are all going to the play, or coming home from it" (OCS xl; 380), gives Chris Brooks grounds for linking an Aristotelian theory of mimesis with Dickens's own "magic reel," a "making strange" of the familiar through a showman's act, in which Dickens represents acts of representations by Sleary's showmen or Mrs. Jarley's Wax-Works that foreground the subjective and aesthetic experience of reality.[60]

This would explain why Dickens chose not to represent the workers mimetically, and it explains why he chose to transfer to the circus the humility and kindness he saw in the workers at the union meeting he attended in Preston. This was a site of the imagination, which the factory could not be (however idealistic Dickens's claim for the "special ineptitude" of the circus performers for any act of dishonesty or deceit). The chasm dividing Blackpool and Bounderby is, however, not bridged in the novel, unlike Thornton's recognition in *North and South* that one human heart united him with Higgins, man with master. The possibility of alleviation of strife lies in a mutual understanding that would bring more humane treatment of the laborers through education and art. In his speech to the Birmingham Polytechnic Institute on 28 February 1844 Dickens avowed that education and art could help to prevent machine operatives from degenerating into machines (*Speeches* 61). This, essentially, is Dickens's criticism of Benthamite utilitarianism,[61] but it is also an attack on instrumentalism and plain villainy. For example, Harthouse's cynicism reveals principles not so different from Gradgrind's; the devotion to "firmness" in the Murdstones runs a common theme, as does cruel despotism in education exemplified by Creakle, or the elimination of love, as practiced by Jane Murdstone who turns all feelings to pen and ink; these ideologies are resisted by David Copperfield's imaginative fantasies and reading of novels.

The performance of Fancy negates the utilitarian system by designifying its metalanguage and challenging its rational basis. Among Sissy's happy mistakes, statistics are exposed as "stutterings" (I, IX; 97), and she confuses national with natural prosperity, thinking they ought to be the same. Sissy is taught that the sign "horse" represents a sum total of facts and figures, not a creature for amusement, as in her father's profession. Such definitions were the stuff of the Logic Jonathan Swift detested at Trinity College, Dublin, and in book 4 of *Gulliver's Travels* he inverts the Enlightenment opposition of man as a rational creature to the horse as a whinnying creature. That is an irony picked up in the description of Astley's horseriding in Pugin and Rowlandson's *The Microcosm of London* (1808), which jokes that for Rousseau the horse in its natural state must be happier than civilized man and therefore a worthy teacher to its dancing instructor! The horse was, in Dotheboy's Hall, a useful beast for the schoolchildren to wash down, and Bitzer can dissect the quadruped creature in a thoroughly utilitarian calculation.

A horse, indeed, cannot be depicted on wallpaper, just as flowers cannot be represented on a carpet, according to the government officer inspecting Gradgrind's model school, because such a thing does not exist in reality.

> "You are to be in all things regulated and governed," said the gentleman, "by fact. We hope to have, before long, a board of fact, composed of commissioners of fact, who will force the people to be a people of fact, and of nothing but fact. You must discard the word Fancy altogether. You have nothing to do with it. You are not to have, in any object of use or ornament, what would be a contradiction in fact. You don't walk upon flowers in fact; you cannot be allowed to walk upon flowers in carpets." ... "You must use," said the gentleman, "for all these purposes, combinations, and modifications (in primary colours) of mathematical figures which are susceptible of proof and demonstration. This is the new discovery. This is fact. This is taste." (HT I, ii; 52)

This absurdly reductionist argument claims representation can only be denotative, not connotative, and that there can be no moral or poetical truth, only the iron laws of Political Economy, to be enforced by coercion. It is of course a parody of the language theory in Bentham's *Theory of Fictions* and has little to do with his use of the term "fictions" in the *Chrestomatia*. Bentham, no less than the author of *Bleak House*, was waging war on legal fictions which were "locked up in an illegible character and in a foreign tongue,"[62] what Conversation Kenge calls the "masterly fictions" of legal practice. Yet Bentham found the key to get out of obfuscation in an instrumentalist view of language which tested figurative statements by their utility, category and statistical probability. Together with his belief in scientific progress, this was the foundation of his moral philosophy. Apparently, Bentham, whose writing was contemporary with Kant's *Critique of Pure Reason*, had reacted to the nursery stories inculcated in him as a child and to the phantasms with which he had been terrorized in just the opposite way to Dickens.

To dismiss aspects of reality, to render unpleasant facts invisible, by controlling representation, as the Government Inspector is doing, cuts to the core of Dickens's own novelistic practice and it is crushed by a plot which depends on the discovery of truth and humanity through the workings of fanciful imagination.

When Gradgrind is unable to save Louisa in her fall down the Giant's Staircase, a parody of the conventional melodramatic tableau of the Fallen Woman, he is forced to admit the failure of the System lying insensible at his feet because it is a lie and as false a representation as Bounderby's self-image is shown to be. The Gradgrind system has taught Tom that crime is no more than a statistical law, one which Tom has obeyed in robbing the bank. When Tom implicates Stephen in his crime, it is the circus people and—supreme irony—a performing horse who save Gradgrind from shame and from another product of the Gradgrind school, Bitzer. For the latter the heart can only be a circulatory pump in a physiological system, not an organ of feeling. Bitzer reminds Gradgrind he has learned the utilitarian lesson of self-interest very well: "... I am sure you know that the whole social system is a question of self-interest.... I was brought up in that catechism when I was very young, sir, as you are aware" (HT III, VIII; 303). It is a society in which everything is to be priced and weighed (as Arthur Clennam's parents taught him), a society in which moral improvement is measured in terms of steam locomotion (as Macaulay measured it). Dickens's novel says differently. Gradgrind's conversion, which fulfills the moral pattern that Barbara Hardy finds in Dickens's novels, is brought about by Fancy, which shows compassion to be stronger than self-interest and the heart to be more than a pump. Fancy can bring about change that makes Gradgrind see and feel more humanely.

Fancy has been squeezed out in Coketown so thoroughly that only the imagination can conceptualize its proscription. What greater affront could there be to Gradgrindery than to represent it in imagery borrowed from fairy tales and in flights of fancy which have no practical use and do not relate literally to facts? What could more efficiently debunk its official rhetoric than to ironically describe factories as Fairy Palaces? In the celebrated schoolroom scene at the beginning of the novel, Dickens shows precisely what is absurd in a utilitarian system of representation. The novel opens in

> a plain, bare, monotonous vault of a schoolroom, and the speaker's square forefinger emphasized his observations by underscoring every sentence with a line on the schoolmaster's sleeve. The emphasis was helped by the speaker's square wall of a forehead, which had his eyebrows for a base, while his eyes found commodious cellarage in two dark caves, overshadowed by the wall. The emphasis was helped by the speaker's mouth, which was wide and thin, and hard set. The emphasis was helped by the speaker's voice, which was inflexible, dry, and dictatorial. (HT I, I; 47)

The scene is packed with metaphors that reinforce the characterization of the facts taught in the schoolroom as useless merchandise destined for futile storage. The geometry of this realm of facts is uniformly regular and its space is closed; all is square. Gradgrind's forefinger, coat, legs, shoulders, his mind, all belie the inhuman inflexibility of his system—even his neckcloth is "trained to take him by the throat with an unaccommodating grasp, like a stubborn fact, as it was" (HT I, I; 47). The deliberate overemphasis stresses the totality of the system, but the effect is rendered ludicrous by the fanciful similes of the "plantation of firs" and the "crust of a plum pie," which describe Gradgrind's balding head as if it "had scarcely warehouse-room for the hard facts stored inside." A vault houses both dead corpses and material valuables. The commodification of the children into vessels filled with "imperial gallons of facts" paradoxically renders the all-important facts quite useless. In a similar schoolroom scene in *Our Mutual Friend* the teachings of Scripture are rendered spiritless and indifferent. The square boundaries, suggesting closure of mind, are a recurrent motif, blatant in the description of Coketown, which is undermined by the very same imagination that it would, in a significantly military metaphor, storm away with its canon of facts and replace with a "grim mechanical substitute" (HT I, II; 48).

Gradgrind's world of Facts is an arid desert of utility into which no human warmth is allowed, no irrational inspiration, no spark of the imagination, just as Chesney Wold is devoid of imagination and therefore of love in *Bleak House*, another site of dead spirit and false representation. The fantasy which Louisa dreams into the embers of the fire, in a more defined sense than the storytelling fire read by the unnamed steel foundry worker in *The Old Curiosity Shop* (a cripple in the manuscript), is a claim to a childhood stolen by industrialization. Her sexuality, an "unwholesome" fire, has been repressed. When Louisa, whose imagination has been systematically starved, looks out at the monotonous chimney stacks she declares, much to the consternation of her father, that "when the night comes, Fire bursts out" (HT I, xv; 135). This is the fire missing in the domestic hearth of Stone Lodge, the fire of imagination and sexuality that has turned to ashes, much as Lizzie Hexam's fireside dreaming in *Our Mutual Friend* indicates a similar will to good in terms of a spatial and structural break from evil, by means of an imaginative reading of the past, present, and future akin to the novel's own. Louisa and Tom, contemplating their fates in the Platonic cave in book I, chapter VIII, can only see the shadows. To come to Reason "through the tender light of Fancy" (II IX; 223) is to preserve the Wordsworthian garden of childhood innocence that, at the end of the novel, fortifies the spirit in adversity—the cold ashes of the dissolved household (as I read the last lines)—and adult mortality, in a neoromantic compassion through imaginative empathy.

Sleary's Horse-Riding establishment has encamped on "neutral ground upon the outskirts of the town, which was neither town nor country, and yet was either spoiled" (HT I, III; 55). Its alien bohemian presence encroaches upon urban territory and threatens the industrial city with its more natural lifestyle and alternate space, not just because it is marginal but because it shows rhetorically how unnatural are the "laws" on which Coketown is built. The very sounds issuing from the *wooden* structure of the circus clash with the mechanical harmony in Gradgrind's heartless, *stony* residence. Tyrolean Flower-acts, tricks by a performing dog, and astounding feats by the Emperor of Japan contradict the teaching of the schoolroom that a horse is a purely functional object and not a creature to pamper the Fancy. The carnivalization of social control is more than a distraction from labor, for its performance frees the body from the mechanization of industrial production, as well as from the rules of bourgeois decency (the ladies are not particular about showing their legs).[63] The parody of the Victorian work ethic and the factory system is of course itself a carnivalesque mode. Yet the wooden pavilion is a temporary tabernacle in the wilderness, and the god enshrined "in an ecclesiastical niche of early Gothic architecture" (HT I, III; 55) is money, whose priest is the self-made man. However, the labor done by Sleary, though not productive, is, like the novelist's, useful: the horse, which for Bitzer is no more than a collection of facts, performs for value of amusement but in dancing the Polka the horse is significantly useful to the resolution of the plot and it teaches Gradgrind a lesson at the end of the novel.

Gradgrind raises his offspring as models of eminent practicality, and he must be disappointed when he discovers his own Louisa and Tom peeping in on Art and Nature, a rebellious Adam and Eve tasting from the forbidden Tree of Fancy in the utilitarian utopia. They have transgressed the boundary marking the circus rabble from the "civilized" urban society which would, if it could, confine them to the House of Correction. What divides the "neutral ground" of the Circus from the Town is a "space of stunted grass and dry rubbish" (HT I, III; 56), a symbolic territory that emphasizes the sexual, spiritual, and ideological aridity of Coketown in which Louisa's imagination and sexuality are starved, "a fire with nothing to burn." Her will is subdued, but what she has seen beyond the fence momentarily enlightens her eyes before she is forcibly led back to the castrating, claustrophobic, cold, damp, dark existence of Gradgrindery in Stone Lodge. Tom calls his home "Jaundiced Jail" and so continues Dickens's satire of the jaundiced injustice of the legal system instanced by *Jarndyce and Jarndyce* in *Bleak House* as well as pointing to the image of the modern city as a prison (which I will discuss in the next chapter). The name of Josiah Bounderby, too, recalls the confining *bounds* of this stifling imprisonment, but also suggests, in English upper-class slang, he might be a dishonest cad, a bounder. On the other hand, Stephen Blackpool is named for a natural place (not yet the popular seaside resort it was to become in the 1860s) on the northern coast, in contrast to the unnatural black chasm that threatens to divide men and masters, though also possibly suggesting the abyss (black as in his name) into which he eventually falls.

The schoolchildren are treated as numbers from an early age, just as the workers are abstracted to the degree of disembodied statistics, "Hands," calculable in the aggregate and useful only in as much as they produce and meet planned ends. The factory and the school operate under strict surveillance. In both, the body is disciplined by the architecture and epistemology of Fact. Anything connected with private life, anything that is at all unaccounted for in the calculation of the happiness of the greatest number, is dismissed into nonexistence. Sissy Jupe's circus life has no place here (it is not even to be mentioned, she is told). Nor do representations of horses on wallpaper or flowers on carpets belong here, because they are not useful in the manufacturers' calculation of production and profits.

On the contrary, they threaten to disrupt the strict control of time in the factory system by distracting workers from their labor. "Hands" can have no separate lives or individual desires at variance with the "natural" laws of political economy, into which no irrational unknown factors of unproductive value may be allowed to enter. Such an application of rationality is the more terrifying because in its own terms it is total, absolute, unquestionable, and infallible. Here Dickens is prescient of the technological and totalitarian dystopias of the twentieth century (Jerome Meckier compares *Brave New World*),[64] for it is a dictatorship that seeks to control both knowledge and representation of the real world. Dickens was engaging in "fantasies of possibilities" (in the manner of H. G. Wells), based on a projection of how contemporary social and economic theories (not necessarily one particular theory among them) could potentially turn into a despotic and inhuman system when taken to logical conclusions and used unscrupulously.

Dickens's argument for Fancy adds a further dimension to the dialogical debate over representation. In the Gradgrind system, knowledge is classified into little cabinets. There can be no unknowns or maybes in an arithmetical "calculated" Stone Lodge where all must conform to $2 + 2 = 4$. Yet the universal system of rule and scientific logic is enclosed and finite, a Leibnizian utopia.[65] Like the schoolroom, the spiritually vacuous mind of Mr. Gradgrind is "cavernous" and bounded by walls. Fortunately, there exists another world of infinite possibilities. The first glimpse we have of this alternate world is through a loophole—a legalistic and spatial metaphor—into Mr. Sleary's Horse-Riding establishment. The loophole hints at a fundamental flaw in the perfect design of Gradgrind's ideological architecture, and Dickens builds up an amusing set of oppositions between the two structures in a double-voiced discourse that mocks the pretensions of the best of all utilitarian worlds. Dostoevsky was later to imagine a different rebellion against the conventional walls of Reason, when he had his Underground Man spitefully declare that $2 + 2 = 5$.

Dickens has been chided for misunderstanding the utilitarian standpoint on education and art, just as he got several other details wrong in the novel. Yet the schoolroom scene was a private joke on Dickens's part aimed at his friend Henry Cole, who was put in charge of the Department of Practical Art when it was set up in 1852. In its attack on the tastelessness of Victorian design, in particular the barrenness of the industrial town, Cole's Department of Practical Art recommended avoidance of the repetition of "men and horses standing on each other's heads" and "flowers and tropical plants" ornamenting carpets so vividly "the feet would fear to tread" upon them.[66] Parliamentary Select Committees had recognized that industry depended on the fine arts for quality design and in 1837 the government set up a School of Design. The Great Exhibition reflected the need to promote an industrial style using the latest technology which would appeal to the middle class, the readers of Dickens's novels, and flower designs on wallpaper were actually encouraged, especially species which represented the latest evolutionary theories of natural history. Moreover, unlike Bounderby, wealthy businessmen and factory owners were prominent among art buyers, and their collections and patronage helped shape aesthetic taste. The topical issues of taste and utility come to the fore in an article Dickens wrote about the depressed East London slum district of weavers, which Mayhew had covered in his 1849 *Morning Chronicle* exposés, "Spitalfields" (*Household Words*, 5 April 1851). Dickens lamented the lack of fancy in English silk manufacturing prior to the 1848 Revolution and expressed the hope that this would be remedied by the new School of Design and the Great Exhibition. The weaver painter whom he visits is an outstanding model of the combination of art and sanitation Dickens would like to see introduced into the workplace.

The schools set up under the 1844 Factory Act were intended for the lower-classes, who needed basic skills of literacy and arithmetic in order to function in an industrial economy and who were not generally considered worthy of such refinements as art. So the schoolroom discussion about carpets and wallpaper would have been unlikely,[67] and Gradgrind's own children would not have been tutored there. Taylor, in his description of factory schools, sets their goal as discipline in the wisdom of the system and the prosperity of the nation, and praises Temperance schools, mechanics' institutes, and reading rooms for inculcating in the worker an intelligent and informed opinion that would counteract the inflammatory influence of agitators, Chartists, and trade-union leaders.[68] Of course, in the dialogical context of the ongoing debate about education in an industrial society, it is not one particular system, such as Lancaster's and Bell's, being examined, but a question of what constituted practical knowledge, especially against the background of the Ashburton movement, in which Dickens's friend Angela Burdett-Coutts was active.[69]

There was a widespread difference of opinion about the relationship of individuality with the social framework, but, although the various applications of Bentham's social theory might look quite different, the implications for the liberty of the individual and formation of character are far-reaching, not least for the design of the new factory town. Robert Owen's experiment at New Lanark, for example, presumed that personality was formed for, not by, the individual.[70] The lesson of the schoolroom in *Hard Times* is made to show the moral consequences of that assumption. The novel, however, is not "about" Facts, but about what happens when Facts become the only permissible mode of representation and a social theory attempts to regulate human behavior according to an abstract theory that is the reigning dogma.

THE MACHINERY OF SIGNS

Foolish Word-monger and Motive-grinder, who in thy Logic-mill hast an earthly mechanism for the Godlike itself, and wouldst fain grind me out Virtue from the husks of Pleasure.

—Carlyle, *Sartor Resartus*

Dickens's novel is itself resisting the texts of Gradgrindery, just as among Coketown's library readers Defoe resists Euclid and Goldsmith resists Cocker, despite the fact that by midcentury anyone denying the principle of the happiness of the greatest number or the principle of profit-and-loss might be thought insane. Taylor considered manufacturers perfectly entitled to decide moral problems mathematically and dictate their workers' personal habits "according to Cocker."[71] In such resistance the novel is making space for its own activity as an agent of moral change, as well as for its claim to give a more accurate representation of what the people of Coketown are really like than the 1851 census or Gradgrind's statistics. Chadwick and other utilitarians saw the conditions of the poor in moral as well as epidemiological terms as a statistical problem, and their reforming zeal did combat bad sanitation and other social evils, as Dickens well knew and appreciated. However, the point is not whether Dickens understood the utilitarians, as supporters of John Holloway's attack on Leavis's reading of *Hard Times* have insisted, but which mode of representation gives more reliable knowledge of human nature and the condition of society.

The novel is in effect carrying out the program of *Household Words*, which set out to blend fact and fiction, and to apply Fancy to knowledge of current affairs and the state of the nation. Dickens's editorial statement on the first page of the inaugural issue of *Household Words* declares:

> No mere utilitarian spirit, no iron binding of the mind to grim realities, will give a harsh tone to our Household Words. In the bosoms of the young and old, of the well-to-do and of the poor, we would tenderly cherish that light of Fancy which is inherent in the human breast; which, according to its nurture, burns with an inspiring flame, or sinks into a sullen glare, but which (or woe betide that day!) can never be extinguished. To show to all, that in all familiar things, even in those which are repellent on the surface, there is Romance enough, if we will find it out:—to teach the hardest workers at this whirling wheel of toil, that their lot is not necessarily a moody, brutal fact, excluded from the sympathies and graces of imagination; to bring the greater and the lesser in degree, together, upon that wide field, and mutually dispose them to a better acquaintance and a kinder understanding—is one main object of our Household Words. ("A Preliminary Word," *Household Words*, 30 March 1850; DJ 2: 177)

Such a manifesto is at once artistic and social.[72] It is artistic in its rehearsal of Dickens's romance of familiar things, later proclaimed in the preface to *Bleak House*, and social in its idealistic platform of bringing the Victorian reader journeying by train through the industrial landscape into imaginative sympathy with the worker and thus to truer knowledge of how the other half lived. This must not be the ironically useless knowledge of collected facts, but a comprehensive vision of the imagination, in a skillfully marketed mixture of practical knowledge (including picturesque accounts of manufacturing processes), current affairs, and fiction.

True, the idyllic descriptions of factory life by Harriet Martineau in Dickens's own *Household Words* combined statistics and the imagination, instruction and entertainment. But when Martineau extolled the "magic" workings of the machines, the fantastic metaphor concealed instead of revealing the horror of the "fairy palaces." For Martineau, the factories induced in the visitor wonder at the cleverness and mysterious magic of machinery. The beauty of the factories and their contributions to progress exhibited in the Crystal Palace fill her with pride because they are making the nation more prosperous and improving living conditions. She saw no contradiction between mechanization and the human worker, whom she exhorted to follow the middle-class Protestant virtues of neat cleanliness and thrift so that there should be no "screw loose" in their domestic affairs. She failed to perceive the effect of machines on the health of the factory women or their home life.[73] However, Martineau's factory sketches do not show the horrendous working conditions (she was herself deaf and had no sense of smell). Dickens, by contrast, resists class and gender constructions of female mill operatives, for example in his description of Lowell, Massachusetts, in *American Notes* IV, which shows what could be achieved in England—the healthy young women work long hours but produce a literary magazine and pursue innocent amusements, though Dickens does note these are not city girls. Dickens's model is not the drunken Mrs. Blackpool, who is the ruin of patriarchal order in the industrial town, but Rachael, who offers an ideal of the love and compassion undaunted by the industrial spirit. Admonishing utilitarian economists and commissioners of fact in *Hard Times*, Dickens warned they would always have the laboring poor with them, "Cultivate in them, while there is yet time, the utmost graces of the fancies and affections to adorn their lives so much in need of ornament; or, in the day of your triumph, when romance is utterly driven out of their souls, and they and a bare existence stand face to face, Reality will take a wolfish turn, and make an end of you" (HT II, VI; 192).

The insistence on Fancy as essential to the prosperity of an industrial society runs a counterargument to the guiding principle of Political Economy that, however much distress and misery there might be in the short term, all must inevitably lead to what Macaulay calls "natural progress." *Hard Times* makes no such assumption that progress is "natural"—Coketown represents all that is unnatural in the factory system—and the anachronism of its title resounds polemically antagonistic for the prosperous midcentury when it appeared, even if the liberty of death in Stockport cellars was still maintained. The subtitle "For These Times" is too frequently ignored. The hardness is a moral indifference that renders Dickens's plea the more urgent. His text punctures the usual complacency of mid-century euphoria and replaces it with a moral vision. Barbara Hardy, for example, finds the psychological characterization of Louisa and Sissy no less serious for its being implied and she suggests that the ending would not ring true if the central protagonists settled down to live happily ever after; the ending is a "sad and sober appraisal" but does look forward to rebirth.[74]

The moral is indeed serious and visionary. Sissy, alone untainted by Coketown morality, is rewarded with happy children. Moved by Sissy's compassion, even

James Harthouse declares himself a Great Pyramid of Failure and sets off for the Nile to go in for camels. Louisa does penance by

> thinking no innocent and pretty fancy ever to be despised; trying hard to know her humbler fellow-creatures, and to beautify their lives of machinery and reality with those imaginative graces and delights, without which the heart of infancy will wither up, the sturdiest physical manhood will be morally stark death, and the plainest national prosperity figures can show, will be the Writing on the Wall,—she holding this course as part of no fantastic vow, or bond, or brotherhood, or sisterhood, or pledge, or covenant, or fancy dress, or fancy fair; but simply as duty to be done,—did Louisa see these things of herself? These things were to be. (HT III, IX; 313)

The visualization of moral space in competing representational models thus undoes the utilitarian claim to absolute knowledge. Instead, by parodying the discourse of economic determinism, the Bakhtinian principle of polyphony in the modern novel is applied. Dickens's language represents—in the Aristotelian definition of the word in the *Poetics*—by imitation of voice; it is a "speaking picture," in Sir Philip Sidney's metaphor, "with this end—to teach and delight." As Valentine Cunningham points out, Cissy's rebuttal of the government inspector's interdiction of Fancy is as forceful a defense of poetry's picture-making as was Sidney's, but Cunningham's conclusion, that "all you need is love, love is all you need" (to quote Paul McCartney), does not quite reach Dickens's own conclusion about the "*unum possum*" of Fancy, without which there cannot be love and compassion in a technological society.[75] In his performance of a grand finale in the chapter "Final," Dickens declares that without fancy there can be no childhood, "the sturdiest physical manhood will be morally stark death, and the plainest national prosperity figures can show, will be the Writing on the Wall." Fancy, then, is the key to knowledge and hence to true representation of the Condition of England. It is Fancy which grants Louisa in the end the vision to love and to know through imaginative empathy the lives of her fellow human beings, to beautify their lives of machinery and factory towns. Art is not just play; but without play, humanity will be reduced to a factor of the division of labor and so much machinery, mere "Hands" in a calculation of production and profits. More than once Dickens rehearsed this Carlylean thesis in his speeches in the industrial towns of Manchester, Liverpool, and Birmingham when arguing for a liberal education as the "one thing needful."[76]

Nevertheless, Dickens was hard put to prove the "relevance of mind and imagination to a culture that claims to pay heed only to 'facts.'"[77] Indeed, Mrs. Gaskell's northern industrial town in *North and South* has no time for classics and literature. E. P. Thompson regards it as a matter of historical tragedy that the resistance of the Romantics, on the one hand, and the radical artisans, on the other, to the acquisitiveness and exploitation of the machine culture bore no fruit.[78] George Eliot's solution of removing her artisan weaver Silas Marner back to the country cottage and Nature sounds in retrospect like an unbelievably Romantic undoing of history. At a time when the definition and proprietorship of culture were in question and Matthew Arnold's Levites of culture felt themselves on the defensive, *Hard Times* dialogizes with utilitarian positions on science and art (or more precisely their imagined consequences) and makes a statement about the usefulness of its performance. In retrospect, Dickens seems to belong to an idealistic minority who thought work and art could be usefully combined.

NOTES

1   Gallagher, *The Body Economic: Life, Death, and Sensation in Political Economy and the Victorian Novel* (Princeton: Princeton University Press, 2006), 72–73.

2   Bakhtin, *Problems of Dostoevsky's Poetics*, trans. R. W. Rotsel (Ann Arbor: Ardis, 1973), 152.

3   Wendell V. Harris, "Bakhtinian Double Voicing in Dickens and Eliot," *ELH* 57.2 (1990): 445.

4   Bakhtin, *The Dialogic Imagination: Four Essays*, trans. Caryl Emerson and Michael Holquist (Austin: University of Texas Press, 1981), 15.

5   Martineau, *The Factory Controversy: A Warning Against Meddling Legislation* (Manchester: National Association of Factory Occupiers, 1855), 45.

6   See K. J. Fielding and Anne Smith, "*Hard Times* and the Factory Accident Controversy: Dickens versus Martineau," in *Dickens: Centennial Essays*, ed. Ada Nisbet and Blake Nevins (Berkeley: University of California Press, 1971), 22–45. For a reevaluation of the competing modes of realism of Dickens and Martineau see Eleanor Courtemanche, "'Naked Truth Is the Best Eloquence': Martineau, Dickens, and the Moral Science of Realism," *ELH* 73.2 (2006): 383–407.

7   E. P. Whipple, "*Hard Times*," *Atlantic* Monthly 34 (March 1877): 354–58. Thomas Babington Macaulay, *Lord Macaulay's Essays and Lays* (London: Longman's, Green, 1885), 325–28.

8   I have dealt with this at greater length in "Dickens and the Pleasure of the Text: The Risks of *Hard Times*," *Partial Answers* 9.2 (2011): 311–30.

9   See A-J. Greimas, "For a Topological Semiotics," in *The City and the Sign: An Introduction to Urban Semiotics*, ed. M. Gottdiener and A. Lagopoulos (New York: Columbia University Press, 1986), 25–54.

10   Mircea Eliade, *The Myth of the Eternal Return*, trans. Willard R. Trask, 2nd corrected ed. (Princeton: Princeton University Press, 1965).

11   For a proposed transformational grammar of this topology see Pierre Boudon, "Introduction to the Semiotics of Space," in *The City and the Sign: An Introduction to Urban Semiotics*, 99–113.

12   Yi-Fu Tuan, *Topophilia: A Study of Environmental Perception, Attitudes, and Values* (Englewood Cliffs, NJ: Prentice-Hall, 1974), 16–18.

13   See *Topophilia*, 43.

14   Efraim Sicher, "Binary Oppositions and Spatial Representation: Towards an Applied Semiotics," *Semiotica* 60.3–4 (1986): 211–24. Greimas's homology has been usefully taken up by Steven Connor in his reading of *Dombey and Son* (*Charles Dickens* [Oxford: Blackwell, 1985], 20–21), and Frederic Jameson has applied it to the binary oppositions in *Hard Times* (*The Prison-House of Language* [Princeton: Princeton University Press, 1972], 166–68), though he is generally critical of the structuralist method.

15   Mary Poovey, *Making a Social Body: British Cultural Formation, 1830–1864* (Chicago: University of Chicago Press, 1995), 29–31. See also Henri Lefebvre, *The Production of Space*, trans. Donald Nicholson-Smith (Oxford: Blackwell, 1991).

16   Melvyn Haberman, "The Courtship of the Void," in *The Worlds of Victorian Fiction*, ed. Jerome Buckley (Cambridge, MA: Harvard University Press, 1975), 38–55.

17   Engels, *The Condition of the Working Class in England*, trans. W. O. Henderson and W. H. Chaloner (Oxford: Blackwell, 1972), 75.

18   Hippolyte Taine, *Notes on England*, trans. Edward Hyams (London: Thames and Hudson, 1950), 219.

19   Michel Foucault, *Surveillir et punir: Naissance de la prison* (Paris: Gallimard, 1975). See Jeremy Tambling, *Dickens, Violence and the Modern State: Dreams of the Scaffold* (London: Macmillan and New York: St. Martin's Press, 1995), 21–22; and see pp. 178–79 below.

20   Lewis Mumford, *The City in History: Its Origins, Its Transformations, Its Prospects* (New York: Harcourt Brace, 1961), 446–81.

21   Taine, *Notes on England*, 219–20; see Asa Briggs, *Victorian Cities* (New York: Harper and Row, 1965), 63, 70–71.

22   "Slavery in Yorkshire," *Leeds Mercury*, 16 October 1830.

23   On the relation of the novel to the Blue Books see Carolyn Berman, "'Awful Unknown Quantities': Addressing the Readers in *Hard Times*," *Victorian Literature & Culture* 37.2 (2009): 561–82.

24   F. R. Leavis, *The Great Tradition* (London: Chatto and Windus, 1962), 228.

25   *Hard Times*, ed. George Ford and Sylvère Monod, 2nd ed. (New York: Norton, 1990), 153 note 5.

26   See Stephen Bornstein, "Miscultivated Field and Corrupted Garden: Imagery in *Hard Times*," *Nineteenth-Century Fiction* 26 (1971): 158–70; see also Alexander Welsh, *The City of Dickens* (Oxford: Oxford University Press, 1971).

27   William Cooke Taylor, *Notes of a Tour in the Manufacturing Districts of Lancashire*, 1842 (3rd ed., London: Frank Cass, 1968), 2–9.

28   *Notes of a Tour*, 40–41.

29   Taylor notes with approval the coercion with which these are applied by contrasting the different standards applied by a woman from the non-industrialized Midlands (*Notes of a Tour*, 35–36).

30   "On the Rise, Progress, and Present State of the British Cotton Manufacture," *Edinburgh Review* 91 (1832), quoted in James Phillips Kay, *The Moral and Physical Condition of the Working Classes Employed in the Cotton Manufacture in Manchester* (London: James Ridgway, 1832), 62.

31   Kay, *The Moral and Physical Condition*, 65.

32   Peter Gaskell, *Artisans and Machinery: The Moral and Physical Condition of the Manufacturing Population Considered with Reference to Mechanical Substitutes for Human Labour* (London: John W. Parker, 1836), 185–87. Gaskell does not report his own clinical examination of the laboring women's bodies, but gives casual impressions of a factory inspector, the report of Dr. Ure, and his own estimate of pelvis and thigh measurements based on casual observation.

33   Gaskell, *Artisans and Machinery*, 186–89.

34   Patrick Brantlinger, *The Spirit of Reform: British Literature and Politics, 1832–1867* (Cambridge, MA: Harvard University Press, 1977), 105–06.

35   Terry Eagleton, "Critical Commentary," in Charles Dickens, *Hard Times*, ed. Terry Eagleton (London: Methuen, 1987), 300–308.

36   Steven J. Spector, "Masters of Metonymy: *Hard Times* and Knowing the Working-Class," *ELH* 51.2 (1984): 365–84. Patricia Johnson has responded that Dickens did portray the harsh reality of working-class conditions by constructing the Factory (in her interpretation) as a controlling metaphor that shaped the novel ("*Hard Times* and the Structure of Industrialism: The Novel as Factory," *Studies in the Novel* 21.1–2 [1989]: 128–37).

37   See Joseph Butwin, "*Hard Times:* The News and the Novel," *Nineteenth-Century Fiction* 32 (1977): 166–87.

38   Nicholas Coles has pointed to internal contradictions in the attack on Gradgrindery in the novel as well as contradictions with some of the positions presented in *Household Words*, where the novel first appeared ("The Politics of *Hard Times:* Dickens the Novelist versus Dickens the Reformer," *Dickens Studies Annual* 15 [1986]: 145–79); for a rebuttal see Grahame Smith "Comic Subversion and *Hard Times*," *Dickens Studies Annual* 18 (1989): 145–60. The implications of facticity are surely paradoxical in view of the satirical thrust of *Hard Times*, although they have much occupied scholars, for example, K. J. Fielding, "The Battle for Preston," in *Twentieth-Century Interpretations of Hard Times*, ed. Paul E. Gray (Englewood Cliffs: Prentice-Hall, 1969), 16–21; Fielding and Smith, "*Hard Times* and the Factory Accident Controversy"; Philip Collins, "Dickens and Industrialism," *Studies in English Literature* 20 (1980): 651–73.

39   See Brantlinger, *The Spirit of Reform*, 81–96. Kate Flint demonstrates the deep complexity of Dickens's position on social change (*Dickens* [Atlantic Highlands NJ: Humanities Press, 1986], 85–110), but the "ideological uncertainty" with which Flint sums up her assessment of Dickens's position on social change reminds us of the politicization of readings of *Hard Times*, various manifestations of which are to be found in the evaluations by Macaulay, Gissing, Ruskin, G. B. Shaw, Raymond Williams, and David Craig.

40   See Nancy Armstrong, "Dickens between Two Disciplines: A Problem for Theories of Reading," *Semiotica* 58.3–4 (1982): 243–75. However, this does not fully answer Josephine Guy's objections that in *The Industrial Reformation of English Fiction* (Chicago: University of Chicago Press, 1985) Gallagher fails to state how the hierarchy of discourse is determined, how its rules are decided, and, finally, if no text is privileged, in what way contemporary Victorians would have read them (*The Victorian Social-Problem Novel: The Market, the Individual and Communal Life* [London: Macmillan, 1996], 58–63).

41   Gallagher, *The Industrial Reformation of English Fiction*, 147–48; cf. Richard Fabrizio, "Wonderful No-Meaning: Language and the Psychopathology of the Family in Dickens's *Hard Times*," *Dickens Studies Annual* 16 (1989): 61–94.

42   Ivan Melada, *The Captain of Industry in English Fiction, 1821–1871* (Albuquerque: University of New Mexico Press. 1970), 110–15.

43   R. Bland Lawson, "The 'Condition of England Question': *Past and Present* and *Bleak House*," *Victorian Newsletter* 79 (1991): 26.

44   Raymond Williams, *Culture and Society* (London: Chatto & Windus and Penguin Books, 1966), 107.

45   David Lodge, *Working with Structuralism* (London: Routledge, 1981), 38.

46   See *Autobiography. Essay on Liberty* (New York: Collier, 1909), 95.

47   However, see Philip Collins, "Queen Mab's Chariot Among the Steam Engines: Dickens and 'Fancy,'" *English Studies* 42 (1961): 78–90; David Sonstroem, "Fettered Fancy in *Hard Times*," *PMLA* 84 (1969): 520–29; and Robert Higbie, *Dickens and Imagination* (Gainesville: University Presses of Florida, 1998). In chapter 5 of his study of popular entertainment in Dickens, Paul Schlicke points to the emblematic value of the imagination (*Dickens and Popular Entertainment* [London: Allen & Unwin, 1985]).

48   See for examples of how scientific discoveries became narrativized in nineteenth-century fiction and reflected crises of belief, Elizabeth Deeds Ermath, *The English Novel in History, 1840–1895* (London: Routledge, 1997).

49   M. H. Abrams, *The Mirror and the Lamp: Romantic Theory and the Critical Tradition* (New York: Oxford University Press, 1953), 306–07.

50   *England and the English* (Paris: Boudry's European Library, 1836), 213.

51   Brantlinger, *The Spirit of Reform*, 24–33.

52   *The Spirit of Reform*, 28.

53   Schlicke, *Dickens and Popular Entertainment*, 265 n. 48.

54   Lodge, *Working with Structuralism*, 27.

55   John Forster, *The Life of Charles Dickens* (London: Dent, 1969), 1: 25.

56   See Schlicke, *Dickens and Popular Entertainment*, 154. Mr. Astley was himself, like Mr. Sleary, a self-made man, and his rise from private soldier to horse-riding was widely documented in guides to the capital.

57   Edwin Eigner, *The Dickens Pantomime* (Berkeley: University of California Press, 1989).

58   Lodge, 42–43. Terence Cave is surely correct in his comment on Lodge's structuralist analysis that the true analogy is the one that can be drawn between the soft-hearted circus-master Sleary and the producer of popular novels (*Recognitions: A Study in Poetics* [Oxford: Oxford University Press, 1989], 411).

59   Schlicke, *Dickens and Popular Entertainment*, 137–89.

60   Chris Brooks, *Signs for the Times: Symbolic Realism in the Mid-Victorian World.* London: Allen & Unwin, 1984), 31–32.

61   Richard J. Arneson, "Benthamite Utilitarianism and *Hard Times*," *Philosophy and Literature* 2 (1978): 60–75.

62   "Fragments of Government," quoted in C. K. Ogden, "Introduction," in Jeremy Bentham, *Bentham's Theory of Fictions*, 2nd ed. (London: Routledge, 1951), xvii.

63   See Helen Stoddard, *Rings of Desire: Circus History and Representation* (Manchester: Manchester University Press, 2000); Katherine Kearns, *Nineteenth-Century Literary Realism: Through the Looking Glass* (Cambridge: Cambridge University Press, 1996), 196–97; Joseph Litvak, *Caught in the Act: Theatricality in the Nineteenth-Century English Novel* (Berkeley: University of California Press, 1992), 117–24.

64   Jerome Meckier, *Hidden Rivalries in Victorian Fiction: Dickens, Realism, and Reevaluation* (Lexington: University of Kentucky Press, 1987), 50–51.

65   See Leona Toker, "*Hard Times* and a Critique of Utopia: A Typological Study," *Narrative* 4.3 (1996): 218–34.

66   *First Report of the Department of Practical Art* (1853), quoted in K. J. Fielding, "Charles Dickens and the Department of Practical Art," *Modern Language Review* 48 (1953): 270–77; Philip Collins, *Dickens and Education* (New York: St. Martin's Press, 1963), 157–58. A further joke might be the modeling of the teacher M'Choakumchild on the writer and statistician J. R. M'Culloch. Incidentally, a J. M. M'Culloch was a headmaster of a school in none other than Circus Place, Edinburgh (*Hard Times*, ed. George Ford and Sylvère Monod, 2nd ed. [New York: Norton, 1990], 303 n.).

67   Collins, *Dickens and Education*, 156–59.

68   Taylor, *Notes of a Tour*, 33–34, 126–39. Taylor notes with some satisfaction that these schools gave industrial training as well as "mere literary education" (33).

69   Fielding, "Hard Times and Common Things," in *Imagined Worlds: Essays on Some English Novels and Novelists in Honour of John Butt*, ed. Maynard Mack and Ian Gregor (London: Methuen, 1968), 183–203.

70   See *Robert Owen on Education*, ed. Harold Silver (Cambridge: Cambridge University Press, 1969).

71   Taylor, *Notes of a Tour*, 113–14.

72   Scholars have not failed to point to the relevance of this to Dickens's aesthetics; see Robert. Newsom, *Dickens on the Romantic Side of Familiar Things: Bleak House and the Novel Tradition* (New York: Columbia University Press, 1977); Alain Bony, "Réalité et Imaginaire dans *Hard Times*," *Etudes Anglaises* 23 (1970): 168–82; Ian Ousby, "Figurative Language in *Hard Times*," *Durham University Journal* (new series), 43 (1981): 103–09.

73   Fielding and Smith, "*Hard Times* and the Factory Accident Controversy," 420–21.

74   *The Moral Art of Dickens* (London: Athlone Press, 1970), 15.

75   Valentine Cunningham, *In the Reading Gaol: Postmodernity, Texts, and History* (Oxford: Blackwell, 1994), 134.

76   Herbert L. Sussman, *Victorians and the Machine: The Literary Response to Technology* (Cambridge, MA: Harvard University Press, 1968), 68–69.

77   John P. McGowan, *Representation and Revelation: Victorian Realism from Carlyle to Yeats* (Columbia: University of Missouri Press, 1986), 19.

78   E. P. Thompson, *The Making of the English Working Class* (New York: Random House, 1963), 832.

5

Labyrinths and Prisons:
Little Dorrit

SHADES OF THE PRISON-HOUSE

> The city is the realization of man's ancient dream of the labyrinth. This reality the *flâneur* pursues without knowing it.
> —Walter Benjamin, *Das Passagen-werk*

> Far aslant across the city, over its jumbled roofs, and through the open tracery of its church towers, struck the long bright rays, bars of the prison of this lower world. (LD II, xxx)

Fancy, we have seen, is essential to Dickens's concept of a healthy childhood and moral education. Without it, the model industrial town will turn into a dystopian nightmare. Suffering the little children to come into the garden of fancy "in the stony ways of this world" (HT II, IX; 223) is the only guarantee of charity in the heart. This is, of course, a Wordsworthian construction of childhood innocence which, in the "Ode: Intimations of Immortality," turned common sight into poetic vision before the shadows of the prison-house of adulthood darkened the world. However, Dickens's invocation of childhood innocence owes perhaps less to Wordsworth's transcendental sensibility of poetic vision than to a paean to childish romance and the arrested growth of a grown-up child later celebrated by Peter Pan.[1]

Always to remember childhood was the secret of never growing truly old, Dickens wrote in a New Year piece, aptly headed "Where We Stopped Growing" (*Household Words*, 1 January 1853). This characteristically sentimental expression of seasonal wishes, typical of Dickens's hearth-side Christmas celebrations of loss as well as bounty, invoked the City of the Dead peopled by spirits of angel-children.[2] Dickens gives pride of place to his childhood reading of *Robinson Crusoe*, *Gulliver's Travels*, and a *Thousand and One Arabian Nights*, to his childhood impressions of the navy dockyards in Chatham and of London with its eccentric characters, but also to the specter of the Bastille in which a suffering old man was locked up. Childhood wonder comes from both reading and from ineffaceable impressions of the city. These are fancies which accompany the adult through life's dreams and nightmares, lending them a sublime sense of wonder but also throwing over them the menacing shadow of the prison. One curious memory Dickens will never outgrow is of special interest: "We have never outgrown the rugged walls of Newgate, or any other prison on the outside. All within, is the same blank of remorse and misery" (DJ 2: 112).

163

It is as if Dickens's adult imagination was haunted by the specter of the prison with which are associated the shame of his visits to the Marshalsea, where his father was imprisoned for debt, and his humiliating experiences at the Blacking Warehouse. Often quoted is the autobiographical fragment dating from Dickens's cathartic working through of his shameful past in the mid-1840s. In this secret document entrusted to Forster, who would later canonize it in the writer's post-humous biography, Dickens recalls visiting his father in prison and being told "to take warning by the Marshalsea, and to observe that if a man had twenty pounds a year, and spent nineteen pounds nineteen shillings and sixpence, he would be happy; but that a shilling spent the other way would make him wretched."[3] That advice, put into the mouth of Micawber (DC xi; 221), is the iron law of Malthusian capitalism that strikes fear in the abject individual and disciplines to hard work and thrift. In the autobiographical fragment, Dickens recalled how he had to manage his pennies, though tempted by puddings and street entertainments on his way to and from work. The Blacking Warehouse is presented by some critics as a "factory," conjuring up scenes of industrial production and abject poverty, rather than the degradation of having to work for a living like most children of his age and mix with members of a lower class, a frustration above all of dreams of school and Cambridge, above all of becoming a gentleman—which acquired all the more the weight of a psychological burden when Dickens did become a great man. The secret knowledge of both the humiliation and the proud struggle to survive imposes itself on the memory-map of the city, and it was with a shudder that Dickens would later pass the places that evoked the "misery" and "remorse" associated with prison walls.

The Marshalsea episode, as is well known, is bound up with resentment at his parents, and Forster rightly points out that there is an element of vengeance in Dickens's portrayal of the debtors' prison in *David Copperfield* for the heartbreak that was caused him.[4] The difference is that, unlike the young Dickens, Copperfield is fantasized as able to help the father figure, Micawber, who is an incorrigible debtor, not just an innocent victim of an unjust system. Another projection of the shame and humiliation which connects the shadow of prison with the Blacking Warehouse is Doctor Manette's obsessive compulsion with shoemaking in *A Tale of Two Cities*, described explicitly as a repressed trauma ("shock") and euphemistically (by Lorry) as a blacksmith's forge. The prison experience is also associated in the fragment of autobiography with initiation into sexuality, when the young Dickens on a visit to Marshalsea has to go and borrow a knife and fork from Captain Porter, whom he finds in a room overhead with his two "wan" natural daughters and the "very dirty lady" who is not married to him. The boy comes away with "knowledge" of what he has seen as certain as the knife and fork in his hand.[5] This is an area that is worth exploring for its biographical and psychological interest, but the present discussion is concerned only with its relevance to the motif of guilt and to the uncanny in the urban psyche.

It is a commonplace of Dickens criticism that prisons loom over so much of his writing. Newgate, the Fleet, and Marshalsea loom darkly in *Sketches by Boz, Pickwick Papers, Oliver Twist, Barnaby Rudge, David Copperfield, A Tale of Two Cities, Great Expectations*, and, most famously, *Little Dorrit*. Newgate stands monumentally at the center of the literary map of London (Defoe was imprisoned there seven times and Moll Flanders was born there), and it stands in the middle of the labyrinth in *Oliver Twist* and *Great Expectations*, hard by the contaminating bestial filth of Smithfield, where slaughter of cattle matches the manslaughter on the gallows. In chapter 4 of *Nicholas Nickleby*, Newgate is found at the center of the capital's powerful currents. In "Dickens: The Two Scrooges," Edmund Wilson attributed to Dickens a split personality of rebel and criminal, and asserted that after the murder in *Martin Chuzzlewit*, the rebel gets the better of the criminal.[6] Since then several critics have sensed something morbidly perverted and sadomasochistic which dominates the "dark side" of Dickens's personality. A. O. J. Cockshut deplores Dickens's flawed attempt to exorcise this "obsession" by universalizing it and asserts that only in *Little Dorrit* does he succeed in transforming personal shame into art.[7] Lionel Trilling's classic analysis of *Little Dorrit* presents a Freudian model of the mind in which the organization of the internal life is likened to a criminal process that turns the mind into criminal, police, victim, judge, and executioner all at once, a model of the mind which "having received the social impress, ... becomes in turn the matrix of society."[8]

The multiple images of imprisonment in the novel thus reflect psychological, not just institutional imprisonment, as in Trilling's example of Arthur imagining his mother's confinement in her wheelchair as equivalent to his own imprisonment, a punishment for the unnamed wrong that lies at the root of his guilt. The imprisoning effect of Mrs. Clennam's Methodism kills the imagination as surely as Gradgrind's equally imprisoning utilitarianism; both maim the child and form its character as it grows up in fear of punishment. The internalization of the prison has been understood in another way, too. Jeremy Tambling reads a Foucauldian inscription of discipline on the body into Dickens's image of the scaffold as a violent effigy connected to a fascination with the monstrous, resulting from an anal fixation and sadomasochistic desires. In this reading, Dickens is said to be reenacting the "deferred trauma" of his father's imprisonment which represses the self.[9] Indeed, F. S. Schwarzbach has suggested that Dickens rewrites this traumatic memory as an urban experience.[10]

In preparation for writing the novel, Dickens did revisit the Marshalsea on his way to Gad's Hill, and he related to Forster how he found the spikes gone, the inhabitants free to go as they please. One room stuck in his memory, and he determined to take it, as Arthur takes Amy's old room, in a revisiting of the repressed past.[11] However, Dickens makes abundantly clear other conscious intentions in plotting the novel. If Dickens was revisiting the Marshalsea only in order to write out that episode in his psyche, then *Little Dorrit* must be judged a dismal failure. Indeed, John Carey, among others, has rejected what he deems to be a simple simile of city and prison because of the author's artistic failure to make it work, for which critics cannot be blamed.[12] Such superficial readings of the novel dismiss any religious or metaphorical interpretation and ignore the strong literary tradition identifying city walls with the prison, so familiar in its transformation in the Nature worship of Rousseau and Wordsworth, who flee from urban imprisonment to the freedom and pastoral innocence of man's true home in a rural paradise. Oliver, recuperating at the Maylies', is far from his former criminal associates and "languishing in a wretched prison" (OT xxxii; 291) and as near as he can be to a Wordsworthian intimation of immortality, a commonplace reference at the time. Traditional studies of *Little Dorrit* have, in fact, drawn attention to the Christian allegory of the postlapsarian world as a vale of tears, or the social critique of England's moral imprisonment. What Gerald Coniffe has insightfully described as "a vision of the human lapse from true humanity" in an imprisoning society where people get trapped by mental fetters of their own making[13] has epistemological implications for the representation of the city, and Chris Brooks aptly calls Dickens's prison imagery in *Bleak House, Hard Times,* and *Little Dorrit* a central "realist property."[14]

The ogre of the city which entraps the innocent with prison bars is inseparable from modern urban consciousness, and the foreboding of death in the footsteps of the crowds pervades the image of the city in *A Tale of Two Cities.* At the same time the prison is both real and, far more horrid, an abstract presence, which haunts Kit Nubbles's dreams when he is jailed awaiting trial and transportation:

> It was a long night, that seemed as though it would have no end; but he slept too, and dreamed—always of being at liberty, and roving about, now with one person and now with another; but ever with a vague dread of being recalled to prison; not that prison, but one which was in itself a dim idea—not of a place, but of a care and sorrow: of something oppressive and always present, and yet impossible to define. At last, the morning dawned, and there was the jail itself—cold, black, and dreary, and very real indeed. (OCS lxi; 556–57)

More ironically, in *Little Dorrit* the real walls of the Marshalsea "asserted their fascination" on Tip who carried the prison wherever he went and who is constantly brought back there. In my rereading of *Little Dorrit*, I shall be exploring the prison-city not merely in a literal sense (the incarcerating city), or in a symbolic pattern (the prison as allegorical city), but in a far-reaching and less reductive metaphysical scheme, in which the prison informs both the meaning of the city and its function in the plot of the novel in a complex relationship between levels of representation that undermines the linearity of the nineteenth-century novel.

The road was conventionally the linear route of the picaresque hero (Bakhtin's chronotope of the journey), and an allegorical progress of the hero in the English realist novel makes an epistemological equivalence of narrative and topographical progression. However, in the modern city the road wound into a mysterious labyrinth, and the plot similarly had to negotiate the twists and turns of city streets, a place of danger where distinctions of rank, gender, and individuality are destabilized and where moral and social barriers are transgressed. In that labyrinth, Oliver Twist gets lost and trapped, like the naive newcomers in Victorian melodrama or popular penny serials, such as Reynolds's *The Mysteries of London*, dragged down into crime and prostitution by wicked lords or vagabonds. The maze of city streets represents the novel's reading of its own hidden connections as it seeks to break out of the claustral, institutionalizing conditions of both the city and of generic form.

The implications for our reading of *Little Dorrit* will be shown in the context of the contemporary debate on crime and prison reform. Crime is an urban problem, if not *the* urban problem. Not for nothing does Henry Mayhew focus on criminality and prison life in the panoramic overview of London that opens *The Criminal Prisons of London and Scenes of Prison Life* (with John Binney, 1862), as if the city was by definition criminal and incriminating. Mayhew devotes the fourth volume of *London Labour and the London Poor* (1861–62) to "those who will not work"—the thieves and prostitutes. On his first day in the great metropolis, Pip too finds that the criminal courts and gallows give him a "sickening idea of London" (GE xx; 170), and this is not only because Newgate's disciplinary architecture, which eclipses St. Paul's, makes him feel guilty for his secret association with criminality (he is ashamed to name the place when he shows Estella the sights on her arrival in London). London was "a vast, hopeless nursery of ignorance, misery, and vice—a breeding-ground for the hulks and jails," as Dickens described the "capital city of the world" (*Daily News*, 4 February 1846). In the nineteenth century, poverty and crime were linked and said to be caused by idleness and drunkenness, though not all related crime to class or saw in the "dangerous class" of London's outcast population a potential disaffection of honest laborers.[15]

BLEEDING HEART OF DARKNESS

> ... youth, and health, and fortune spent
> Thou fliest for refuge to the wilds of Kent.
> —Samuel Johnson, "London"

The prison is an enclosing space at multiple levels of *Little Dorrit*, and it is connected at each level of the novel with the labyrinth. The imprisoning maze of the city streets serves as a metaphor for the inextricable tangle in which the affairs of the "prison of the lower world" are muddled, as well as a metaphor for life's journey on which a person is lost, like Dante on his way to visit Hell. J. Hillis Miller has described the Circumlocution Office, the center of the labyrinth through which all government matters pass and get tangled up, as an expression of the individual's hopeless search for judgment in a Kafkaesque bureaucracy in which appeal to authority is impossible and the applicant is held guilty, "though without quite Kafka's deliberate universalization of the labyrinth as a symbol of the metaphysical alienation of man."[16] Chancery and the "muddle" of Coketown are both memorable images of the tangle of modern urban life. In *Little Dorrit*, the prison and the labyrinth are overlapping and interconnected chronotopes, and each represents a topology of knowledge and power which in nineteenth-century Britain are vested in the city. The prison and the labyrinth belong to the same social, moral, and legal cartography; both are traps, with this difference: one is lost in the latter and tries to get out, and one tries to avoid getting in the former.

In *Little Dorrit*, we enter the city with Arthur Clennam, who has returned to England and will discover a dark secret in his murky family past:

> He crossed by St. Paul's and went down, at a long angle, almost to the water's edge, through some of the crooked and descending streets which lie (and lay more crookedly and closely then) between the river and Cheapside. Passing, now the mouldy hall of some obsolete Worshipful Company, now the illuminated windows of a Congregationless church that seemed to be waiting for some adventurous Belzoni to dig it out and discover its history; passing silent warehouses and wharves, and here and there a narrow alley leading to the river, where a wretched little bill, FOUND DROWNED, was weeping on the wet wall; he came at last to the house he sought. (LD I, III; 70–71)

The crookedness, the constriction, the obsolescence, the fathomless depths of a maze that would, as in "Seven Dials," challenge the Egyptian explorer Giovanni Belzoni—all this prefigures the plot that will entrap Arthur in its urban mysteries. It is both a topography of getting lost (as in the disorienting view from Todgers's) and an archeology of loss, an unearthing of a city of ruins and tombs, like Nineveh or other lost civilizations which reminded Londoners of the fate of a great metropolis.[17] In a striking counterimage to the bustling streets of the world's business center, in the City, the isolation and disuse reflect Arthur's own loss of selfhood and identity on his return from exile. The disorientation is underscored by the reification of the waiter's truncated speech ("Gelen box num seven, not go sleep here, gome") and by his "passing" the silent buildings through the slanting rain and the slanting streets until he comes to that "home," which turns out, like its owner, to be a cripple. True to the city-body analogy of disease, the house had slipped down sideways but had been "propped up, however, and was leaning on some half-dozen gigantic crutches; which gymnasium for the neighbouring cats, weather-stained, smoke-blackened, and overgrown with weeds, appeared in these latter days to be no very sure reliance" (LD I, III; 71). The house serves as synecdoche for the city's diseased and deformed organism and it hides secret knowledge in the labyrinth of its crooked passageways, but its imprisoning labyrinth points also to a necropolis.

The labyrinth represents the city's underside of uncontrollable violence and anarchy. The orderly citadel that contains and controls through rationality and law is disclosed as a Dionysian chaos.[18] St. Augustine reminds us the earthly city was founded by the nomadic murderer Cain, just as Rome was founded on fratricide, an archetype staining the image of the city for centuries to come. In his metamorphosis into the Wandering Jew, Cain lurks murderously in the city's labyrinthine alleys and passageways. The reptilian Jew slinks through the labyrinth of London's underworld in *Oliver Twist*, and in *Little Dorrit* it is Rigaud who is the diabolical Cain "let loose" from the city, haunting the low flat landscape of the Saône (a figure to be met again in Magwitch's ghoulish appearance in the flat marshes of Kent in the opening of *Great Expectations*). The myth is transformed by Romantics such as Eugène Sue into the demonic bogeyman of the modern city and scapegoat for its evils. This leaves an unsettling and primeval presence in the city, so that the bourgeois lives in fear of the *unheimlich*. When Rigaud accosts Mrs. Flintwich locked out of doors, frightened out of her wits by the melodramatic storm in the adjacent graveyard, he is identified by the red tinge of his hair and hooked nose, as well as by his demonic identity of the Wandering Jew/Cain stalking the twisted lanes of the modern city. Later it is an elderly Jew who is the agent of Arthur's confinement to the Marshalsea, a detail reinforcing the stereotypical association of the Jew with the fiendish entanglement of loans, debts, and speculation, an identification with Judas and Shylock that we can recognize in Fagin's role as bogey of urban capitalism.

The secrets of the city's mysteries cannot be revealed without penetrating the maze, a convention that introduces the numinous in Gothic stories. In the menacing encounter with the unknown, with the Other, the labyrinth forms a closed space that brings to an end the quest of the wanderer seeking to transcend evil and seek truth.[19] Unlike the mock-Gothic construction and destruction of the House of Usher, however, the House of Clennam is itself a labyrinth haunted by secrets that are explicitly associated with the city, a mystery that pervades the secret byways of the City of London when Clennam is on his way to the encounter with Rigaud at his mother's. That episode illustrates how Dickens imbues place with meaning that is structuring and symbolic, characterizing protagonists and events, rather than giving topographic information, while stretching the figurality of imprisonment beyond the strictly literal or sociological, so that the prison and the labyrinth become emanations of psychological states and moral development.

The urban labyrinth is above all a place of danger. The hustle and bustle of the streets near the Marshalsea are not a "safe resort" for an old man like Frederick Dorrit, who is later described as "lost" in a labyrinthine world (LD I, xix; 266). Yet, when negotiated by a trustworthy guide, the labyrinth can serve as a secret escape path from the necropolis. As in *The Old Curiosity Shop*, the guide is an angelic girl-woman, sufficiently innocent to shock the suicidal prostitute by her presence with Maggy on the streets at night, but also experienced enough to know the ways of the city.

Dickens locates the "heart" of the city's darkness at the junction of Newgate and Smithfield, sites of execution and slaughter:

> There, at the very core of London, in the heart of its business and animation, in the midst of a whirl of noise and motion: stemming as it were the giant currents of life that flow ceaselessly on from different quarters, and meet beneath its walls: stands Newgate; and in that crowded street on which it frowns so darkly—within a few feet of the squalid tottering houses—upon the very spot on which the vendors of soup and fish and damaged fruit are now plying their trades—scores of human beings, amidst a roar of sounds

to which even the tumult of a great city is as nothing, four, six, or eight strong men at a time, have been hurried violently and swiftly from the world, when the scene has been rendered frightful with excess of human life; when curious eyes have glared from casement and house-top, and wall and pillar; and when, in the mass of white and upturned faces, the dying wretch, in his all-comprehensive look of agony, has met not one—not one— that bore the impress of pity or compassion. (NN IV; 30)

In *Little Dorrit*, the bleeding heart is an oblique metaphor for a true heart in pain. This is not just because of the associations of Bleeding Heart Yard with the legend of the murder of Lady Elizabeth Hatton (and with the Virgin Mary in a nearby pub sign). The "bleeding heart of iron" of the manufacturer is in this case not the "malefactor" of one of Plornish's malapropisms (as astute as Sissy Jupe's), whose factory bears a childish association with the murder of Abel. Unlike the hardhearted Gradgrind and Bounderby clinking their coins, Doyce is himself a powerless, bleeding victim of the System which kills initiative, even at the cost of ignoring safety and the public interest, a point to which Dickens returns time and again (as he does in "A Poor Man's Tale of a Patent," UT 461–66).

In the description of Bleeding Heart Yard, the repression of a rural past, a historical memory of hunting lodges, and a cultural memory of Shakespeare lie just behind and beyond the archetypal labyrinth of urban poverty off Theobald's Road, a pastoral and ludic space antipodal to the city of *homo faber* which again points to a trace of loss of natural innocence and the historical past:

> As if the aspiring city had become puffed up in the very ground on which it stood, the ground had so risen about Bleeding Heart Yard that you got into it down a flight of steps which formed no part of the original approach, and got out of it by a low gateway into a maze of streets, which went about and about, tortuously ascending to the level again. At the end of the Yard and over the gateway, was the factory of Daniel Doyce, often heavily beating like a bleeding heart of iron, with the clink of metal upon metal. (LD I, XII; 176)

Bleeding Heart Yard is one of several contiguous spaces of the city that are connected centripetally—through Doyce with the Circumlocution Office, through Arthur with the Marshalsea and Plornish, and through Plornish to an exposition of poverty and administrative incompetence which inexorably must lead to the debtors' prison or institutionalized do-nothing-ism, or both. Like Stephen Blackpool, Plornish minds his own piecework and only knows

> that it wasn't put right by them what undertook that line of business, and that it didn't come right of itself. And, in brief, his illogical opinion was, that if you couldn't do nothing for him, you had better take nothing from him for doing of it; so far as he could make out, that was about what it come to. Thus, in a prolix, gently-growling, foolish way, did Plornish turn the tangled skein of his estate about and about, like a blind man who was trying to find some beginning or end to it; until they reached the prison gate. (LD I, XII; 184)

The historical context of the Crimean War points to another sense of the bleeding heart, too, since it was do-nothing-ism which Dickens indicted for that bloody debacle, thundering with Carlylean anger against the denial by government of any legal or moral culpability, as if it was, like everything else that went wrong, "Nobody's Fault," the original title of the novel.[20]

DEATH IN LONDON AND VENICE

> Stone walls do not a prison make,
> Nor iron bars a cage . . .
> —Richard Lovelace, "To Althea, from Prison"

> I stood in Venice on the Bridge of Sighs,
> A palace and a prison on each hand.
> —Byron, *Childe Harold's Pilgrimage*

The connection with the prison is both a metaphorical and a topographical link in the mystery plot Arthur is trying to solve: what connects Amy and the Marshalsea with himself? But at the semiotic and semantic levels, the connection helps to unravel the "tangled skein" of the web which links the demonic presence of Rigaud and the cities of Europe with what the novel is saying about the imprisoning city, indeed with the labyrinthine form of the novel itself.

Such a link can be seen in another example of how the streets of London knot together the lives and destinies of diverse characters in a dense labyrinth of plot. In book I, chapter xiii, Clennam steps out into the night, leaving behind Flora and his youthful love, and encounters John Baptist injured by the Mail Coach, literally knocked down by progress and the speed of the city streets, before contemplating his life's journey, on which he has learned from cruelty to be kind. The answer that knocks at his door is, of course, Little Dorrit. She can read the streets of Covent Garden better than he, and can see, behind the wealth and luxury, the arches hiding ragged children, who "like young rats, slunk and hid, fed on offal, huddled together for warmth, and were hunted about" (LD I, xiv; 208). These "rats," protests the narrator, were "eating away our foundations, and will bring the roofs on our heads!" (LD I, xiv; 208). This Carlylean plea to the deaf ears of the Barnacles points to the collective responsibility implicit in such interconnectedness, as well as to similar analogies of social and structural collapse in the melodramatic climax of the novel, when the House of Clennam collapses, burying the monstrous city-rat Rigaud. In the romantic image of Venice as a city of spectacle, a dream image which would appear and dissolve, as Dickens described it in *Pictures from Italy*, we have a figural representation of the political reality of London.[21] And the analogy with London's archetypal metropolis is not far away when Austrian soldiers occupying Italian palaces bring ruin to the foundations on which the city stands. That undermining of the city recollects the collapsing ruins of Tom-All-Alone's and points to a larger meaning of Abbau in imperialist discourse. As in *Bleak House*, the ideology of domesticity is undermined by the homelessness on the streets of the city. The desolation of the Adelphi Steps offers a stark contrast to familiar busy streets, infamous for suicides of fallen women, as in Augustus Egg's painting *Past and Present* (1858). This is a London represented by emptiness and absence:

> There is always, to this day, a sudden pause in that place to the roar of the great thoroughfare. The many sounds become so deadened that the change is like putting cotton in the ears, or having the head thickly muffled. At that time the contrast was far greater; there being no small steam-boats on the river, no landing places but slippery wooden stairs and foot-causeways, no railroad on the opposite bank, no hanging bridge or fish-market near at hand, no traffic on the nearest bridge of stone, nothing moving on the stream but watermen's wherries and coal-lighters. Long and broad black tiers of the latter, moored fast in the mud as if they were never to move again, made the shore funereal and silent after dark; and kept what little water-movement there was, far out towards mid-stream. At any hour later than sunset, and not least at that hour when most of the people who have anything to eat at home are going home to eat it, and when most of those who have nothing have hardly yet slunk out to beg or steal, it was a deserted place and looked on a deserted scene. (LD II, IX; 586)

As an inverted form of imprisonment, the labyrinth is contiguous with quarantine on John Baptist's map at the beginning of *Little Dorrit*, a site of surveillance and inspection where foreigners and criminals alike may be isolated to protect society from contamination and contagion.

Quarantine, however, also tells us that the city has been not only a Vetruvian refuge but also a necropolis. This should not be understood as merely an allegorical or metaphorical transition to truth, which Alexander Welsh has explicated as Dickens's sentimental domestication of death.[22] In the description of London matching that of the staring heat of Marseilles, the bells sound the knell in a plague city, warning of both spiritual and physical death in an epidemic of both speculation fever and jail fever:[23]

> Melancholy streets, in a penitential garb of soot, steeped the souls of the people who were condemned to look at them out of windows, in dire despondency. In every thoroughfare, up almost every alley, and down almost every turning, some doleful bell was throbbing, jerking, tolling, as if the Plague were in the city and the dead-carts were going round. (LD I, III; 67)

We think of the city of Perdition in Arthur's childhood gospel readings, or the "smoke and fly plagues" dimming the framed Plagues of Egypt (LD I, III; 72) in the Clennams' house of the dead, a dead trading house that represents the commercial City of London and represents moral death in the city.

The "labyrinth" of the world (LD I, II; 57), as Arthur Clennam calls it in the second chapter of *Little Dorrit*, is an allegorical quest for truth, like Bunyan's

Christian walking through "the wilderness of this world" or Robinson Crusoe musing on providential faith on his prison-island. But like Bunyan's reference to the author's own experience of jail in *Pilgrim's Progress*, Dickens sets against consciousness of the real prison the falsity of the freedom of this world as a Dantean wilderness of sin that forms a space which mediates between the real and the symbolic. Looking out as a traveler at the dismal labyrinth of the city, Arthur muses how the ghosts must think with pity of their former "places of imprisonment"—their earthly homes but also their earthly bodies—and his journey takes on a metaphysical significance without his leaving the real city.

These different levels of reading the city in *Little Dorrit*, literal and figurative, spiritual and physical, are informed by the cultural paradigm rooted in Western culture of Adam and Jesus going out into the wilderness and the biblical tradition of the city as destroyed Babel or Jerusalem, a spiritual wasteland awaiting resurrection. Significantly, in *Pilgrim's Progress* Christian learns of the destruction of the city by reading a book containing the Word of God, so that he is, like Little Dorrit, a reader of the city. The city is a bewildering confusion of paths whose rhyme and reason are unfathomable to the wanderer on the "pilgrimage of life" (LD I, ɪɪ; 67), on which there are people, as Miss Wade warns ominously, who will do things to you. It is in a "labyrinth" of "parasitic" streets off Park Lane (another wilderness disguised as civilization) that Miss Wade is found by Meagles and Arthur in pursuit of Tattycoram.

Leaving London behind is not to leave behind the prison, and its metaphorical as well as psychological presence pursues the traveler. In the icy atmosphere of the Great St. Bernard monastery and with the black figure of Rigaud in pursuit, the prison past is not far behind. As the palazzo, the prison, and the city coalesce, the palaces of Italy become "labyrinths" of absurdly spacious proportions measured in Little Dorrit's mind by the prison confines of the Marshalsea. Echoing Dickens's disdain in *Pictures from Italy* for "pleasure-travellers through life" who were not moved by the sublime truth of nature concealed in the rugged mountains, Amy is particularly struck by the resemblance of the leisured classes touring Europe to her experience of prison—a "superior sort of Marshalsea. Numbers of people seemed to come abroad, pretty much as people had come into prison; through debt, through idleness, relationship, curiosity, and general unfitness for getting on at home. They were brought into these foreign towns in the custody of couriers and local followers, just as the debtors had been brought into the prison. They prowled about the churches and picture galleries, much in the old, dreary, prison-yard manner. They were usually going away again to-morrow or next week, and rarely knew their own minds" (LD II, vɪɪ; 565). The analogy suggests a Johnsonian satire on the vanity of human wishes, with a sharp barb at idlers; these are not purposeful travellers like Clennam and Doyce. However, the frozen corpses of travelers who did not manage to complete their journey cast a grim shadow over such meditations. The Swiss Alps, the Wordsworthian site of David Copperfield's recuperation in Nature where Dickens had also gone to get away from London, are a monstrous landscape of death that resists domestication. This is the mental abyss facing the poet in the sixth book of *The Prelude*, who reads in the Book of Nature the apocalyptic Book of Revelation. With its Miltonian resonance, the passage in Wordsworth describes another form of wilderness which is here assimilated to the savagery in urban civilization, rather than the Noble Savage. Dickens described his stay at the convent in a letter to Forster of September 1846 in ghoulish terms after an ascent through a "valley of desolation" which was "very awful and tremendous" (*Letters* 4: 618).[24]

When the specter of the Marshalsea catches up with William Dorrit himself, a return of the repressed triggered by Young John, that voyeur at the lock with his phallic cigars, he addresses the assembled dinner party guests as if he were still the Father of the Marshalsea. The prison is no longer confinable in symbol or analogy, but is being worked into a thematic construction, just as *Martin Chuzzlewit* was built on another Johnsonian theme, selfishness, in a labyrinthine connection of plot. Dorrit's delusion that he is still in the Marshalsea is not merely a paranoiac obsession with the shadow of the prison or a projection of Dickens's complex relations with his importunate father, but connects seemingly disparate levels of the novel's meaning. The "gloomy bridge" in Venice, for example, which leads from the Doge's Palace to the dungeons, indirectly recalls the prison for Mr. Dorrit, who stands, like Byron's hero in *Childe Harold*, "A palace and a prison on each hand."

> There is a dungeon, in whose dim, drear light
> What do I gaze on? Nothing: Look again!
> Two forms are slowly shadow'd on my sight—
> Two insulated phantoms of the brain:
> It is not so; I see them full and plain—
> An old man, and a female young and fair,
> Fresh as a nursing mother, in whose vein
> The blood is nectar:—but what doth she there,
> With her unmantled neck, and bosom white and bare? (4: 148)

We recall Dombey and his abuse of Florence's breasts, and once more we find the ideal feminine figure nurturing a sick body imprisoned in the city.

FATHERING THE PRISON

> Come, let's away to prison:
> We two alone will sing like birds i' the cage
> —Shakespeare, *King Lear*

> "a prison is a world within itself, and has its own business, griefs, and joys, peculiar to its circle."
> —Sir Walter Scott, *The Heart of Midlothian*

In a celebrated essay in *The Dyer's Hand*, W. H. Auden once described Pickwick's entry into the Fleet debtors' prison as a Fall which expelled him from the Eden of Dingley Dell and introduced him to the experience of reality, a religious parable that differentiated Law from Grace.[25] John Lucas has objected that, in choosing to go to prison, because of his gentleman's code of honor, Pickwick chooses the world of experience over the atemporal Eden.[26] He is a victim of the prison he makes for himself, and, in some ways, so are the characters in *Little Dorrit*. Like Pickwick guided through the subterranean dungeons of the modern inferno of the lower world, Arthur's innocence must be tested, and, though he needs no Sam Weller to dispel Quixotic delusions, he must also redraw his map of the city.

The prison's social fabric represents a truer division of society than the official hierarchy of "good" and "bad," the more grotesque for the normalcy of the lives of these imprisoned debtors. Mr. Dorrit is reassured on his imprisonment that he can be as comfortable there as can be, for he has reached the bottom rung and is therefore relieved of the constant anxiety of falling. The prison is a city within a city (as the Fleet prison is described in *Peregrine Pickle*, a childhood favorite of Dickens) and therefore can form an allegorical setting for the dangers and traps of the urban labyrinth. The debtors are innocent criminals who have offended against the economic laws of the city and are supposed to be separated from the inner prison of the offenders against the tax laws, the "smugglers." The homogeneity of the prison population serves a narrative of inner freedom reflected in the mirror-like "cells" and "blind alleys" of the prison-city within the city-prison.

> It was an oblong pile of barrack building, partitioned into squalid houses standing back to back, so that there were no back rooms; environed by a narrow paved yard, hemmed in by high walls duly spiked at top. Itself a close and confined prison for debtors, it contained within it a much closer and more confined jail for smugglers. Offenders against the revenue laws, and defaulters to excise or customs who had incurred fines which they were unable to pay, were supposed to be incarcerated behind an iron-plated door closing up a second prison, consisting of a strong cell or two, and a blind alley some yard and a half wide.... In practice they had come to be considered a little too bad, though in theory they were quite as good as ever; which may be observed to be the case at the present day with other cells that are not at all strong, and with other alleys that are stone-blind. (LD I, vi; 97)

As an analogue of the city and of the home, the prison completes another circle of the bureaucratic hell managed (if that is the right word for doing nothing) by the Circumlocution Office. The Circumlocution Office, which has a claim on Dorrit and which criminalizes debtors and inventors alike, is one segment in the labyrinth of different transformations of the prison in the convoluted web of the plot. The prison is, moreover, a typically British institution inspected from time to time by someone from some office who goes away after doing his nothing, "neatly epitomizing the administration of most of the public affairs in our right little, tight little, island" (LD I, vi; 97). It is, therefore, a branch of the Circumlocution Office in what Carlyle called in *Latter-Day Pamphlets* the "red-tape jungle."

The metonymic quality of Arthur's view of the ragged population in and around the prison, much less joyful than the dancing clothes sketched by Boz in

Monmouth Street, is indicative of the way the prison moves outside the walls into the mind of the observer of the city:

> There was a string of people already straggling in, whom it was not difficult to identify as the non-descript messengers, go-betweens, and errand-bearers of the place. Some of them had been lounging in the rain until the gate should open; others, who had timed their arrival with greater nicety, were coming up now, and passing in with damp whity-brown paper bags from the grocers, loaves of bread, lumps of butter, eggs, milk, and the like. The shabbiness of these attendants upon shabbiness, the poverty of these insolvent waiters upon insolvency, was a sight to see. Such threadbare coats and trousers, such fusty gowns and shawls, such squashed hats and bonnets, such boots and shoes, such umbrellas and walking-sticks, never were seen in Rag Fair. All of them wore the cast-off clothes of other men and women, were made up of patches and pieces of other people's individuality, and had no sartorial existence of their own proper. (LD I, ix; 130)

This dismal scene presents to Arthur on the morning of his first (accidental) imprisonment in the Marshalsea the affinity of poverty inside and outside the prison and exposes the way the city has dissolved subjectivity itself. These were men and women "made up of patches and pieces of other people's individuality, and had no sartorial existence of their own proper." Almost anticipating modernism, the metonym becomes the person: "Mendicity on commission stooped in their high shoulders, shambled in their unsteady legs, buttoned and pinned and darned and dragged their clothes, frayed their button-holes, leaked out their figures in dirty little ends of tape, and issued from their mouths in alcoholic breathings" (130). This dissolution of selfhood reflects Arthur's own conscious state, and his story is the story of resistance to it as the child of parents who allowed him no will in a society which allowed no individuality.[27]

The debtors are not isolated as in the penitentiary, but can receive visitors and traders and can otherwise make themselves comfortable. Liberty is relative and confinement universal, a capitalistic venture and power structure under the franchise of the Father of Marshalsea, himself a prisoner. Dorrit has fled the confusion and incoherence of the affairs of this world to the Marshalsea, a refuge in a way from the everyday troubles of life though a false one, because Amy keeps secret from him the source of his food and income, as well as the fact that her "streety" brother cannot hold down a job. Dickens, who has set the novel in the time of his father's imprisonment for debt and is writing some years after the Marshalsea ceased to be a debtors' prison, gives birth in his imagination to his own father, the Father of the Marshalsea himself and to the Child of the Marshalsea. The Lacanian absence of the father may be sensed in his castration as family supporter and his emasculation, while Arthur's visits to the prison and his own imprisonment in it lead him quite literally to the name of the father. Another Dickensian angel, Little Dorrit, is one of those innocent child-martyrs and diminutive sexless women who parent their own fathers, along with Little Nell, Agnes, and other domestic saints. There is also in Little Dorrit something of Dickens's own experience of negotiating the city outside the walls of his family's secret home. For example, her furtiveness reflects his own visits to the Marshalsea, hidden from Bob Fagin in the autobiographical fragment, his determination to manage his own and his family's finances better than his father, and, perhaps, a working through of envy of his sister's musical talents in the depiction of the "professional" Fanny in the theater.[28]

The prison scene that opens *Little Dorrit* emerges out of the staring heat of Marseilles, a site of revolution in a Carlylean view of history, which carries overtones of the Marshalsea in the city's name, a hellish trap for anyone who falls afoul of the cruel laws of the city into poverty. Both Arthur and Little Dorrit must experience a literal and metaphysical prison in order to overcome the discourse which condemns them to commodification. Little Dorrit is the ideal repository of resistance to the cruel ethics of the city, and in her there resides an unspoiled and incorruptible innocence that turns prison walls into a metaphysical refuge from the corruption of the city. As for Arthur, when the walls close around him, he faces a choice that rereads the moral boundaries of the city as he seeks clues to the mystery of the inheritance plot.

If Lord Decimus Tite Barnacle's "labyrinths of sentences" are a minor comic eccentricity, the "gloomy labyrinth" of Mrs. Clennam's mind is far from humorous. However, Mrs. Plornish's comic attempts at Tuscan succeed in breaking out of the prison-house of language, just as much as Jo's idiolect. As in the legal labyrinth of *Bleak House*, language must escape the imprisoning "exigencies of representation itself"[29] and excite a compassion deriving from a different reading of the city in a linguistic series of differences that assumes an alternative construction of subjectivity. A playful perversity in naming opposes the harsh law of prisons and foundling hospitals, as in the substitution of the changeable and absurd Tattycoram for the harsh regime of the arbitrary naming of "Harriet Beadle," a substitution of the subjective for the solipsistic that (as in Bumble's naming of Oliver Twist) opposes two sign systems and two philosophies of life: the real-life Thomas Coram's philanthropy in founding a children's hospital and the self-interested pomposity of a Bumble. When Miss Wade rescues Tattycoram from the paternalistic philanthropy of Meagles, her opposition to Jarndyce-type charity is shown to be a perversion in league with the city's demon Rigaud (though Meagles's sermon at the end of the novel that Little Dorrit is a lesson in "Duty" hardly sounds like a convincing endorsement of Victorian domesticity).

Fashionable society in *Little Dorrit* is all veneer and no content, corrupted by perverted logic (such as Mrs. Merdle's or Miss Wade's) and by a demonic obsession with money, the contagion of speculation that infects Arthur as well. This will be a theme of *Our Mutual Friend*. The difference between official irresponsibility in the Circumlocution Office (expounded by Ferdinand Barnacle as a justifiable practice of government) and the criminal deceit of swindlers like the worthless idol Merdle is seen to be one of degree. This necessarily complicates an understanding of criminality, especially if we consider it in the context of Dickens's complex attitudes towards crime, which the Victorians regarded as the potential undoing of their civilization.

THE PUNISHMENT OF DISCIPLINE

> ... this astonishing increase in human depravity has taken place during a period of unexampled prosperity and unprecedented progress.... If this is the progress of crime during the days of [the British empire's] prosperity, what is likely to become in those of its decline...?
>
> —*Blackwood's Magazine*, July 1844

> The Newgate Calendar may belong to the history of London, but it is not that history.
>
> —Robert Vaughan, *The Age of Great Cities*

Fagin's den, the workhouse, and the prison run on similarly dishonest principles. It is no wonder that Bentham, back in 1791, thought his "Panopticon" suited both jail and workhouse because it corrected the same problem of unemployment and poverty. "Morals reformed," he boasted, "—health preserved—industry invigorated—instruction diffused—public burdens lightened—economy seated, as it were, on a rock—the Gordian knot of poor laws not cut but untied, all by a simple idea in Architecture."[30] Pugin mocked Bentham's "Panopticon" in his *Contrasts*, attacking the "Modern Poor House" as inferior to monastic charity and satirizing the efficient recycling of the bodies of the poor for dissection (fig. 16). Pugin understood the architectural principles behind the ideology of the utilitarian model city, and a Benthamite jail stands in the foreground of Pugin's modern town in his contrast of a medieval Catholic city with a modern factory town, which, like Coketown, is built to a uniform architecture.

The "Panopticon" was influential not only in the design of such prisons as the Philadelphia penitentiary, but also in the equation of crime and poverty in the 1834 Poor Law Amendment Act which intended the workhouse to operate as a deterrent to idleness and wanton increase of the unproductive elements in the population.[31] The Poor Law Bastille was attacked in *The Times* in the second half of 1836 for its inhuman conditions and for encouraging crime and prostitution, since no other means of subsistence were possible outside the workhouse, so that Dickens was not saying anything substantially new when he published the first installment of *Oliver Twist* in February 1837. He was in fact criticized for anachronism in depicting abuses of power which had been ended by the commissioners of the new Poor Law who were responsible for the efficient administration of a rationalized, centralized system.[32]

Meanwhile, the prison was being gradually reformed between 1832 and 1868 into a centralized unified system with some semblance of clear policy. The savagery of punishment, particularly its public spectacles of corporal and capital punishment, was also becoming a thing of the past, because it did not serve the interests of the landowning classes, who might hesitate to prosecute for a minor offense that was punishable by execution or transportation (perhaps that is one reason why Brownlow is unwilling to prosecute Oliver for pickpocketing); besides, execution of sentence was notoriously unpredictable. Dickens campaigned against public hangings, which were ended by the 1868 Capital Punishment Amendment Act. Dickens's letters in the *Daily News*, in 1846, argued that capital punishment was inhumane and archaic; far from deterring crime, it depraved public morals and provided the kind of public spectacle depicted in Hogarth's *The Idle Apprentice*, which encouraged lewd behavior and pickpocketing.

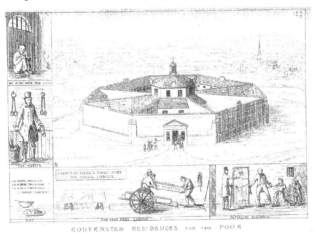

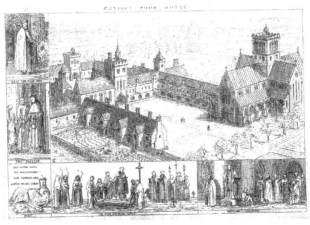

Fig. 16: Pugin, "Contrasted Residences for the Poor" (1841)

The public spectacle of violence performed on the body usually afforded carnival enjoyment and sadistic pleasure of the sort imagined being meted out in eighteenth-century London and Paris in *A Tale of Two Cities*, including the painful execution inflicted on Robert-François Damiens in 1757. That execution is cited by Foucault as an illustration of the public spectacle that was replaced by the institution of an unseen punishment no less dreaded or certain for being carried out behind walls, a step toward punishment by an efficient modern administrative system in which only the condemnation was visible and shameful.[33] In "Going to See a Man Hanged" (*Fraser's Magazine*, August 1840), Thackeray noted the crowd's carnivalesque mood and sensed empathy for the hanged man, though there is little evidence such scenes or descriptions in the *Newgate Calendar* and *Jonathan Wild* actually aroused sympathy for hardened villains. Ainsworth's Jack Sheppard enjoys popular solidarity, but Fagin stands in danger of being lynched by the riotous mob before he is safely executed. Compared with Thackeray's expression of shame at participating in what he felt to be a judicial murder, witnessed moreover by children, Dickens's arguments are less emotional and more reasoned. The death penalty, he thought, was too terrible a sentence to leave to fallible human judges, and execution could not be reversed if new evidence turned up exonerating the accused. Of particular interest is the clash of Dickens's imaginative sympathy with a utilitarian position: to Macaulay's sexist remark in Parliament that anyone who questioned the usefulness of capital punishment must be a victim of "effeminate feeling," Dickens responds sarcastically that this makes the hangman the manliest person in the kingdom.[34] It was the public visibility of the hanging that Dickens found most objectionable, and it pinpointed for him the savagery within Victorian civilization. Nonetheless, Dickens is in sympathy with the mob no more than Thackeray, for their carnival possession of the street on such occasions threatens riot and disorder.

Bentham's optimism that a "Panopticon" could control wrongdoing is not matched by Dickens's treatment of surveillance; when Pickwick sits for his "likeness" in the Fleet we are made to feel the discomfort of the operation. "La visibilité est un piège," Foucault has said.[35] Visibility is something which is constantly threatening Oliver, who hoped he'd be able to disappear in the huge metropolis, although he does not comprehend what is the precise danger of the gaze of Monks and Fagin. In *Household Words* the discipline of prison architecture was mocked as quite ineffective and inhuman. Echoing Dickens's own abhorrence of corporal punishment and his treatment of crime and punishment in *Oliver Twist* and *Little Dorrit*, R. H. Horne (in "London Sparrows," *Household Words*, 19 April 1851) tells an old gentleman's story of being pickpocketed like Mr. Brownlow by children and expresses his indignation at the elaborate and expensive ritual of whipping at a London Bridewell, a punishment carried out in view of the awesome prison buildings. Horne pleads for compassion and prevention instead of statistical reassurances and the cruel discipline of the prison inscribed on the body by a paternalistic society.

One reason why crime and prostitution occupied Poe, Balzac, Hugo, Dickens, and, later, Dostoevsky is their attempt in their fiction to understand the psychology of law and society. These were real facts of city life which gripped the reader's imagination with terrifying tales of disgrace, poverty, and sudden death, the calamities of modern life which could be visited on anyone who ran afoul of the law or fell victim to conniving villains, a psychological fear which needed to be released through fantasized projection. Fagin, Rigaud, and Vautrin are attractive monsters, yet when misdeeds are rationalized by a Heep, a Rastignac, or a Raskolnikov, crime becomes an intellectual problem, the problem of Macbeth and Iago, as in Edward Bulwer-Lytton's portrait of Eugene Aram, which he claimed (in the preface to the novel) was entirely distinct from the "profligate knavery" and "brutal cruelty" of the literature of Newgate and the Hulks. Hugo, groping towards the motivation of criminality in *Les Misérables*, chooses to characterize the lower depths of Paris by stringing together stories of different characters connected in a labyrinth of coincidences that shows no escape from poverty and the most unrelenting, persecuting injustice in a dark cosmos of city and nation; all France, Hugo tells us, is a suburb of Paris.

Writing in an age of utilitarianism, Dickens knew the philosophy behind the system and behind crime was equally amoral, as did Dostoevsky, with his own bitter disillusion in the idealism of the forties, in *Crime and Punishment*. It is not so much that the way of the world changed between Moll Flanders and Vautrin and society came to be regarded as criminal, as Burton Pike has it,[36] but that the rationality of the Enlightenment was itself exposed as criminally amoral. Sikes does not become a Macbeth,[37] for all the terror of the corpse's eyes which pursue him and drive him to his own death: he bears the stamp of the wanted criminal, lacking only fetters to complete his police description. However, the fact that Fagin and Sikes come alive in the imagination in all their spinechilling horror lends a sinister, almost paranoiac and nightmarish atmosphere to the city in which the novel imprisons us without any sense of possible release.

The only escape is into natural virtue and compassion, associated with a romanticized, absent Nature and what one early critic of *Oliver Twist* unkindly called a "*feelosophy*"[38] which is opposed to everything the utilitarian system of rational self-interest stands for. The utilitarians who wrote in *The Westminster Review* in the 1820s were aware of such hostile attitudes toward what was perceived as the hard-hearted aspect of utilitarian rationalism, which ruled out social change except by economic laws. J. S. Mill recalls in his *Autobiography* that they "retorted by the word 'sentimentality,'" a term of opprobrium in their vocabulary since "cultivation of feelings" was not held in high esteem. Ricardo and Malthus might sound dreary and despairing to the layman, who might not appreciate J. S. Mill's point that "While fully recognizing the superior excellence of unselfish benevolence and love of justice, we did not expect the regeneration of mankind from any direct action on those sentiments, but from the effect of educated intellect, enlightening the selfish feelings."[39] That is a retrospective confession, and it does not mitigate the thrust of the dialectic. For the utilitarians, charity could never be in line with social justice. W. R. Greg, writing in *The Westminster*

Review in June 1845, complained of the benevolence behind Lord Ashley's factory and mining legislation and liberal proposals to relieve poverty: "We are weary of this cuckoo-cry—*always charity, never justice,*—always the *open purse,* never the *equal* measure."[40] It is nevertheless Oliver's instinctive compassion that disproves a theory which excludes any spontaneous or altruistic feeling; even the hardened prostitute Nancy answers some hidden wellspring of her being and denounces the gang to save the child. Dickens castigates Fagin's parodic social contract because its scientific model of society is dishonest and inhuman and because it outlaws the compassion of charity, much like that other sinful city of destruction, Sodom.

The "wickedness and guilt" of the city can be redeemed only as long as the soul remains uncorrupted. Rose (herself of "doubtful birth") pleads on behalf of Oliver, "think that he may never have known a mother's love, or the comfort of a home; that ill-usage and blows, or the want of bread, may have driven him to herd with men who have forced him to guilt ... think of this, before you let them drag this sick child to a prison, which in any case must be the grave of all his chances of amendment" (OT xxx; 268). Rose's plea for mercy, on the grounds that it could equally have been her as this innocent child, chimes with the narrator's earlier words that if only the imagination would awaken our sympathy with our fellows, how many stories of human cruelty the dead could tell us. This anti-determinist romanticized appeal to an intimation of immortality in the innocent child attacks an inhuman, wicked system that punishes children rather than preventing what drives them to crime. Resistance to evil is not possible when utilitarianism or evangelicalism cripples the individual will, but once the falsity of the system is recognized, the will to good can be regained. Mr. Gradgrind's conversion and Mrs. Clennam's Lazarus-like dash through the streets to make up with Amy are fictional miracles that offer the possibility of resurrection in the necropolis. On the other hand, poetic justice is done to Sikes, Bitzer, and Casby, and no sympathy is found for monstrous villains like Fagin and Rigaud, not even the Christian compassion with which the bishop Monsieur Myriel in Hugo's *Les Misérables* purchases the penance of Valjean, who in turn redeems the prostitute Fantine shortly before her death and adopts her illegitimate daughter.

Little Dorrit confirms the view in *The City of God* of the fallen sons of Adam treading the maze of the lower world, afflicted by the deeds of wicked men like Merdle. Yet Dickens clearly did not agree with Augustine's conclusion that evil desires and ignorance could only be restrained by "the birch, the strap, the cane," which are the scripturally endorsed instruments of education, an education by punishment recalled by Arthur and satirized in the Grinders' School and elsewhere. Dickens's novels mock the discipline and punish philosophy of education that works by internalization of a doctrine of guilt which criminalizes the child, just as it criminalizes the poor.

The prison serves as both a toponymical space in the urban labyrinth and a figure for metaphorical imprisonment, in the city's legal system in *Bleak House* (Chancery *is* London), in Coketown's industrial utilitarianism in *Hard Times*, or the professional amorality of money and law in *Great Expectations*. The ambiguity of the relations between different levels of representation helps in establishing connections between Pip's sense of being stained by Newgate and Jaggers's secret knowledge, Oliver Twist's capture by Fagin and his relationship with Monks, or the affinity of Arthur and Little Dorrit. The effect is to imbue the city with an atmosphere of menacing evil, whose precise identity is veiled, though understood to be demonic and inhuman in *Oliver Twist* and *The Old Curiosity Shop*. In *Little Dorrit*, J. Hillis Miller finds for the first time a consciousness of anxiety in the characters' psyche and thoughts[41] that may suggest an urban consciousness which allows us to perceive the psychological portrait of Arthur's mental confrontation with his mother's imprisoning house and the imprisoning city, or Miss Wade's self-tormenting complexes, though nothing so obsessively introspective as Raskolnikov's sick mind.

We have thus moved beyond the prison as setting and symbol to the presentation of character and society in the ideational discourse of the novel, which raises the question, how human nature may be corrected, if it can be. In *David Copperfield*, Copperfield, now the mature writer, visits Creakle's prison to inspect the solitary system, a system first tried out at Pentonville in 1842 and one to which Dickens was vigorously opposed. In "Pet Prisoners" (*Household Words*, 27 April 1850) Dickens had engaged in a Swiftian dialogue with reformers such as the Reverend John Field (chaplain of Reading County Jail) and Harriet Martineau by ridiculing their trust in discipline to reform criminals into useful members of the labor force. For his part, in his *Prison Discipline: The Advantages of the Separate System of Imprisonment* (2nd ed., 1848), Field had repeated Joseph Adshead's mockery of Dickens in *Prisons and Prisoners* (1848) as a "fugacious prison inspector" who had the audacity to question the wisdom of experienced experts.[42] The sneer at "petting prisoners" (repeated in *Great Expectations*) reinforced Dickens's earlier conclusion, drawn from the Philadelphia experiment, that it was based on a misunderstanding of the human mind and tended to drive inmates insane if confined for too long a period. Dickens preferred the silent system as practiced at Coldbath Fields in London, because it reduced the association between convicts that contaminated them with further temptation without the cruelty of long-term solitary confinement. By contrast, Mr. William Barker in "The Last Cab-Driver and the First Omnibus Cad" very much enjoys solitary confinement in preference to laboring at the wheel and spends the rest of his sentence on his back singing comic songs (SB 175).

Dickens seems to have felt that some exercise of self-denial and restraint was essential to moral reformation and praised, albeit not without reservation, the Marks System, advocated by penal reformer Captain Alexander Maconochie, which gave rewards for good behavior, later introduced in English prisons, as well as in Urania Cottage, the home for Fallen Women established by Dickens and funded by Angela Coutts (despite the policy to avoid anything punitive and to educate toward virtue by choice). Appealing to the middle-class taxpayer's pocket and respect for law and order, Dickens attacked the perversion of government priorities which invested vast sums on a system that was ineffective, wrongheaded, and un-Christian, since it failed to promote remorse for the crime or true repentance, and, moreover, prepared criminals for transportation rather than applying the same resources to alleviate starvation and poverty on the streets (DJ 2: 214).

Unfortunately, Dickens's criticism of the inordinate expense of the Model Prison was read as supporting Carlyle's second *Latter-Day Pamphlet*, "Model Prisons," launched on an outraged public just a few weeks before. Passages from Carlyle's diatribe against Exeter Hall philanthropy were laid side by side in *Fraser's Magazine* with those from *David Copperfield*, and the comparison tended to the conclusion that Dickens thought with Carlyle that the prisoners were better cared for than an English duke and that the scoundrels deserved nothing better than a "collar round the neck, and a cartwhip flourished over the back."[43] Nevertheless, a glance at the comic treatment of the prison in *David Copperfield* dispels any confusion of Carlyle's reactionary condemnation of false pity for those "diabolic" specimens of "animalism" with Dickens's conviction, echoed in "The Demeanour of Murderers" (*Household Words*, 14 June 1856), that men who poisoned their wives deserved no pity because they had none themselves. The prison in this novel is an all-too-obvious transformation of Salem House, where Copperfield was schooled in discipline and punishment (the school as a penal institution of discipline and punishment will be recalled from Miss Monflather's establishment and Squeer's Academy). As such, the school shadows forth the adult prison-house which dims the Wordsworthian innocence of childhood in "Ode: Intimations of Immortality," to which I referred in the opening of this chapter, that commonplace of Victorian writing that drew on an ancient metaphor of the imprisoned soul.

The Benthamite theory of discipline and punishment, taken up by Foucault as a model of eighteenth- and nineteenth-century social theory, is scathingly satirized by Dickens because it is System—absolute and infallible, which cannot be discussed or criticized, though the warders exchange knowing looks in *David Copperfield*. It is hypocrisy to pretend the likes of Heep and Littimer have really mended their ways. On the contrary, Uriah Heep is mouthing once more the lesson of being humble drummed into him at school, in a ranting discourse of the penitence with which he has been indoctrinated. In the evangelizing spirit of John Styles's letter to his mother (satirized in "Pet Prisoners"), Heep begs the gentlemen to come and join him in order that they too can mend their sinful ways. He is so forceful that Copperfield is glad when he is safely locked away. Dickens's solution in the novel is to transform Micawber into a benevolent magistrate alongside a radiant Mell in Australia, an acting-out of Dickens's own earlier ambition to be a London magistrate, a post for which he lacked the necessary qualifications.[44] Curiously, this utopian plan is feasible only in that vast dumping ground overseas where hardened criminals and prostitutes were transported for reformation.

Turning around the medical trope for crime, Dickens argued in "Lying Awake" (*Household Words*, 30 October 1852) that cruel punishments such as public whipping were "contagious" devices. As in any other disciplinary institution, they made the whole culture barbaric, from workhouses to madhouses, from schools to families. Dickens was opposed to reactionary measures that returned England to torture in dungeons for the same reason that he was against "petting" prisoners in Pentonville, because it did not answer the social ills. What did answer better than that, he wrote, were "hard work, and one unchanging and uncompromising dietary of bread and water" (DJ 3: 94).[45] This may seem unpalatable to those who would regard Dickens as a liberal reformer, but it reaffirms the more strongly the asssumption that society is not going to be changed by reforming institutions instead of dismantling a system based on inhuman principles of discipline and punishment.

THE PRISON-HOUSE OF THE NOVEL

> *Hamlet*: Denmark's a prison.
> *Rosencrantz*: Then is the world one.
> *Hamlet*: A goodly one; in which there are many confines, wards and dungeons, Denmark being one o' the worst.
> —Shakespeare, *Hamlet*

> *Duke Vincentio*: Correction and instruction must both work
> Ere this rude beast will profit.
> —Shakespeare, *Measure for Measure*

The prison exerts its discipline and inscribes its mark on the body, which is thereby ideologized and subjected, as Foucault sees it,[46] whether in the quarantined city during plague or under the surveillance of Bentham's "Panopticon"—the two are (as I have shown) closely connected.[47] My analysis of *Little Dorrit*, however, has tried to show that its narrative resists a discourse of discipline by a rational authoritarian society and its plot subverts the design of the prison, interpreted by Bender as a similar narrative structure of confinement and reformation.[48] *Little Dorrit* redefines criminality and challenges the discourse of discipline which attempts to reform the individual in a cruel misconception of pain and happiness that puts Jeremy Bentham in unexpected affinity with Mrs. Clennam's religion of punishment for sin. Its novelistic practice, moreover, responds to the prison-city by positing the ludic and the pastoral, at least as imaginary spaces in the minds of the beleaguered innocents of the prison and of Bleeding Heart Yard.[49]

Panoptic control of a panoramic view exposes the carcereal conditions of the city at the heart of the commercial system, revealed in Mayhew's balloon view, but, as noted in a previous chapter, it shows the ideological control in such a distancing of the city's conditions of crime and prostitution. In Pierce Egan's *Life in London* (II, v), after previously passing the debtors in the Fleet as quickly as possible, Tom and Jerry note the harrowing scene of the condemned men's yard at Newgate Prison and admire their masculine fortitude, yet they return for a bird's-eye view of the praiseworthy order. Discipline is achieved by classifying the criminals according to a typology of their crimes and constant surveillance, which makes escape impossible. However, Boz has too much humanity not to feel compunction at such scenes, nor can the narrator of *Nicholas Nickleby* turn away from the "all-comprehensive agony" of "the dying wretch" in Newgate, in the "very core" of London, where there is nobody to feel compassion or pity.

Dickens's novels should not been seen as the agent of ideological law enforcement but as a house of correction of such ideology. The English novel was accused of fraternizing with popular street culture and was indicted from the early eighteenth-century onwards for encouraging immorality and social unrest, but that, as Lennard Davis contends, was because the theoretical and structural assumptions of the novel were in a sense "criminal in nature."[50] Language must break out of the claustral confines of conventional representation and show it to be false. The tensions between the figurative and literal spaces of the city subvert any black and white, either/or representation. If *Sketches by Boz* explored the commonplace in order to shift our sympathies down-market and to test the possibilities of representing the quirky and eccentric aspects of the everyday, we have in the marriage of Amy and Arthur, which concludes *Little Dorrit*, the apotheosis of sympathy exclusively with those who go down into the lower world transformed by knowledge of the city, and Pancks's public punishment of Casby, a latterday shearing of Samson which emasculates the rack-renting landlord in a symbolic castration scene, provides a radical example of fantasized possibilities.

The test of the novel is not, as D. A. Miller would understand this term, police realism. In *Oliver Twist*, Losberne realizes that the Bow Street runners Duff and Blathers, who are comic but not dull-witted, will not read Oliver's story with Rose Maylie's imaginative compassion because the facts will incriminate him, unless he meddles with the evidence. Such a mode of realism is beyond the understanding of police constables in *Great Expectations* who "took up several obviously wrong people, and ... ran their heads very hard against wrong ideas, and persisted in trying to fit the circumstances to the ideas, instead of trying to extract ideas from the circumstances" (GE xvi; 149). This is hardly what Dr. Watson later called the realism of police reports in Arthur Conan Doyle's "A Case of Identity."[51] In Dickens's day these were a source of information for reformers and writers alike, a statistical representation that criminalized the poor and placed prostitutes under police surveillance. Charles Knight's *London* cites police statistics not only of convicted and habitual criminals, but also of vagrants and bearers of begging-letters, as well as no less than three classes of prostitutes, all of whom were under police observation and jurisdiction, a classification typical of statistical representations of the homeless and outcasts in police reports.[52] Instead, like Sherlock Holmes, Dickens's narrator lifts the lid off reality with a truth "better than any novel-book" as Blathers would say (OT xxxi; 278), that is, a representation which rejects all others as "fiction."

Observation and surveillance are keys to knowledge ("intelligence") and therefore control in the city, where there are no neighbors or community to keep watch (as Chadwick stressed in his 1829 Benthamite pamphlet "Preventive Police"). The British police were famous for their discreet and invisible surveillance, often noted by foreign visitors like Max Schlesinger, who (in *Saunterings about London*, 1853) recognized that effective prevention of crime and protection of the middle classes from London's criminal hordes guaranteed the illusion of untrammeled liberty. Yet Dickens's narrators are not policemen, however much the Uncommercial Traveller treads an amateur beat around the streets of London, regarding himself "as a higher sort of police-constable" (UT 345). Dickens detested the abuse of police powers to control pauperism, though he had harsh words for policemen who didn't go down dark alleys.[53] In fact, if we are to judge by a whimsical sketch written in the manner of *A Sentimental Journey*, "Please to Leave Your Umbrella" (*Household Words*, 1 May 1858), Dickens resented the police's usurping of powers of caretakers of private thought and of truth in public places.

True, in "On Duty with Inspector Field" (*Household Words*, 14 June 1851), Dickens admires the "regulation" of the poor and the Inspector's ability to penetrate the labyrinth of squalid lodging houses in St. Giles', the Borough, and Whitechapel. These he patrols just like the imperial treasures of the British Museum, the displayed artifacts of colonialism which form a body of knowledge that controls representation of empire. Yet control and surveillance are subordinate to the interest of the detective as an agent of discovery of an unknown world, a "roving eye" at home everywhere and able to penetrate the secret passages of London's underworld:

> How many people may there be in London, who, if we had brought them deviously and blindfold, to this street, fifty paces from the Station House, and within call of Saint Giles's church, would know it for a not remote part of the city in which their lives are passed? How many, who amidst this compound of sickening smells, these heaps of filth, these tumbling houses, with all their vile contents, animate and inanimate, slimily overflowing into the black road, would believe that they breathe *this* air? (DJ 2: 360; emphasis in the original)

The interest the scene has for the author is the shared moral responsibility for this neglected blight, whereas for the policeman it is a matter of clearing the way on pain of detention and punishment. In response to the awful slum conditions in *Oliver Twist*, *Bleak House*, and *Little Dorrit*, Esther's sheltering of Jo and the quasilegal activities of Messers Brownlow, Losberne, and Maylie would suggest that individual initiative could, at least in the imagination, ignore reasons of state and circumvent the long arm of the law.

The activities of novelists and policemen, which have seemed so similar to some scholars,[54] seem here to be at odds with each other. In "Detective Police" (*Household Words*, 27 July 1850), Dickens is careful to distinguish between the constabulary (the old Bow Street Runners) and the new detectives from Scotland

Yard, and Dickens accords the new type of detective much respect in *Bleak House* and *Household Words*. Inspector Bucket belongs to the new genre of investigating detectives (constituted with the Metropolitan Police in 1842), who prove Peel's constabulary incompetent fools, because like the judiciary and the legislature which they serve, they are blind to the connections that can be made only in the imagination, connections which are equivalent to narrative devices in the novel. The authority to have the Jos of this world "moved on" or removed makes the police, like Mrs. Pardiggle, invasive agents of the new public order, whereas the secret knowledge of the detective places him as guardian of the middle-class home—a Lacanian *lieu-tenant* of paternity and inheritance (Jaggers the lawyer is another such "lieutenant" of other people's secrets).

Violating the sacred principle of the impenetrability of the home in the name of protection of middle-class domesticity, Inspector Bucket himself intrudes into homes under false pretenses and has excluded himself from his own domestic space in order to trap Hortense, though he manages to warm his feet by the fire of that ultimate public place, the police station. Inspector Bucket is an agent of narration who embodies the novelist's drive to uncover motivation and resolve plots, but, unlike the police constable, the detective possesses the tact and discretion essential in uncovering family mysteries which must not be subject to the public gaze. This, incidentally, is a point made in W. H. Wills's Freudian joke about the "rape of the lock" when the lady's jewel box in her bedchamber is "wiolated," reminding us of Bucket's relations with locks and door-handles ("The Modern Science of Thief-Taking," *Household Words*, 13 July 1850). Bucket is the ultimate private eye because there is no barrier to his knowledge of the city and in this he is like the real Inspector Field who is "equally at home everywhere" (DJ 2: 367) and cannot be said to belong to one place or class. Field was Dickens's "Night-Guide" to London's nocturnal dens and denizens. Dickens patronized the detectives, who would, he boasted, do anything for him; they provided him with a good story and a "character," as well as protecting him on his slumming expeditions, as he informed Bulwer-Lytton and the Duke of Devonshire (*Letters* 6: 377–81).

Dickens has been accused of turning reactionary with the conservative trend toward harsher discipline after 1850 and of sharing the authoritarian sentiments of Carlyle's *Latter-Day Pamphlets*, which warned of the threat of anarchy.[55] Humphry House asserts, rather inaccurately, that Dickens had scarcely a word of criticism for the police, which he explains by worship of authoritarian power after Dickens realized the failure of individualist competition and fell prey to Freudian impulses.[56] Actually it was the failure of the police to keep the streets safe and prevent sexual harassment that prompted Dickens's call for the "Ruffian" to be kept out of the way of decent people and to have his "back scarified often and deep" ("The Ruffian," *All the Year Round*, 10 October 1868; UT 302). The zealousness of the Uncommercial Traveller in prosecuting a young woman for foul language sets him up as the public guardian of middle-class law and order. But it also proposes deterrence as a means of prevention, not moral reformation, which might indicate pessimism about the possibility of change in human nature reflected in some of Dickens's villains. Dickens repeatedly singled out one type of repeating offender who could not be reformed, the hard convict who should not be "petted," quite in line with earlier criticism of prison as a Benthamite reformatory instead of a place where convicts were punished.[57]

If Sikes, Fagin, and Rigaud are irredeemably bad, there seems to be a level of redeemability below which they have sunk. Carker's brother John does penance and makes restitution, and even Alice Marwood allows Harriet to read to her on her death bed from the Christian scriptures. It depends, of course, whether criminality is defined as an offense against laws or against Nature. A characteristic passage in *Dombey and Son* is eloquent on this issue. Having drawn lessons from the pride of Dombey and Edith, on the one hand, and the ex-convict Alice Marwood, on the other, the narrator wonders whether this is not a natural characteristic when the mind is prisoner to a master-vice, whether it is not "natural to be unnatural" when one is blind to the truth of Nature. Dickens then goes on to speak of the moral pestilence which would shock us if we could see it in the polluted air of the "unnatural outcasts" of society, urging us to think of the consequences of being born and bred in hell and to see the depravity and nameless sins against human nature festering in the city. "Then should we stand appalled to know, that where we generate disease to strike our children down and entail itself on unborn generations, there also we breed, by the same certain process, infancy that knows no innocence, youth without modesty or shame, maturity that is mature in nothing but in suffering and guilt, blasted old age that is a scandal on the form we bear. Unnatural humanity! When we shall gather grapes from thorns, and figs from thistles; when fields of grain shall spring up from the offal in the by-ways of our wicked cities, and roses bloom in the fat churchyards that they cherish; then we may look for natural humanity, and find it growing from such seed" (D&S XLVII; 620). Despite the determinist implications of the metaphor of disease, the insistence on moral responsibility is a call to make the world a better place and not add to the legion of the Destroying Angel by further perversion of Nature. Dombey and Edith take their course to doom, while Florence and Walter, who marry in a city church in a labyrinth of lost souls, respond to natural affection and heed the voice of eternity.

The repetitive motif in Dickens's novels of moral reformation within the city looks increasingly to the transcendental and spiritual as capitalism tightens its hold on the city—the referential background to *Little Dorrit* is of course the proliferation of financial scandals and the attempt to regulate the banking system. Obsession with money in the portrait of Dorrit motivates a transformation of Dickens's earlier reworking of the Lear motif in *The Old Curiosity Shop* as a distinctly urban nightmare (like Old Goriot's deluded obsession with his daughters). The bleak city of the later novels is malignant and merciless. The question, of course, is whether one must submit to Pope's "mighty maze" once it has been shown to be disorder in reality and not just in appearance.[58] More importantly, once the human condition is recognized for what it is, what meaning, if any, can be assigned to salvation in the city?

NOTES

1   See Malcolm Andrews, *Dickens and the Grown-Up Child* (Iowa City: University of Iowa Press, 1994), 56–70.
2   See, for example, Dickens, "What Christmas Is As We Grow Older," *Household Words*, (Extra Christmas Number, 1851): 1–3.
3   John Forster, *The Life of Charles Dickens* (London: Dent, 1969), 1: 16.
4   *The Life of Charles Dickens*, 1: 16.
5   *The Life of Charles Dickens*, 1: 16–17.
6   Edmund Wilson, *The Wound and the Bow: Seven Studies in Literature* (London: Methuen, 1961), 26.
7   A. O. J. Cockshut, *The Imagination of Charles Dickens* (London: Methuen, 1965), 26–49.
8   Lionel Trilling, "*Little Dorrit*," in *Dickens: A Collection of Critical Essays*, ed. Martin Price (Englewood Cliffs, NJ: Prentice-Hall, 1987), 150.
9   *Violence and the Modern State: Dreams of the Scaffold* (London: Macmillan, and New York: St. Martin's Press, 1995).
10   *Dickens and the City* (London: Athlone Press, 1979).
11   Forster, *The Life of Charles Dickens*, 2: 185.
12   John Carey, *The Violent Effigy: A Study of Dickens's Imagination* (London: Faber and Faber, 1973), 113–17.
13   Gerald Coniffe, "The Prison of the Lower World," in *Charles Dickens: New Perspectives*, ed. Wendall Stacy Johnson (Englewood Cliffs, NJ: Prentice-Hall, 1982), 115.
14   Chris Brooks, *Signs for the Times: Symbolic Realism in the Mid-Victorian World* (London: Allen & Unwin, 1984), 70–71.
15   J. J. Tobias, *Urban Crime in Victorian England* (New York: Schocken, 1972).
16   J. Hillis Miller, *Charles Dickens: The World of His Novels* (Cambridge, MA: Harvard University Press, 1958), 232.
17   On the connection between archeological discoveries and the novel's representation of London, see Nancy Metz, "*Little Dorrit's* London: Babylon Revisited," *Victorian Studies* 33.3 (1990): 465–86.
18   Gerald Bruns, "Cain: Or the Metaphorical Construction of Cities," *Salmagundi* 64–65 (1987): 74.
19   See Manuel Aguirre, *The Closed Space: Horror Literature and Western Symbolism* (Manchester: Manchester University Press, 1990).
20   Dickens links the general corruption and incompetence with financial fraud and the collapse of a bank in "Nobody, Somebody, and Everybody" (*Household Words*, 30 August 1856), written after the suicide of a Treasury official and Irish M.P., John Seidler, the model for Merdle. See Forster, *The Life of Charles Dickens*, 2: 183; John Butt and Kathleen Tillotson, *Dickens at Work* (London: Methuen, 1957), 223–30. For a reading of financial crisis and suicide in *Little Dorrit* see Paul A. Jarvie, *Ready to Trample on All Human Law: Financial Capitalism in the Fiction of Charles Dickens* (London: Routledge, 2005), 79–113.
21   See Ronald R. Thomas, "Spectacle and Speculation: The Victorian Economy of Vision in *Little Dorrit*," in *Dickens, Europe and the New Worlds*, ed. Amy Sadrin (London: Macmillan, 1999), 34–35.
22   Alexander Welsh, *The City of Dickens* (Oxford: Oxford University Press, 1971), 196–212.
23   Edwin B. Barrett, "*Little Dorrit* and the Disease of Modern Life," *Nineteenth-Century Fiction*, 25.2 (1970): 199–215.

24   In George Levine's reading of the episode, this is a Ruskinian landscape of snow-white Nature, except that what it portrays is not transcendence (as in Ruskin's "Mountain Glory"), but death (*The Realistic Imagination: English Fiction from Frankenstein to Lady Chatterley* [Chicago: Chicago University Press, 1981], 224–26).

25   "Dingley Dell & the Fleet," reprinted in *Dickens: A Collection of Critical Essays*, ed. Martin Price (Englewood Cliffs, NJ: Prentice-Hall, 1987), 78–82.

26   John Lucas, *The Melancholy Man: A Study of Dickens's Novels* (London: Methuen, 1970), 1–2.

27   For a different reading of this passage see Carol Bernstein, *The Celebration of Scandal: Toward the Sublime in Victorian Fiction* (University Park: Penn State University Press, 1991), 156–57.

28   The transferal of guilt at that secret knowledge from Bob Fagin to the Jew in *Oliver Twist* is suggested by Steven Marcus in his *Dickens: From Pickwick to Dombey* (London: Chatto & Windus, 1965), 358–78.

29   John Romano uses this expression in an attack on the dichotomy in New Criticism between coherence and correspondence (*Dickens and Reality* [New York: Columbia University Press, 1978], 106).

30   Bentham quoted in Stephan Oettermann, *The Panorama: History of a Mass Medium*, trans. Deborah L. Schneider (New York: Zone Books, 1997), 42; see also Anthony Vidler, "The Scenes of the Street: Transformations in Ideal and Reality," in *On Streets*, ed. Stanford Anderson (Cambridge, MA: MIT Press, 1978), 54.

31   Actually the prison was originally an Elizabethan institution designed to regulate out-of-work paupers (Henry Mayhew and John Binny, *The Criminal Prisons of London and Scenes of Prison Life* [London: Griffin, Bohn, 1862], 274), and its architectural design was meant to deter and discipline well before Bentham; see John Bender, *Imagining the Penitentiary: Fiction and the Architecture of Mind in Eighteenth-Century England* (Chicago: University of Chicago, 1987). Certainly, Chadwick in his Poor Law Report followed the language and principles of Bentham's Panopticon quite closely (S. E. Finer, *The Life and Times of Sir Edwin Chadwick* [New York: Barnes and Noble, 1952], 74–75).

32   Unsigned review of *Oliver Twist*, *The Spectator*, 24 November 1838; excerpted in *Dickens: The Critical Heritage*, ed. Philip Collins (London: Routledge, 1971), 42–43.

33   Michel Foucault, *Surveillir et punir: Naissance de la prison* (Paris: Gallimard, 1975), 9–15.

34   Fifth Letter, *Daily News*, 16 March 1846, reprinted in *Selected Letters of Charles Dickens*, ed. David Paroissen (London: Macmillan, 1985), 245–46.

35   *Surveillir et punir*, 202.

36   Burton Pike, *The Image of the City in Modern Literature* (Princeton: Princeton University Press, 1981), 15.

37   John Bayley, "Oliver Twist: Things as They Really Are," in *Dickens in the Twentieth Century*, ed. John Gross and Gabriel Pearson (London: Routledge, 1962), 49–64.

38   Unsigned review of *Oliver Twist*, *The Spectator*, 24 November 1838; excerpted in *Dickens: The Critical Heritage*, 42–43.

39   John Stuart Mill, *Autobiography. Essay on Liberty* (New York: Collier, 1909), 75.

40   Quoted in Humphry House, *The Dickens World*, 2nd ed. (Oxford: Oxford University Press, 1942), 73 (emphasis in the original). House's point is that Dickens's ignorance of economic theory led him to "pauperizing" charity which sought to relieve rather than remove poverty. In having Dickens ascribe to a Marxist analysis of reification by capitalism,

John Romano (*Dickens and Reality*, 128) similarly fails to recognize Dickens's attack is directed at reification by theory itself.

41   J. Hillis Miller, *Charles Dickens*, 236.

42   Philip Collins, *Dickens and Crime*, 2nd ed. (London: Macmillan, and New York: St. Martin's, 1965), 118–19.

43   See Butt and Tillotson, *Dickens at Work*, 174–75; Collins, *Dickens and Crime*, 155–56; Michael Goldberg, *Dickens and Carlyle* (Athens, GA: University of Georgia Press, 1972), 151–52, 154. If Carlyle's "model prison" was not that noble building from which the ladies averted their gaze as Boz rowed down the river, Millbank Penitentiary, but Coldbath Fields during George Chesterton's command, as Collins suggests, it seems to me inconceivable Dickens would consciously have agreed with an attack on the silent system and the man he admired. Goldberg (in *Dickens and Carlyle*) guesses that Dickens characteristically accepted Carlyle's influence impulsively and uncritically without pausing to consider how much it contradicted his own commitment to reformation through love or to pity for the humanity of the convicts, for which Carlyle had no patience. However, it is unlikely he would have argued with Carlyle's basic critique of the utilitarians' false remedy of social disease and disorder by building a utopian city—the prison—when outside its walls there was cholera and starvation. Dickens continued his attack on false sympathy for the prisoner as part of his critique of the general reign of speechifying do-nothing-ism, which ignored victims of bank frauds, murders, and Divorce Laws (see "The Murdered Person," *Household Words*, 11 October 1856).

44   According to Collins, *Dickens and Crime*, 1. There is a further reference to the "Uriah Heeps of our day" in an attack on eighteenth-century cruelty and corruption at the Marshalsea and Fleet prison in "Prison Discipline," *All the Year Round*, 7 September 1867.

45   Collins argues for an attachment to the treadmill in what he describes as Dickens's bourgeois reactionary attitude, at least until the 1853 Birmingham prison scandal showed firm discipline and hard labor could be counterproductive in the correction of indolence and the defense of middle-class interests; Dickens is judged by Collins on this and other points to be "foolish," "irresponsible," and "wrong" (*Dickens and Crime*, 75).

46   *Surveillir et punir*, 30.

47   *Surveillir et punir*, 199–229.

48   Bender, *Imagining the Penitentiary*.

49   In a Nabokovian reading of the text, Mark M. Hennelly has argued that in *Little Dorrit* the ludic impulse of earlier novels is overshadowed by the prison and that playfulness itself (intertextuality, actual games, or figures of playing) dehumanizes because game has turned into delusion ("'The Games of the Prison Children' in Dickens's *Little Dorrit*," *Nineteenth-Century Contexts* 20.2 [1997]: 187–213).

50   Davis, *Factual Fictions: The Origins of the English Novel* (Philadelphia: University of Pennsylvania Press, 1996), 123–24.

51   *Sherlock Holmes: The Complete Short Stories* (London: John Murray, 1928), 53–54.

52   J. C. Platt, "Prisons and Penitentiaries," in *London*, ed. Charles Knight (London: Charles Knight, 1841–44), 5, 323. Dickens was not alone in questioning the efficacy of police statistics (as he did in "Ignorance and Crime," *The Examiner* 22 April 1848, DJ 2: 92–95). In 1816 the indefatigable statistician Patrick Colquhoun was mocked in evidence before a parliamentary Select Committee for claiming precision in estimating criminal activities in the metropolis when such activities were by their nature secret and often undetected (Tobias, *Urban Crime in Victorian England*, 15).

53   See Welsh, *The City of Dickens*, 33–53.

54   Adam Zachary Newton, *Narrative Ethics* (Cambridge, MA: Harvard University Press, 1995), 260–65; D. A. Miller, *The Novel and the Police* (Berkeley: University of California Press, 1988), 128–32.

55   See Collins, *Dickens and Crime*, 18–22.

56   *The Dickens World*, 201–02. See also Collins, *Dickens and Crime*, 196–219, for an account of Dickens's almost hyperbolic admiration of the detective force.

57   See, for example, the review of the prison inspector Frederic Hill's *Crime: Its Amount, Causes, and Remedies*, written with Henry Morley and W. H. Wills, "In and Out of Jail," *Household Words*, 14 May 1853; UW 2: 478–88.

58   Flora manages to work Pope's "An Essay on Man" into her loquacious prattle when she considers the natives Arthur would have met on his foreign travels, but the comic relief of Flora's affection for Arthur should perhaps not be taken as seriously as some critics have taken these scenes, which were partly inspired by the reappearance in the maze of Dickens's own life of his former sweetheart Maria Beadnell, now forty, plump, and silly.

6

The Waste Land: Salvage and Salvation in *Our Mutual Friend*

RECYCLING AND THE ECONOMY OF *OUR MUTUAL FRIEND*

> London is the heart of your commercial system, but it is also
> the hot-bed of corruption. It is at once the centre of wealth
> and the sink of misery; the seat of intellect and empire ... and
> yet a wilderness wherein they, who live like wild beasts upon
> their fellow creatures, find prey and cover.
> —Robert Southey, *Colloquies*

Bella's "money, money, money" and Twemlow's "waste, waste, waste" are two
obsessions that reflect a carnivalesque inversion in *Our Mutual Friend* (1865)
between a wasteful leisure-class and the filthy scavengers of the capitalist city. It is, I
believe, in *Our Mutual Friend* that Dickens tackles head-on the question of what to
do about money. What Henry James criticized as a product of permanent exhaustion
of mind, though possibly also an exhausted mine,[1] may be seen as a brilliant grand
finale of Dickens's plots and themes, which satirizes a society of scavengers feeding
off each other. The shallow Veneerings, the xenophobic Podsnap, the sham Lammles,
the artificial Lady Tippins—these are civilized cannibals feeding off their guests in
their scramble for a conspicuous display of consumption. At the bottom end of the
scale, Fascination Fledgeby, Rogue Riderhood, Gaffer Hexam, Boffin, Wegg, Venus,
and even the crippled doll's dressmaker, Jenny Wren, are all on the make: they are
making money out of society's waste—a gruesome list of dead bodies, live bodies,
body parts, rubbish heaps, and cloth remnants.

Underlying the novel is a discourse that questions the value of money in a
waste-producing society. The comic description of the "bran-new" Veneerings, for
example, shows how money has bought the nouveaux riches their place in society.
Their reification of people (as in Twemlow's representation as a dining table) robs
the living of their identities, while their circulation in society is shown to be an
empty and base coin. The Veneerings are fishers of men in ways Hexam could not
be, parasites who feed on the important connections invited to dinner, just as they
feed on the Harmon murder. Their guests are so much heavy plate, and the mirror
above the Veneerings' dinner table reflects reification itself, veneered surfaces hiding
useless and non-productive speculation by the "prosperously feeding" Podsnap and
other "new" people of the money-producing economy of the 1860s.

The scavengers of the urban wasteland in *Our Mutual Friend* feed on each
other like cannibals, putting us in mind of Swift's savage satire of the English

devouring the Irish or Kingsley's description of the farm laborers in *Alton Locke*. The usual opposition of civilization and savagery has been reversed. Charley Hexam provides yet another example of moral ambiguity in the process of civilization: despite his cleanliness and literacy there is "a curious mixture in the boy, of uncompleted savagery, and uncompleted civilization" (OMF I, III; 60); later, like Tom Gradgrind, he learns the lessons of his school only too well. Lady Tippins derides the newly married Eugene and Lizzie as "savages," to which Mortimer responds sarcastically that they were "eating each other" when he left them, a sure sign they were becoming civilized (OMF IV, XVII; 888)! Lady Tippins herself is an example of how Dickens subverts this colonialist construction of class and, as in the keynote description of Coketown, exposes the savage below the fashionable mask of "civilization." Below the expensive Bond Street dresses there is nothing genuine in her: "in the bonnet and drapery announced by her name, any fragment of the real woman may be concealed, is perhaps known to her maid; but you could easily buy all you see of her, in Bond Street; or you might scalp her, and peel her, and scrape her, and make two Lady Tippinses out of her, and yet not penetrate to the genuine article" (OMF I, x; 164).

This carnivalesque inversion of the social hierarchy is analyzed by the anatomist who, like Mr. Venus, scalps and scrapes the civilized body and finds it artificial. The living are reduced to something less than corpses, to the sum of their parts like Venus's "miscellaneous human," to be scalped and scraped (like Mrs. Podsnap [OMF I, II; 52]) by the famous palaeontologist Professor Richard Owen, head of the Natural History Section at the British Museum and formerly professor of comparative anatomy and physiology at the Royal College of Surgeons. Dickens had known Owen since 1842, the year he coined the term "dinosaur," and featured his discoveries in *All the Year Round*.[2] Dickens's co-opting of Owen (who had been drawn into bitter controversy and public mockery for his disagreement with Darwin over natural selection) responds to Darwinian evolution by suggesting a regressive descent of the species to primeval savagery, as does the Megalosaurus waddling up Ludgate Hill in the description of London's mud swamp in *Bleak House*.[3] Dickens seems to suggest here, as in *Bleak House*, that modern London is submerged in a primeval "Dismal Swamp" (the title of the chapter describing the greedy mass descent on the newly rich Boffins), indicating a universal regression rather than an evolutionary progress in the bleak chaos of the modern city, where rapacious beasts of prey (like Riderhood, but also the upper-class cannibals) fed on unsuspecting victims. This departure from social Darwinism is met again in "On an Amateur Beat" when the Uncommercial Traveller points to the mud-prints that will show future paleontologists "the public savagery of neglected children" in the streets of the capital (UT 347), but it also represents a resistance to the anthropomorphic analogy in social realism adopted by George Lewes and George Eliot, which was based on evolutionary theory, which, together with market exchange value, Foucault regards as the central episteme of nineteenth-century scientific and social discourse.[4]

In our disposable, throw-away commodity culture, we tend to forget how important thrift was to the Victorians. They understood that the organic and inorganic waste choking the arteries of the metropolis was part of a larger problem. Dust was not only a euphemism; money could be made out of waste. This recycling of waste highlights the circularity of the effluence of the nation and its recycling into affluence, though the relation can be inverted too: in Mandeville's *Fable of the Bees* (preface to the 2nd ed., 1714) the streets of London are said to be filthy in relation to the production of wealth, so that its "dirty streets are a necessary Evil inseparable from the Felicity of London."

Money was understood to circulate in the economy on the analogy of the natural body, which assumed that an unimpeded blood-flow was essential to ensure the distribution of wealth.[5] The trope was a discursive and conceptual analogy both in the economy and in descriptions of the social organism by investigators of the living conditions of the poor in nineteenth-century English cities who advocated medical policing and regulation in order to ensure free ventilation of water and air in order to prevent disease. This may be seen against the background of the shift described by Michel Foucault towards institutionalization of illness and treatment of the body as a system.[6] In his 1842 report on *The Sanitary Condition of the Labouring Population of Great Britain*, Chadwick presented the modern city as a mechanical and economic system that depended on efficient supply of water and drainage. In the physiological analogy, the products of the human body are recycled in the system, so that waste is salvaged and converted into money value that is in turn recycled back into the economy. This was an engineering solution to the problem of epidemic disease that was the scourge of the inhuman conditions in the slums of the big cities, and also a typically bureaucratic solution to the economic problem of how to increase national prosperity by cutting down the cost of disease, high mortality, and wasted productivity.

This revaluation of money draws attention to the efficiency of circulation. Dirt, the sign of poverty and low class, can be made useful, and in Henry Mayhew's descriptions of dustmen and dredgermen in *London Labour and the London Poor*, we meet hale and hearty men whose dirt is evidence of useful labor.[7] The economic value of waste was, for example, praised in Dickens's *Household Words* in an article by R. H. Horne aptly headed "Dust; or Ugliness Redeemed."[8] In this description, "a huge Dust-heap of a dirty black colour, – being, in fact, one of those immense mounds of cinders, ashes, and other emptyings from dust-holes and bins, which have conferred celebrity on certain suburban neighbourhoods of a great city" is shown to be both redeemable and redeeming. A deformed ex-chimney-sweep, Jem Clinker, who has had visions of angels that sound as if they were straight out of Blake, old Gaffer Doubleyear, and Peg with her wooden leg dream of treasures in the dust-heap and find a gilded miniature and parchment which partly restore the fortunes of a talented gentleman who has lost his money and thrown himself in the nearby canal; the suicide is revived by the dust-sifters after being covered by the warmth of the heap. The coincidence with some of the characters in Dickens's

Our Mutual Friend (especially the one-legged Wegg) is striking and has been noted more than once. Apart from "Gaffer," a genial dust contractor marries his daughter off to the talented but unfortunate gentleman, just as Bella, adopted by Boffin, marries John Harmon, who has likewise survived drowning.[9]

However, Horne is more concerned with showing that his characters are all virtuous and dirt is useful, rather than pursuing the religious theme of salvation and resurrection. The Victorian ingenuity for classification makes the human scavengers far more thorough than the predatory birds or animals scrounging in the dust-heaps. The waste is sifted for its usefulness and converted back into manure, fuel, or bricks, with the additional value of monetary exchange. The dust-heaps are thus literal monuments of the British economy, and grow according to the laws of supply and demand. Even their nuisance value could be converted into cash: in 1832, recounts Horne, one dustman in the London parish of St. George's agreed to remove the nuisance for five hundred pounds per annum in addition to what he got for selling it! In *Our Mutual Friend*, by contrast, recycling brings into play a complex symbolic pattern of personal redemption and national salvation.

The plot of *Our Mutual Friend* must be read in the context of the capitalist economy of the 1860s, in which everything and everyone had a price. Amidst a number of banking scandals, this was a time of much debate over uncontrolled speculation and unregulated investment. It was, moreover, a society confronting demands for enlarging the franchise to disaffected working men. *Our Mutual Friend* is radical in the way it undermines the class hierarchy based on money made out of speculation. Speculation, like the other kind of speculation in Mr. Dolls's eyes, is dead, and, instead, the filth of laborers is extolled as work that is not only productive but is both economically and morally useful. The novel offers transformation through conversion of value and meaning, not commodity exchange, through ocular and intellectual, not monetary, speculation. Its stock in trade is mutual benevolence, an ethical capitalism practiced elsewhere by the Cheeryble Brothers.

In its rather grim and morbid tale of drowned corpses and anatomical models, *Our Mutual Friend* reveals a faith in mutual benevolence and love that could reverse the Midas touch which Carlyle believed had blighted labor relations. By substituting the organic body of romantic harmony for the utilitarian physiology of anatomical inquiry (as Carlyle had done in "Characteristics"), it attempts to turn Chadwick's terminology of national prosperity and waste recycling to the good. The redemptive figure is John Harmon, who remakes the Victorian domestic economy into a rainbow-colored harmony and converts Bella into an Angel of the House more after Ruskin's "Queen's Gardens" than Coventry Patmore and Mrs. Beeton (she doesn't get on too well with *The Great British Housewife*, the bible of Victorian domesticity). John's "Harmony" in the home may get us no further than a mawkish Wordsworthian romanticism, but when it reaches the workplace (as in the Paper Mill, a veritable New Jerusalem in a green and pleasant land), it is all there is to prevent the laboring classes from being reduced to statistics of disease and mortality. By contrast with the treatment of avarice in *Le Père Goriot* and *The*

Old Curiosity Shop, or George Eliot's conversion of Silas Marner's gold worship into nature worship, money is not intrinsically bad and the ugly can be redeemed.

Is the hope for salvation in salvage merely a romantic ideal? This may depend on the effectiveness of any response to a commonplace rhetoric in the 1850s and 1860s that advocated solutions to London's environmental problems in accordance with a circulatory conception of the city-body, arguing that reform had been impeded by the lack of a unified metropolitan authority that could tackle the pollution of the Thames, source of much of London's drinking water, and the unsanitary housing conditions of the poor laboring classes.

RECYCLING WASTE

Then *Cloacina* (goddess of the tide
Whose sable streams beneath the city glide)
Indulg'd the modish flame; the town she rov'd,
A mortal scavenger she saw, she lov'd;
The muddy spots that dry'd upon his face,
Like female patches, heighten'd every grace.
—John Gay, "Trivia, or the Art of
Walking the Streets of London"

Go, scented Belgravian! and see what London is! and then go
to the library which God has given thee—one often fears in
vain—and see what science says this London might be!
—Charles Kingsley, *Alton Locke* (1850)

Writing under the sign of T. S. Eliot, Edgar Johnson has given symbolic pride of place in the urban wasteland of *Our Mutual Friend* to Boffin's dustheaps.[10] Although they form a brief mock-panorama in the descriptive landscape and cast their shadow no further than Boffin's backyard or on Wegg's false prospects, they have yielded their weight in gold to critics sniffing out excrement.[11] Fecal imagery is not hard to find elsewhere either. In *Bleak House* the streets are fouled by horse droppings, which Jo has to sweep in order to maintain circulation of traffic, and we are reminded in *Our Mutual Friend* of that ubiquitous and euphemistic mud in the joke at Podsnap's expense about the horse droppings, which the Frenchman identifies as marks of the British Constitution, which reminds some readers and critics of Swift's "excremental vision."[12] Given the vast quantities of dung deposited by London's horse traffic, the urgent need to vacate the Augean stables that were the capital's main streets could not be exaggerated. In *London Labour and the London Poor*, Henry Mayhew gives tables of the average daily excretions of London's horses showing the total deposited per annum in the capital amounted to a staggering 36,662 tons.[13] Yet, in his thorough classification of London's dust-men and the people who earned money from the dustheaps, Mayhew gives little attention to human waste, which after the new sanitary regulations of 1848 would have been disposed of separately. Considering his treatment of sewage and prostitution, Mayhew can hardly be accused of prudery or censorship, and he is not hesitant in giving revolting details of the sewers, where a living is made from salvaging precious metal and from rat catching.

The human and animal sewage flowing in London's streets and river point to something more important than an anal fixation. Victorians understood that the organic and inorganic mud choking the arteries of the metropolis was part of a larger problem of waste in Victorian society. The dustheaps were made up of a varied and lucrative assortment of the garbage and debris of society—largely, as Henry Mayhew testifies, comprising ashes and cinders from coal fires, of great value for brick making or fertilizing marshy soil, the rest being used for landfill or other purposes.[14] This was collected by the dustmen under contract with the parish, while the emptying of cesspools and privies was carried out at night by dustmen willing to do the work by arrangement with local landlords. The dustmen, nightmen, and sifters are regular or casual unskilled laborers and might double as scavengers, but their productivity is indisputably useful to the economy, not just in the removal of waste but in its sorting and recycling into material of immense value. The dust contractors are wealthy, and though the dustmen are largely ignorant and illiterate, they are healthy men with a taste for the popular theater and social gatherings at the pub.[15]

Waste was the enemy of Chadwick's typically Victorian thrift drive to optimize efficiency and to recycle the byproducts of a modern industrial city, yet waste was also a problem because of its part in causing and spreading disease, which was a drain on the nation's capital assets and manpower. As his biographer S. E. Finer puts it, "His motive was neither religious nor benevolent—it was horror of waste."[16] In this, Finer believes, he was exactly like Charles Kingsley's Dr. Tom Thurnall in *Two Years Ago* (1857), who raged against disease in the same way others raged against sin. In explaining why he believed in self-interest yet fought so hard to destroy the disease of others and made himself so unpleasant in doing so, he answered, "Don't you understand me? You hate sin, you know. Well, I hate disease. Moral evil is your devil, and physical evil is mine." But most of all he hates waste, "I hate to see anything wasted, anything awry, anything going wrong; I hate to see water-power wasted, manure wasted, land wasted, muscle wasted, pluck wasted, brains wasted; I hate neglect, incapacity, idleness, ignorance, and all the disease and misery which spring out of that."[17] Waste, then, is symptomatic of inefficiency in the system, and this outburst, occasioned by a cholera outbreak in the West Country, would have met a sympathetic response from middle-class readers who, concerned with public health and municipal reform, would have approved of Thurnall's practical measures to prevent disease such as cleanliness and disinfection of houses.

The Malthusian phobia of waste is derided in the parody of tripe production in *The Chimes*, but in the common usage of the word, waste of time, energy, words, and lives all indicate disease in a well-regulated body of society that depends on free circulation of capital. In a specialized industrial production plant, argued William Cooke Taylor in his *Tour in the Manufacturing Districts of Lancashire*, no waste could be afforded. The inhuman housing conditions of the poor exposed in Chadwick's report led to a "profligate waste" and improvidence.[18] A diseased system in turn produced diseased bodies. Unhealthy housing conditions produced the unhealthy bodies of Spitalfields weavers, and women were singled out for neglecting the rules of domestic economy.[19] Like Thurnall, Chadwick did not think of the individual but of the wealth and efficiency of society at large. He was above all a systemizer, and where there existed different municipal authorities whose responsibilities for street cleaning, water, drainage, and waste disposal overlapped or fell short, he conceptualized an integrated system that was self-financing and self-maintaining. This was made possible by the egg-shaped sewer into which the improved modern W. C. flushed human waste to flow under pressure out of the city.[20] The loop in the cycle was completed when Chadwick learned from the German chemist Justus Liebig of the economic value of human waste as fertilizer and followed the example of Edinburgh. There the liquid gold was pumped straight to cultivated fields,[21] thus improving productivity while keeping the rivers clean from pollution by the waste which was usually dumped there, though making it unbearable for Queen Victoria to reside at the neighboring Holyrood Palace. It was in Edinburgh, too, that residents were reported to pay their rent by production of dung heaps, which accumulated in dwellings that were worse than pigsties.[22] This private enterprise of converting biological output into raw materials and profits was suited to the practice of dustmen in large cities to let the dung accumulate before carting it away. Chadwick was merely rationalizing the productivity of waste and making its removal efficient and cost-effective.

For Chadwick, disease was primarily an engineering and not a medical problem, a matter of "practical means of prevention" rather than treatment of illness or understanding its causes and infection.[23] The conception of a mechanical and economic system of efficient supply of water and drainage at low cost nevertheless shared with Robert Vaughan's *Age of Great Cities* (1843) the assumption in William Cooke Taylor's *Natural History of Society* that the city was a body subject to scientific investigation and correction. In a letter of 1 October 1845 to Lord Francis Egerton, Chadwick boasted he had found an engineering solution in the "venous and arterial system of Towns" from the piping of water, through the flushing of excreta to its recycling into liquid manure.[24] The human body is a producer of waste that is then recycled in the system, so that waste is salvaged and converted back into money value that is in turn recycled in the economy. The medical view of the problem was nevertheless influential not just for shocking the public into supporting radical solutions but also for its construction of the city as a diseased body that was connected to a social system. Although Chadwick's name alone appeared on the 1842 report, it depended for its facts on a number of observers and investigators who brought their opinions and views with them, chief among them the miasmic theory that incorrectly described the transmission of epidemic disease as olfactory, the fever being "excited," as Thomas Southwood Smith wrote in his 1830 *Treatise on Fever*, by the gases given off by decaying organic matter. Chadwick subscribed to this view, which gave further impetus to his obsession with the removal of smelly waste.

The moral analogy between the animal organism and the susceptibility of the city to contagious disease figures the city/body as a dynamic organism in perpetual flux of renewal and waste recycling. Social reformers believed urban ills could only be healed by scientific investigation and regulation. A model of such investigation of disease (in this case cholera) was James Kay's highly influential 1832 pamphlet on Manchester's laboring poor, *The Moral and Physical Condition of the Working Classes Employed in the Cotton Manufacture in Manchester*. Just as in the animal organism, pain alerts us to the diseased parts that threaten to convulse the entire body, so Kay found scientific investigation by means of close inspection and surveillance necessary for the health of the social body. It is not the capitalist industrial system that is at fault, according to Kay's biological model, but its failure to alleviate the problems of the laboring poor, caused by the demoralization resulting from mechanical and exhausting work in the factories, the bad influence of the improvidence and sloth of Irish immigrants (a foreign contagion infecting the body of the nation in Kay's racialized language),[25] and faulty domestic values such as malnutrition, insanitary housing, poor personal hygiene, promiscuity, and intemperance ("the unrestrained licence of animal appetite").[26] All these predispose the lower classes to disease. Cholera epidemics or typhus outbreaks thus become a metaphor as well as an explanation for the danger to the nation's economic, social, and physical health of moral and political disorder, in particular Luddism and working-class agitation, but also crime, which threatened both property and personal liberty. Chronic disease and the "moral leprosy" it represents are shown to be potentially fatal in the case of Manchester, the "metropolis of the commercial system." Therefore, "errors and diseases" in part of the social body must be removed by medical and police regulation for the "ultimate welfare of the whole social system."[27] In addition, Kay recommends the "remedy" of free trade, town planning, and ideological control (through education in domesticity), if the vitality and energy of the system was to be maintained. Rejecting empiricism as "dangerous" in *Artisans and Machinery* (1836), Peter Gaskell similarly calls for the nation's moral, social, and economic relations to be examined in the light of current medical theory like a diseased body in need of remedies.[28] In his report, Chadwick, too, diagnoses pestilence as a sign of moral disorder,[29] and is no less aware than Kay of its threat to the wealth and power of the nation and the health of the entire social body, to capitalist "civilization" itself.[30]

Besides Kay, doctors of the Edinburgh school, including Hector Gavin, Leonard Horner, Thomas Southwood Smith, William Alison, and Neil Arnott, were among the chief investigators of public health in the big cities, and the changing face of physiology and clinical practice with which they are identified influenced such reformers as Chadwick and radical thinkers like Charles Bray.[31] A critical change in medical thinking, according to Michel Foucault in his study of the institutionalization of the body, *The Birth of the Clinic*, had occurred in the early nineteenth century. Instead of "sympathies" with no specific location in the body, disease came to be understood as deformations or lesions in a localized sequence within the body that was now a three-dimensional *system* subject to the scientific gaze which rendered the invisible *readable*. Disease was described in a grammar of signs (symptoms) within the institution of the clinic and hospital, where the body was scientifically treated and studied in morbid anatomy. The medical topography of the turn of the century which had applied theological models of a natural organism to the city was now being replaced by such pioneers as Southwood Smith with sanitary science. After his conversion to Bentham's utilitarianism, Smith advocated the study of the body as a machine governed by principles analogous to social and moral systems; only such an understanding of the organism could identify and treat its dysfunction. The circulation and chemical reaction of fluids in the system constituted the vital processes that were "either processes of supply or processes of waste."[32] Applied to public health, the construction of the body as a dynamic system in perpetual flux led to a view of the relationship between the body and the urban environment in terms of a constant circulation of fluids and the renewal of vital functions by the introduction of fresh particles and by the elimination of waste. A healthy city depended on free circulation of air and water in its arteries and the efficient disposal of garbage or recycling of waste. Epidemic disease resulted from malfunctions in the system, such as overcrowding, clogged drains, or broken sewers.[33] It could be treated by collecting vital statistics and mapping the diseased areas of the city; health inspectors reported the locations of epidemic outbreaks, and the machinery of medicine was policed (a word used more than once in its sense of regulation in Chadwick's report) by administrative measures or removal of nuisances.[34] As we saw in chapter 3, circulation was all-important if disease was to be controlled because, according to the ruling miasmic theory, it spread through the air where ventilation was inadequate; as a consequence, for too long the contamination of water supplies was ignored.[35]

Dr. Arnott pointed to the economic implications in his far-reaching reciprocal analogy of city and body:

> We know that as the Thames water spreads over London in pipes, to supply the inhabitants generally, and to answer the particular purposes of brewers, bakers, tanners and others, and is then in great part returned to where the current sweeps away the impurities; so, nearly, in the human body, does the blood spread in the arteries from a central vessel in every direction, to nourish all the parts and to supply such material of secretion to the liver, the kidneys, the stomach and other viscera, and returns from these by the veins, towards the heart and lungs, and to have its ways replenished, that it may renew its course.[36]

It was therefore a sound principle of Political Economy in Chadwick's Town Improvements Company that the flow of water and sewage was integrated (the project flopped with other speculations in the collapse of the railway boom of 1845). Chadwick did not disguise his debt to French models of sociological investigation and centralized social control (the latter anathema to *The Times* and Mr. Podsnap, who thought it "not English"). Yet the interventionist centralization in Chadwick's recommendations for the reform of public health does not in any way contradict the principle of laissez-faire in trade; on the contrary, it ensures material prosperity by making the system flow more efficiently. Indeed, the "sanitary idea" owed its impetus to the inability of the Poor Law administrators to account for financing of public health schemes. Together with other reforms, it introduced the idea of society as a self-sufficient organism, administered by professionals on economic principles, uniform in "legislation and in the executive machinery," so that the nation would become one body, instead of diverse laws in different towns and regions, which was both economically wasteful and against the interest of "choosing the best" for a national, not local prosperity.[37] Hence the rhetorical strategy in Chadwick's report of stressing the economic, moral, and social cost to the nation of illness and pointing to administrative models in order to save public money.

Despite Dickens's satire of the New Poor Law in *Oliver Twist*, Chadwick failed to appreciate he had been branded as a heartless Malthusian and turned to Dickens for support through Dickens's brother-in-law Henry Austin, who was secretary of the Sanitary Commission. Dickens was important to Chadwick as an opinion shaper, and although Dickens favored Chadwick's report with a bare commendation in *American Notes*,[38] he was nonetheless to become a fervid supporter of the public health campaign in the 1850s. Dickens worked with Henry Austin to publish a series of articles in *Household Words* and supported him in the struggle against "vestryization" by local aldermen such as Sir Peter Laurie who resisted the Commissioners' reform of London's waterworks and sewers. Dickens shared with Chadwick an almost obsessive concern for circulation and eliminating waste, and his fastidiousness with tidiness and order at home is well known. Dickens declared in the preface to *Martin Chuzzlewit* that all his writing highlighted the unsanitary housing conditions of the poor wherever possible. In his 1851 speech to the Metropolitan Sanitary Association, Dickens dutifully acknowledged his debt to the reports of Chadwick and Southwood Smith (*Speeches* 128–29). And advising Angela Burdett-Coutts on her "Nova Scotia" housing project in Bethnal Green, Dickens recommended she consult Southwood Smith, whom he knew and trusted, for his fever practice and reports gave him a reliable knowledge of the poor's housing needs (letter of 13 January 1852, *Letters* 6: 573–74; 16 March 1852, *Letters* 6: 626–27).

Nevertheless, Dickens transforms the medical construction of a circulatory system and applies recycling to very different purposes. Moreover, by the time Dickens wrote *Our Mutual Friend*, the attitude toward the unwashed poor had changed, and they were being represented without the sentimentality that had romanticized or marginalized them in previous decades. James McNeill Whistler's Thames etchings of 1859–61, *Pictures of the Scenes of the Working River* (so much admired by Baudelaire), for example, were observations of the London not visited by the middle-class gentleman who bought the engraving; from his vantage point in the salubrious Wapping district, the artist gave almost photographic focus to the buildings and figures along the shoreline and on the river. *Our Mutual Friend* turns similar ethnographic material into a vision of mythical proportions, but what Dickens's novel has in common with the documentary record of London life in Henry Mayhew's *London Labour and the London Poor* is an underlying assumption that the "want and vice" of the "first city in the world" is a shared social reality.

Mayhew's sociological and economic analysis of the languages, customs, and breeding patterns of the seminomadic race of the street folk who feed on the city represents the streets and subterranean world of outcast London as part of the city with its own diverse and divergent voice, not merely a statistical product of official reports and surveys. Nor can Mayhew's descriptions be easily dismissed as a projection of bourgeois disgust at the cloacal conditions of city streets and the subversive nomads' lack of domestic values of cleanliness, family, and religion. Cultural historians have identified in this disgust the "fascinated gaze" which drew middle-class readers to scenes of obscene filth, prostitution, and crime, thus controlling both fears of contamination of domestic space and illicit desires.[39] However, apart from shaming the rich into feelings of charity and subtly undermining class definitions of nationhood and Englishness, this "cyclopedia" of the capital's secret knowledge uncovers a change in ways of human life unique to the metropolis that has produced previously unknown occupations useful to the urban economy.[40]

Indeed, in taking the lid off the sewers (quite literally), Mayhew extends the primordial world of hunters and gatherers underground and reveals the nightmarish underside of the city where rats are said to have devoured men and civilization is forced to face its repressed secrets. The sewers are the repository of what lies beneath the surface of bourgeois "decency" and "home comforts," yet Mayhew disarms class prejudice and identifies public, rather than private, filth with immorality.[41] Filth is not a simple equation of class, for in the Westminster drainage district he finds the sewers of the smart streets of Belgravia worse than under St. Giles', a fact Mayhew uses to argue against the relation of poor sanitation and housing to disease.[42] The functions of waste recycling are shown to be integral to the social organism, and therefore scavengers are essential to the productivity of the urban economy, not idle parasites. Just as the sewers revealed enormous hordes of valuable waste material for recycling, Mayhew recycled material from Dickens and Dickens, in turn, may have recycled Gaffer Hexam and Betty Higden from Mayhew's descriptions of a dredgerman and an old woman who collected dog turd ("pure") for tanneries.[43] This demonstrates the circularity of the discourse, but also shows how honest labor can avoid dependence on public charity and destitution.

We have already met Krook in *Bleak House*, another salvage collector who buys all kinds of household refuse to resell at a profit or for scrap metal and wastepaper. However, Krook's warehouse differs from Jenny Wren's making dolls out of rags and scraps in *Our Mutual Friend* in its contrast of the self-ingesting closed system of Chancery with a covetous greed for the power of possession.

In fact, Krook's interest in waste invests it with uneconomic sentimental value, since it is hoarded instead of being recirculated, and it is the novel that has to read value into the writing chalked on the wall, for Krook cannot read legal documents and their significance escapes him. His disregard of the meaning of the papers he collects puts him into the class of Mayhew's rag-and-bottle man for whom print is so much pulp.[44] A more malicious version of this type who reduces everything to undifferentiated salvage is Fledgeby, for whom the debts on Queer Street are so much "waste-paper" to be bought up by the pound.

In *Our Mutual Friend*, the scavengers of society are reclassified in an inversion of the relation of class to dirt. This carnivalesque inversion questions the place of nonproductive accumulation of wealth at the top of the social hierarchy, while questioning the commodification of the body, and thus revises Chadwick's model of industrial production and recycling of waste which disciplines the body. Gaffer Hexam is literally a fisher of men who lives off the bodies of the drowned. That he may be one of the most reliable observers of London life and a source of knowledge, like Jack the odd "odd-job" man in *Great Expectations*, may be judged from the fact that Inspector Bucket takes Esther downriver in *Bleak House* on the chance of gaining some gruesome information from such a man. Dickens wraps his portrayal of Hexam in sinister overtones of a murder mystery which has to be deciphered. Hexam is neither a waterman nor a lighterman, and he gives "no clue" to the object of his search, except that his boat is "of dirty and disreputable appearance." In contrast to this sun-browned "half-savage" with "ragged grizzled hair," sits his daughter shivering with horror and dread at his intent gaze.

> Trusting to the girl's skill and making no use of the rudder, he eyed the coming tide with an absorbed attention. So the girl eyed him. But, it happened now, that a slant of light from the setting sun glanced into the bottom of the boat, and, touching a rotten stain there which bore some resemblance to the outline of a muffled human form, coloured it as though with diluted blood. This caught the girl's eye, and she shivered. (OMF I, I; 44)

The studied ambiguity of the scene—the darkening hues of a river sunset and the contemporaneity of time and place (the deflating "these times of ours")—deepens the mystery. The procedure by logical deduction places the reader in the position of a detective "on the look out" for the plot, but also trying to identify the "muffled human form" that lies at the bottom of the boat. One clue to the mystery is Hexam's bright-eyed gaze of a bird of prey and the girl's hiding of her face from the nameless terror in tow. Hexam scorns her fastidiousness for what the river provides her with—"meat and drink" (living off the dead and feeding on them)—and justifies his robbing of the corpses in rather different terms than Mayhew's informant: the dead have no use for money, unlike the living whom Rogue Riderhood has robbed.

These "high moralities" reflect the underlying discourse around the value of money in a waste producing society. At one level, they motivate the deadly jealous enmity between Hexam and Riderhood; at another they lead directly into the comic description of the "bran-new" Veneerings, whose money has bought them their place in society and who are fishers of men in ways Hexam could not be. Their use of people as objects (Twemlow's representation as a dining table, for example) robs the living of their identities, which are confused or vague, while their circulation in society depends on empty and base coin. The Veneerings are parasites who feed on the important connections who come to dinner (as they earlier fed on the Harmon murder). The living are reduced to something less than corpses, the sums of their parts, veneered surfaces. They are prey to the unproductive speculation by the "prosperously feeding" Podsnap and other "new" people of the money-producing economy of the 1860s, for whom the unidentified body is the Man from Somewhere in the romantic plot of some novel related by the idle Mortimer Lightwood (a rival "Society" narrative). The opening scene is crucial for introducing the symbolic relation between salvage and salvation. The "muffled human form" must not be allowed to remain a stain or a statistic, but must be given an identity by the novelist so that human value can be redeemed from waste above that of a price for the reward and the coins in the pockets.

RESURRECTION, RESUSCITATION, REDEMPTION

I am the Lock.
—Rogue Riderhood (OMF III, VIII; 571)

Resurrectionist, in search of a subject.
—(Visiting card, once sent by the aspiring Dickens as a youthful prank)[45]

The detective plot revolved around a murdered man, but here the missing body motivates a mystery of identity in the menacing anonymity of the urban crowd. The novelist must, like the detective, give the corpse an identity within the city's labyrinth of mysteries, but also must conjure up an act of resurrection that will animate the drowned man, like Venus the "articulator" who puts skeletons into artistic and anatomical shape.[46] This secular resurrection restores the body to meaning as semantic sign in the plot and in the city's necropolis, unlike the corpses "shot" as rubbish in clearance of overcrowded pestilential burial-grounds (fig. 17), or the corpses snatched by the Resurrection Men from graveyards for anatomical dissection which provided a ghoulish figure for such sensationalist urban Gothic as G. W. M. Reynolds's *Mysteries of London*, as well as the somewhat less ghoulish Jerry Cruncher in *A Tale of Two Cities*. Death was only too real in the city, but the public health debate did little to bring the city's dead and dying to life as human in the imagination.

The filth of Hexam's body and abode parodies the class approbation of outcast London as barbaric in much of the public health debate. He lives in a tumbledown former mill in a jumble of dwellings and shipping on the riverside where "accumulated scum of humanity seemed to be washed from higher grounds, like so much moral sewage, and to be pausing until its own weight forced it over the bank and sunk it in the river" (OMF I, III; 63). The disorder of the "moral sewage" contrasts with the monastic order of the police station, where Mr. Inspector is busy with the statistical bookkeeping of law and order (later it is described as Pickford's warehouse, where inmates are ticked off and shipped like goods). Yet, in common with Mayhew, Dickens recognizes the productivity of outcast London, though he is more interested in the usefulness of the poor in the moral economy. This contrasts with the wasted lives of the idle and useless Mortimer and Eugene and with Twemlow's painful awareness of his own unloved insignificance as "a waste, a waste, a waste" (I, x; 164). The "moral sewage" can be saved from crime by literacy, and sure enough Charlie Hexam is sent by his sister to school to better himself. Lizzie, though at first ignoring Miss Abbey's advice to leave her father and be "happy and respectable," later excels (as does Betty Higden) in thrift and cleanliness as a dutiful worker. Nevertheless, it is the illiterate dredgerman's daughter who dreams in the fire and proves to be the redemptive force in the story when she turns her rowing skill and brute strength "to good at last" (OMF IV, VI; 768) by saving Eugene. It is she who watches that her father does no wrong (more effectively than the police) and she who is rewarded for being not only "as industrious as virtuous" (II, v; 332)—a worker after Harriet Martineau's heart!—but being as good as she is handsome.

Fig. 17: "Modern Resurrection—East London, 19th Century" (1846)

The ugly could be made attractive in Horne's moral tale of a dustheap, and Maggy's ugliness is redeemed by her smile in *Little Dorrit*. Redeeming the ugly but useful waste of the urban economy characterizes the double efficiency in Jenny Wren's waste recycling, since she recycles the remnants of Pubsey & Co. and uses up her waste by making pen-wipers (presumably for stone-headed teachers such as Headstone or indolent solicitors like Wrayburn). She is a model of thrift and banks up her fire with damp cinders that it might last longer and waste less when she is out (OMF III, II; 492). Her chief occupation is to make effigies of society: she surreptitiously takes the images for her dolls from society ladies at evening parties and displays them in the toy-shop window. This is a speculation in gazing that, like the novelist's, is profitable though illicit (Jenny peeks out from behind a policeman's cape, just like Boz evading the policeman's suspicion in "Meditations in Monmouth-Street"). Dickens puns on the speculation missing from the dolls' eyes and the speculation that has gone out of the eyes of Mr. Dolls (OMF IV, IX; 801) with reference to Macbeth addressing the ghost of Banquo:

> Thou hast no speculation in those eyes
> Which thou dost glare with!
>
> (*Macbeth* III, IV)

There is the playful hint in Jenny of a murderous witch who sticks pins in her enemies' eyes and effigies. Yet speculation in the novel is both financial (as in *Little Dorrit*) and ocular, in the sense of feeding on the object of the gaze, as in Boz's speculative gaze that is quite different from the "speculation" of Richard Steele's privileged spectator of London's streetlife, which he values for the aesthetic pleasure it gives the gentleman and its improvement of his mind ("The Hours of London," *The Spectator*, 11 August 1712). The dolls' eyes are not, however, an empty speculation but provide an animated mask salvaged from the dead waste of society. Jenny is thus a true Resurrection Artist, for she revives the dead souls of London by representing society to itself in far more vivid mimesis than the Veneerings' self-reflective mirror. The fun, as she explains to a bewildered Riah, is in the trying-on, for the society ladies are quite unconscious that their images are being recycled from idle waste for the useful amusement of children. In a similar fashion, Dickens recycles Lady Tippins's idle dinner talk into a comedy of manners which shows how little of genuine value there is below her doll-like exterior.

The much abused poor little dolls' dressmaker seems in no way related to Mayhew's seller of artificial dolls' eyes, nor does Mayhew record an unusual occupation which provides the occasion for another guess-my-trade game in book I, chapter VII. The taxidermist's shop supplies skeletons for medical students and artists, as well as body parts, like Wegg's, for dissection.[47] Venus is thus another purveyor of representations, which happen to be constructed out of the dead waste of society (including human corpses and amputations). However, this hapless lover with "the patience to fit together on wires the whole framework of society" (OMF III, VI; 540), as Wegg puts it, alluding "to the human skelinton," cannot put together a complete figure. His collection of "human warious" resists the organicist concept of society, embraced by Huxley and Spencer and popularized by G. H. Lewes and George Eliot, the epistemological implications of which underlie Eliot's "natural history" of society in *Felix Holt* and *Middlemarch* and are spelled out in the analogy of the social body and disease in the "Address to Working Men by Felix Holt" (1867).[48] Mr. Wegg's leg cannot be made to fit, for all the anatomist's exquisite art of reconstructing a skeleton from "miscellaneous" items (a veritable recycling of spare parts!). Neither the national construction of the English body (as distinct from the French gentleman), nor the anatomist's skill at artistic embellishment can fit the "me" of Wegg into a whole. This has been taken as an expression of anatomization and fragmentation,[49] which misses the comic mockery of the mean and unscrupulous Wegg who gets his due (waste valued to the fraction) when he is thrown (with a "prodigious splash") into a scavenger's dust cart (OMF IV, xiv; 862)! His leg does not fit into the organic body, but it might have value as a "Monstrosity," presumably to be exhibited for the entertainment or education of the public, like the freaks at fairs whose carnivalized bodies at once transgressed and stabilized the boundaries of the natural.[50] We cannot miss the humor of Venus regretting he had ever made the purchase of the amputated leg, or of his threatening to articulate the boy who buys the stuffed bird because some teeth got mixed up in the change. All this mocks of paleontology which classified fossils into a synecdochal representation of the species so important for the science of natural history (Dickens must have been aware that Professor Owen had fabricated his dinosaurs from fragments).

What the misanthropic Venus comically represents (his own much abused "me") is what is missing in the classificatory systems of natural history and so sacred to Dickens's own humanistic sensibilities: love and benevolence. In Carlyle's "Scavenger Age" of speculators like Hudson or the Veneerings, the "me" that will constitute a moral self can only be articulated in the love that is denied Venus and later redeems him. The unscientific moral scruples that stop Venus wasting his "time on groping for nothing in cinders" (OMF III, vi; 539) make him a functional organ in the metaplot of double-deceit. In that scheme, Boffin outwits Wegg in a revision of the inheritance plot that redeems dust by freeing it from the money-nexus. Bella likewise undergoes a moral conversion and is weaned from her money fetish.

In a similar comparison to the one that Chadwick had employed in his report,[51] the recycling effected by the plot puts Paris in far better light than the wasteful capital of the British empire, because it makes efficient use of its dust to feed its scavengers. The dust flying around in London does not just pollute the air with particles that irritate and blind,[52] but paradoxically opens our eyes to both the moral worthlessness of the euphemistic dust and the invisible process by which it eats away at the social and human fabric:

> That mysterious paper currency which circulates in London when the wind blows, gyrated here and there and everywhere. Whence can it come, whither can it go? It hangs on every bush, flutters in every tree, is caught flying by the electric wires, haunts every enclosure, drinks at every pump, cowers at every grating, shudders upon every plot of grass, seeks rest in vain

behind the legions of iron rails. In Paris, where nothing is wasted, costly and luxurious city though it be, but where wonderful human ants creep out of holes and pick up every scrap, there is no such thing. There, it blows nothing but dust. There, sharp eyes and sharp stomachs reap even the east wind, and get something out of it.

The wind sawed, and the sawdust whirled. The shrubs wrung their many hands, bemoaning that they had been over-persuaded by the sun to bud; the young leaves pined; the sparrows repented of their early marriages, like men and women; the colours of the rainbow were discernible, not in floral spring, but in the faces of the people whom it nibbled and pinched. And ever the wind sawed, and the sawdust whirled. (OMF I, xii; 191)

The circulation of paper currency is worthless in terms of moral productivity, so much sawdust flying about in this "hopeless city, with no rent in the leaden canopy of its sky" (OMF I, xii; 191), as it seems to Lightwood and Wrayburn, those two legal dust contractors (in Boffin's joking expression). It is the false currency of the Veneerings and other speculators in stocks and shares, as well as countless tradesmen and begging-letter writers who attach themselves to the gold of the Golden Dustman. In the end, the Golden Dustman scatters the dust that he has been throwing in everyone's eyes and reveals the true worth of his benevolence, in contrast to a society which can read into his dust mounds only cash value. In the end, the dust mounds are unsentimentally carted away for what they are worth, no more then their exchange value.

Boffin may be a stereotypically rich dust contractor, but more than any other character he is responsible for redeeming meaning, rather than money, from waste. Boffin is the schemer who engineers Bella's conversion and John Harmon's resurrection. He is another dissembler of false representations in his acting of the miser, and, like Riah, he is a sheep in wolf's clothing. Both Boffin and Riah dissemble avaricious worship of money and both parody a social discourse which privileges money. Money's corrupting influence on society is unmasked, and the characteristics of a national Podsnappery are exposed as hard-heartedness and compulsive acquisitiveness. Selfishness must be exchanged for the currency of a mutual friendship, which is proposed as an agency of change and circulation far more efficacious than the charitable institutions which plague the Golden Dustman. Benevolence can redeem the ugly dustheaps, and in real life Dickens encouraged Angela Burdett-Coutts's conversion of a dustheap into model housing at Nova Scotia Gardens in Bethnal Green, a squalid slum neighborhood in the East End of London (fig. 18).

Fig. 18: "Nova Scotia Gardens and What Grew There" (1859)

In the penultimate chapter, there is a general tidying up and cleaning, when Mr. and Mrs. John Harmon "set right all matters that had strayed in any way wrong" in the fiction of the murder, including untangling the disfigured Eugene's affairs (accounting for his figures, but also for his changed identity). This achieves an efficiency parallel to the neat office management of Boffin's secretary and the novelist's efficient management of the plot. The story ends with the removal of the dustheap that undoes the philosophy of "money, money, money" which obsessed Bella until Boffin's mimicry of great misers awakened in her disgust at its dehumanizing corruption. Boffin proves his lack of avarice by being satisfied with his little mound. Similarly, Eugene's dissolute inability to feel sympathy for other classes in an economy that makes nonsense of affections has to be converted into true love for Lizzie.

In the debate between exchange and speculation, Dickens seems to be proposing the novel as a transformative agent of exchange of natural value.[53] In his public speeches, Dickens pointed in terms not so different from the social reformers and medical men to a far more efficient recycling in the circulation of knowledge among the laboring classes, who would otherwise be redundant or, worse, "what might otherwise easily become waste forces" (*Speeches* 281–82). Speaking in Manchester in 1858 to the Institutional Association of Cheshire and Lancashire, Dickens praised the true mutual benevolence of the association, in contrast to the usual pretensions of such institutions, because the mutual benevolence of encouraging working-class education could have far-reaching benefits in the reduction of waste and in the efficiency of productivity, though the responsibility and initiative lie clearly with the middle classes and not, as Felix Holt believed, with the radical artisans. Addressing the Birmingham and Midland Institute in 1869, Dickens spelled out the benefits not only of educating artisans but teaching them to think:

> Suppose that one of your industrial students should turn his chemical studies to the practical account of extracting gold from waste colour water, and of taking it into custody, in the very act of running away by the thousand pounds worth, down the town drains. Suppose another should perceive in his books, in his studious evenings, what was amiss with his master's until then inscrutably defective furnace, and should go straight at it—to the great annual saving of that master—and put it right. (*Speeches* 401–02)

An alchemist's dream, perhaps, and it required a faith in individual enterprise to overcome the system (which Doyce, in his struggle with the Circumlocution Office fails to do). But more than the rehearsal of a Carlylean theme, it is the redemptive narrative of the novel which must turn Chadwick's terminology of national prosperity and waste recycling to the good and reconstitute the social body in terms of the capital P of Dickens's much misunderstood conclusion to his Birmingham speech in which he declared, "My faith in the people governing is, on the whole, infinitesimal; my faith in the People governed, is, on the whole illimitable" (*Speeches* 407).

London Underworld and Netherworld

> There are more ways than one of looking at sewers.... There is a highly romantic point of view, from which they are regarded as accessible, pleasant, and convivial hiding-places for criminals flying from justice, but black and dangerous labyrinths for the innocent stranger.
>
> —John Hollingshead, *Underground London*

Such moral regeneration may be applied to the three-dimensional model of circulation in the city. The three-dimensional model of the city as a circulatory system figures in several of the visionary schemes which proposed underground passages segregating commercial traffic and the working classes from neo-classical mansions and banks above ground (fig. 19). Sir Joseph Bazalgette's unified sanitary system incorporates this concept in the building of the Victoria Embankment as a lid for both sewers and the new underground railway.[54] But the metonym of the national economy as a sewer system was not simply a medical or engineering trope. Carlyle's first *Latter-Day Pamphlet* ("The Present Time," February 1, 1850; 20: 27–28) makes the very real cesspools into a figure for the excremental state of society at large, while in *Sartor Resartus* urban pollution is a symptom of a national disease that can only be cured by curbing the competition and money worship of a laissez-faire economy and by reconnecting with organic nature. By recycling the value of filth, Dickens's novel escapes from a synecdochal relationship of plot and

Fig. 19: Metropolitan Traffic Relief (1850)

characters and develops a metaphorical reading of the city's economy of relations that reclassifies society into two categories: those who will work by turning filth into a moral good—like Boffin, Jenny Wren, Lizzie Hexam, and the novelist himself in his useful work of representing them—and those who make money by not working—the true parasites and misers responsible for a sterile, fossilized state of affairs that is undermining the moral fabric of society.

Underground London exerted a fascination with sewers because it ripped the veil off civilization, revealing to middle-class readers the invisible world of the city and its oral and archeological history beneath the surface. John Hollingshead's 1862 book, called *Underground London*, based on essays in Dickens's *All the Year Round*, demythicizes the sewers and excavates the invisible city of the modern Nineveh.[55] However, Hollingshead looks to the future promised in the underground railway, which was designed to link the major railway termini and create a further link in the circulatory system. Charles Knight's celebration of the neoclassical grandeur of London's waterworks in *London* exulted in the great progress made in the capital's sanitation,[56] and readers of *The Illustrated London News* were treated to detailed drawings of the engineering works in the Fleet sewer, whetting their curiosity about the wondrous metropolitan world below ground which supplied the needs of bourgeois comfort but which also threatened the city, as when the Fleet sewer burst in 1862. Yet what was not shown in such descriptions were the collapsing walls, rotten timbers, and faulty gradients of London's drainage arrangements, unsanitary housing, or the lack of coordination between different administrative bodies responsible for street cleaning, waste removal, and water supply. Progress could mean ventilating the overcrowded houses of the poor by demolition, which left many homeless, or, as happened after the Town Improvement Clauses Act of 1847, flushing London's drains into the river, which was both drinking supply and sewer, so that the cholera epidemic became waterborne. Waste was being disposed, not removed,[57] and what was needed was a modern drainage system that would prevent further epidemics instead of wasting money on poisoning the Thames.[58]

We have to pick our way through the open drains in Manchester's streets in chapter 6 of Mrs. Gaskell's *Mary Barton*, and we smell the disgusting condition of that city's streets in Engels's notorious description in *The Condition of the Working-Class in England in 1844* (though the English translation appeared only in 1892). In Dickens's *Our Mutual Friend*, Dickens heeds the warning of Carlyle's first *Latter-Day Pamphlet* and combines the literal description with a figurative representation of moral and metaphysical significance which recognizes that the streets are sewers and the sewers are streets in a multidimensional model of the city in which conflict takes place above and below the surface. Published three years after Victor Hugo's *Les Misérables*, *Our Mutual Friend* does not take us down the common-shore of John Gay's sewers, but remarkably it does, like Hugo's tale of subterranean Paris, imply both its literal and figurative meaning beneath the surface in order to show the connection between recycling and redemption in the city. Hugo extends the metaphorical dimension of the underground city in a backward look at the sewers before they were modernized and sanitized, at the rotten foundations of a revolutionary upheaval. The sewers, it is stressed, are an inverted labyrinth of the streets above, with a similar architectural decline from Louis XVIII, and bring into contaminating contact all classes and ranks of society. Without departing from a mimetic representation of the Paris underworld, Jean Valjean's excursion through the Paris sewers suggests a Dantean journey from darkness to light, from a prison existence to liberty. Burdened with the wounded body of Marius, his struggle through the quicksand is a test of endurance. The robber-innkeeper Thénardier acts as mythical tollgate keeper for the fugitive Theseus, an unrecognized Odysseus, out of the funneled grating, a secret passage like other gratings in Hugo's novel leading to love and death. The movement is upward toward redemption. *Our Mutual Friend* turns the social hierarchy upside down and excavates beneath the surface in order to enable us to discern mythical structures in everyday life and, as in *Bleak House*, to feel the human contact with the poor and needy, the outcasts who inhabited the underworld charted by Mayhew in *London Labour and the London Poor*.

Dickens's moral sensibility, in contrast to Hugo's, extends sympathy to the respectable poor,[59] but both novels have strong redemptive themes: the redemption of a convict and a fallen woman, the redemption of the silver candlesticks, the bearing of Marius as a cross though the underworld, and the ascent to the land of the living are matched by the drowning of Rogue Riderhood and John Harmon's resurrection, the general motif of the redemption of money and money values, and Lizzie's redemption of Eugene through love.

Fig. 20: "The 'Silent Highway'-Man: Your Money or Your Life!" (1858)

In *Our Mutual Friend*, the river, rather than the underworld, is the vehicle for this mythical and metaphysical symbolism, but the desired purification from contamination cannot help also being literal. In contemporary images, such as the *Punch* cartoon "The 'Silent Highway'-Man" (fig. 20), the shipping highway to the emporium of the Empire is a stream of ineffable effluence plied by Charon's barge. Gaffer Hexam is another Charon, who scavenges the waterway for the corpses of its victims and exacts coins for their passage to the netherworld. This is no mere trope for the plague city, for, until the 1859 drainage improvements, the river was a real carrier of death. Although Swinburne counted the river as a protagonist in *Our Mutual Friend*, there has been no critical consensus on what it symbolizes or whether it is a symbol. Critics such as F. S. Schwarzbach have lamented Dickens's weakness for watery imagery, while John Carey has regretted a muddled and unfortunate attempt to imbue the Thames with religious significance. J. Hillis Miller, however, claims the river, along with dust and wind, as the prime movers of the novel's symbolization of otherness.[60]

Our Mutual Friend opens on the river, as the mysterious figures in the boat proceed downstream from the iron Southwark Bridge to the new stone London Bridge. The river winds through the novel in a complex imagery of death and resurrection, waste and salvage, that is riddled with far greater ambivalence than in *Little Dorrit* or *Dombey and Son*,[61] but may still resemble a street housing mysterious secrets, as well as a commercial highway. Because of the great incidence of suicides, the black Thames in "Down With the Tide," "seems an image of death in the great city's life" (DJ 3: 114). It is the urban site of violent death in the dreamworld of the Uncommercial Traveller's "Night Walks": "the river had an awful look, the buildings on the banks were muffled in black shrouds, and the reflected lights seemed to originate deep in the water, as if the spectres of suicides were holding them to show where they went down. The wild moon and clouds were as restless as an evil conscience in a tumbled bed, and the very shadow of the immensity of London seemed to lie oppressively upon the river" (UT 129). Unlike the pastoral memory of childhood revisited in "Chatham Yard," the river in *Our Mutual Friend* is painted as a dreary landscape in the gloomy prospect that opens to Lizzie's mind in a vivid impressionism worthy of Whistler's later *Nocturnes*, which emphasized the visual effects of night light, though here perhaps more reminiscent of Turner's *The Fighting Téméraire*:

> The white face of the winter day came sluggishly on, veiled in a frosty mist; and the shadowy ships in the river slowly changed to black substances; and the sun, blood-red on the eastern marshes behind dark masts and yards, seemed filled with the ruins of a forest it had set on fire. (OMF I, VI; 118)

The mood is lugubrious and fantastic. In Eugene Wrayburn's inebriated, somnambulant imagination the river looms like a fairytale monster; it threatens to suck in and submerge in its debris and waste all that is human, as it sucks in Gaffer.

Not a sluice gate, or a painted scale upon a post or wall, showing the depth of water, but seemed to hint, like the dreadfully facetious Wolf in bed in Grandmamma's cottage, "That's to drown *you* in, my dears!" Not a lumbering black barge, with its cracked and blistered side impending over them, but seemed to suck at the river with a thirst for sucking them under. And everything so vaunted the spoiling influences of water—discoloured copper, rotten wood, honey-combed stone, green dank deposit—that the after-consequences of being crushed, sucked under, and drawn down, looked as ugly to the imagination as the main event. (OMF I, xiv; 219–20)

Rarely is the river calm, but stormy and menacing with the prospect of death in a necropolis:

The squall had come up, like a spiteful messenger before the morning; there followed in its wake a ragged tear of light which ripped the dark clouds until they showed a great grey hole of day.

They were all shivering, and everything about them seemed to be shivering; the river itself, craft, rigging, sails, such early smoke as there yet was on the shore. Black with wet, and altered to the eye by white patches of hail and sleet, the huddled buildings looked lower than usual, as if they were cowering, and had shrunk with the cold. Very little life was to be seen on either bank, windows and doors were shut, and the staring black and white letters upon wharves and warehouses "looked," said Eugene to Mortimer, "like inscriptions over the graves of dead businesses." (OMF, I, xix; 219)

Even upstream, in contrast to *Little Dorrit*, the river no longer resembles Nature's tranquil stream, or "gentle spring ethereally mild," as in Thomson's *Seasons*, but, in the case of the residence of the indolent lawyers on its brink, is imagined as "nipping spring with an easterly wind" (OMF I, xii; 191).

In another example of a thematic use of setting, the Thames reflects the ripple of Eugene's emotions and suggests to Betty Higden, fleeing from the terror of entering a workhouse, a redemptive passage out of her misery and despair:

In those pleasant little towns on Thames, you may hear the fall of the water over the weirs, or even, in still weather, the rustle of the rushes; and from the bridge you may see the young river, dimpled like a young child, playfully gliding away among the trees, unpolluted by the defilements that lie in wait for it on its course, and as yet out of hearing of the deep summons of the sea. It were too much to pretend that Betty Higden made out such thoughts; no; but she heard the tender river whispering to many like herself, "Come to me, come to me! When the cruel shame and terror you have so long fled from, most beset you, come to me! I am the Relieving Officer appointed by eternal ordinance to do my work; I am not held in estimation according as I shirk it. My breast is softer than the pauper-nurse's; death in my arms is peacefuller than among the pauper-wards. Come to me!" (OMF, III, viii; 567)

In the rural riverside towns where Betty Higden plies her wares, she finds little compassion and she flees the "Good Samaritan" of the Poor Law.[62] The angry

Carlylean tones offer a solemn sermon that the honorable gentlemen of the boards and commissions should roll up their sleeves if the dust mounds of the Poor Laws are to be cleared. Yet it is not through the National Dustmen, as members of Parliament are called in *Hard Times*, that society will be redeemed, but through the kindness and faithfulness represented by Lizzie in her merciful act of rescuing Betty Higden's honesty at the last. These moral qualities are reflected in Lizzie's beauty, as discerned by John Harmon, in the guise of Rokesmith educating Bella.

Betty Higden follows the allegorical path of the suffering Christian fallen afoul of the laws that deny her freedom and dignity, an advanced version of Dickens's earlier "Parish-Boy's Progress." If this was not a charade, Riderhood could be a type of obstacle or vice on the road to salvation. In a reversal of John 11.25 he tells Betty Higden "I am the Lock" (OMF III, VIII; 571)—he is surely anything but the Life and the Resurrection! Riderhood robs Betty before she flees again, coming to rest in an Ascension in front of the lights of the glass-windowed Paper Mill, at the foot of the Cross at her long journey's end, where the angel Lizzie finds her and lifts her to Heaven (III, VIII). The Paper Mill offers a vision of a Blakean New Jerusalem with its ideal working conditions in a green and pleasant land blessed by the mutual benevolence of the Jews who, in reversal of the usual stereotyped relations (though no more "real" Jews than Fagin), are a foil to the unredeemed Christians blind to moral regeneration.[63] The Paper Mill is a recycling plant like the one praised, in an article which Dickens wrote with Mark Lemon (*Household Words*, 31 August 1850; UW I, 137–42), as holding out hope against taxation and for forbearance, mercy, and progress. As such, it strengthens the argument for moral recycling and offers a glimpse of the edenic bliss which previously Dickens had sought in childhood innocence (in *Oliver Twist*), the pastoral countryside (*The Old Curiosity Shop*), or, more furtively, in America (*Martin Chuzzlewit*).

In *Our Mutual Friend*, the otherworldly space of the celestial city seeks a redeeming vision on Mr. Riah's rooftop where Jenny Wren's vision of angels suggests transcendence of a quasi-Blakean "experience" *in* the city: "And you see the clouds rushing on above the narrow streets, not minding them, and you see the golden arrows pointing at the mountains in the sky from which the wind comes, and you feel as if you were dead" (OMF II, V; 334). When she calls Riah to come back up and be dead in his garden on the roof-tops, he sees her "looking down out of a Glory of her long bright radiant hair, and musically repeating to him, like a vision: 'Come up and be dead! Come up and be dead!'" (OMF II, V; 335). The scene in the rooftop paradise offers another version of Paul Dombey's dreamy floating out to eternity and Little Dorrit's reading in the city of a pastoral idyll; significantly, both Lizzie and Jenny are engaged in reading, suggesting a reading that transcends the earthly city. We recall the gardens atop the Delectable Mountains after Christian and Hopeful leave Vanity Fair, and like the Arcadian bower enjoyed by Adam, Eve, and Raphael in *Paradise Lost*, it offers a rural innocence unpolluted by Satan "long in populous City pent, / Where Houses thick and Sewers annoy the Air" (9: 445–56).[64] Admittedly, this rooftop vision of eternity merely hints in its scriptural references

(John 3; Revelation 11, 12) at the possibility of a spiritual transcendence. The glory of the divine clouds trailed by Jenny's soul is a poor travesty of Wordsworthian intimations of immortality, but the "rainbow" display of her dolls in the shop window confirms her child-woman's vision is the truer one, just as it is the prophet Riah, the true Good Samaritan, who is admitted to the kingdom of heaven on the rooftop, while Fledgeby, like Milton's Satan, must go down in unredeemed and unenlightened darkness to the illegible streets of Mammon's City below, where he can only read pounds, shillings, and pence.

Later in the novel, after Bella has told the rechristened John she is going to bear him a baby, the redemptive plot returns us to the vision of the factory at evening, the factory made over to the good, of the city but not in it. That vision reads into the river landscape a transcendence no longer accessible to much Victorian social thought, taking us beyond and away from a visionary landscape to a hereafter which is nevertheless close at hand, to something like Jenny Wren's rooftop celestial city of the spirit. It also offers a rare glimpse of Coketown's ugly citadel made beautiful:

> The Paper Mill had stopped work for the night, and the paths and roads in its neighbourhood were sprinkled with clusters of people going home from their day's labour in it. There were men, women, and children in the groups, and there was no want of lively colour to flutter in the gentle evening wind. The mingling of various voices and the sound of laughter made a cheerful impression upon the ear, analogous to that of the fluttering colours upon the eye. Into the sheet of water reflecting the flushed sky in the foreground of the living picture, a knot of urchins were casting stones, and watching the expansion of the rippling circles. So, in the rosy evening, one might watch the ever-widening beauty of the landscape—beyond the newly-released workers wending home—beyond the silver river—beyond the deep green fields of corn, so prospering, that the loiterers in their narrow threads of pathway seemed to float immersed breast-high—beyond the hedgerows and the clumps of trees—beyond the windmills on the ridge—away to where the sky appeared to meet the earth, as if there were no immensity of space between mankind and Heaven. (OMF IV, vi; 756–57)

The passage precedes the plea not to outlaw the workers' depraved pleasures in the statistical reality of disease, but also leads into a love scene in which Lizzie martyrs herself to the lesson of Betty Higden's death.

Lizzie, whose eyes have long been open to visions of transcendence, swears to keep to her principles and distance herself from Eugene. She will not allow her body to be subjected to a class oppression that would render her inferior. It is Eugene who must change for the class divide to be breached. Nevertheless, Lizzie droops under the masterful gaze of the upper-class male. Before they part, he forces on her a sacramental kiss, "almost as if she were sanctified to him by death" (IV, vi; 764), a christological allusion that should not pass us by. They will marry on his deathbed in a macabre last sacrament that unites Eros and Thanatos. We recognize

Lizzie as one of Dickens's otherworldly figures who shows Eugene a way out of his crisis to a significant and symbolic act of salvation. Lizzie's rescue of Eugene raises him, Lazarus-like, from the dead and summons supernatural assistance to bring the disfigured body to shore. Lizzie's role curiously parallels Little Dorrit's in raising the crippled Mrs. Clennam from her catacomb existence. Yet Lizzie is actually reenacting her father's skilled raising of the dead, in his raising of the "Harmon" body in the opening scene (which Charley told Mortimer no Lazarus could raise), except that she discovers love, not coins, in the corpse, and this time she does not avert her eyes from the disfigured face, but kisses it in imitation of Salome, in a further reinforcement of the parallel of John the Baptist.

Eugene's resurrection is a moral and physical rebirth, a disfigurement and refigurement, no less than Esther Summerson's, in a sentimental but symbolic transition from one state of being to another. It is a transfiguration through death which enables Eugene to share Jenny's fancy of flowers and children which eases bodily pain. The transformative recycling from cynicism and *ennui* to productivity and benevolence brings about a regeneration which changes both Eugene's and Mortimer's view of society and converts them from participation in its unscrupulous calculation and mocking amorality to recognition of its hypocrisy and vacuity. The unrelieved, amoral view of the "hopeless" city can change when they "turn to in earnest"—a telling phrase in Dickens for productive labor that is honest and diligent. Eugene does "turn to in earnest" (IV, xvi; 885), substituting vocation and work for the moribund, wasteful culture of a leisure class which can afford limitless idleness and which avoids doing anything serious.

Eugene defies the voice of society by marrying a "horrid female waterman" turned factory-girl and is suitably rewarded, in Lady Tippins's mock Parliamentary Committee, with Twemlow's knighting him a true gentleman. Eugene has learned a similar lesson to Pip's in *Great Expectations*, that portable property and wasteful spending do not make a gentleman and only altruism pays its rewards. The ending thus invests in an alternate moral economy which converts worthless dust to socially useful purpose and challenges class divisions which prevent the love and benevolence that alone can transform individuals.

Eugene Wrayburn and John Harmon are each baptized in the river and each emerges different in spirit and body. Gaffer Hexam, however, cannot be resurrected. He is said to be "baptized unto Death" (OMF I, xiv; 222) in a playful reference to Paul's expression of salvation and atonement for sins through the crucifixion of Jesus (Romans 6.3).[65] This allusion to a passage central to the baptismal rite might hint that Hexam was more sinned against than sinning, that he too might not be beyond reach of atonement.

> Father, was that you calling me? Father! I thought I heard you call me twice
> before! Words never to be answered, those, upon the earth-side of the grave.
> The wind sweeps jeeringly over Father, whips him with the frayed ends of
> his dress and his jagged hair, tries to turn him where he lies stark on his
> back, and force his face towards the rising sun, that he may be shamed the

more. A lull, and the wind is secret and prying with him; lifts and lets fall a rag; hides palpitating under another rag; runs nimbly through his hair and beard. Then, in a rush, it cruelly taunts him. Father, was that you calling me? Was it you, the voiceless and the dead? Was it you, thus buffeted as you lie here in a heap? Was it you, thus baptized unto Death, with these flying impurities now flung upon your face? Why not speak, Father? Soaking into this filthy ground as you lie here, is your own shape. Did you never see such a shape soaked into your boat? Speak, Father. Speak to us, the winds, the only listeners left you! (OMF I, xiv; 221–22)

This is Lizzie's consciousness, though not her voice, praying for her father's soul to be redeemed from the mocking wind and the "impurities" hailing down upon him in this foul earth-bound existence where he is shamed and repudiated, despite his calling out twice, unanswered.

The river is a key actor in the redemptive plot as a source of both pollution and metaphysical cleansing, though it cannot cleanse Headstone's foul deed, when he takes a dip in a futile propitiatory act. Riderhood, who later retrieves from the river the clothes that provide evidence of bloody guilt and exchanged identities, is himself "Found Drowned" and resuscitated in the Six Jolly Fellowship Porters. That is an occasion for the narrator to muse on the death that irresistibly pulls all of us. Riderhood deserves no moral resurrection, for the encounter with death, which has excited our common empathy with mortality, proves a "sweet delusion" that the evil will be "drowned out" of him. However, despite his belief that a drowned man cannot be drowned twice, Bradley Headstone calls him (in the opposite direction of Jenny Wren's summons) to Hades, "Come down!" Both villains are found locked in an iron grip in the ooze and scum in a pit behind one of the rotten gates of the Lock, which Riderhood has drained, so that neither is drowned in water but die without any chance of rebirth or cleansing (IV, xv).

The "solemn river" that flows outside the window of the dying Eugene (IV, xi; 822) follows the inexorable path of Father Time, which reminds us of our mortal destiny and mutual responsibility in a society ruled by railway time and unnatural values (as we saw in chapter two). The river functions as both a mythical transformation or resurrection and a crossing point from one semiotic field to another, from the earthly to the celestial city. Like Riah, the fairy godmother of transformations, the river cannot itself bring about the transformation. The living-dead John cannot rationalize how he came up on the other side of the river, but he has crossed the river like Bunyan's pilgrims and he has been reborn in accordance with the Christian myth of rebirth in spirit and water (John 3.1–6).[66]

Now John must decide whether to resurrect himself and come into his money or remain incognito after burying himself under mounds of earth, as well as mounds of dust, so that the Boffins can continue to enjoy their inheritance. His decision to test Bella is a decision also to reject the evil uses to which money is put and to repudiate the dead legacy of his father's testament which (like Dombey) acquires a woman like any other commodified object. The redemption of dust, like Florence Dombey and

Arthur Clennam's redemption of their parents' avarice, echoes the explicit reference to resurrection in Carlton's substitution for Darney's atonement for his family's evil past in *A Tale of Two Cities*; resurrection is to be sought through a spiritual as well as social union in *Our Mutual Friend* by Eugene's story.

Rebirth in the river is, however, only the beginning of the recovery of a self—the "I" that separates from the drowning John Harmon (OMF II, xiii). The fact that he is drugged and "shot" into the river (like rubbish shot into the dust mound for sifting) at the same spot as the murdered man indicates a splitting of self. This dissolution of identity suggests, besides much else, the struggle to maintain moral autonomy in the polluted flow of modern city life which sucks in bodies and submerges them in its libidinous, cannibalistic economy.

The test of faith (marital and moral) is not complete until John Harmon clears himself of suspicion (another charade, because his "game," as Mr. Inspector puts it, has been to cast suspicion over himself). He has put Bella through a trial of proving she is more than a doll in a dollhouse and can exercise the power of money to do good to others, for which abstinence and poverty will not do. The plot must reconcile money and morals, love and lucre.

Conclusion, in a Rainbow

Highgates heights & Hampsteads, to Poplar Hackney & Bow:
To Islington & Paddington & the Brook of Albions river
We builded Jerusalem as a City & a Temple; from Lambeth
We began our Foundations; lovely Lambeth! O lovely Hills
of Camberwell, we shall behold you no more in glory & pride
For Jerusalem lies in ruins & the furnaces of Los are builded there
You are now shrunk up to a narrow Rock in the midst of the Sea
But here we build Babylon on Euphrates, compell'd to build
And to inhabit, our Little-ones to clothe in armour of the gold
Of Jerusalems cherubims & to forge them swords of her Altars
I see London blind & age-bent begging thro the Streets
Of Babylon, led by a child, his tears run down his beard

Blake, *Jerusalem*

"Better to be Abel than Cain," declares a chapter title in *Our Mutual Friend* (IV, vii). Eugene Wrayburn is an ambivalent Abel, in view of his designs on Lizzie's body. Nevertheless, the murderous duality of sinful mankind can transform the experience of suffering and death into salvation within the city like the Christian parable of the seed which must first die, though without the dark Dostoyevskyan mysticism of descent into sin and expiation from crime.[67] This is a further dimension of the motif of the potential of dust to transform bodies from death to more life-giving properties (rather than bodies as property). However, if any salvation can be discerned in Eugene's "hopeless city," it works by a mythopoeic transformation of realities in which there is no contradiction between the literal and the figurative.[68]

J. Hillis Miller has difficulty in accepting transcendence in *Our Mutual Friend* because it is limited by the human condition in a city where there is no unity of experience.[69] This difficulty can be met by appreciating a polyphonic performance of different voices that express multiple consciousness in the city—Harmon's split self, Wrayburn's insomniac nocturnal excursion on the river in a hailstorm, his alienated view of St. Paul's from the monotony of his office, Headstone's stormy depths of passion, Lizzie's prayers on the river, and Betty Higden's feverish imagination. It is a heteroglossia that, like Sloppy's newspaper reading, does the police in different voices (OMF I, xviii). Yet the dialogical discourse, far from distancing itself in despair at any stable meaning in an unredeemed world, does not preclude belief in another world beyond empirical verification and in a Creator to whom there is moral responsibility. On the contrary, it suggests the possibility of transcendence, as well as the consequences of blindness to it. The insistence on the certainty of death and the meting out of reward and punishment within the novelistic universe point to a belief in an otherworldly accountability that lends unseen meaning to the city's financial and moral economy. Dickens, declared Ruskin in *Modern Painters*, was one of those popular authors who set themselves against religious form but pleaded for "simple truth and benevolence";[70] if this is dressed up as the duty to do good which privileges the poor and meek, it is no less subversive of the fog of words and dead Mammon-worship of the necropolis of ashes and dust.[71]

Dickens's representation of the city looks at first glance depressingly gloomy. It is a city of fog and dust which chokes the mind and spirit, as if the grating wind were sawing instead of blowing, blinding and choking the pedestrians with dust (OMF I, xii; 191). The London fog served Carlyle as simile of how the English should grope their way out of the midday darkness in the modern doomed Jerusalem, which he also saw as choked by dust and wasting its natural resources under the Midas spell of Mammonism. But the blinding and choking sawdust never gathers into the damning storm-cloud of Ruskin's 1884 lecture (a storm-cloud which he dated no earlier than 1871). Instead, salvation can only be sought in the fallen city, in a vision of the city which shows to those blind to the truth the consequences of their blindness, the harvest of the grim reaper, Death. The vision is radical not in the narrow political sense but in its Carlylean rejection of the utilitarian model of the diseased body of the city, arguing instead for its reformation into an organic body that ideally responds to all its parts with mutual benevolence.

In his unpopular series in the *Cornhill Magazine*, "Unto This Last" (1860), Ruskin insisted on Christian principles of benevolence in response to the cruelty of Political Economy, an ideology in which wealth was power and price was detached from value. In adopting the utilitarian analogy of physiological circulation, Ruskin was arguing that Political Economy encouraged unequal distribution of wealth at the expense of the poor, whereas the health of the nation depended on an equal flow throughout the body: "There is one quickness of the current which comes of cheerful emotion or wholesome exercise; and another which comes of shame or of fever. There is a flush of the body which is full of warmth and life; and another which will pass into putrefaction."[72] In opposing Political Economy, Ruskin seeks to reinscribe the human body into economic discourse as other than a dead commodity of productive or exchange value and to reunite wealth with well-being. Dickens takes up this common Victorian antithesis of prosperity and disease (Ruskin's "wealth and illth") in the national body to reanimate (resurrect) John Harmon as a body that can be reinvested with the moral as well as economic and legal power to divest inherited wealth.[73] *Our Mutual Friend* similarly reconstitutes the organic body through its revaluation of society's waste, the outcasts and scavengers of the city, at the expense of the idle rich, showing comically how waste scraps can be given value as dolls (objects of amusement and of representation) and, more gruesomely, how drowned bodies or amputated and dissected bodies can be turned to cash. The novel begins with a body in the city's necropolis, but the mystery of whose body it is remains unsolved. Instead, John Harmon rises out of death in the river to assume a new identity that transforms the relation of money to bodies and to the body of the city. However, this transformation of the deadening money-economy appears to lie in the ability to conceptualize moral agency in the imprisoning wasteland of Harmon's house, or the littered Sahara of suburbia, through which Wilfer makes his way home.

The putative pastoral in the arbor atop Boffin's dust mound is pleasant but facetious. The romanticized or neo-romantic idyll of escape from the city, glimpsed at the Maylies' in *Oliver Twist* and in Little Nell's flight and death, or later located in the pastoral cottage that displaces Bleak House, gradually narrows down to Plornish's Bleeding Heart Yard and Mr. Riah's rooftop. Major improvements were nevertheless under way at the close of Dickens's life, chief among them Joseph Bazalgette's monumental sewage construction which modernized the city by constructing a *system* of waste disposal and treatment that replaced the poorly maintained medieval sewers and cleaned up the Thames.[74] It is, however, in the city's self-destruction ("Abbau") that there is any hope of building the New Jerusalem. Dickens's rereading of the city re-inscribes moral agency, albeit in an increasingly bleak realization that no magic wand is going to transform London's dust-heaps into an ethics not dependent on money without society believing in the possibility of regeneration. The resurrected Eugene is transformed by love, as is Bella, and John connives to subvert the coercion of a father's will (another turning of dust to value), but in its weak apocalypse *Our Mutual Friend* does not bear great promise that the New Jerusalem will be reached any time soon.

On his excursion into the wasteland of Stepney and Radcliffe down by the "impure river" in "A Small Star in the East," the Uncommercial Traveller encounters a scene from the medieval woodcuts of the "Dance of Death" in the "mud-desert" of unemployed "hewers of wood and drawers of water" (UT 319). It is a mocking skeleton, not a whole and immortal political body, which presents these starving scavengers with electoral promises

> for staying the degeneracy, physical and moral, of many thousands (who shall say how many?) of the English race; for devising employment useful to the community for those who want but to work and live; for equalising rates, cultivating waste lands, facilitating emigration, and, above all things, saving and utilising the oncoming generations, and thereby changing ever-growing national weakness into strength. (UT 320)

The description of the barest conditions of subsistence juxtaposes the ideological assumptions of the campaign for enfranchisement of the working classes with uncomplaining, even hopeful people starving to death in filth and disease. The woman lying in the "horrible brown heap" on the floor dying from lead poisoning, with her brain seeping out at her ears, the dock porter with withered legs and the woman making peajackets for a pittance—all form a dark tableau. They do not beg but are happy to receive the gentleman's interest and sympathy, despite the reader's class prejudice against them as parasites living off public charity. They hardly touch outdoor relief and have a horror of the workhouse as great as Mrs. Higden's. Yet the Uncommercial Traveller can only hope to gain the hostile reader's empathy by pitying the suffering children and so takes us into the East London Children's Hospital—the true and lonely star in the east—which is remedying malnutrition and disease with nourishment, cleanliness, and ventilation in a voluntary mission of compassion and self-denying dedication. It is to such a heavenly haven that little Johnny is taken in his sickness in *Our Mutual Friend* (II, ix) and where he dies, comforted by a scene of angels and bequeathing a kiss to the "boofer lady." The Uncommercial Traveller nevertheless rejects narrow constructions of himself as a charitable do-gooder (he has decided he will give no handouts) or as a patronizing interferer and agitator (he hears no complaint or resentment at the lot of the poor). Instead, he invites the reader to retrace his steps with the shortest of train rides that measures the unfathomable distance between the construction of public health in the fashionable representation of the poor by the Podsnaps or the Veneerings and the horrific reality of London's "moral sewage" awaiting salvation.

NOTES

1   Review of *Our Mutual Friend*. *The Nation* (New York), 21 December 1865, 786–87.

2   See "Owen's Museum," *All the Year Round*, 27 September 1862. In *Hard Times* each of the little Gradgrinds has "dissected the Great Bear like a Professor Owen" (I, iii; 54)—a comic example of how Science has banished the nursery rhymes and Fancy of childhood.

3   Victor Sage, "'Negative Homogeneity': *Our Mutual Friend*, Richard Owen and the 'New Worlds' of Victorian Biology," in *Dickens, Europe and the New Worlds*, ed. Amy Sadrin (London: Macmillan, 1999), 217–24. For the Darwinian context of *Our Mutual Friend* see Pam Morris, "A Taste for Change in *Our Mutual Friend*: Cultivation or Education?" in *Rethinking Victorian Culture*, ed. Juliet John and Alice Jenkins (London: Macmillan, 2000), 180–82; Howard W. Fulweiler believes *Our Mutual Friend* follows the pattern of the "mutual

relations" of species in Darwin's *The Origin of Species* (1859) but, far from applauding the success of natural selection, Dickens opposes both Malthusian and Darwinian theories of evolution to project a moral community of individuals. Yet Darwin was equally reading Dickens's anatomy of the bleak competitive chaos of Victorian society at the mercy of rapacious beasts of prey ("'A Dismal Swamp': Darwin, Design, and Evolution in *Our Mutual Friend*," *Nineteenth-Century Literature* 49.1 [1994]: 55–56). See also George Levine, *Darwin and the Novelists: Patterns of Science in Victorian Fiction* (Chicago: University of Chicago Press, 1991), 124–51; Virginia Zimmerman, *Excavating Victorians* (Albany: State University of New York Press, 2009), 167–70; Ernest Fontana, "Darwinian Sexual Selection and Dickens's *Our Mutual Friend*," *Dickens Quarterly* 22 (2005): 153–71; Natalie McKnight, "Dickens and Darwin: A Rhetoric of Pets," *The Dickensian* 102 (2006): 131–43; Adelene Buckland, "'The Poetry of Science': Charles Dickens, Geology, and Visual and Material Culture in Victorian London," *Victorian Literature and Culture*, 35 (2007): 679–94.

4   Michel Foucault, *The Order of Things: An Archeology of the Human Sciences* (London: Tavistock, 1974), 206–08, 367–73.

5   For a survey of the trope of circulation, see Trotter, *Circulation: Defoe, Dickens, and the Economies of the Novel* (New York: St. Martin's, 1988).

6   *The Birth of the Clinic: An Archaeology of Medical Perception*, trans. A. M. Sheridan (London: Tavistock, 1973).

7   Dickens may have borrowed from Mayhew (see Nelson, "Dickens's *Our Mutual Friend* and Henry Mayhew, *London Labour and the London Poor*," *Nineteenth-Century Fiction* 20.3 [1965]: 207–22), but the influence also worked in the other direction, and Mayhew recycled descriptions by Dickens in *London Labour and the London Poor*. The differences between the two authors are quite apparent when Dickens has harsh words for the watermen and dredgermen as criminal outcasts of the river in "Down With the Tide" (*Household Words*, 5 February 1853).

8   *Household Words*, 13 July 1850. This article also circulated widely in the American press.

9   Joel J. Brattin has adduced evidence from the manuscript and proofs of Dickens's novel to support the influence of Horne's article, arguing that Boffin is opposed to the corrupt Wegg as an agent of conversion, an alchemy resisted by the English aversion to change ("Constancy, Change and the Dust Mounds of *Our Mutual Friend*," *Dickens Quarterly* 19.1 [2002]: 23–30). See also Zimmerman, *Excavating Victorians*, 163–66.

10   Edgar Johnson, *Charles Dickens: His Tragedy and Triumph* (London: Gollancz, 1953), 2: 1043–44.

11   Many critics and readers assume that most of London's dust was dung, and the symbolic association in the public mind of dust with both excrement and money should not be discounted in Dickens's depreciation of filthy lucre (Harvey Sucksmith, "The Dust-Heaps in *Our Mutual Friend*," *Essays in Criticism* 23 [1973]: 206–12); see also Ellen Handy, "Dust Piles and Damp Pavements: Excrement, Repression, and the Victorian City in Photographs and Literature," in *Victorian Literature and the Victorian Visual Imagination*, ed. Carol T. Christ and John O. Jordan (Berkeley: University of California Press, 1995), 111–33.

12   For an analysis of anality in *Bleak House* see Michael Steig, "Dickens's Excremental Vision," *Victorian Studies* 13.3 (1970): 339–54. The term "excremental vision" was coined by Professor J. M. Murry for Jonathan Swift's satire and it is discussed at length in Norman O. Brown's chapter on Swift in *Life Against Death: The Psychoanalytical Meaning of History* (Middletown: Wesleyan University Press, 1959).

13   *London Labour and the London Poor*, 2: 194–95.

14   *London Labour and the London Poor*, 2: 170–71.

15   *London Labour and the London Poor*, 2: 175.

16   S. E. Finer, *The Life and Times of Sir Edwin Chadwick* (New York: Barnes and Noble, 1952), 3.

17   *Two Years Ago* (London: Macmillan, 1892), 212. Significantly, this passage was reproduced in the *British Medical Journal*, 21 March 1857, 245.

18   Edwin Chadwick, *The Sanitary Condition of the Labouring Population of Great Britain*, ed. M. W. Flinn (Edinburgh: Edinburgh University Press, 1965), 309.

19   Chadwick, *Sanitary Condition*, 251–52.

20   Chadwick, *Sanitary Condition*, 124–33.

21   Chadwick, *Sanitary Condition*, 117–18; 121–22.

22   Chadwick, *Sanitary Condition*, 98.

23   Chadwick, *Sanitary Condition*, 214.

24   Chadwick Papers, University College London, quoted in Schoenwald, 679; see Finer, *The Life and Times of Sir Edwin Chadwick*, 223.

25   James Phillips Kay, *The Moral and Physical Condition of the Working Classes Employed in the Cotton Manufacture in Manchester* (London: James Ridgway, 1832), 6–7.

26   Kay, *Moral and Physical Condition*, 15–16. Peter Gaskell also points to absence of home comforts and sexual depravity as reasons for the ill-health and brutalization of factory workers; see his *Artisans and Machinery: The Moral and Physical Condition of the Manufacturing Population Considered with Reference to Mechanical Substitutes for Human Labour* (London: John W. Parker, 1836).

27   Kay, *Moral and Physical Condition*, 3–4.

28   Gaskell, *Artisans and Machinery*, 3.

29   Chadwick, *Sanitary Condition*, 199.

30   In her analysis of the cultural logic of Kay's pamphlet, Mary Poovey does not relate to medical constructs of the body (*Making a Social Body: British Cultural Formation, 1830–1864* [Chicago: University of Chicago Press, 1995], 55–72). On Chadwick's representation of the poor in panoptic terms and his attempt at moral policing in order to contain the threat of the lower-class body see Joseph W. Childers, *Novel Possibilities: Fiction and the Formation of Early Victorian Culture* (Philadelphia: University of Pennsylvania Press, 1995), 88–121.

31   Graeme Davison, "The City as a Natural System: Theories of Urban Society in Early Nineteenth-Century Britain," in *The Pursuit of Urban History*, ed. Derek Fraser and Anthony Sutcliffe (London: Edward Arnold, 1983), 357.

32   "Lectures on Animal Economy at the London Institution" (1833), quoted in Davison, "The City as a Natural System," 361–62.

33   Smith, cited in Davison, "The City as a Natural System," 362.

34   On the political overtones of the policing of public health in France under the ancien régime see Foucault, *The Birth of the Clinic*, trans. A. M. Sheridan (London: Tavistock, 1973), 25–26. In Britain, a medical police was established only in the second half of the nineteenth century, when the appointment of public health inspectors became mandatory, but these were hampered by the vested interests of their employers, who were often landlords, and by inefficient administration or the lack of any practical solutions for slum dwellers evicted from condemned housing (Anthony S. Wohl, "Unfit for Human Habitation," in *The Victorian City: Images and Realities*, ed. H. J. Dyos and Michael Wolff [London: Routledge, 1973], 2: 606–07).

35   Stephen Halliday, *The Great Stink of London: Sir Joseph Bazalgette and the Cleansing of the Victorian Capital* (London: Sutton, 1994),17–18.

36 "Elements of Physics," quoted in Davison, "The City as a Natural System," 363–64.

37 Chadwick, *Sanitary Condition*, 425.

38 See Childers, *Novel Possibilities*, 72–74.

39 See, for example, Peter Stallybrass and Alison White, *The Politics and Poetics of Transgression* (Ithaca: Cornell University Press, 1986), 140.

40 "Preface," *London Labour and the London Poor*, 1: iii–iv.

41 *London Labour and the London Poor*, 2: 383–452. Stallybrass and White relate the filth of the sewers to Freud's analysis of the "Rat Man" and identify an anal eroticism in a vertical axis of the middle-class body and urban topography (*The Politics and Poetics of Transgression*, 138–48).

42 *London Labour and the London Poor*, 2: 395.

43 Nelson, "Dickens's *Our Mutual Friend* and Henry Mayhew's *London Labour and the London Poor*." Mayhew's "pure" lady is reduced to this occupation by poverty, as Betty Hidgen is forced to earn her living as a street-seller, but it is as much love of open air as of independence that keeps Betty out of the workhouse (*London Labour and the London Poor*, 2: 144–45).

44 *London Labour and the London Poor*, 2: 100. See Richard J. Dunn, "Dickens and Mayhew Once More," *Nineteenth-Century Fiction* 25.3 (1970): 348–53.

45 J. C. Hotten cited in Andrew Sanders, *Charles Dickens Resurrectionist* (New York: St. Martin's, 1982), ix.

46 Albert Hutter, "Dismemberment and Articulation in *Our Mutual Friend*," *Dickens Studies Annual* 11 (1983): 135–75. For the analogy of the Resurrection Men and their grisly trade to *A Tale of Two Cities* see Hutter, "The Novelist as Resurrectionist: Dickens and the Dilemma of Death," *Dickens Studies Annual* 12 (1983): 1–39.

47 It was his illustrator Marcus Stone who introduced Dickens to this extraordinary trade in St. Giles' (John Forster, *The Life of Charles Dickens* [London: Dent, 1969], 2: 292); Mayhew was interested in the street folk, not storekeepers, but a kindly taxidermist can be found in Black Jack, rat-catcher and rodent exterminator to Her Majesty the Queen (*London Labour and the London Poor*, 3: 11–20).

48 See Sage, "'Negative Homogeneity,'" 220–23.

49 See Nancy Metz, "The Artistic Reclamation of Waste in *Our Mutual Friend*," *Nineteenth-Century Fiction* 34.1 (1979): 59–72.

50 See Stallybrass and White, *The Politics and Poetics of Transgression*, 39–44.

51 Chadwick, *Sanitary Condition*, 238–39.

52 Kate Flint relates dust particles to Victorian concepts of dirt and aesthetic beauty at the end of the century, and extrapolates these to the ubiquitous dust mounds of *Our Mutual Friend* and contemporary journalism (*The Victorians and the Visual Imagination* [Cambridge: Cambridge University Press, 2000], 40–63).

53 See Michal Peled Ginsburg, *Economies of Change: Form and Transformation in the Nineteenth-Century Novel* (Stanford: Stanford University Press, 1996), 138–56.

54 See Halliday, *The Great Stink of London*. David Trotter examines the trope of circulation in *Bleak House* but presumes it was exhausted by the 1860s, when *Our Mutual Friend* was published (*Circulation*, 133–36).

55 *Underground London* (London: Groombridge, 1862). See Flint, *The Victorians and the Visual Imagination*, 153–61.

56 J. C. Platt and J. Saunders, "Underground," in *London*, ed. Charles Knight (London: Charles Knight, 1841–44), 1: 225–40.

57 "Drainage and Health of the Metropolis," *The Examiner*, 14 May 1849, 1–2; "The Sewers' Commission," *The Examiner*, 4 August 1849, 482–83.

58   "The Main Drainage of London," *The Times*, 19 July 1859, 5.

59   As Rosalind Williams concludes from her comparison of Hugo's novel and Dickens's *Christmas Carol* (*Notes on the Underground: An Essay on Technology, Society, and the Imagination* [Cambridge, MA: MIT Press, 1990], 157–58).

60   F. S. Schwarzbach, *Dickens and the City* (London: Athlone Press, 1979), 197; John Carey, *The Violent Effigy: A Study of Dickens's Imagination* (London: Faber and Faber, 1973), 108–09; J. Hillis Miller, *Charles Dickens: The World of His Novels* (Cambridge, MA: Harvard University Press, 1958), 312–13. John Lucas insists there is no symbolism whatever in the river (*The Melancholy Man: A Study of Dickens's Novels* [London: Methuen, 1970], 340). See Karl Ashley Smith, *Dickens and the Unreal City: Searching for Spiritual Significance in Nineteenth-Century London* (Houndmills and New York: Palgrave Macmillan, 2007), 148–77.

61   As Elizabeth Deeds Ermath has commented in relation to the opposition of nature and society in Dickens's works (*The English Novel in History, 1840–1895* [London: Routledge, 1997], 37).

62   William Cooke Taylor reports similar resistance to the Poor Laws among out-of-work factory operatives in Bolton in the forties and declares that the gradual submission to the workhouse was a moral "contagion" which would eventually affect the middle classes too (*Notes of a Tour in the Manufacturing Districts of Lancashire*, 3rd ed. [London: Frank Cass, 1968], 42–46).

63   Janet L. Larson also glimpses the Celestial City, but interprets the passage as a stylization of Betty's diseased mind in a grim reference to Matthew 11.28–30 which affirms death is the terminal destination (*Dickens and the Broken Scripture* [Athens, GA: University of Georgia Press, 1985], 296–97).

64   On this conventional anti-urban paradigm in provincial novels by George Eliot, Charlotte Brontë, and Thomas Hardy see U. C. Knoepflmacher, "The Novel Between City and Country," in *The Victorian City: Images and Realities*, ed. H. J. Dyos and Michael Wolff (London: Routledge, 1973), 2: 517–36.

65   See Smith, *Dickens and the Unreal City*, 163–64. Smith reads this allusion as ironic, considering the river's pollution (*Dickens and the Unreal City*, 164–68, 175–77).

66   In his discussion of baptismal regeneration in *Our Mutual Friend*, Sanders points out the relevance of this passage, where Jesus tells Nicodemus of rebirth through water and spirit, to the naming of Nicodemus Boffin (*Charles Dickens Resurrectionist*, 175–77). For a deconstructive reading of the baptismal motif see Larson, *Dickens and the Broken Scripture*, 293–99.

67   Eugene does not suffer in his rebirthing the psychic torments of Raskolnikov in *Crime and Punishment* (conceived the same year, but published one year later than *Our Mutual Friend*); Lizzie is not a prostitute and Headstone is not driven by an obsessive ideology. See Robert Alter, *Imagined Cities: Urban Experience and the Language of the Novel* (New Haven: Yale University Press, 2005), 81; Donald Fanger, *Dostoevsky and Romantic Realism: A Study of Dostoevsky in Relation to Balzac, Dickens, and Gogol* (Chicago: University of Chicago Press, 1967); N. M. Lary, *Dostoevsky and Dickens: A Study of Literary Influence* (London: Routledge, 1973).

68   Robert Alter sees figurative language as the key to Dickens's apocalyptic understanding of the city in *Our Mutual Friend* (*Imagined Cities*, 43–81).

69   *Charles Dickens: The World of His Novels*, 293.

70   John Ruskin, *Modern Painters, Of Many Things. Part IV* (New York: Wiley & Halsted, 1859), 259.

71 See on this Carlylean note Larson, *Dickens and the Broken Scripture*, 286–89. For cogent reasons why the promise of salvation should be taken seriously in Dickens's fictional deaths see Sanders, *Charles Dickens Resurrectionist.*

72 Ruskin, *Unto This Last and Other Writings*, ed. Clive Wilmer (London: Penguin, 1985), 183.

73 See Catherine Gallagher's reading of Ruskin's essay as an interpretive key to *Our Mutual Friend* (*The Body Economic: Life, Death, and Sensation in Political Economy and the Victorian Novel* [Princeton: Princeton University Press, 2006], 86–117). Gallagher alleges Ruskin and Dickens were closer than they thought to theories of labor value in Political Economy.

74 See Halliday, *The Great Stink of London*; Rosalind Williams, *Notes on the Underground*, 70–73.

Index

"Abbau" 13, 63, 69–70, 108, 131, 172, 224;
  see also mining; Mumford; Wheeler
Aberdeen 97
Ackroyd, Peter 5
Addison, Joseph 10
Adshead, Joseph 183
Ainsworth, Harrison 96, 180
Albert, Prince Consort 112, 141
Alison, William 202
All the Year Round 67, 188, 196, 214
America 44, 67, 113, 156, 218
Arac, Jonathan 107
architecture 9, 17, 25, 41, 87–88, 93,
  109, 113–14, 126, 129–30, 152, 153,
  167, 178, 180
Aristotle 148
Arkwright, Sir Richard 135
Armstrong, Nancy 88
Arnold, Matthew 158
Arnold, Thomas 61
Arnott, Neil 202, 203
Arnout, Jules 31
Ashburton, Baron William Bingham
  Baring 154
Ashley, Lord (seventh earl of
  Shaftesbury) 182
Ashworth brothers 136
Asmodeus 28–29, 42
Athens 108
Auden, W. H. 174
Augustine 168, 182
Austen, Jane 10, 12, 20, 52; Mansfield
  Park 88; Northanger Abbey 52
Austin, Henry 204
Australia 184
Babylon 10, 25, 28, 42, 44, 52, 55, 69,
  75, 108, 135, 222
Bagehot, Walter 1, 15
Bakhtin, Mikhail 12, 16, 56, 88, 124,
  142, 148, 157, 166
ballooning 29–31, 38, 44, 185
Balzac, Honoré de 3, 5, 6, 19 n. 2, 28,
  32, 42, 43, 87, 180; Le Père Goriot 5,
  28, 46, 181, 189, 198
Barthes, Roland 1, 8

Baudelaire, Charles 16, 26, 33, 34, 35,
  36, 40, 41, 46, 113, 204; Les Fleurs
  du Mal 40, 41
Bayly, Mary 95
Bazalgette, Joseph 213, 224
Beadnell, Maria 193 n. 58
Beames, Thomas 95
Beeching, Richard 67
Belzoni, Giovanni 168
Bender, John 185
Benjamin, Walter 12, 16, 26, 27, 33,
  34–37, 38, 40, 41, 42, 58, 113, 163
Bentham, Jeremy ix, 2, 29, 114, 123,
  130, 134, 143, 148, 149, 154, 178,
  180, 184, 185, 187, 189, 191 n. 31,
  203; see also utilitarianism
Berman, Marshall 12
bildungsroman 2, 88
Birmingham 67, 69, 145
Blackpool 152
Blackwood's Magazine 178
Blake, William 41, 55, 56, 59, 197, 218;
  Jerusalem 222; "London" 49 n. 63, 56
Booth, Henry 61
Bosanquet, Charles 95
Bourne, John Cooke 69, 70
Bradford 129, 131
Brantlinger, Patrick 144
Bray, Charles 144, 202
Brighton (Sussex) 82
British Museum 116, 187, 196
Broadstairs 35
Brodie, Sir Benjamin 6
Brontë, Anne 61
Brontë, Charlotte 2; Jane Eyre 2
Brontë, Emily 88; Wuthering Heights
  2, 88
Brontë sisters 20 n. 4, 88
Brooks, Chris 92, 148, 166
Brooks, Shirley 81
Brown, Tom 51
Browne, Hablot ("Phiz") 32, 146
Browning, Elizabeth Barrett 135
Brunel, Isambard Kingdom 66
Buckle, Henry Thomas 132

Bunyan, John 172–73, 221; *Pilgrim's Progress* 8, 173

Burdett-Coutts, Lady Angela 111, 143, 154, 183, 204, 211

Burke, Edmund 56

Burke, Thomas 5

Bury, Thomas Talbot 69

Byron, Lord George Gordon 134, 171, 174

Cambridge 144, 164

Capital Punishment Amendment Act (1868) 179

Carey, John 165, 216

Carlyle, Thomas 8, 28, 59, 60, 61, 62, 70–71, 76, 98, 99, 101, 104, 116, 131, 132, 141, 154, 157, 171, 175, 177, 184, 188, 192 n. 43, 198, 210, 212, 213, 214, 218, 223; "Chartism" 59; *Latter-Day Pamphlets* 62–63, 70, 104, 116, 175, 188, 213; *Past and Present* 60, 61, 98, 99, 116, 131, 132, 141, 172; *Sartor Resartus* 104, 133, 146, 154, 213, 214

Cartwright, Edmund 135

Certeau, Michel de 30

Chadwick, Sir Edwin 18, 57, 94, 97, 98, 102, 112, 116, 142, 155, 187, 191 n. 31, 197, 198, 200, 201–02, 203–04, 206, 210, 212

Chalmers, Thomas 126

Chatham 20, 38, 72, 163, 216

Chatsworth 112

Chernyshevsky, Nikolai 113

Chesterton, G. K. 38

Chesterton, George 192 n. 43

Chichester, Frederick 64

childhood 5, 6, 8, 18, 36, 72, 124, 139, 143, 151, 157, 163, 163, 172, 175, 184, 216, 218; and maternal deprivation 72; memories of — 8, 72, 216

China 114-15, 122 n. 91

Christianity 99

circus 29, 113, 123, 127, 133, 143, 145–52; Astley's — 29, 146, 147, 149, 161 n. 56

city 4–7, 8, 9–15, 25–28, 33, 39, 40–41, 51–61, 87, 89, 90, 94, 98, 100–04, 108–09, 113, 123, 125–27, 129–30, 131, 132, 134–35, 136, 142, 163–68, 169–70, 171–72, 178, 181, 189, 197, 200, 202, 213, 214, 215, 218, 220, 222, 223, 224; as body 7, 51–61, 100, 168, 199, 201, 202, 203, 205, 223, 224; celestial — 44, 217–19, 221, 229 n. 63; and country 8, 39, 45, 46, 53, 61, 62, 63, 74, 107, 127, 133, 134, 157, 224; invisible — 26, 44–45, 64, 96, 133, 214; — as labyrinth 3–4, 5, 7, 17–18, 35, 37–38, 42–43, 44, 76, 78, 93, 97, 106, 167–70, 171, 172, 173, 175, 181, 182, 187, 189, 207, 215–216; as monster 10–11, 52, 54; as necropolis 163, 172, 207, 216–17, 224; as prison 164–68, 171, 173–78, 182–83, 185–88; and subjectivity 14, 17, 56, 176–77; *see also* crime; legibility; sexuality

Clough, Arthur 56

Cobbett, William 51

Cocker, Edward 155

Cockshut, A. O. J. 165

Cole, Henry 110, 138, 153

Coleridge, S. T. 144

Collins, Wilkie 68, 109

colonialism 92, 102, 131, 187

Colquhoun, Patrick 192 n. 52

Comte, Augustus 1

"Condition of England" 2, 17, 64, 100, 101, 140, 157

Coniffe, Gerald 166

Conrad, Joseph 83

Constable, John 66

Conway (Wales) 72

Coram, Thomas 177

Corn Law repeal 68, 115, 135, 136

Coutts, Angela: *see* Burdett-Coutts, Lady Angela

Cowper, William 54, 55

Craig, David 160 n. 39

crime 2, 4, 7, 11, 14, 18, 25–26, 29, 30, 36, 94, 95, 97, 98, 99, 101, 118, 119–20 n. 31, 150, 165–67, 172, 175, 178–89, 202, 205, 208, 213, 222

Crimean War 116, 140, 171

Index

233

Cruikshank, George 3, 10, *11*, 26, 29, 30, *30*, 71, *73*, 116, *117*, 143
Cruikshank, Isaac 26
Cruikshank, Robert 26
Crystal Palace 17, 109–18, 128, 156; *see also* Great Exhibition; Paxton
Cunningham, Valentine 107, 157
Daily News 38, 39, 68, 114, 138, 167, 179
Daleski, H. M. 96–97, 107
Damiens, Robert-François 180
Dante, Alighieri 167, 173, 215
Darwin, Charles 196, 225–26 n. 3
Davis, Lennard 186
Defoe, Daniel 19, 78, 83, 155, 165; *Moll Flanders* 165, 185; *Robinson Crusoe* 83, 163, 173
Denman, Lord Thomas 6
De Quincey, Thomas 35, 40
Derrida, Jacques 13, 21 n. 17
detective 10, 37, 42, 103, 107, 187–88, 206, 207
Devonshire, sixth duke of (William George Spenser Cavendish) 112, 114, 187
Dickens, Catherine 93
Dickens, Charles; in Warren's Blacking Warehouse 6, 8, 136, 146, 164; as reporter 26, 40; move to London 16, 46; father's imprisonment for debt 72, 165, 176; in Bayham Street 6; in Doughty Street 7; at Gad's Hill 165; individual works: *American Notes* 67, 156, 207; *Barnaby Rudge* 7, 37, 165; *Bleak House* 2, 4, 7, 10, 13, 14, 17, 39, 40, 42, 44, 46, 49 n. 63, 53, 54, 79, 57, 87–122, 128, 129, 132, 135, 137, 141, 149, 151, 152, 155, 166, 172, 177, 182, 187, 188, 189, 196, 199, 205, 206, 214, 224, 228 n. 54; *Christmas Books* 138, 200; *Christmas Carol* 229 n. 59; *David Copperfield* 6, 39, 46, 88, 93, 103, 148, 164, 165, 173, 177, 181, 182, 183, 184; *Dombey and Son* 5, 10, 17, 28, 35, 51–86, 89, 107, 108, 114, 128, 130, 174, 185, 189, 216, 221; *Great Expectations* 4, 7, 8, 18, 39, 88, 100, 101, 108, 165,

169, 183, 185, 206, 220; *Hard Times* 10, 17, 18, 20 n. 4, 43, 52, 57, 63, 76, 98, 110, 123–162, 166, 182, 218, 225 n. 2; *Little Dorrit* 3, 4, 6, 7, 14, 16, 18, 41, 53, 70, 77, 93, 101, 105, 108, 116–118, 120 n. 44, 128, 141, 163–93, 209, 212, 216, 217, 218, 220, 222, 224; *Martin Chuzzlewit* 42–43, 50 n. 70, 165, 174, 204, 218; "Master Humphrey's Clock" 41, 51, 68, 85 n. 29; "The Mudfog Papers" 133, 143; *The Mystery of Edwin Drood* 7; *Nicholas Nickleby* 6, 30, 58, 67, 136, 139, 165, 184, 186; *The Old Curiosity Shop* 6, 7, 10, 44, 50 n. 69, 58, 93, 98–99, 104. 128, 130, 131, 137, 138, 146, 148, 151, 163, 166, 177, 189, 198–99, 218, 224; *Oliver Twist* 2, 3–4, 7, 14, 21 n. 18, 39, 43, 91, 95, 96–97, 99, 119–20 n. 31, 134, 143, 147, 165, 167, 168, 169, 177, 178, 180, 181, 183, 185, 186, 187, 191 n. 28, 204, 218, 224; *Our Mutual Friend* 4, 13, 18, 20 n. 4, 41, 45, 48 n. 36, 80, 81, 98, 101, 103, 107, 128, 134, 142, 151, 177, 195–230; *Pickwick Papers* 3, 6, 30, 75, 133, 147, 165, 175; *Pictures from Italy* 79, 171, 173; *Sketches by Boz* 3, 15, 26–42, 102, 103, 165, 168, 175–76, 183, 186, 209; "Stray Chapters" 147; *A Tale of Two Cities* 18, 164, 165, 180, 207, 222; *The Uncommercial Traveller* 39, 187, 188, 196, 216, 224, 225; *see also All the Year Round*; childhood; *Household Words*
Dickens, Charles, Junior 21 n. 17
Dickens, Fanny 177
Dickens, John 72, 119 n. 21, 164–65, 174, 176–77
Dijon 58, 76, 80
Disraeli, Benjamin 139; *Sybil* 139
domesticity 6, 7, 10, 17, 52, 75, 77–78, 87–93, 94, 95, 97, 99, 100, 104, 109, 110, 136, 172, 177, 188, 198, 204, 205, 202; *see also* homelessness
Donald, James 15

Doré, Gustave *frontispiece*, 5, 64, *64*,
    108, 116, *117*
Dostoevsky, Fyodor 113, 124, 153,
    180, 181, 222, 229 n. 67; *Crime
    and Punishment* 181, 183, 229
    n. 67; *Winter Notes of Summer
    Impressions* 113
Doyle, Sir Arthur Conan 186
Dryden, John 19, 59
Edinburgh 72, 135, 201
education: *see* schools
Egan, Pierce 26, 28, 31; *Life in London*
    26, 33, 186
Egerton, Lord Francis 201
Egg, Augustus 172
Eliade, Mircea 126
Eliot, George (Mary Ann Evans) 1, 2,
    12, 14, 78, 79, 144, 157, 196, 199,
    210; *Adam Bede*, 14; *Felix Holt*, 210,
    212; *Middlemarch* 210; *Mill on the
    Floss* 88; "The Natural History of
    German Life" 78, 79; *Silas Marner*
    157, 199
Eliot, T. S. 13, 109, 199
Elton, Esther 103
Engels, Friedrich 40, 64, 129, 140, 214
epistemology 1, 16, 34, 42, 55, 58, 70,
    103, 124, 126, 127, 152
Ermath, Elizabeth Deeds 82
Euclid 155
evangelicalism 182
factories 2, 10, 12, 15, 16, 40, 54, 63, 67,
    72, 75, 90, 94, 107, 112–113, 114,
    123–62, 164, 170, 178, 182, 202,
    219, 220
Factory Act (1844) 140, 154
Fancy: *see* imagination
Feuerbach, Ludwig 1
Field, Charles Frederick 117, 187, 188
Field, John 183
Fielding, Henry 14, 16; *Jonathan Wild*
    180; *Tom Jones* 88
Finer, S. E. 200
Fisher, Philip 12
flâneur 16, 33–42, 46, 48 n. 34, 49 n. 62,
    106, 163
Flaubert, Gustave 13
Flint, Kate 79, 89

Forster, John 6, 7, 12, 35, 38, 79, 80, 81,
    164, 165, 174
Foucault, Michel 114, 130, 180, 184,
    185, 196, 197, 203
Fourier, Charles 113, 114
Fowler, Roger 142
Francis, John 62, 71
Fraser's Magazine 135, 141, 180, 184
Freud, Sigmund 9, 39, 52, 72, 83 n. 8,
    92, 105–06, 121 n. 51, 165, 188, 228
    n. 41
Gallagher, Catherine 20, 123, 140–41
Gaskell, Elizabeth 14, 40, 88, 96, 126,
    134, 138–39, 140–41, 144, 157, 214;
    Mary Barton 40, 96, 126, 134, 139,
    144, 214; *North and South* 138, 140,
    141, 157
Gaskell, Peter 131, 136, 201, 227 n. 26
Gavarni, Paul (Sulpice Guilliame
    Chevalier) 26, *34*
Gavin, Hector 94, 97, 102, 202
Gay, John 19; *Trivia* 26, 199, 215
gender 8, 17, 18, 61–62, 83 n. 7, 88–90,
    110, 111, 124, 142, 156, 166
geography 16, 26, 44; human — 127;
    "literary —" 5–6
Gibbon, Edward 108
Giedion, Siegfried 113
Gissing, George 160 n. 39
Gladstone, William 68
Godwin, George 95, 99
Goethe, Johann Wolfgang von 36
Goldsmith, Oliver 75, 155
Goncourt brothers 90
Goodair, John 146
Gothic 4, 5, 13, 17, 39, 41–44, 104–06,
    108, 112, 144, 152, 169, 207
Goujon, Jean 86 n. 52
Grant, Daniel and William 136
Grant, James 32
Gray, Thomas 75
Great Exhibition 109–11, 114–118,
    144, 153, 154; *see also* Crystal
    Palace
Greene, Graham 4
Greenwood, James 95
Greg, W. R. 181–82
Greimas, A.-J. 126–27

Grimaldi, Joseph 147
Halliday, M. A. K. 142
Hardy, Barbara 18, 91, 150, 156
Hardy, Thomas 12
Harvey, William 51
Hatton, Lady Elizabeth 170
Haussmann, Baron Georges Eugène 13, 26, 90, 113
Hawthorne, Nathaniel 28
Hazlitt, William 32, 33
Hobbes, Thomas 58, 128, 131
Hoffmann, E. T. A. 54, 106
Hofmannsthal, Hugo von 106
Hogarth, Georgina 93
Hogarth, Mary 8
Hogarth, William 26, 179
Hogg, John 28, 44, 94
Holbein, Hans 59
Hole, James 53
Hollingshead, John 95, 213, 214
Hollington, Michael 32
Holloway, John 155
homelessness 10, 87, 98, 104, 106, 107, 172
homes: *see* domesticity
Hood, Thomas 77
Horne, R. H. 114, 180, 197, 198, 202, 209
Horner, Leonard 125
House, Humphry 2, 188
Household Words 138, 139, 140, 143, 154, 155, 156, 163, 180, 183, 184, 187, 188, 197, 204, 218
Howard, Ebenezer 113
Hudson, George 62, 68, 70–71, 210
Hugo, Victor 41, 43, 67, 180, 181; *Les Misérables*, 21 n. 18, 41, 181, 182, 214–215; *Notre-Dame de Paris* 43
Hunt, Leigh 78, 119 n. 21
Huxley, T. H. 210
Illustrated London News 101, 214
imagination 14, 17, 19, 26, 35–36, 72, 79, 83, 114, 123–62, 163, 165, 181, 182, 188, 189, 207, 220, 225 n. 2
industrialization: *see* factories
Jaloux, Edmond 35
James, Henry 107, 195
Jenks, Chris 41

Jerrold, Blanchard 5, 108
Jerusalem 129, 173, 198, 218, 222, 223, 224
Johnson, Edgar 199
Johnson, Samuel 78, 167, 173, 174
Jones, Gareth Stedman 27, 96
Kafka, Franz 167
Kant, Immanuel 149
Kay, James Phillips (Kay-Shuttleworth) 94, 131, 136, 202
Keats, John 144
Kew Gardens 112
Kingsley, Charles 40, 94; *Alton Locke* 40, 95–96, 196, 199; *Two Years Ago* 200; *Yeast* 141
Klotz, Volker 15, 37
Knight, Charles 137; *Knight's Cyclopedia of Useful Knowledge* 144; *London* 186, 214
Knox, John 95
Lacan, Jacques 92, 106, 176, 188
Lamb, Charles 32
Lamb, Robert 135
Laurie, Sir Peter 204
Leavis, F. R. 133, 155
legibility 13, 15, 16, 27, 28, 37, 38, 44, 45, 76, 87, 101, 103
Lehan, Richard 92
Leibniz, Gottfried Wilhelm von 153
Lemon, Mark 218
Lesage, Alain René 28
Lévi-Strauss, Claude 126
Lewes, George 2, 33, 120 n. 45, 196, 210
Liebig, Justus 201
Lively, Penelope 7
Liverpool 112, 135, 157
Lockwood and Mawson 129
Lodge, David 142, 148
London 1–123 passim, 163–230 passim; Great Fire of — 19, 44; growth of — 11, 13, 51; — as site of modernity 9–19, 25, 26–27, 29, 33–34, 39, 40, 42, 43, 44, 52, 69, 72, 75, 106, 108–09, 113, 166–67, 169, 175, 181, 196, 222; postmodern — 6–7, 27
London County Council 13

London Zoo 112
Lovelace, Richard 171
Lowenthal, David 5
Lucas, John 1, 175
Lukács, Georg 106
Lynch, Kevin 5
Lytton (Bulwer-Lytton), Edward 28, 96, 114, 144, 181, 188; *Eugene Aram* 36, 87, 181
Macaulay, Thomas Babington 9, 78, 108, 124, 125–26, 130–31, 139, 144, 150, 156, 160 n. 39, 180
McCartney, Paul 157
McCulloch, J. M. 161 n. 66
McCulloch, J. R. 136
Maconochie, Alexander 183
Malthus, Thomas 53, 78, 94, 95, 123, 140, 164, 181, 200, 204, 225–26 n. 3
Manchester 64, 94, 116–17, 127, 129, 130, 131, 133, 135, 136, 157, 202, 212, 214
Mandeville, Bernard 197
Marcus, Steven 8, 107
Marseilles 172, 177
Martin, G. H. 7
Martineau, Harriet 124–25, 133, 139–40, 144, 156, 183, 208
Marx, Karl 33, 76, 137
Masson, David 51
Mayhew, Henry 4, 29, 94, 101, 111, 116, 154, 167, 185, 197, 199–200, 205, 206, 208, 209, 215, 226 n. 7, 228 n. 43, 228 n. 47
Meckier, Jerome 153
melodrama 7, 13, 26, 32, 144, 150, 167, 169, 171
Methodism 165
Metropolitan Board of Works 13, 27
Metropolitan Sanitary Association 98, 116, 204
Mighall, Robert 104
Mill, John Stuart 108, 143, 181
Millais, Sir John Everett 14
Miller, D. A. 88, 186
Miller, J. Hillis 3, 26, 101, 103, 167, 183, 216, 223
Miller, Thomas 44, 95
Milton, John 29, 144, 174, 219; *Paradise*

Lost 50 n. 70, 218
Mitford, Mary Russell 6
Mitford, William 108
modernism 5, 10, 27, 37, 106, 109, 176
Moncrieff, W. T. 7
More, Sir Thomas 124
Morley, Henry 29, 79, 138, 139
Morning Chronicle 29, 34, 154
Mudie, Robert 28, 42, 52, 55, 56
Mumford, Lewis 13, 108, 130, 131
Murray, John Fisher 39
Musil, Robert 106
Nabokov, Vladimir 192 n. 49
Nadar (Gaspard-Félix Tournachon), 30
Nead, Lynda 27
New Lanark 129, 154
Newcomen, Thomas 135
Newgate Calendar 178, 180
Newman, Cardinal John Henry 1, 144
Newsom, Robert 105
Newton, Adam Zachary 107
Newton, Sir Isaac 38, 54, 65
Nietzsche, Friedrich 21 n. 17
Nineveh 168, 214
novel 150, 151, 152, 154–55, 157, 165–67, 171, 180–81, 183, 185, 186–89, 195, 206, 207, 209, 212, 213–14, 216, 223; "Newgate —" 181; "railway —" 78–79
Oastler, Richard 131, 133
orientalism 86 n. 63
Owen, Sir Richard 196, 210, 225 n. 2
Owen, Robert 53, 129, 154
Paine, Thomas 56
painting 9, 14, 66, 93; Dutch genre — 14, 77; landscape — 20 n. 9, 66
Paley, William 53
panorama 16, 28, 29, 30, 43, 114, 199
pantomime 147–48
Paris 3, 5, 6, 13, 14, 16, 26–27, 28, 33, 38, 41, 43, 44, 46, 53, 67, 68, 75, 76, 80, 90, 113, 180, 181, 210–11, 215
Parliament, Houses of 46, 104; as institution 62, 71, 75, 91, 103, 153, 180, 218, 220
pastoral 4, 6, 7, 16, 17, 66, 76, 112, 166, 170, 185, 216, 218, 224
Patmore, Coventry 89–90, 198
Paxton, Joseph 68, 111–12, 114

Peel, Sir Robert 126, 188
Penny Illustrated Paper 80
photography 5, 12, 27, 58
Pictorial Times 101
picturesque 3, 5, 29, 40, 69, 70, 71–72, 101, 105, 155
Pike, Burton 181
Pitt, William 56
Plato 151
Poe, Edgar Allan 25, 35, 36, 180; "The Fall of the House of Usher" 105, 108; "The Man of the Crowd" 25, 34, 35, 27, 29; "The Philosophy of Composition" 107–08
police 15, 26, 37, 38, 40, 42, 95, 98, 101, 107, 111, 115, 125, 139, 165, 181, 186, 186–88, 202, 208, 209, 223
Political Economy: *see* utilitarianism
Poor Laws 134, 178, 204, 217–18 229 n. 62
Poovey, Mary 20, 128
Pope, Alexander 189, 193 n. 58
Pre-Raphaelites 14
Preston 129, 137, 138, 146, 148
prison 7–8, 15, 16, 18, 29, 42, 43, 72, 92, 106, 114, 130, 152, 163–89 passim, 215; Birmingham — 192 n. 45; Coldbath Fields — 183, 192 n. 43; Fleet — 165, 174, 175, 180, 185, 192 n. 44; Marshalsea — 6, 7, 164–66, 169, 170, 171, 173, 174, 176–77, 192 n. 44; Millbank Penitentiary 192 n. 43; Newgate — 7, 163, 165, 167, 169, 181, 183, 186; Pentonville — 183, 185; Philadelphia Penitentiary — 178; Reading (UK) — 183
prostitution 18, 95, 96, 167, 178, 180, 185, 200, 205
Pugin, Augustus 112, 146, *147*, 149, 178, *179*
Punch 71, 85 n. 29, 101, 114, *115*, *215*, 216
Quarterly Review 62, 63
railways 7, 9, 10, 12, 13, 15, 16, 17, 33, 51–86 passim, 111–12, 113, 114, 115, 127, 138, 204, 221; underground — 69, 213, 214

Reach, Angus B. 33, *34*
reading: *see* legibility
realism 1–3, 5, 9, 10, 12, 14–15, 19, 20 n. 9, 30, 36–39, 41, 43, 54, 66–67, 79, 126–27, 140–41, 166–67, 186; critical — 1; social — 36, 79, 196; "urban —" 1, 9, 126, 127
Reform Bill (1832) 26, 56, 126
Reform Bill (1867) 126, 198
Regulation of Railways Bill (1844) 68
religion 4, 11, 18, 98, 185, 205; *see also* Christianity
Reynolds, G. W. M. 4, 96, 167, 207
Ricardo, David 182
Richardson, Samuel 88
river, 7, 18, 37, 52, 63, 66, 81, 82, 101, 130, 200, 201, 205, 206, 207, 208, 214, 216–18, 219, 220, 221–22, 223, 224, 229 n. 60; — Fleet 214; — Saône 169; — Thames 31, 55, 66, 81, 96, 101, 108, 115, 199, 203, 204, 214, 216–17, 219, 220, 221–22, 223, 224
Rockingham Castle 105
Romanticism 5, 8, 9, 10, 17, 19 n. 2, 25, 33, 38, 39, 40, 41, 52, 62, 68, 74, 82, 95, 106, 108, 124, 131, 139, 144, 148, 151, 157, 169, 171, 181, 182, 198–99, 204, 207, 224
Rome 25, 168
Rousseau, Jean-Jacques 77, 149, 166
Rowlandson, Thomas 146, *147*, 149
Ruskin, John 12, 28, 66, 67, 69, 79, 89–90, 114, 125, 169 n. 39, 191 n. 24, 198, 223–24; "Fiction, Fair and Foul" 79; *Modern Painters* 223; "Queens' Gardens" 198; *Sesame and Lillies* 90; "The Storm-Cloud of the Nineteenth Century" 223; "Unto This Last" 223–24
Sadleir, John 71
Said, Edward 83
Saint-Simon, Comte Henri de (Claude-Henri de Rouvroy) 41
Salt, Sir Titus 129
Saltaire 129
sanitary reform 51, 94–98, 116, 204, 213, 214–15; *see also* Chadwick

Schivelbusch, Wolfgang 66
Schlesinger, Max 187
Schlicke, Paul 148
Schnitzler, Arthur 106
schools 72, 111, 130, 131, 134, 142, 149,
    150–54, 161 n. 68, 182, 184, 185, 196,
    208; Ragged — 95
Schwarzbach, F. S. 8, 165, 216
Scott, Sir Walter 144, 174
Sedley, Charles 28
Sennacherib 10
sexuality 8, 52–53, 76–77, 83 n. 8, 88,
    90–93, 106, 107, 115, 124, 136, 139,
    151, 152, 164, 176–77, 180, 188,
    227 n. 26
Shakespeare, William 6, 82, 147,
    170, 174, 185; *Hamlet* 185; *King
    Lear* 174, 189; *Macbeth* 181, 209;
    Measure for Measure, 185; *The
    Merchant of Venice* 4, 169; *Othello*
    181
Shelley, Mary 54; *Frankenstein* 1, 54, 74
Sidney, Sir Philip 157
Simmel, Georg 33, 60, 67
Smiles, Samuel 62, 114
Smith, Adam 51, 123, 139, 140, 144
Smith, Thomas Southwood 98, 202,
    203, 204
Smith, W. H. 78
Smollett, Tobias 16; *Peregrine Pickle*
    88, 175
Sodom 182
Southey, Robert 9, 62, 124, 126, 131,
    134, 135, 144, 185; *Colloquies* 124,
    135, 195; *Letters from England* 9,
    124
Spencer, Herbert 210
Spenser, Edmund 142
Steele, Sir Richard 32, 209
Steig, Michael 71
Stendhal (Marie Henri Beyle) 34
Stephenson, George 62
Sterne, Laurence 16
Stone, Frank 133
Stone, Harry 80
Stone, Marcus 228 n. 47
Styles, John 184
Sue, Eugène 14, 28, 109

Swift, Graham 7
Swift, Jonathan 19, 149, 183, 195, 199,
    226 n. 12; *Gulliver's Travels* 149,
    163
Swinburne, Algernon Charles 216
Taine, Hippolyte 104, 113, 130, 131
Tambling, Jeremy 165
Taylor, William Cooke 53, 135–36, 154,
    155, 201, 229 n. 62
Ten Hours Bill 139
Tennyson, Lord Alfred 75, 109, 143; *In
    Memoriam* 109
Ternan, Ellen 81
Thackeray, William Makepeace 33, 51, 109,
    146, 180
Thomas, T. M. 76
Thompson, E. P. 157
Thomson, James (eighteenth-century
    poet) 55, 217
Thousand and One Arabian Nights 163
Times, The 178, 204
Tocqueville, Alexis de 131
Town Improvement Clauses Act (1847)
    214
Trilling, Lionel 165
Trollope, Anthony 70
Trotter, David 116
Tuan, Yi-Fu 126
Turner, J. M. W. 66, 216
Tyler, Wat 95
utilitarianism 18, 51, 60, 68, 71–72,
    114, 123–38, 144–56, 165, 181,
    182–83, 203–04, 223–24, 230 n. 73;
    see also Bentham; Chadwick
Urania Cottage 183; *see also*
    prostitution
van Ghent, Dorothy 43
Vaughan, Robert 9, 25, 178, 201
Venice 12, 134, 171, 174
Viardot, Pauline 81
Victoria, Queen 9, 87, 112, 201, 213
Vienna 44, 106
Walpole, Horace 105
Ward, John 26
Watkins, Gwen 8
Watson, Mrs. Lavinia 110
Watt, James 135, 143
Weber, Jean-Jacques 142

Welsh, Alexander 2, 8, 172
Westminster Review 181
Wheeler, William Morton 13
Whipple, E. H. 125
Whistler, James McNeil 204, 216
Whitely, William 110
Whittington, Dick 4
Williams, Raymond 2–3, 10, 36, 141–42, 160 n. 39
Wills, W. H. 29, 78, 111, 112, 118, 188
Wilson, Edmund 8, 165
Wirth-Nesher, Hana 10
Wolfreys, Julian 27

Woolf, Virginia 89
Wordsworth, William 25, 32, 33, 46, 56, 62, 71–72, 74, 81, 144, 151, 163, 166, 173–74, 184, 198, 219; "Composed upon Westminster Bridge" 56, 74; *Lyrical Ballads* 144; "Ode: Intimations of Immortality" 8, 163, 184, 219; *The Prelude* 25, 32, 173–74
Wornum, Ralph 110
Wren, Sir Christopher 44
Wyatt, James 135
Zola, Emile 14, 19 n. 2